Coal,
Iron,
and Slaves

Isaac Jefferson in the 1840s. *Reproduced with the permission of the University of Virginia Library, Charlottesville, Virginia.*

COAL, IRON, AND SLAVES

Industrial Slavery in Maryland and Virginia, 1715-1865

RONALD L. LEWIS

CONTRIBUTIONS IN LABOR HISTORY, NUMBER 6

GREENWOOD PRESS

WESTPORT, CONNECTICUT • LONDON, ENGLAND

Library of Congress Cataloging in Publication Data
Lewis, Ronald L., 1940–
   Coal, iron, and slaves.

   (Contributions in labor history; no. 6 ISSN
0146-3608)
   Bibliography: p.
   Includes index.
   1. Slave labor—Maryland. 2. Slave labor—
Virginia. 3. Factory system—Maryland—History.
4. Factory system—Virginia—History. 5. Mines
and mining—Maryland—History. 6. Mines and
mining—Virginia—History. 7. Maryland—History.
8. Virginia—History. I. Title. II. Series.
E445.M3L48   331.1'1734'09752   78-55333
ISBN 0-313-20522-1

Library of Congress Catalog Card Number: 78-55333
ISBN: 0-313-20522-1
ISSN: 0146-3608

First published in 1979

Greenwood Press, Inc.
51 Riverside Avenue, Westport, Connecticut 06880

Printed in the United States of America

10 9 8 7 6 5 4 3 2 1

TO MY FATHERS
LORAN LEWIS, who perished in a
coal mine while pursuing the American Dream,
and MELVIN LEWIS, who abandoned the mines and found
it.

Contents

Illustrations

Tables

Acknowledgments

During the preparation of this study, I received assistance from many patient and generous people. Because they are too numerous to thank individually, I would like to extend my appreciation to them collectively. Especially helpful over a long period of time were the staffs of the Maryland Historical Society in Baltimore; the Alderman Library of the University of Virginia in Charlottesville; the Virginia Historical Society and the Virginia State Library in Richmond; and the Perkins Library of Duke University in Durham, North Carolina. Many others assisted as well, such as the staffs of the Manuscript Division at the Library of Congress in Washington, D.C.; the Cyrus McCormick Library of Washington and Lee University in Lexington, Virginia; the Maryland Hall of Records in Annapolis; the Historical Society of Pennsylvania in Philadelphia; the Southern Historical Collection at the University of North Carolina in Chapel Hill; and the Wisconsin State Historical Society in Madison.

Numerous scholars have shared their views with me on various portions of this study. In particular, I would like to express my appreciation to Professors George Knepper of the University of Akron, Charles B. Dew of the University of Missouri at Columbia, August Meier of Kent State University, Stanley Engerman of the University of Rochester, Randall Miller of Saint Joseph's College (Philadelphia), Philip S. Foner of Lincoln University (Pennsylvania), as well as Mark Schmitz and Raymond Wolters of the University of Delaware. In his characteristically unselfish manner, Professor Robert Zangrando of the University of Akron has been unflagging in his support and friendship. He has been an adviser worthy of emulation.

Finally, I formally acknowledge the valiant efforts of Ms. Gail Brittingham in rendering my scrawl into a clean typescript, the University of Delaware Research Foundation for its timely financial support, and the Black American Studies Program, not only for material assistance, but also for providing me with an invigorating atmosphere in which to work. Expressions of gratitude to my wife Susan for her years of tedious proofreading and constant companionship will remain private.

November 1977
NEWARK, DELAWARE

Coal,
Iron,
and Slaves

Introduction

Upon graduation from the University of Vermont in 1839, Jason Niles journeyed south in search of a teaching position. Along the way he spent the night at a Nashville hotel and, at the bar, overheard two patrons debate the relative virtues of careers in agriculture and in business enterprise. One disputant declared the independent farmer ten times more an aristocrat than a businessman because "the merchant lived by being complaisant and civil to all; and when he ceased to be so he starved; while the farmer who was not dependent on others for his living, could be as aristocratic and haughty as he pleased with perfect impunity."[1]

There can be little doubt that the agrarian ideal mirrored in this statement, along with its corollary tendency toward the "aristocratic and haughty," hampered the growth of a strong business class in the antebellum South. Businessmen of the region lacked the social prestige enjoyed by their northern counterparts and, as a group, ranked beneath planters, politicians, military officers, and professionals. This agrarian spirit was reflected in the general disdain for "Yankees" as unprincipled men who only lusted for the dollar, in the tendency for successful businessmen to purchase plantations and thereby attain the ultimate distinction, and in the disinclination of intelligent young men to enter upon a business career.[2]

The distinctive qualities of business and industry in the Old South have been obscured by the pervasive shadow of the plantation. The roar of a blast furnace, or the din of a cotton factory, was more likely to jar the southern imagination than to capture it, given the South's traditional idealization of itself as an arcadian paradise. Much less specialized than their northern peers, southern factory owners often blended their careers with those of planter and politician. This propensity constituted one of the most striking characteristics of industrial development in the South. Since they owned a disproportionate share of the region's surplus wealth, planters who themselves did not become businessmen often invested capital in that industrial expansion which did occur. Whether managed and financed by planters, businessmen, or both, however, established social and economic imperatives predetermined that slaves would be relied upon to turn the wheels of industry just as surely as they were to pick cotton. In fact, slavery became one of the characteristic features of southern industry.

Most southern cotton and woolen factories utilized a slave work force, either exclusively or alongside poor white workers. The first southern textile mill was probably established in South Carolina during the American Revolution, but by the 1840s, Georgia's remarkable expansion in productive capacity led that state to distinction as the "New England of the South." The textile industry followed a unique employment pattern. Piedmont factories generally utilized poor whites rather than blacks, while lowland mills almost universally employed only slave labor. This practice is at least partially explained by the fact that poor whites predominated in the Carolina uplands; their well-known class antagonism toward the institution of slavery and the relatively scant number of slaves in the district precluded reliance on bonded factory operatives. On the other hand, lowland slaves often outnumbered whites by a wide margin. Political and economic necessity, therefore, dictated that excess slaves be put to useful employment in the lowland mills. Unlike William Gregg's famous experiment with poor white workers at the Graniteville cotton mills, most factories followed the example of South Carolina's Saluda factory, which employed 158 bondsmen in 1851. Even though owners of southern textile factories began to shift from slave to free white operatives during the 1850s, in 1860 they still employed more than five thousand slave factory hands.[3]

By contrast, tobacco factories relied on slave labor almost exclusively. Two centers of production dominated the market—the eastern district of Virginia and North Carolina, and the western district of Kentucky. In the eastern district, most tobacco factory slaves were hired hands, although the employers always owned a sizable portion of their operatives. Whether owned or hired, however, the number of slave operatives at tobacories in the district was always large until, by 1860, they totaled 12,843. The most successful Richmond tobacconist, James Thomas, Jr., utilized 150 bondsmen who produced over one million pounds of chewing tobacco annually.[4]

Hemp production represented another leading industry of the Old South. During the eighteenth century, Virginia hemp became a major staple from which osnaburg, linsey-woolsey, linen, rope, and sail were manufactured. Many Virginia planters, such as Robert Carter of Nomini Hall, erected small establishments for the commercial production of cloth and, even in these first small transitionary shops between the homespun and factory stages, slaves spun and wove the finished products. During the Revolutionary War, numerous slaves worked at Virginia's public ropewalk and at the other establishments erected during the period to produce hemp products. By the turn of the nineteenth century, the center of the American hemp industry had shifted westward to Kentucky, where the fiber became a staple of major importance. In fact, according to the preeminent authority on the topic, James F. Hopkins, "Without hemp, slavery might not have flourished in Kentucky, since other agricultural products of the state were not conducive to the extensive use of bondsmen."[5] So thoroughly did blacks dominate labor in the industry that white Kentuckians tagged hemp a "nigger crop." By the Civil War, nearly two hundred Kentucky hemp factories utilized five thousand bondsmen. At the same time, another twenty-five hundred slave operatives toiled in the hemp factories of Missouri.[6]

The northern sojourner J. H. Ingraham observed in 1835 that, in the South, "slaves are trained to every kind of manual labor. The blacks, cabinet-maker, carpenter, builder, wheelright [sic] — all have one or more slaves laboring at their trades. The negro is a third arm to every working man, who can possibly save money to purchase one."[7] Actually, this large representation of southern blacks in the various skilled crafts had deep roots in the colonial period when free artisans were in chronically short supply, particularly in the southern colonies. Not surprisingly then, many slaves became sawyers, carpenters, blacksmiths, coopers, tanners, shoe-makers, cabinet-makers, wheelwrights, weavers, and practitioners of at least nineteen additional trades, according to the files of the *South Carolina Gazette*. This wide range of crafts practiced by colonial slaves begs the question whether the eighteenth-century plantation society could have survived at all without slave artisans.

During the nineteenth century, southern blacks not only continued to practice traditional crafts but learned new ones as well. Bondsmen became machinists or "engineers," cobblers were grouped into shoe factories, and slaves operated the innumerable tanneries, bakeries, and printing presses. They also labored by the hundreds in southern brickyards, and by the thousands in the small local gristmills which ground flour throughout the South. Similarly, commercial mills, such as the Gallego and Haxall mills (the world's largest) of Richmond, Virginia, operated with slave manpower. Throughout the South Carolina and Georgia Tidewater, hundreds of slaves labored at the rice mills concentrated in that area. Likewise, Louisiana and Texas sugar mills worked bonded labor exclusively.[8]

Southern salt production was centered primarily in the Kanawha River Valley of western Virginia. The constant demand for salt, a vital food preservative, led to a steadily increasing capital investment into its manufacture. Between 1810 and 1850, the industry grew dramatically, and as production increased, the slave population grew to 3,140 in 1850. Since so few bondsmen resided in the district, surplus hands from eastern Virginia and from Kentucky formed the backbone of the labor force at the Kanawha saltworks.[9]

The South possessed an abundance of forest resources. Out of the Mississippi and Louisiana swamps black bondsmen chopped, trimmed, and rafted cyprus to New Orleans and Natchez, where still other slaves operated the steam-powered saw mills which could be found in most southern cities. Some of these mills became sizable operations which frequently employed more than one hundred slaves. Many bondsmen disappeared into southern swamps for months at a time to cut wooden shingles and barrel staves. On the eve of the Civil War, most of the sixteen thousand men who labored in the region's lumbering operations were slaves. Similarly, the naval stores industry relied on blacks almost entirely. The industry was centered in the Carolinas, an area that produced over 90 percent of the nation's tar and turpentine in 1850. Large turpentiners such as Daniel W. Jordan of North Carolina utilized slave work forces which totaled two hundred or more. By 1860, the South's turpentiners worked fifteen thousand bondsmen.[10]

The South's fisheries yielded a very important protein supplement to the diet of slaves and masters alike, and exports of the product reached significant if undetermined proportions. The famous traveler Frederick Law Olmsted observed that fishing constituted an important branch of industry and a "source of considerable wealth." Like most industries, fisheries also employed "mainly negroes, slave and free."[11] It has been estimated that by 1861 upwards of twenty thousand slave-operated fisheries existed in the South.

Although the South lagged far behind the North in internal improvements, the region's turnpikes, bridges, canals, levees, railroads, city sewers, and waterlines were all built by slave labor. Probably a total of twenty thousand slaves toiled on southern railroads alone during the antebellum period. Numerous blacks also worked at shipyards, the most famous being the runaway slave from Baltimore, Frederick Douglass. Bondsmen also piloted the countless boats large and small which plied southern rivers, inlets, and bays; they operated the ferries and manned canal boats; they labored on steamboats as deckhands, porters, firemen, and engineers; and they performed countless other tasks which had nothing to do with picking cotton.[12]

Few nonagricultural occupations in the Old South, however, made use of slaves so universally, and over such an extended period of time, as the production of iron and the mining of coal. For a half century prior to the American Revolution, Maryland and Virginia iron dominated the colonial export market. Although the Chesapeake region lost its preeminence after the Revolution, within the South it remained the most important single center for the production of iron. Similarly, the eastern Virginia coal field yielded the major supply of coal for homes and industries along the Atlantic Coast, from the development of the first commercial mine in the 1760s until the 1840s, when railroads made it economically feasible to develop the enormous reserves of bituminous coal in western Virginia and Pennsylvania. Until the late 1850s, however, when the Alabama and Tennessee fields assumed a minor degree of importance, commercial coal mining in the South was almost exclusively a Virginian affair. Since slaves played a crucial role in the growth and development of both industries in that region over an extended period of time, a primary purpose of this study is to define the extent to which bonded labor was employed in the coal and iron enterprises of Maryland and Virginia.

Even though inadequate manuscript and statistical data render a precise enumeration of slave workers in the iron and coal industries of Maryland and Virginia nearly impossible, a reasonably accurate approximation may be projected. At least sixty-five ironworks were erected in the region during the colonial era, and the typical ironworks of that period required an average labor force of seventy workers. Thus, a minimum of forty-five hundred hands would have been required at one static point in time during the eighteenth century. By the nineteenth century, slave-operated ironworks increased to about eighty, most of which were now concentrated in Virginia, and the average labor force had risen to about ninety hands. Collectively, these ironworks would have utilized approximately seven thousand workers at any given moment during the period from 1800 to 1865.

Between the American Revolution and the Civil War, a minimum of forty coal companies operated in the Richmond Coal Basin of eastern Virginia. Individual mines varied in size and importance, of course, but a few, such as the Midlothian and Dover mining companies, were extensive operations and employed work forces of 150 workmen or more. Other companies employed twenty-five or fewer hands. The average mine probably utilized between fifty and sixty bondsmen. The actual number of mines operating in the field varied over time, but can be grouped into three stages of development. Between the American Revolution and the late 1820s, no more than ten or twelve companies worthy of note operated in the Basin. During the 1830s and 1840s, that number burgeoned to between twenty-five and thirty, but the total had declined again to about ten on the eve of secession. Since the larger and better financed enterprises either absorbed or overwhelmed the smaller companies in the marketplace, mines operating in the Basin during the 1850s were usually larger and more sophisticated than their predecessors. During the initial stage of growth, the slave miners employed at these pits averaged between five hundred and seven hundred, a little over two thousand during the peak production years, and about sixteen hundred to nineteen hundred just prior to the Civil War.

Two industries, of course, do not constitute the entirety of industrial slavery. Neverthelesss, where the cliometricians' macrocosmic approach has stirred intense controversy about the nature of slave life, the utility of microcosmic studies takes on new significance. They provide a valuable tool for testing the universality of the social, economic, and racial imperatives imposed by the slave regime; that is, the applicability of broad generalizations to specific local cases. In so doing, microcosmic studies remind us that generalizations must be drawn from life rather than from a synthetic historical paradigm.

Looking backward tends to flatten time into a single dimension. Through this historical lens, the details of everyday life are freqently obscured and moderns are thus apt to forget that personal adjustments to specific circumstances were often extremely complex, for masters as well as slaves. The highly skilled and trusted ironworker who suddenly rebelled and made a dash for freedom, for example, first had to achieve his "privileged" slave status. It is doubtful, therefore, that our understanding of the dynamics of slavery can be enhanced by forcing slaves onto a continuum from "accommodation" to "resistance," or masters onto a unilinear gradient from "benevolent" to "brutal." Generally, historians have denounced industrial slavery as the most brutal phase of the regime.[13] They usually attribute this harshness to the hiring-out system because it separated the slave from the owner's protection and exposed slaves to the notorious practices of industrialists whose only interest consisted of extracting labor from the hired hands. With that assumption in mind, it is easy to gather examples of harsh treatment and then to conclude that industrial slavery brutalized blacks. Industrial slaves often received harsh treatment, but so did plantation slaves. Accordingly, this kind of analysis reveals little about life as an industrial slave. Only by examining the web of interpersonal relations between employers, slaves, and owners of hired hands can we ever understand the nature of human existence under industrial bondage. While slave codes and court proceedings provide valuable indices to southern white ideals with regard to race relations, daily life often varied from the institutional and legal superstructure of slavery. Consequently, a significant portion of this study examines the day-by-day patterns of human affairs at Chesapeake ironworks and coal mines.

Finally, I have attempted to develop a model of causation which explains the linkage between the industrialists' preference for black labor to white, and the cultural milieu in which that predilection evolved. Some scholars have concluded that slave labor provided more economic advantages than free white labor.[14] Others have argued that, as the foundation of southern culture, slavery was in various degrees uneconomical but that whites could conceive of no other way to deal with blacks than within the controlling mechanism of slavery.[15] Whatever the case with other southerners, industrialists concerned themselves with considerations of both profit and control. Sufficient evidence to prove the profitability of slavery in the coal and iron industries simply does not exist. But entrepreneurs *believed* slaves preferable to whites and acted affirmatively on that assumption. In this light, actual profitability becomes somewhat academic. Like most people, ironmasters and colliers were products of their culture. Conditioned by the values and assumptions of their society, like the planter oligarchy, the operators of ironworks and coal mines clung tenaciously to their "peculiar institution" when they felt it to be threatened. Any menace to that system of labor organization and race relations jeopardized their view of the proper status of blacks in society. Far from a "new breed" of progressive industrialists smothered in a region dominated by powerful planters, ironmasters and colliers felt, as did their plantation counterparts, a paranoiac devotion to the established arrangements in southern society.

NOTES

1. Diary of Jason Niles, November 23, 1839, quoted in Clement Eaton, *The Growth of Southern Civilization, 1790–1860* (New York: Harper & Row, Publishers, 1961), p. 244.

2. Ibid., p. 221.

3. Robert S. Starobin, *Industrial Slavery in the Old South* (New York: Oxford University Press, 1970), pp. 12–13; E. M. Lander, Jr., "Slave Labor in South Carolina Cotton Mills," *Journal of Negro History* 38 (April 1953):161–73; Eaton, *Growth of Southern Civilization*, Chap. 10; *Hunt's Merchants' Magazine* 15 (1846):417, and 17 (1847):323; *Niles' Weekly Register* 40 (1831):281.

4. Joseph Clarke Robert, *The Tobacco Kingdom: Plantation, Market, and Factory in Virginia and North Carolina, 1800–1860* (Gloucester, Mass.: Peter Smith, 1965, originally 1938), p. 197; Starobin, *Industrial Slavery in the Old South*, p. 17; Richard C. Wade, *Slavery in the Cities: The South, 1820–1860* (New York: Oxford University Press, 1964), pp. 22, 33–35; Eaton, *Growth of Southern Civilization*, pp.229–30.

5. James F. Hopkins, *A History of the Hemp Industry in Kentucky* (Lexington: University of Kentucky Press, 1951), p. 4.

6. G. Melvin Herndon, "A War-Inspired Industry: The Manufacture of Hemp in Virginia During the Revolution," *Virginia Magazine of History and Biography* 74 (July 1966):301–11; Louis Morton, *Robert Carter of Nomini Hall: A Virginia Tobacco Planter of the Eighteenth Century* (Charlottesville: University Press of Virginia, 1941). Chap. 7; Thomas B. Moore, *The Hemp Industry in Kentucky* (Lexington: University Press of Kentucky, 1905), Appendix 5; Eaton, *Growth of Southern Civilization*, pp. 239–40.

7. Joseph Holt Ingraham, *The South-west. By a Yankee* (New York: Harper & Brothers, 1835), p. 249.

8. Marcus Wilson Jernegan, *Laboring and Dependent Classes in Colonial America, 1607–1783* (Chicago: University of Chicago Press, 1931), pp. 13, 23; Starobin, *Industrial Slavery in the Old South*, pp. 19–21; *Debow's Review* 2 (1846):331, and 14 (1853):611; V. A. Moody, "Slavery on Sugar Plantations," *Louisiana Historical Quarterly* 7 (April 1924):201–07, 232–53.

9. John Edmund Stealey III, "Slavery and the Western Virginia Salt Industry," *Journal of Negro History* 59 (April 1974):105–31; Edna Chappell McKenzie, "Self-Hire Among Slaves, 1820–1860. Institutional Variation or Aberration?" (Ph.D. dissertation, University of Pittsburgh, 1973), pp. 52–76; Eaton, *Growth of Southern Civilization*, p. 239.

10. Starobin, *Industrial Slavery in the Old South,* pp. 25–26; Frederick Law Olmsted, *A Journey in the Seaboard Slave States, with Remarks on Their Economy* (New York: Mason Brothers, 1859), pp. 149–56; John Hebron Moore, "Simon Gray, Riverman: A Slave Who Was Almost Free," *Mississippi Valley Historical Review* 49 (December 1962):472–84.

11. Olmsted, *Journey in the Seaboard Slave States,* p. 351.

12. Starobin, *Industrial Slavery in the Old South,* pp. 27, 29–30; Frederick Douglass, *Life and Times of Frederick Douglass Written by Himself: His Early Life as a Slave, His Escape from Bondage, and His Complete History* (London: Collier-Macmillan Ltd., 1962, originally 1892), pp. 178–93; "Slave Labor upon Public Works at the South," *DeBow's Review* 17 (1854):76–82; William Wells Brown, *Narrative of William W. Brown: A Fugitive Slave* (Boston: The Anti-Slavery Office, 1848), as reproduced in Robin W. Winks et al. (eds.), *Four Fugitive Slave Narratives* (Reading, Mass.: Addison-Wesley Publishing Co., 1969), passim; Moses Grandy, *Narrative of the Life of Moses Grandy, Late a Slave in the United States of America* (Boston: Oliver Johnson, 1844), reproduced in William Loren Katz (ed.), *Five Slave Narratives* (New York: Arno and the *New York Times,* 1969), pp. 6–25; Joseph A. Goldenberg, "Black Labor in Colonial Shipyards," paper presented at the 1973 Annual Meeting of the Association for the Study of Afro-American Life and History, New York. For a study of planters' involvement in southern manufacturing, see Fred Bateman, James Foust, and Thomas Weiss, "The Participation of Planters in Manufacturing in the Antebellum South," *Agricultural History* 48 (April 1974): 277–98. For a study of the comparative economic development in the North and South, see Fred Bateman and Thomas Weiss, "Comparative Regional Development in Antebellum Manufacturing," *The Journal of Economic History* 35 (March 1975): 182–215.

13. See, for example, Charles Sackett Sydnor, *Slavery in Mississippi* (Gloucester, Mass.: Peter Smith, 1965, originally 1933), p. 179; Kenneth M. Stampp, *The Peculiar Institution: Slavery in the Ante-Bellum South* (New York: Alfred A. Knopf, 1956), p. 84; Samuel Sydney Bradford, "The Ante-Bellum Charcoal Iron Industry of Virginia" (Ph.D. dissertation, Columbia University, 1958), Chaps. 4 and 5, and his article, "The Negro Ironworker in Ante Bellum Virginia," *Journal of Southern History* 25 (May 1959):201–04.

14. See, for example, Alfred H. Conrad and John R. Meyer, *The Economics of Slavery; and Other Studies in Econometric History* (Chicago: Aldine Publishing Co., 1964), p. 82; and Starobin, *Industrial Slavery in the Old South,* pp. 186–89.

15. See, for example, Ulrich B. Phillips, *Life and Labor in the Old South* (Boston: Little, Brown & Co., 1929), Chaps. 10 and 11; and Eugene D. Genovese, *The Political Economy of Slavery: Studies in the Economy and Society of the Slave South* (New York: Random House, 1965), pp. 13–36.

"The Blur of the Coals, the Blast of the Bellows" 1

All my life is full of sorrow,
   Welcome seems the grave;
Oh when will freedom's bright to-morrow
   Dawn on the factory slave?
               —"The Factory Slave"

Although the southern economy of the eighteenth century was predominantly agricultural, the seeds of industrialization took root during the
half century prior to the American Revolution. Between 1716 and 1733, the
Chesapeake Bay region gave birth to the first southern ironworks. By 1775,
the American colonies were the world's third largest producer of unfinished iron and accounted for about 15 percent of the total world output,
or an estimated thirty thousand tons annually. Sweden was second, and
Russia first, in the total production of raw iron.[1] Prior to the War for
Independence, the Chesapeake iron industry produced the vast bulk of
colonial iron for export. Together, Virginia and Maryland exceeded all the
other colonies combined at a ratio sometimes as large as 10 to 1 (see
Appendix 1). That ratio does not tell the whole story, however, for it is
based only on iron exports from the respective colonies and does not
indicate actual production. Since most records for early ironworks no
longer exist, the raw data are simply unavailable. Thus, by 1771 colonial
production had risen to an estimated total of thirty thousand tons annually,
although only about seven thousand of that total were shipped to Britain.
Most of the iron found its way into domestic consumption via ironworks
forbidden by law to manufacture iron wares.[2] Because such production and
distribution of iron remained illegal, official public records were not maintained.

Before the outbreak of the Revolutionary War, an estimated total of 257
furnaces and forges had been built in the colonies.[3] By 1775, Maryland and
Virginia possessed about 25 percent of those installations, while Pennsyl-

vania alone had over one-quarter of the total.[4] Numbers can be deceiving, however, for while Pennsylvania had a larger number than Maryland and Virginia, it had no ironworks that could compare in production capacity to such Chesapeake works as the Principio Iron Company or the Baltimore Iron Company, two of the largest industrial enterprises in colonial America.[5] It was not until the Revolutionary War and after that Pennsylvania ironworks, such as Colebrook Furnace and Cornwall Furnace, began to produce iron at a rate comparable with that of the Principio and Baltimore companies. Expansion of the Pennsylvania iron industry during and after the Revolution was nothing short of phenomenal. During the six decades from 1716 to 1775, seventy-three ironworks were erected in Pennsylvania; in the quarter century from 1775 to 1800, however, ninety-four furnaces and forges were built in that state.[6]

Maryland and Virginia became important producers of iron in America for several reasons. The Chesapeake Bay and its extensive network of rivers enabled ironmasters to overcome the difficulties of overland transportation during this era of inadequate roads. Furnaces and forges were located so that ironmasters could take advantage of the water transportation provided by the Chesapeake system.[7] This was especially significant since the Chesapeake exported so much pig iron to Britain during the colonial period.

Tobacco cultivation also influenced this pattern, for the tobacco trade provided regular, although seasonal, shipping between Chesapeake plantations and England, as well as the opportunity for shipping iron as ballast in tobacco ships.[8] In addition, readily available iron ore close to navigable waterways, a plentiful supply of timber for charcoal, and abundant oyster shells for lime flux from the Chesapeake Bay, all proved important advantages in developing an iron industry in Maryland and Virginia. At least sixty-five ironworks were erected in the Chesapeake region during this era: thirty-six in Maryland and a minimum of twenty-nine in Virginia (see Appendixes 2 and 3). Quite probably, other ironworks were erected, operated, and abandoned in the Chesapeake region during the eighteenth century without leaving any historical traces.

The natural expansion of the region's population and its movement westward·spurred the need for additional production of iron wares. More importantly, the Revolutionary War created an unprecedented demand for iron. Decreasing supplies of wood for charcoal, the depletion of easily accessible iron ore in the Tidewater, and the corresponding increase in production costs had forced many Tidewater iron plantations to suspend operations. When the Revolutionary War began, those furnaces and forges in the eastern part of the colonies were saved by the demand for cannon, shot, camp utensils, and other articles of war. At the same time, new ironworks appeared in the western sections of Maryland and Virginia.[9] The demands of war proved so great that Isaac Zane, owner of Marlboro Ironworks in the Shenandoah Valley, was prompted to proclaim that "had we ten Furnaces and Forges the demand is more than equal to what could be made."[10]

The mixture of war and politics also resulted in the confiscation of several ironworks operated by loyalists and English sympathizers. Thus, American officials seized the Principio Iron Works during the Revolution and converted it to the manufacture of cannon and balls for the war.[11] Elk Forge in Maryland was also confiscated and put to the production of cannon and swivel guns for the patriots, and a similar fate befell the Nottingham Iron Works. Most ironmasters, however, supported the struggle for independence. In the Baltimore area, for example, several works, such as the Elk Ridge Furnace and the Northampton Furnace, manufactured ammunition for the struggle.[12] Furnaces and forges erected farther west in the rebellious colonies also produced cannon, shot, and utensils. Two years before the Revolution, Thomas Johnson and his brothers James and Baker began operating Catoctin Furnace, located in Frederick County, Maryland. Catoctin probably produced cannon and ammunition for the war.[13] One of the largest and steadiest suppliers of weaponry for the patriots was Antietam Furnace, located seven miles north of Harpers Ferry.[14] The owner, Samuel Hughes, became Maryland's foremost manufacturer of heavy weapons. Following hostilities, Hughes continued to make cannon and purchased the Principio Furnace site in 1790, where he erected Cecil Furnace. In 1818, Hughes offered his works for sale. The advertisement mentioned "a Boring mill with most perfect machinery to bore five canon [sic] at a time."[15]

Soon after the fighting began, the Virginia legislature authorized the loan of £5,000 for the construction of a furnace, and in 1777, it loaned £2,000 to the Albemarle Furnace Company to rejuvenate its ironworks.[16] Virginia also passed a series of acts exempting forge and furnace workers from military service.[17] Finally, Virginia itself entered the iron industry by building Westham Foundry, one of the best cannon foundries in America.[18] The Chesapeake iron industry not only provided vital supplies for the war but a number of Revolutionary leaders as well. Many Maryland families, for example, were involved in the iron industry and participated on the patriot side of the struggle. These included such well-known figures as Charles Ridgely, a colonel in the Continental Army, Charles Carrollton, one of the major political leaders in the movement for independence, and Thomas Johnson, who became the first governor of Maryland.[19]

Despite the early advantages enjoyed by the Chesapeake region, the industry there came under serious challenge by the late eighteenth century. Thereafter, improved technological developments found ready acceptance in Pennsylvania and spawned a dynamic growth, unparalleled elsewhere, in that state's iron industry. Although the Chesapeake lost its preeminence to Pennsylvania, the loss was relative, and Chesapeake iron production expanded without serous interruption until the Civil War.[20]

The Chesapeake region is comprised of four major geographic areas. The *Tidewater* is that portion from the Atlantic Ocean, the Chesapeake Bay and its numerous inlets, to the falls of the Potomac, Rappahannock, James, Appomattox, and Roanoke rivers where the water is briny. The section between the falls into the eastern spurs of the Blue Ridge Mountains, where the water runs swift and fresh, is known as the *Piedmont*. The *Great Valley of Virginia* stretches between the Blue Ridge Mountains to the east and the Allegheny Mountains to the west, and extends from Maryland to North Carolina and Tennessee. The fertile Valley of Virginia itself is further subdivided into those of the Shenandoah, James, Roanoke, New, and Holsten rivers. Finally, that mountainous area west of the Allegheny Mountains crest, which now constitutes the state of West Virginia, is known as the *Trans-Allegheny region*.[21] Following the successful struggle for independence, the Chesapeake iron industry went into a short period of recession but soon recovered and entered an era of expansion that continued until the Civil War decade. This growth was especially evident in the western part of the region where ironworks sprang up even on the other side of the Allegheny Mountains. Within less than a century, the iron industry had moved from the Tidewater into the outermost reaches of the Chesapeake states (see Figure 1).[22]

Before the American Revolution, growth in the iron industry was not limited strictly to the Tidewater area. As in Pennsylvania, furnaces and forges came into existence to meet the immediate needs of settlers moving into the interior.[23] For example, Pine Forge appeared in Shenandoah County within nine years after Alexander Spotswood had erected the first ironworks in 1718.[24] In the region bounded by the Blue Ridge and Allegheny mountains, and the counties of Shenandoah, Rockbridge, Botetourt, Allegheny, and Wythe, there was a similar, though more significant, expansion of the industry after the Revolution. Shenandoah County had at least thirteen furnaces and forges;[25] Rockbridge County had eight furnaces and forges;[26] Allegheny and Botetourt counties possessed a total of nineteen ironworks;[27] and in Wythe County eleven ironworks were constructed between 1800 and 1861.[28]

On the other side of the Allegheny Mountains, in western Virginia, Mount Pleasant Furnace was built in Monongalia County in 1789, three years prior to the construction of the first ironworks near Pittsburgh.[29] On the Ohio River, Wheeling enjoyed a location near extensive coal fields that offered cheap and abundant fuel and easy transportation of its products to the growing towns of the Ohio River Valley. By 1853, Wheeling had become a rival to Richmond and was dubbed "Nail City" because of the

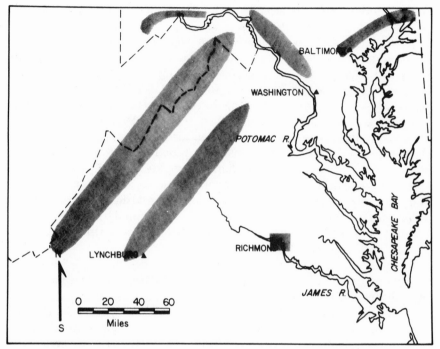

BALTIMORE

WASHINGTON

POTOMAC R.

CHESAPEAKE BAY

LYNCHBURG

RICHMOND

JAMES R.

S

0   20   40   60

Miles

1.   Important Iron-Producing Districts. *Drawing by Karen Woods.*

products of its five extensive rolling mills.[30] Early that year, the *Wheeling Daily Intelligencer* commented that "the various manufactures of iron, glass, silk paper, etc., were visited by intelligent men from all quarters of the East and West, who were surprised at the perfection to which those manufactories have been brought up in a place whose rise is comparatively so recent."[31]

A similar process was underway in western Maryland. Allegheny County, near Cumberland, contained the richest coal and iron deposits in Maryland. During the 1830s, the Baltimore and Ohio Railroad Company and the Chesapeake and Ohio Canal stimulated development of the area's mineral resources and, by providing the necessary transportation, created a ready acceptance among iron men of western Maryland after the 1830s for the new production techniques developed earlier in Great Britain.[32] As the frontier pressed westward, iron manufacturing followed close at hand. In the process, the industry lost the characteristics of relatively isolated local operations and acquired the larger focus of the region itself. Increasingly, the economies of the Ohio and Mississippi river basins, along with their tributaries in Kentucky and Tennessee, were integrated by improved river transportation and the construction of canals and railroads into a relatively unified system directed toward specific markets within a new regional economy.[33]

Enlarged marketing patterns took hold throughout the Chesapeake region during the same period. The most significant expansion and integration occurred in the Valley of Virginia. Valley ironmasters sought and found profitable outlets for their iron down the Shenandoah and Potomac rivers to Baltimore, and eastward down the James River to Richmond and Norfolk. Consequently, the Valley played the role of producer of crude iron for eastern Virginia and remained rural while helping to build urban centers in the east.[34] The same was true in Maryland where iron was shipped down the Susquehanna and Potomac rivers and a variety of smaller streams to Baltimore. This system of integrated waterways flowing to the Bay gave the iron industry of the region the characteristic of a Chesapeake iron industry.[35] Although the industry found greater prosperity as a result of integration with broader market outlets, in times of general depression it also suffered more. The national boom in railroad construction from the early 1840s on made for dramatic fluctuations in the business cycle with irregular periods of "booms" and "busts." Other disruptive factors included foreign competition from British iron, overextension of credit, and occasional inventory surpluses.[36]

Unlike western Maryland, the Valley of Virginia did not contain the natural resources necessary to convert to mineral coal fuel; it, therefore, relied on charcoal. Nevertheless, by the 1830s the iron industry in the Valley of Virginia had undergone a great expansion.[37] Even though the

Panic of 1837 halted this movement temporarily, by the 1840s the capital invested in Virginia's ninety-odd ironworks totaled $1,246,650.[38] Much of this large investment was both the result of, and the reason for, the major attempts to improve transportation between eastern and western sections of the Chesapeake region. The James River and Kanawha Canal Company, created in the 1830s, strengthened the economic bonds of the Valley ironmasters with the industrial entrepreneurs of Richmond in the same way that the Chesapeake and Ohio Canal and the Baltimore and Ohio Railroad tied together western Maryland and Baltimore. These improvements in transportation to the Tidewater greatly stimulated the establishment of secondary manufactures and the rise of urban centers on the Bay.[39] This symbiotic relationship, however, could last only so long as charcoal iron could compete in the broader marketplace, and technological developments long underway in the industry were squeezing charcoal iron out of the urban centers it had helped create.

Toward the end of the eighteenth century, the British iron industry underwent a technological revolution that changed the nature not only of iron manufacture, but eventually of all industry and society itself. It began with the introduction of coke as a blast furnace fuel in place of charcoal. Once adopted, coke swiftly transformed the British iron industry. During the American Revolution, perhaps, most British furnaces used charcoal. By 1806, only 11 out of 173 iron furnaces in Britain still fired with charcoal.[40] In the process, Britain was transformed from a high-cost to a low-cost producer of unfinished iron. In the United States, however, the old technology continued. Now the positions of the two countries were reversed as America became a high-cost producer of iron. Nevertheless, this was a *relative* change in the status of American iron, and the industry continued to grow until by the 1830s U.S. production of pig iron had increased to about two hundred thousand tons, nearly a 700 percent increase over production at the beginning of the Revolutionary era.[41]

During the eighteenth century, the so-called indirect process of smelting and forging prevailed in England and America. The first step in the process involved a blast furnace, a large stone structure the inside of which was a bottle-shaped container for smelting iron ore and fuel (see Figure 2). Under intense heat the oxygen was banished from the ore, and carbon from the charcoal took its place. The resultant alloy, known as pig iron, could be reheated and worked into various shapes.[42]

At the forge, pig iron was refined by alternately heating it in a hearth until malleable and then beating it with a large water-powered hammer that pounded out the impurities in the form of slag. The process required a great deal of labor, and only a small quantity of iron could be produced at one time. By the end of the eighteenth century, English inventors had altered both steps of the iron-making process. Coke replaced charcoal as a fuel, and refining pig iron by hammering gave way to the technique known as "puddling." This technique involved the use of a new kind of furnace, called the "reverberatory" furnace. In it, iron was separated from the fuel by a low wall, and because the fuel and iron did not come into contact, a fuel less pure than charcoal, such as coke, could be used without contaminating the metal. Although too impure to use for traditional methods of refining, coke was ideal for puddling. Instead of removing the iron from the fire for hammering, now the furnaceman, or "puddler," manipulated the iron through ports in the furnace wall, performing a sort of stirring motion, or "puddling."[43] Moreover, the great increase in the amount of heat permitted by the new reverberatory furnace made it possible to replace the hammering phase with a new system that forced the malleable iron through grooved rollers, known as the "rolling mill," which could be adjusted to press the desired shape. The rolling mill and the technique of puddling were usually adopted together in the United States since puddling produced an iron with a high slag content which had to be literally "squeezed" out as it passed through the rolling operation.

Puddling and rolling cut labor and fuel costs. While England had generally accepted the new technology by the end of the eighteenth century, the United States retained the traditional charcoal blast furnaces. Until technical refinements in furnace construction during the second decade of the nineteenth century, puddling furnaces wasted too much of the blast.[44] Also, charcoal was nearly free of sulphur, and, once burned, its ash consisted mostly of the lime needed to smelt iron. Moreover, good anthracite coal and coke were difficult to find in the early nineteenth century, and coal or coke did not produce iron as hard as that made with charcoal. The

2. Cross Section of a Charcoal Blast Furnace. *Drawing by Karen Woods.*

lack of adequate overland transportation facilities for shipping large quantities of iron, and the inertia of tradition, also constituted strong deterrents to the adoption of the new technology by American ironmasters. Perhaps the most important reason coke did not find ready acceptance in America was the abundance of timber for charcoal. However, even the seemingly endless forests of early America could not continue to supply the insatiable demand of the charcoal iron industry. Only the growing scarcity of wood in traditional iron-producing centers precipitated a conversion to coke in the United States.[45]

Although few technological changes took place in the American iron industry prior to the 1830s, by the late antebellum era earnest experimentation began with anthracite and coke fuels, steam power for blowing engines, and hot-blast furnaces. Unlike the traditional charcoal furnaces erected in western Virginia after the Revolution, some western Maryland ironworks quickly adopted the new technological innovations.[46] One of the largest and most sophisticated ironworks in the nation, Mount Savage Iron Works, built in 1840 near Cumberland, consisted of three very large hot-blast coke furnaces, a rolling mill with twenty-seven furnaces to heat the iron, and two trains of rollers. The entire operation was powered by steam rather than the traditional waterwheel.[47] In 1844, the Mount Savage Iron Works also produced the first heavy railroad track ("T" rails) manufactured in the United States. And not far from the Mount Savage Works near Frostburg, Lonaconing Furnace had already successfully used coke as a fuel in 1837.[48]

During the two decades before the Civil War, increasing demands from railroads, building construction, and the general quickening of the industrial pulse stimulated the adoption of the new technology in other areas as well.[49] The machinery and supplementary works that constituted rolling mills tended to appear in cities where profitable markets existed and trade with the countryside could be conducted with facility and profit. In the Chesapeake region, rolling mill centers developed at Richmond and Baltimore, where railroad and port facilities were readily available. Other ironmasters chose to erect rolling mills near the ore fields in close proximity to furnaces and forges, such as in the Cumberland, Maryland, area.[50] Adoption of the new technology reflected the trend of manufacturing toward the large-scale unit of production and the centralization of the new ironworks at strategic points within the transportation network.[51] Between 1800 and 1860, a total of at least 115 ironworks had been erected —80 in Virginia and 35 in Maryland (see Appendixes 4 and 5).

Despite its earlier successes, the Chesapeake iron industry declined rapidly after the Civil War. The war itself decimated some of the ironworks and seriously disrupted the normal channels of trade. The boom in American railroad construction after the Civil War sealed the industry's downfall. By 1874, the four major railroads, the New York Central, Pennsylvania, Erie, and Baltimore and Ohio, had consolidated lesser lines into intricate systems connecting the eastern urban centers with the western markets at Chicago, Omaha, and St. Louis. West of the Mississippi Valley numerous short lines were built, and four transcontinental lines spanned the West before the turn of the twentieth century. As early as 1868, the Union Pacific and the Central Pacific met at Promontory Point, Utah, linked East and West, and symbolized the beginning of a truly national market system connected by railroads. This extensive railroad construction created a boom in the iron industry, which in turn adopted new techniques for the mass production of cheaper iron. The Chesapeake iron industry, however, failed to adapt to the new technology, partly from conservatism, but mostly because the dictates of efficiency shifted the main centers of iron manufacture farther west. The city of Pittsburgh became the nation's major iron producer because it was located at the optimum point between the new western markets, the Great Lakes ore ranges, and the rich Pennsylvania coal fields—all linked by efficient railroad transportation. Thus, while initially the railroads were good customers for charcoal iron, the Chesapeake iron industry helped lay the track for its own demise.[52]

As the South slowly began to develop an embryonic industrial base, there was a corresponding increase in the dependency upon black slaves to supply the labor for this movement. Unfamiliar with American slavery and under the impression that black workers provided only brute labor for tobacco plantations, J. D. Schoepf, a German physician touring Virginia in the 1780s, was amazed to find that blacks performed all types of skilled labor. He observed that "there is hardly any trade or craft which has not been learned and is carried on by negroes."[53] The same observation held true for the iron industry in Maryland and Virginia. In the 1790s, the Irish traveler Isaac Weld, Jr., noted that in Chesapeake iron production "the forges and furnaces are all worked by negroes, who seem to be particularly suited to such an occupation."[54] Although Weld exaggerated, that general impression was often gained by foreign travelers. From the very beginning of southern iron manufacture, slaves were the key ingredient in the labor force. Whenever possible, masters owned their skilled black artisans to insure stability at key positions in the production process. Common laborers were often owned as well, but as time wore on, they were increasingly hired from local owners and from slave-hiring marts which arose in various parts of the region. This pattern hardened into a tradition that lasted until it was destroyed by the Civil War.

On the morning of June 20, 1710, Alexander Spotswood, the newly commissioned lieutenant governor of Virginia, arrived in the colony from England. Spotswood's career as governor, however, was far less signifi-

cant than his private business endeavors, for he was the first ironmaster in
America to see that black slaves could be productively employed in the
manufacture of iron. The exact year in which Spotswood erected the
South's first successful ironworks remains unknown, but in 1714 the governor paid the passage of a group of destitute German miners and settled
the immigrant families along the Rapidanna River at Germanna. Here he
constructed the Tuball (Virginia) Iron Works. The Germans, who operated
the iron mines and erected the furnace, soon grew dissatisfied and in 1720
evacuated the iron community for greater opportunities elsewhere. The
governor's response to the problem of an unstable labor supply was to
purchase a large number of African slaves to operate his installation.[55]

Most of what is known about Spotswood's ironworks historians must
glean from a careful reading of one of eighteenth-century Virginia's most
famous residents. A man of diverse interests and accomplishments in the
Enlightenment mold, William Byrd of Westover journeyed to Germanna in
1732 to learn something about the "mystery" of making iron. Perhaps the
most poignant observation Byrd recorded in his journal during that visit
was the ironmasters' nearly complete dependency upon slave workers.

On his way to Germanna, Byrd paused briefly to inspect a furnace at
Fredericksville, Virginia, which was operated by a Mr. Chiswell. As Byrd
discovered, the Fredericksville works depended on a slave force of considerable size. Chiswell believed that 120 slaves were necessary for the
operation of an ironworks, and "the more Virginians amongst them the
better."[56] Only about eighty bondsmen were employed at that time, however, for Chiswell observed that the works needed "forty Negroes more to
carry on all the business with their own force."[57]

Byrd found that slave labor was heavily relied upon at Spotswood's
Tuball works as well, and that remained true throughout its existence. In
1725, at least eighty slaves toiled at the installation, and by 1739, when
Spotswood drew up a proposal to lease the works, he stipulated that he
would "deliver up Sixty able Working Slaves with 12 or 15 of their children
which . . . have all been trained up and Employed in the Iron Works."[58]
Spotswood died in 1740, and his estate passed to his oldest son. The Tuball
works continued to operate for the next two generations with the toil of
"eighty working slaves."[59] Alexander Spotswood's example set the pattern for the charcoal iron industry in the Chesapeake region, which
suggests that his ideas fell on fertile ground and provided a realistic adapta-
tion to the economic realities and social milieu of the area. As the first to see
the value of black slaves in the manufacture of iron, Spotswood was the
initiator of one of the most striking characteristics of the Chesapeake iron
industry.[60]

Another booming enterprise, the Principio Iron Works, located along
Principio Creek in Maryland not far from present-day Baltimore, also

attracted Byrd's attention. The association of British ironmasters, merchants, and capitalists who owned Principio sent ironmaster John England to Maryland to oversee the completion and supervision of the works.[61] The company began operations in 1718 when it shipped about three tons of bar iron to England as a test sample, the first American crude iron exported to the mother country.[62] Between 1722 and 1751, the Principio Company prospered and built four additional installations. Three of them, the North East Works, Kingsbury Furnace, and Lancashire Furnace, were constructed in Maryland.[63] The Accokeek Furnace was built in Stafford County, Virginia, on the plantation of Augustine Washington, who became the father of George ten years later, in 1732.[64] By 1751, the Principio Company was the sole proprietor of four furnaces, two forges, and nearly thirty thousand acres of land, and became one of the largest producers of iron in the American colonies.[65]

At first, the Principio partners were wary about using slave workers. Unaccustomed to slaves, for a time they preferred to rely upon traditional sources of free and indentured employees.[66] It was not long, however, before the severe shortage of white labor in the colonies forced the partners to change their minds. Acquiescing to the force of necessity, in 1721 they purchased at least eighteen hands.[67] By 1723, the infant Principio Company employed twenty-six free whites, ten white servants "without wages," and, after the death of several blacks, thirteen slaves.[68] In 1725, the company agent in London invested the Principio ironmaster with "full power to buy at any time 40 or 50 blacks, or what number you think proper."[69] Whether or not the manager used this authority remains unknown. Over the years, however, the company not only grew in productive capacity, but in doing so also augmented its slave force, until by 1751, Principio "owned slaves and live-stock in abundance."[70]

During the three decades following midcentury, the fortunes of the Principio Company declined appreciably. Its timber resources began to dwindle and its farmlands yielded less and less. Moreover, the slaves grew old, many of them becoming superannuated.[71] All of these difficulties increased operating costs. The War for Independence proved the final disruption for the company's operations. In 1780, the Maryland General Assembly confiscated all British property in the state, and the Principio ironworks passed under the auctioneer's hammer.[72] Even though the company had been in a gradual decline for thirty years, its confiscated assets included at least 136 black bondsmen: from the Lancashire Furnace 54 Negroes, from the Kingsbury Furnace 40 blacks, and from the North East Forge 42 bondsmen.[73]

In 1731, several prominent Maryland residents—Daniel Dulany, Dr. Charles Carroll, Benjamin Tasker, Charles Carroll of Annapolis, and Daniel Carroll—formed a partnership and, along the Patapsco River near

Baltimore, constructed the third major iron company in the Chesapeake region. The Baltimore Iron Company represented the first locally owned and operated works in the colony. The company expanded over time, and by the 1760s it became one of the largest industrial enterprises of any kind in colonial America.[74]

Unlike the Principio Company, the Baltimore Iron Works utilized a large contingent of black slaves from the beginning. After all, in contrast to those of the Principio Company, the owners were resident Maryland aristocrats who already had extensive slaveholdings prior the erection of the works.[75] The company began operations in 1733 with a labor force of forty-seven white men, thirty-eight of whom were free men on wages and nine indentured servants. On the other hand, the company owned forty-two black slaves.[76] A year later, the labor force at the Baltimore works numbered eighty-one. Forty-three were black slaves, although the company also employed many part-time white workmen from the surrounding area on a seasonal basis.[77] At the height of its development, in 1764, the Baltimore Iron Works owned 150 blacks and hired still others.[78] Little is known of the company's history after this period, but its operations must have been extensive. In 1785, one-fifth of the Baltimore works was put up for sale "consisting of a Furnace and Two Forges, with upward of 28,000 acres of land, and more than 200 Negroes, and also Stock of every kind."[79] Few iron companies in the Chesapeake area operated on the magnitude of the Baltimore Iron Works or used as many slave operatives. To some degree, however, they all followed the same pattern in assuming it both natural and necessary to utilize slaves in the production of iron.

It is impossible to arrive at the precise number of blacks employed at most of the other ironworks which operated in the Chesapeake area during the colonial period. Nevertheless, they all utilized slave labor. For example, at Neabsco Furnace, owned by the wealthy Virginia planter John Tayloe, about thirty-five or forty hands labored in 1741, year for which records still exist.[80] John Tayloe was also the controlling partner in the Occoquan Iron Works from 1755 to 1760. He kept a ledger for those years, and although it is not in good order, it does establish that Occoquan employed a number of slave laborers. Purchases for the years 1755, 1756, and 1758 indicate that the Occoquan company purchased at least twenty-eight hands for their furnace.[81] In 1760, the partnership agreement for the works lapsed, thrusting the operation of Occoquan into the hands of John Ballendine, a Virginian who dabbled in many speculative enterprises. Ballendine soon lost control of the furnace to his creditors, and after liquidating what he could of the estate, he filed bankruptcy in 1767. Even after the sale of an unknown number of company slaves, Negroes at Occoquan still numbered forty.[82]

The nature of employment patterns at other colonial ironworks in the region are even more difficult to ascertain because the evidence is so fragmentary. For example, few records remain for the various furnaces and forges erected in Virginia's Shenandoah Valley during the pre-Revolutionary period. Several Shenandoah ironmasters were Quakers who had emigrated from Pennsylvania, and their religion may have temporarily dampened their desire for slaves. The Quaker Isaac Zane, owner of Marlboro Iron Works, listed only one slave in 1771.[83] But before long, Zane apparently acquired assumptions similar to the Chesapeake slave-owners and attempted to cut his costs by converting to a larger slave labor force. By 1795, he owned twenty Negroes valued at £1120 and hired an undetermined number of others.[84]

One relatively small company, Patuxent Iron Works, which operated a few miles south of Baltimore, utilized a remarkably stable slave crew. Managed by brothers Samuel, John, and Thomas Snowden, the company averaged about forty-five slave hands per year throughout the period between the 1760s and the 1780s.[85] Other companies employed work forces which were amalgams of convicts, indentured servants, and black slaves, as did Elk Ridge Furnace located a few miles from Patuxent.[86]

Throughout the slave era, a number of important ironworks operated north of Baltimore in the area of the Big Gunpowder River. In 1762, Charles Ridgely began construction of Northampton Furnace and two forges along the Big Gunpowder. Three years later, James Russell headed a group that established nearby Nottingham Furnace. Both of these companies conducted extensive operations before the American Revolution. During the war, Northampton produced munitions for the patriots, while Maryland confiscated the Nottingham Company because of the loyalist sympathies of its owner.[87] Although the evidence does not indicate what percentage of the company's work force the slaves constituted, an inventory of Nottingham's confiscated assets in 1780 listed 161 black slaves.[88] Nottingham Furnace was auctioned by the state a year later, and Charles Ridgely, the owner of Northampton, purchased the furnace along with fifty-eight of its bonded workmen.[89] Ridgely's Nottingham Furnace was an operation of considerable scale during the 1760s and 1770s. Although only a few blacks were present, in 1772 he employed a fairly large force of at least eighty-five white indentured servants.[90] But in 1781 Ridgely committed himself to slave labor, as we have seen. By 1788, the company must have relied primarily upon black slaves, for when one-eighth of the partnership was put up for sale, that portion of the property consisted of about sixty Negroes.[91]

By the beginning of the War for Independence, the use of slave labor at Chesapeake ironworks clearly was a well-established practice. Slaves not only constituted the backbone of the Chesapeake iron industry, but they also worked in every occupation associated with the production of iron. Almost from the beginning, they provided not merely common labor, but service in the most skilled crafts as well. Thus, in 1732 Alexander Spotswood did "everything with his own people, except raising the mine and running the iron," and in doing so he felt that he had reduced his expenses significantly. Moreover, Spotswood was so enthusiastic over the black workers that he believed that "by his directions he could bring sensible Negroes to perform those parts of the work" as well as the skilled whites who now held those positions.[92] By 1739, however, when Spotswood drew up a proposal to lease the works, he used slaves in every occupation, for he wrote that except for the "chief founder and General Overseer the whole Business of my Iron Works is carried on by Slaves who have no Wages."[93]

The Principio Company also used slave workers in every capacity. Unfortunately, no roster has survived which indicates the occupations of the blacks employed by the company; hence, there is no way of knowing what kind of work slaves performed at Principio during its many years of operation. As early as 1725, however, the owners of the works consented to the use of blacks at skilled positions, for the company's spokesman in Britain exhorted manager John England to "encourage the Blacks and all Such workmen as teach them anything."[94] When the Maryland General Assembly confiscated the company's holdings during the Revolution, its list of assets included slaves of many skills, including founders, stock-takers, fillers, colliers, blacksmiths, watermen, miners, and others.[95]

Of the ninety-six-man work force at the Baltimore Iron Works in 1736 and 1737, forty-three slaves constituted a large segment of the miners, colliers, woodchoppers, farm hands, cooks, and at least one was a blacksmith.[96] No doubt existed in Dr. Carroll's mind about the use of skilled bondsmen at ironworks. Actively involved in the management of the Baltimore works for many years, in 1753 when he enumerated his "Proposals" for erecting a furnace to "run iron," Dr. Carroll suggested that the prospective owner

> as soon as he Can conveniently do it to get Young Negro Lads to put under the Smith Carpenters Founders Finers & Fillers as also to get a certain number of able Slaves to fill the Furnace Stock the Bridge Raise Ore & Cart and burn the same. Wood Cutters may for some Time be hired there. There should be Two master Colliers one at the Furnaces another at the Forge with a Suitable Number of Slaves or Serv[an]ts under Each who might Coal in the Summer and Cut wood in the winter.[97]

Similarly, Occoquan slaves were among the fifty-five blacks offered for sale to liquidate an estate in 1768. Included in the group of blacks sold were several of the most skilled craftsmen to be found at an ironworks. For example, Billy was "a very trusty good Forgeman, as well at the Finery as under the Hammer, and understands putting up his Fire." Also advertised in the estate sale were Ralph, "an exceeding good Finer," Isaac, a Hammerman and Finer, Abraham, "an exceeding good Forge Carpenter, Cooper, and clapboard carpenter," and Ben and Toby, both "very fine master Colliers." Also offered for sale were five blacksmiths, four colliers, and other skilled hands.[98] Before John Tayloe bowed out of the Occoquan venture, he hired to the works a slave with dexterity seldom equaled, for Billy was so ingenious that he was "capable of doing almost any Sort of Business, and for some Years past has been chiefly employed as a Founder, Stone Mason, and a Miller as occasion required."[99]

This pattern of slave employment in all branches of the industry apparently held true for those other furnaces and forges in the region about which little or nothing is known. For example, James Hunter's iron and steel works located near Fredericksville, Virginia, employed a large number of slaves during the early years of the Revolution. Beginning operation in 1776, Hunter advertised for a "Number of Hands who understand the File, also Anchor Smiths, Blacksmiths, and Nailors." Because Hunter, like ironmasters generally, preferred to own his most skilled craftsmen, he advertised that "Negro Tradesmen in any of the above Branches," as well as other categories, "would be preferred on Purchase, for ready Money."[100] When Hunter's ironworks was sold in 1790, the estate included "a number of valuable Slaves, such as Hammermen, Refiners, Colliers, Forge-Carpenters, Wheelwrights, Smiths, Millers, Waggoners, etc."[101]

Colonial newspapers carried many descriptive references to blacks skilled in some labor connected with the iron industry. Among the thirty-two blacks sold from the estate of one deceased ironmaster in 1760 were "about 18 or 20 tradesmen vis. smiths, forgemen, colliers, carpenters, & such."[102] In another newspaper advertisement, approximately one hundred bondsmen, including a blacksmith and several miners and furnace men,[103] were offered for sale by an ironmaster in 1769. And a 1771 estate sale advertised two hundred slaves, among which were many "good Furnace Men, Forgemen, Colliers, Carters, and Watermen."[104]

Heavy reliance on slave labor at Chesapeake ironworks persisted beyond the American Revolution to the Civil War. Following the struggle for independence, the demand for war material declined and many ironworks were forced to shut down. Even though much of the evidence is fragmentary, it is apparent that those which continued to operate did so with black labor. Moreover, both owned and hired slaves continued to perform every kind of occupation required at an ironworks.

John Blair, an iron founder in Grayson County, Virginia, employed at least nine black hands at his ironworks, although it is not clear whether they were owned or hired.[105] Redwell Furnace, in Shenandoah County, Virginia, also utilized many black workmen. The account book that remains is not in good condition, but inevitably the names of such people as "Reuben Negroe," "Black Joseph," "Moses Negroe," and "Moses Negroe Little" appear throughout the pages.[106] Ridwell Furnace (not Redwell), located in New Market, Virginia, also utilized black hands. In 1808, about twenty white workers and twenty-four hired slaves labored at Ridwell.[107] Cumberland Forge of Maryland dates back to the 1740s. Although there is no indication that slaves were employed in the beginning,[108] by 1796, Cumberland Forge utilized at least forty-four slave hands.[109]

Most of these early ironworks were unknown beyond their own localities, but a few attained national importance. Because the company correspondence and business records have been preserved, it is possible to examine the operations of several ironworks in detail. One of these belonged to David Ross of Bedford County, Virginia. With its own coaling grounds, ore banks, furnace, forge, farms for food production, and carpenter and blacksmith shops, the Oxford Iron Works was a relatively self-sufficient iron community. According to the tax lists for 1787 and 1788, Ross owned four hundred slaves and over one hundred thousand acres of land, and, according to Jackson T. Main, was the "richest of all planters" who lived in Virginia at that time.[110] Precisely when Ross erected and began operation of the Oxford Iron Works is uncertain. In 1765, he had entered into partnership with Joseph Chapline, Samuel Beall, Jr., and Richard Henderson to erect the Antietam Iron Works on the Potomac River. Ross and Henderson built an ironworks, at that time known as Frederick Forge,[111] but what role Ross played in the enterprise thereafter is unknown. By February 1777, Ross must have completed work on the Oxford works, for in that month he advertised that he wanted to hire "50 stout Negro Men for the use of his ironworks in Bedford County (Virginia) and will give ready money for twenty Young Negro Fellows from 16 to 20 years of age."[112] In November 1777, Ross once again ran an advertisement in the *Virginia Gazette:*

> I will give ready Money for likely young Negroes from 15 to 20 Years of Age. I would also hire between this and the first of January 50 or 60 Negro men for one, two, or three Years. One half the first Year's Hire will be paid down, if required. The Situation of the Works is very healthy, the Labour of the Slaves moderate, and they shall have a plentiful Diet. I will allow an advance Price for Carpenters and Wheelwrights, but will not be concerned with any that are noted Runaways.[113]

By 1811, Ross employed 220 black bondsmen at his Oxford works. Although he owned many of these slaves, a large but undetermined number

Table 1

SLAVES AT OXFORD IRONWORKS, JANUARY 15, 1811

	Men	Boys	Women	Girls	Total
Coaling ground	13	7	3	1	24
Ore bank	3	2	1	2	8
Furnace & forges	19	1	10	1	31
Waggoners	6	0	0	0	6
Carpenters	6	2	0	0	8
Smiths	5	4	0	0	9
Odd hands	3	0	0	0	3
Plantations	7	3	14	1	25
House	0	1	1	1	3
Old people & children	7	41	14	41	103
TOTAL	69	61	43	47	220

Source: "List of Slaves at Oxford Iron Works," William Bolling Papers, Duke University.

were hired.[114] During the last few years of his life, Ross's fortunes entered into a decline because of a series of financial problems. Nevertheless, he still owned numerous slaves: 195 in 1816, 144 in 1817, and 130 in 1818, the year of his death. Following the partial settlement of his estate in 1819, Ross's estate included only forty slaves over twelve years of age.[115]

Ross worked his slaves at every occupation required at an ironworks (Table 1). In fact, many had multiple skills. After reprimanding one of his agents for not sending to Oxford the tools he had ordered, Ross explained his concern:

> You must know then that many of my servants at Oxford have double trades, some of them treble, most of my Blacksmiths are also potters, and part of them go into the pot houses when the furnace is in blast, last August the commencement of the blast, Nat Senr, Ben, King, Alexander and Jack resumed their potting business, their strikers were very little inferior to themselves, some of them had been 7 years in the trade, & I promoted four of them to fill the place of the four potters, when the furnace blew out there was no tools for these servant potters and have since been employed in common labour & must continue so until I get tools.[116]

Black youths, working under the guidance of black craftsmen, acquired the skills of blacksmiths, colliers, founders, and forgemen. Not infrequently, women worked in the mine banks; less often, they labored in the furnace and forge. Women also assisted in the charcoal-making process. Usually employed as unskilled hands, they helped to make charcoal and, along with black children, were designated "leaf-rakers." In that capacity, they gathered damp leaves for the charcoal pit. There is no indication precisely what the women did at the furnace and forge.[117]

In March 1824, the Virginia General Assembly authorized a $400,000 loan to construct a canal through the Blue Ridge Mountains as part of a scheme designed to connect the James River on the east and the Kanawha River on the western side of the mountains.[118] By facilitating the movement of western products to the Virginia seaboard and giving Virginia a share of that lucrative trade, the western portion of the state would more quickly attract new settlers. The contract for the first leg of the internal improvement was awarded to two men from the Shenandoah Valley, John Jordan and John Irvine.[119] Jordan and Irvine used large numbers of slaves for constructing the canal; some they owned, but most were hired. Although the number of black hands employed at the canal was probably higher, in 1825 Jordan and Irvine paid taxes on forty-eight black slaves.[120]

The profits Jordan and Irvine received for their work on the canal were invested in an ironworks.[121] The Lucy Selina Furnace was erected in 1827 about twenty miles east of Covington in Alleghany County, Virginia.[122] In 1827, Jordan and Irvine extended their business to include the operation of Clifton Forge, located a few miles west of Lucy Selina Furnace,[123] and put to work eighty or ninety slaves annually at the two installations. The company owned fourteen but hired the remainder from year to year. In 1830, Jordan and Irvine employed forty-seven slaves at Clifton Forge, thirty-six of them on hire. The five most skilled artisans were the hands who worked at the forge itself. The company owned these men, but the other slaves worked in every facet of the business.[124]

William Weaver was another well-known and powerful ironmaster whose personal and company papers have been preserved. The large collection of extant Weaver papers provides an excellent opportunity to study the labor force of another important ironworks of the region. Little is known of Weaver's early life. Apparently, he had been a merchant in Philadelphia before migrating to Rockbridge County, Virginia, in 1814.[125] By 1827, he was living at and operating Buffalo Forge in Rockbridge County. In 1825, Weaver had already purchased Lydia Furnace, located in the same county, and in 1828, he renamed the two facilities Bath Iron Works.[126] Little is known about his iron interests between 1840 and 1855. By the mid-1850s, however, two nephews, William W. Rex and Charles K. Gorgas, managed Etna Furnace, while Weaver and his nephew-in-law, Daniel C. E. Brady, operated Buffalo Forge. When Weaver died on March 25, 1863, his personal assets included seventy slaves.[127]

From his entrance into the iron business in 1827, Weaver relied upon the labor of black bondsmen. Some of these hands he owned, but many he hired annually. From 1827 to 1829, Buffalo Forge utilized 53 different slaves,[128] and between 1830 and 1840, that number rose to 114.[129] Between the years 1845 and 1850, Buffalo Forge annually employed an average of about 30 slaves.[130] Even after the Civil War, Weaver continued to rely on black labor; between 1865 and 1873, his works employed 101 black people.[131]

The same circumstances prevailed at Weaver's Bath Iron Works where an average of between sixty and seventy slaves labored at the furnace and forge. A total of fifty-four black hands were employed in 1829,[132] and the same number were worked in 1837.[133] Since the 1829 figure referred only to hired hands, while Weaver himself owned a number of slaves outright, this figure did not include all of the blacks at the works. Moreover, the figure for 1837 related only to those slave hands who received cash for working extra time. A more accurate estimate can be derived from the Bath Forge Negro Books, which list all of the slave hands employed at the works. From 1839 to 1842, they show that Weaver utilized seventy blacks per year,[134] and sixty-four in 1846.[135] Etna Furnace also employed a large number of slave workers. From 1854 to 1856, a total of ninety-six different slaves labored at the furnace.[136] Similarly, from 1857 to 1859, the works utilized the labor of ninety-three individual slaves,[137] while the white labor force averaged between twenty and twenty-five hands during the 1850s.[138] Weaver had to rely on a sizable number of hired blacks each year to sustain his operations.[139]

Slave labor played a large role in all phases of production at Weaver's Etna Furnace. In addition to several skilled white artisans and a few white supervisors, sixty or seventy black slaves labored as colliers, miners, teamsters, founders, and general furnace hands. As mentioned earlier, at Buffalo Forge, Weaver employed an average of thirty skilled slaves annually, most of whom he owned in order to insure stability at key production posts. Several additional semiskilled and unskilled black hands were also hired each year to work the forge.[140]

Although southern ironworkers normally were assigned specific tasks, under extenuating circumstances even skilled artisans, free and slave, turned their attention to the needs of the hour. For example, at Buffalo Forge in April 1852, Warder and Sam were hauling saw logs and fire wood. A few days later, there were four hands cutting oats rather than doing forgework. The road to the forge apparently needed repair, so on April 19, 1852, Weaver had two teams and eight hands employed hauling cinders, and the next day Weaver noted in his Time Book that "logs got cut, fixed saw mill, 2 Teams & 10 hands making rails, Mitch & hands making rails." The following day, April 21, the forge hands were chopping wood, and a few days later the forgemen were planting corn rather than plying their particular skills at the forge. Most iron plantations grew crops, and at harvest-time all hands became farmers. Thus, on July 12, 1852, all the forgemen turned to threshing. The weather sometimes took the forgemen from their normal occupations. Because of the sporadic and seasonal nature of production at rural iron plantations, the wide variety of tasks required greater flexibility in individual workers than was the case at urban ironworks such as those in Richmond.[141]

There were several reasons for Richmond's late antebellum rise as the leading iron center of the South. Increased demand for finished iron products, abundant water power, ready access to raw materials, and the construction of railroads and canals all contributed to the city's rapid industrial expansion from the late 1830s to the Civil War.[142] Richmond's most important iron establishment, the Tredegar Iron Works, differed in organization from the rural charcoal iron plantation model. Concentrated in an urban commercial and transportation center, the Tredegar Iron Works represented, both physically and symbolically, the emergence of the modern corporate organization in the upper South.

Founded in 1836 by several Richmond businessmen and industrialists, the Tredegar Company suffered as the Panic of 1837 forced prices downward and undermined the railroad boom. To salvage the firm, the company gave Joseph R. Anderson the task of managing its operations.[143] Only twenty-eight years old when he assumed control in 1841, Anderson transformed Tredegar into the most important ironworks in the South. By 1848, he assembled sufficient capital to buy the works for $125,000.[144] The nearby Armory Iron Company came under Anderson's control in the form of a partnership in 1859 and became known as Joseph R. Anderson and Company.[145] The demands of the Civil War, as well as the need for assurance that Tredegar would receive the quantity and quality of unfinished iron for the production of arms, cannon, plating for ironclads, and railroad stock, resulted in Anderson and Company's acquisition or control of nine furnaces in the Valley of Virginia, two coal mines, nine canal barges, three blockade runners, a tannery and shoe shop, a grist-mill, a firebrick plant, and a large, well-stocked farm.[146]

When Anderson became commercial agent for the Tredegar Company in 1841, he sought a cut in operating costs; among other steps, he introduced black slave labor into skilled rolling mill positions.[147] Anderson decided that by pairing blacks and skilled white ironworkers, a crew of slaves could be trained for the most skilled and high-paying positions at the works. This move also had the advantage of providing a means of control over white workers who could stop production at the works, if they became sufficiently disgruntled. For the most part, the iron industry in the South had lagged behind that of the North and Great Britain in the development of a modern iron technology. The result was a scarcity of skilled workers capable of operating the modern facility that Anderson managed. He explained to the company directors:

> It has always been considered an object of primary impor-
> tance in our Country to introduce slave labour generally in
> the several branches of Iron manufacture. The difficulty has
> been that certain operations, as Puddling, Heating, Rolling
> &c. are known only to foreigners and a few Americans who
> have been from interest opposed to imparting this knowledge
> to Negroes.[148]

He estimated that either hiring or purchasing slave apprentices would result in substantial savings to the company. The directors apparently agreed, for Anderson's plan was soon implemented.[149]

Over the next five years, slaves entered the mill in subordinate capacities, but when Anderson tried to install black hands at the highly skilled positions, the white workers refused to accept them. On May 23, 1847, skilled whites decided to strike rather than yield to the company's plan. Clearly, they hoped "to prohibit the employment of colored people in the said works." Anderson confronted the workers directly and on May 26, 1847, informed them that by their actions they had "discharged them-selves."[150] After an interview with Anderson, the *Richmond Enquirer* reported that

> those who enter into his employment must not expect to
> prescribe to him who he shall be at liberty to employ; and that
> he would not consent to employ men who would unite and
> combine themselves into an association to exclude slaves
> from our factories. It was because the late workmen asserted
> such a pretension that he determined that their employment
> should cease. . . . In that aspect, he regarded it as a matter in
> which the whole community was conceived; it must be evi-
> dent that such combinations are a direct attack on slave
> property; and, if they do not originate in abolition, they are
> pregnant with evils.[151]

The city's newspapers stood squarely behind Anderson on the matter. The *Times and Compiler* commented that "the principle is advocated, for the first time we believe in a slave-holding state, that the employer may be prevented from making use of slave labor." If permitted, the foundation of the master's rights would be undermined, and the value of slave property destroyed.[152] After the white strikers had failed to influence either Ander-son or the city officials to whom they appealed, large numbers of blacks went into the Tredegar and the Armory rolling mills. Referring to the rolling mills, Anderson noted that in 1848 he was "employing in this establishment . . . almost exclusively slave labor except as to Boss men."[153]

During the 1850s, the Tredegar Company increased its operations, and its labor force rose from 250 to about 800 by 1860.[154] Although the Civil War accelerated Tredegar's growth, as the Confederate demand for war material grew, there was a corresponding decline in available manpower. Consequently, the need for black labor increased enormously, and by 1862, the Tredegar plant employed a total of 131 bondsmen and 4 free blacks.[155] A newspaper advertisement in late 1862 and early 1863 indicated the extent of the company's labor requirements: "Wanted—*Five Hundred Hands*—We wish to hire for the ensuing year five hundred able-bodied Negro Men to be employed by us at our Blast Furnaces, in Botetourt County, and at our Coal Mines, on James River, seventeen miles above the city."[156] A year later, Anderson used 226 bondsmen at his Richmond works, and between 500 and 600 additional blacks in the company's furnaces, forges, coal mines, and fleet of boats elsewhere. Still, this number was insufficient, and the company advertised for one thousand hands.[157] By November 1864, the Tredegar Richmond works employed about four hundred white men and two hundred blacks,[158] while, as Table 2 indicates, blacks comprised the vast majority of the labor force at the company's outlying facilities.

Table 2

WORKERS AT THE TREDEGAR'S FURNACES IN THE
VALLEY OF VIRGINIA, DECEMBER 1864

Furnace	Number of Black Men	Number of Women and Children	Number of White Men
Mt. Torry	55	40	20
Australia	53	60	29
Catawba	90	76	38
Cloverdale	105	60	30
Glenwood	99	32	17
Rebecca	71	68	34
Grace	78	60	29
Boats:			
8 canal			
6 mall	58	12	9
TOTAL	609	408	206

Source: Adapted from Tredegar Letter Book, December 17, 1864, Virginia State Library, and Kathleen Bruce, *Virginia Iron Manufacture in the Slave Era* (New York: Augustus M. Kelley, 1960, originally 1930), p. 463. These data do not indicate, of course, the number of blacks among the women and children.

Because the Tredegar works was an urban establishment, it differed in organization and occupational categories from the traditional charcoal ironworks that supplied it with raw iron. Still, slaves were employed in a wide variety of positions. Before the Civil War, Tredegar slaves found themselves largely confined to the rolling mills and the blacksmith shop. Over one-third of the eighty slaves working at the Richmond plant in 1860 were skilled puddlers, heaters, and rollers. About twenty were blacksmiths, strikers, smith's helpers, and teamsters, while twenty or thirty served as common laborers. A white foreman supervised the cooper shop where a group of black youths built kegs.[159] As Confederate military demands reduced the number of free laborers available to private industry, slaves began to play a broader role in all Tredegar occupations. For example, in 1862 the Richmond plant employed a total of 135 blacks at varied occupations (Table 3).

During the last two years of the Civil War, the Tredegar works became more and more dependent on slave labor, and blacks entered departments which had previously been closed to them. In 1863 and 1864, ten or eleven slaves went to work in the machine shops and about thirty blacks entered the foundry for the first time, while forty-two blacks worked as crewmen on the company's iron barges.[160]

The Tredegar Iron Works, the most dramatic example of the heavy reliance upon slave labor that characterized the Chesapeake iron industry

Table 3

NEGROES HIRED AT TREDEGAR IRONWORKS IN RICHMOND, JANUARY 1, 1862

Slaves		Free Blacks	
Rolling mill hands	48	Rolling mill hands	1
Blacksmiths	6	Blacksmiths	1
Blacksmiths' helpers	7	Blacksmiths' helpers	1
Strikers	12	Carpenters	1
Smith shop laborers	19		
Foundry laborers	6	*TOTAL*	4
Teamsters	7		
Boatmen	1		
Common laborers	21		
TOTAL	131		

Source: "List of Negroes Hired, January 1, 1862," Tredegar Contract Books, Tredegar Company Records, Virginia State Library, as adapted from Charles B. Dew, *Ironmaker to the Confederacy: Joseph R. Anderson and the Tredegar Iron Works* (New Haven, Conn.: Yale University Press, 1966), p. 92.

generally, provided a fitting climax to a tradition that spanned nearly 150 years. The large percentage of slaves employed at ironworks in the area from the 1720s through the end of the Civil War indicates that ironmasters throughout the slave era assumed that slaves constituted a desirable source of labor. This assumption applied not only to menial or back-breaking labor, but also to the most skilled and critical positions associated with the work of making iron.

Although it is impossible to establish a definite percentage of black to white workers at Chesapeake ironworks, the ratio was high at all of them. In 1739, Alexander Spotswood's entire labor force was composed of slaves, except for the general overseer and chief founder.[161] By the 1750s, the Principio Company "owned slaves . . . in abundance,"[162] and well over half the permanent workers of the Baltimore Iron Company were probably black slaves.[163] The Patuxent Iron Works employed a labor force which was almost totally slave between 1767 and 1783,[164] and by the 1790s, the Northampton Furnace utilized forty-six blacks and sixteen whites, or a work force that was about 75 percent black.[165] The Oxford Iron Works was operated by a labor force which was probably over 90 percent black in 1811.[166] By the 1850s, William Weaver's iron manufacturing establishments required from 100 to 120 blacks who constituted at least 80 percent of the work force at Etna Furnace and Buffalo Forge;[167] the overall system employed about 800 blacks in 1864, comprising well over half of its total workers in Richmond and the Valley of Virginia.[168]

NOTES

1. Arthur Cecil Bining, *British Regulation of the Colonial Iron Industry* (Philadelphia: University of Pennsylvania Press, 1933), pp. 122, 134.

2. Peter Temin, *Iron and Steel in Nineteenth-Century America: An Economic Inquiry* (Cambridge, Mass.: MIT Press, 1964), p. 14.

3. Bining, *British Regulation,* pp. 5–14.

4. It is uncertain whether Bining listed every ironworks whether or not they went into blast. Some might have existed only on paper. The data provided here from Maryland and Virginia relate only to those works that actually produced iron.

5. Michael Warren Robbins, "The Principio Company: Iron-Making in Colonial Maryland, 1720–1781" (Ph.D. dissertation, George Washington University, 1972), pp. 55–56; Keach Johnson, "The Genesis of the Baltimore Ironworks," *Journal of Southern History* 19 (May 1953):177, 157.

6. Arthur Cecil Bining, *Pennsylvania Iron Manufacture in the Eighteenth Century* (Harrisburg: Pennsylvania Historical Commission, 1938), pp. 187–92.

7. Michael W. Robbins, *Maryland's Iron Industry During the Revolutionary War Era* (Annapolis: Maryland Bicentennial Commission, 1973), p. 9.

8. Robbins, "The Principio Company," p. 18.

9. James L. Bishop, *A History of American Manufactures, from 1608–1860* (Philadelphia: Edward Young & Co., 1866), pp. 588–89; Robbins, 'The Principio Company," p. 281.

10. Isaac Zane to Sarah Zane, May 19,1777, the Isaac Zane Papers, Historical Society of Pennsylvania, hereafter cited as HSP.

11. William H. Browne et al., *Archives of Maryland* (Baltimore: Maryland Historical Society, 1883–1930), 21:536; *Journal of the Proceedings of the Commissioners Appointed to Preserve Confiscated British Property, 1781, 1782*, Hall of Records, Annapolis, Maryland, hereafter cited as HR.

12. *Archives of Maryland* 12:512; Robbins, "The Principio Company," pp. 284–85; and *Journal of the Proceedings of the Commissioners*, HR.

13. *Archives of Maryland* 12:92; Robbins, "The Principio Company," p. 286.

14. Bishop, *History of American Manufactures*, p. 588.

15. John C. Fitzpatrick (ed.), *The Writings of George Washington* (Washington, D.C.: U.S. Government Printing Office, 1944), 14:329; Miscellaneous item, the Robert and William Smith Papers, Maryland Historical Society, hereafter cited as MHS. Also see Robbins, "The Principio Company," p. 288.

16. Kathleen Bruce, *Virginia Iron Manufacture in the Slave Era* (New York: Augustus M. Kelley, 1968, originally 1930), pp. 45, 65–66; Samuel Sydney Bradford, "The Ante-Bellum Charcoal Iron Industry of Virginia" (Ph.D. dissertation, Columbia University, 1958), p. 10.

17. William Waller Hening (ed)., *The Statutes at Large, Being a Collection of All the Laws of Virginia* (Richmond: By the Editor, 1810–1823), 9:28, 267, 275, 342, 452, 592, and 11:21. An act of May 1780 repealed the militia law exempting men at privately owned ironworks (ibid., 10:262). However, the act of 1781 once again exempted such people from military service, although not before ruining at least one vital works (Bruce, *Virginia Iron Manufacture*, p. 75).

18. Bruce, *Virginia Iron Manufacture*, pp. 45–46; Bishop, *History of American Manufactures*, p. 607. It was this works that Benedict Arnold destroyed during his raid into Virginia in 1781; James M. Swank, *History of the Manufacture of Iron in All Ages* (Philadelphia: American Iron and Steel Association, 1892), p. 268.

19. Robbins, *Maryland's Iron Industry*, p. 12. For an example of how one such leader blended his industrial and political interests, see Edward S. Delaplaine, *The Life of Thomas Johnson: Member of the Continental Congress, First Governor of the State of Maryland, and Associate Justice of the United States Supreme Court* (New York: Frederick H. Hitchcock; Grafton Press, 1927).

20. Swank, *History of Iron in All Ages*, p. 255; Bining, *British Regulation*, pp. 128–32; Temin, *Iron and Steel in Nineteenth-Century America*, p. 280.

21. Bruce, *Virginia Iron Manufacture*, pp. 24–25.

22. Swank, *History of Iron in All Ages*, pp. 256, 269–70; Bradford, "Charcoal Iron Industry of Virginia," pp. 12–13.

23. Swank, *History of Iron in All Ages*, pp. 170, 184–85; Bradford, "Charcoal Iron Industry of Virginia," p. 8.

24. John B. Pearse, *A Concise History of the Iron Manufacture of the American Colonies Up to the Revolution and Pennsylvania Until the Present Time* (Philadelphia: Allen, Lane & Scott, 1876), p. 14.

25. John W. Wayland, *A History of Shenandoah County, Virginia* (Strasburg,

Va.: Shenandoah Publishing House, 1927), pp. 178, 237, 239, 242.

26. J. P. Lesley, *The Iron Manufacturer's Guide to the Furnaces, Forges and Rolling Mills of the United States; with Discussions of Iron as a Chemical Element, an American Ore, and a Manufactured Article, in Commerce and in History* (New York: John Wiley, Publisher, 1859), pp. 70–71, 131.

27. Ibid., pp. 71–72, 181, 183.

28. Ibid., pp. 74, 183–84.

29. Swank, *History of Iron in All Ages,* p. 225.

30. Lesley, *Iron Manufacturer's Guide,* pp. 254–55.

31. Cited in Bradford, "Charcoal Iron Industry of Virginia," p. 15.

32. J. Thomas Scharf, *History of Maryland: From the Earliest Period to the Present Day* (Hatboro, Pa.: Tradition Press, 1967, originially 1879), 3:183–86; Bishop, *History of American Manufactures,* p. 590.

33. Lester J. Cappon, "History of the Southern Iron Industry to the Close of the Civil War" (Ph.D. dissertation, Harvard University, 1928 microfilm copy of earlier draft, University of Virginia Library), p. 107, and his article "Trend of the Southern Iron Industry Under the Plantation System," *Journal of Economic and Business History* 2 (February 1930):356, 367–71.

34. Cappon, "History of the Southern Iron Industry," p. 141.

35. This regional perspective has been developed in Arthur Pierce Middleton, *Tobacco Coast: A Maritime History of Chesapeake Bay in the Colonial Era* (Newport News, Va.: Mariner's Museum, 1953). For a discussion of iron, see ibid., pp. 167–71.

36. Cappon, "History of the Southern Iron Industry," p. 107b.

37. Ibid., p. 142; Lesley, *Iron Manufacturer's Guide,* pp. 63–74, 178–86.

38. James D.B. DeBow (ed.), *DeBow's Review and Industrial Resources, Statistics, Etc., of the United States and More Particularly of the Southern & Western States* (New York: Augustus M. Kelley, 1966, originally January 1846 through April 1862), 10:542; Richard Swainson Fisher, *The Progress of the United States of America from the Earliest Periods: Geographical, Statistical, and Historical* (New York: J. H. Colton & Co., 1854), p. 289.

39. Bishop, *History of American Manufactures,* p. 590; Cappon, "History of the Southern Iron Industry," p. 142.

40. H. R. Schubert, *History of the British Iron and Steel Industry* (London: Routledge & Kegan Paul, 1957), p. 335; Thomas Southcliffe Ashton, *Iron and Steel in the Industrial Revolution* (New York: Augustus M. Kelley, 1968, originally 1924), p. 99; Temin, *Iron and Steel in Nineteenth-Century America,* p. 14.

41. Temin, *Iron and Steel in Nineteenth-Century America,* p. 15.

42. Ibid., p. 16.

43. Ibid., p. 17. Coke is bituminous coal from which the gas has been expelled, leaving a mineral more closely resembling pure carbon (ibid., p. 52).

44. Ibid., p. 18; Harry Scrivenor, *History of the Iron Trade, from the Earliest Records to the Present Period* (London: Longman, Brown, Green & Longmans, 1854), pp. 252–53.

45. Bining, *Pennsylvania Iron Manufacture,* p. 73.

46. Robbins, *Maryland's Iron Industry,* p. 12.

47. Bishop, *History of American Manufactures,* p. 591; Swank, *History of Iron*

in All Ages, p. 256. The term *hot blast* referred to air passed through a chamber where it was heated and then forced into the furnace by a "blowing engine" composed of one or several pistons driven by water or steam power. The hot air rose faster from the bottom to the top of the furnace than cold air and made the furnace more efficient by increasing the draft and, therefore, the heat. Scrivenor, *History of the Iron Trade,* pp. 84–86.

48. Robbins, *Maryland's Iron Industry,* p. 12.

49. *DeBow's Review* 20:641–42; Victor S. Clark, *History of Manufactures in the United States 1607–1860* (New York: Peter Smith, 1949, originally 1929), 1:285–86, 260–62, 452, Chap. 14.

50. Bishop, *History of American Manufactures,* pp. 590–91; Swank, *eistory of Iron in All Eges,* p. 256.

51. Cappon, "History of the Southern Iron Industry," pp. 9, 107c, 107d, 107f; Johnson, "Genesis of the Baltimore Ironworks," pp. 178–79.

52. John F. Stover, *American Railroads* (Chicago: University of Chicago Press, 1961), Chaps. 3–4; George R. Taylor and Irene D. Neu, *The American Railroad Network, 1861–1890* (Cambridge, Mass.: Harvard University Press, 1956), pp. 26–34, 49–76.

53. A. D. Schoepf, *Travels in the Confederation, 1783–84,* Alfred J. Morrison (ed.) (Philadelphia: University of Pennsylvania Press, 1911, originally 1785), 2:221.

54. Isaac Weld, Jr., *Travels Through the States of North America and the Provinces of Upper and Lower Canada During the Years 1795, 1796, and 1797* (London: John Stockdale, 1800), pp. 178–79.

55. Bruce, *Virginia Iron Manufacture,* pp. 8–11. For a mid-eighteenth century discussion of Spotswood's ironworks, see Hugh Jones, *The Present State of Virginia: From Whence Is Inferred a Short View of Maryland and North Carolina,* Richard L. Morton (ed.) (Chapel Hill: University of North Carolina Press, 1956), pp. 90–91. The earliest full-scale ironworks in the English colonies, known as Falling Creek, was erected in 1619 seven miles below the James River falls. On March 22, 1622, the Indians destroyed the installation, and no further successful attempts to produce iron were undertaken in Virginia for nearly a century. Charles E. Hatch, Jr., and Thurlow Gates Gregory, "The First American Blast Furnace, 1619–1622: The Birth of a Mighty Industry on Falling Creek in Virginia," *Virginia Magazine of History and Biography* 70 (July 1962):261–65.

56. Bruce, *Virginia Iron Manufacture,* p. 12; William Byrd, "Progress to the Mines," as reproduced in Louis B. Wright (ed.), *The Prose Works of William Byrd of Westover: Narratives of a Colonial Virginian* (Cambridge, Mass.: Belknap Press of Harvard University Press, 1966), p. 348.

57. Byrd, "Progress to the Mines," pp. 348, 352; Pearse, *Concise History of the*

58. Spotswood, "Terms and Conditions," as reproduced in Lester J. Cappon (ed.), *Iron Works at Tuball: Terms and Conditions for Their Lease as Stated by Alexander Spotswood on the Twentieth Day of July 1739* (Charlottesville: Tracy W. McGregor Library of the University of Virginia, 1945), pp. 20, 27.

59. Ibid., p. 16.

60. Bruce, *Virginia Iron Manufacture,* p. 11.

61. Byrd, "Progress to the Mines," p. 354; William G. Whitely, "The Principio Company: A Historical Sketch of the First Iron-Works in Maryland," *Pennsyl-*

vania Magazine of History and Biography 11 (1887):63, 68.

62. Johnson, "Genesis of the Baltimore Ironworks," p. 159; Earl Chapin May, *Principio to Wheeling, 1715–1945: A Pageant of Iron and Steel* (New York: Harper & Brothers, Publishers, 1945), p. 13.

63. Whitely, "The Principio Company," pp. 66–67, 193–96; May, *Principio to Wheeling*, pp. 45–46.

64. Byrd, "Progress to the Mines," pp. 368–69. Augustine Washington became a partner in the Principio Company in 1727, with a one-twelfth share. William Chetwynd to John England, September 15, 19, 1725, and John Lightfoot to John England, October 2, 1730, in the John England Letterbook, Principio Company Papers, 1723–1730, MHS.

65. Whitely, "The Principio Company," p. 197; Johnson, "Genesis of the Baltimore Ironworks," p. 160.

66. May, *Principio to Wheeling*, p. 11.

67. Ledger in the Principio Company Papers, 1723–1730, MHS. In a reference to an accident at the works, William Chetwynd, one of the partners in London, wrote the company's ironmaster, John England, saying that "as for the misfortune of the blacks, we must expect such accidents. . . . " Apparently, some slaves were lost, for Chetwynd went on to urge England to buy more slaves "as money comes in from Principio iron." William Chetwynd to John England, August 19, 1726, Principio Iron Company Papers, 1725–1726, Virginia State Library, hereafter cited as VSL.

68. Ledger in the Principio Company Papers, 1723–1730, MHS.

69. William Chetwynd to John England, September 19, 1725, cited in Swank, *History of Iron in All Ages*, p. 247.

70. Whitely, "The Principio Company," pp. 196–97.

71. Ibid., p. 291.

72. Ibid., pp. 292–93.

73. *Journal of the Proceedings of the Commissioners,* HR. Accokeek Furnace ended operations in 1753 and along with the works were sold an uncertain number of black slaves. Swank, *History of Iron in All Ages*, p. 264.

74. Bishop, *History of American Manufactures*, p. 586; Pearse, *Concise History of Iron Manufacture*, p. 18; Johnson, "Genesis of the Baltimore Ironworks." pp. 157, 162.

75. Unsigned memorandum in Dr. Carroll's handwriting, undated, Box 3, Carroll-Maccubbin Papers, MHS. Charles Carroll, cousin to Dr. Charles Carroll, was probably the most affluent of the original owners. In 1764, his total worth was £88,380. Included in his estate were "285 slaves, each worth, on an average £30 sterling." Charles Carroll to his son, January 9, 1764, in "Extracts from the Carroll Papers," *Maryland Historical Magazine* 12 (March 1917):27.

76. "A List of Taxables . . . Belonging to the Baltimore Iron Company for the Year 1733," Box 3, Carroll-Maccubbin Papers, MHS.

77. "Account of Persons Employed at the Baltimore Iron Works, April 30, 1734," Carroll-Maccubbin Papers, MHS. References to seasonal white workers are scattered throughout the records of colonial iron companies, including the Baltimore Iron Works.

78. Charles Carroll to his son, January 9, 1764, in "Extracts from the Carroll Papers," p. 27.

79. *Maryland Journal,* April 8, 1785.

80. John Tayloe was also a partner in the Bristol Iron Works Company, built during the 1720s in Virginia, on the Rappahannock River, but almost no details are known of this venture. G. MacLaren Brydon, "The Bristol Iron Works in King George County," *Virginia Magazine of History and Biography* 42 (April 1934): 97.

81. "Occoquan Company Account Book," Box 1, Tayloe Family Papers, Virginia Historical Society, hereafter cited as VHS.

82. *Virginia Gazette* (Purdie & Dixon), November 16, 23, 1769; Bruce, *Virginia Iron Manufacture,* p. 18.

83. Bruce, *Virginia Iron Manufacture*, p. 21; Roger W. Moss, Jr., "Isaac Zane, Jr., A 'Quaker for the Times,' " *Virginia Magazine of History and Biography* 77 (July 1969):296, n. 18.

84. Inventory of Negroes and Their Value belonging to I. Zane, May 26, 1795, Isaac Zane Papers, HSP.

85. Ledger of the Executors of the Estate of Thomas Snowden, December 24, 1775, Patuxent Iron Works, HR: Robbins, "The Principio Company," p. 302.

86. Robbins, "The Principio Company," p. 304; Journal for Ledger C, 1758–1761, and Journal CC, October 15, 1764–June 27, 1772, Elk Ridge Furnace, HR.

87. Robbins, *Maryland's Iron Industry,* pp. 36–37;*Journal of the Proceedings of the Commissioners,* HR.

88. Journal of the Proceedings of the Commissioners, HR.

89. *Sale Book of Confiscated British Property, 1781–85,* HR.

90. Furnace Workmen's Book, B–28, Ridgely Account Books, MHS.

91. Time Book, 1792–1794, B–26, Box 10, Ridgely Account Books, MHS; *Maryland Journal and Baltimore Advertiser,* July 18, 1788.

92. Byrd, "Progress to the Mines," p. 358.

93. Spotswood, "Terms and Conditions," pp. 20, 27.

94. William Chetwynd to John England, October 5, 1725, Principio Company Papers, Library of Congress, hereafter cited as LC.

95. *Journal of the Proceedings of the Commissioners,* HR.

96. "Account of Persons Employed at the Baltimore Iron Works, April 30, 1734," "Copy of List of Taxables for the Yr 1736—Wm. Hammond Sheriff," and "Inventory of Ben Tasker, Negroes at the Furnace, 1737," Carroll-Maccubbin Papers, MHS.

97. Charles Carroll (Dr.), "Proposals . . . for erecting one Furnace to Run Iron Ore into Pig Metal and one or more Forges for making it into bar iron. . . ," dated February 1753, in "Extracts from Account and Letter Books of Dr. Charles Carroll of Annapolis," *Maryland Historical Magazine* 25 (1930):299.

98. *Virginia Gazette* (Rind), April 14, 1768.

99. Ibid., August 4, 1768; ibid. (Purdie & Dixon), April 14, 1774.

100. Ibid. (Dixon & Hunter), November 16, 1776.

101. *Maryland Journal and Baltimore Advertiser,* July 16, 1778.

102. *Maryland Gazette,* August 21, 1760.

103. *Virginia Gazette* (Rind), November 17, 1769.

104. Ibid. (Purdie & Dixon), October 3, 1771.

105. Ledger of John Blair, 1795–1797, College of William and Mary.

106. Redwell Furnace Account Book, 1791–1813, VHS.

107. Ridwell Furnace Record Book, June 6, 1805–May 23, 1809, #234, Vol. 1, Southern Historical Collection, University of North Carolina, hereafter cited as UNC.

108. Account Book, 1744–1786, John Stump and Company, LC.

109. Cumberland Forge Account Book, 1796–1797, LC.

110. See references to Oxford facilities throughout the David Ross Letterbook, January 14, 1812–October 29, 1813, VHS; Jackson T. Main, "The One Hundred," *William and Mary Quarterly* 11 (July 1954):363, 384. A study of property-holding and slaveownership in Virginia during this era is most easily found in Jackson Turner Main, "The Distribution of Property in Post-Revolutionary Virginia," *Mississippi Valley Historical Review* 41 (September 1954):241–58.

111. Robbins, *Maryland's Iron Industry,* p. 60.

112. *Virginia Gazette* (Pinkney), February 14, 1777.

113. Ibid. (Dixon & Hunter), November 7, 1777.

114. "List of Slaves at the Oxford Iron Works in Families & Their Employment, January 5, 1811," William Bolling Papers, Duke University, hereafter cited as Duke.

115. Campbell County Personal Tax Books, 1816–1819, VSL.

116. D. Ross to Davis, July 25, 1813, David Ross Letterbook, January 14, 1812–October 29, 1813, VHS. "Potters" were highly skilled artisans who molded hollow iron wares.

117. "List of Slaves at Oxford Iron Works," William Bolling Papers, Duke.

118. *A Collection of All Acts and Parts of Acts of the General Assembly of Virginia, From October, 1784, Down to the Session of 1829–30, Inclusive, Relating to the James River Company* (Richmond: Samuel Shepherd & Co., 1830), p. 66.

119. John Jordan and John Irvine, Articles of Agreement, June 9, 1824, Jordan and Irvine Papers, McCormick Collection, State Historical Society of Wisconsin, hereafter cited as SHSW.

120. Tax Receipt, 1825, and "Register of Hands who are at Work on the Canal for Jordan & Irvine," Jordan and Irvine Papers, SHSW.

121. "Copy of Canal Settlt. for Colo. John Jordan up to 30th Dec. 1826," Jordan and Irvine Papers, SHSW.

122. Lesley, *Iron Manufacturer's Guide,* p. 71.

123. Ibid., p. 182; Oren F. Morton, *A Centennial History of Alleghany County, Virginia* (Dayton, Va.: J. K. Ruebush Co., 1923), pp. 81–82.

124. "Register of Forge for 1830," Jordan and Irvine Papers, SHSW.

125. Francis R. Holland, Jr., "Three Virginia Iron Companies, 1825–1865" (M.A. thesis, University of Texas, 1958), p. 69.

126. Ibid., p. 70.

127. See numerous references to Weaver's managers throughout the William Weaver Papers (Duke) and the Weaver-Brady Papers (University of Virginia—hereafter cited as UVa); Holland, "Three Virginia Iron Companies," pp. 84, 102.

128. Negro Book, 1827–1829, Ledger Box 1, Buffalo Forge, Weaver-Brady Papers, UVa.

129. Negro Book, 1830–1840, Buffalo Forge, Weaver-Brady Papers, UVa.

130. Journal, 1845–1850, Buffalo Forge, Weaver-Brady Papers, UVa.

131. Negro Book, 1865–1873, Ledger Box 6, Weaver-Brady Papers, UVa.

132. "Memorandum of Hired Negroes at Bath Iron Works for 1829," William Weaver Papers, Duke.

133. "Memo Cash to Negroes, Dec. 23, 1837," William Weaver Papers, Duke.

134. Negro Book, 1839–1842, Ledger Box 3, Bath Forge, Weaver-Brady Papers, UVa. Although it is unknown how many slaves Weaver owned earlier, he held thirty-one in 1860. Manuscript Population and Slave Schedules, Rockbridge County, Virginia, Eighth Census of the United States, 1860, National Archives Microfilm Publications, M653.

135. Negro Book, 1846, Ledger Box 3, Weaver-Brady Papers, UVa.

136. Negro Book, 1854–1856, Etna Furnace, Weaver-Brady Papers, UVa.

137. Negro Book, 1857–1859, Etna Furnace, Weaver-Brady Papers, UVa.

138. White Hands Book, 1857, Etna Furnace, Weaver-Brady Papers, UVa.

139. William Weaver to James D. Davidson, January 10, 1855, James D. Davidson Papers, SHSW.

140. See numerous entries for skilled slaves throughout Negro Books, 1827–1829, 1830–1840, 1846, 1854–1856, 1857–1859, and 1865–1873, Weaver-Brady Papers, UVa.

141. See entries in Time Book, 1843–1853, Buffalo Forge, Weaver-Brady Papers, UVa.

142. Charles B. Dew, *Ironmaker to the Confederacy: Joseph R. Anderson and the Tredegar Iron Works* (New Haven, Conn.: Yale University Press, 1966), p. 3; Charles W. Turner, "The Early Railroad Movement in Virginia," *Virginia Magazine of History and Biography* 55 (October 1947):350–71.

143. Bruce, *Virginia Iron Manufacture,* pp. 150–64; Dew, *Ironmaker to the Confederacy,* p. 4.

144. Clay Bailey, "Joseph R. Anderson of Tredegar," *The Commonwealth* 12 (November 1959):36.

145. Bruce, *Virginia Iron Manufacture,* pp. 214–23; Dew, *Ironmaker to the Confederacy,* pp. 16–17.

146. Bailey, "Anderson of Tredegar," p. 38.

147. Dew, *Ironmaker to the Confederacy,* p. 22.

148. Minutes of the Directors and Stockholders of Tredegar Iron Company, June 1842, Tredegar Company Records, VSL.

149. Ibid. Joseph Anderson first used large numbers of blacks when he supervised the construction of the Shenandoah Valley Turnpike during the late 1830s and early 1840s. In the fall of 1840, he wrote to his brother that he preferred to use slaves for construction because "We don't wish to rely on white labor" (Joseph Anderson to F. T. Anderson, October 11, 1840, Anderson Family Papers, UVa).

150. *Richmond Times and Compiler,* May 28, 1847. The skilled whites feared they would be discharged once the blacks had been trained (Bruce, *Virginia Iron Manufacture,* pp. 224–25). That skilled white artisans traditionally opposed the use of black labor, slave or free, in their particular crafts has been thoroughly documented by historians. For the colonial period, see, for example, Richard B. Morris, *Government and Labor in Early America* (New York: Columbia University Press, 1946), pp. 182–88. For the antebellum era, see, for example, Robert S.

Starobin, *Industrial Slavery in the Old South* (New York: Oxford University Press, 1970), pp. 211–14. Many of the slave narratives note the hostility that ex-slaves encountered when attempting to practice their skills. The most well known instance was that recorded by Frederick Douglass in his autobiography.

151. *Richmond Enquirer,* June 12, 1847.

152. *Richmond Times and Compiler,* May 28, 1847.

153. Anderson to Harrison Row, January 3, 1848, cited in Bruce, *Virginia Iron Manufacture,* p. 237; Dew, *Ironmaker to the Confederacy,* p. 26. Most southern ironworks relied on black labor. For example, in Tennessee's Cumberland Valley, where ironworks were numerous, *Hunt's Magazine* 28 (1953):644–55, reported that 1,045 whites and 1,360 slaves worked the nineteen furnaces, while 260 whites and 410 black slaves operated the nine forges, and 90 whites and 140 blacks operated the rolling mills.

154. Dew, *Ironmaker to the Confederacy,* p. 28; Bruce, *Virginia Iron Manufacture,* p. 239.

155. "List of Negroes Hired, January 1, 1862," Tredegar Contract Books, Tredegar Company Records, VSL.

156. *Richmond Dispatch,* November 22, 1862–January 15, 1863.

157. *Richmond Examiner,* November 14, 1863; "Negroes and Rations at Catawba, 1863," and "List of Negroes at Furnaces, 1863," Tredegar Letters re: Furnaces, Tredegar Company Records, VSL; Dew, *Ironmaker to the Confederacy,* p. 258.

158. Anderson & Co. to Morton, deBree, and Brown, November 5, 1864, Tredegar Letterbooks, Tredegar Company Records, VSL.

159. *Richmond Dispatch,* January 11, 1859; *Richmond Enquirer,* September 5, 1860; Bruce, *Virginia Iron Manufacture,* p. 239; Dew, *Ironmaker to the Confederacy,* p. 27.

160. "Hands Hired for the Smith Shop in 1863," Tredegar Letterbooks, and "List of Hands Employed on Canal Boats," Tredegar Letters re: Furnaces, Tredegar Company Records, VSL; Dew, *Ironmaker to the Confederacy,* pp. 253, 262–63. For other skilled slaves at Tredegar from 1862 to 1865, see James H. Brewer, *The Confederate Negro: Virginia's Craftsmen and Military Laborers, 1861–1865* (Durham, N.C.: Duke University Press, 1969), p. 64.

161. Spotswood, "Terms and Conditions," p. 20.

162. Whitely, "The Principio Company," pp. 196–97.

163. Charles Carroll to his son, January 9, 1764, in "Extracts from the Carroll Papers," 12 (March 1917):27.

164. Journal A & B, 1767–1794, Patuxent Iron Works, HR.

165. Time Book, 1792–1794, B-26, Box 10, Ridgely Account Books, MHS.

166. "List of Slaves at Oxford Iron Works," William Bolling Papers, Duke.

167. William Weaver to James D. Davidson, January 10, 1855, James D. Davidson Papers, SHSW.

168. "Negroes and Rations at Catawba, 1863," MSS, Tredegar Volume; "List of Negroes at Furnaces, 1863," Tredegar Letters re: Furnaces, Tredegar Company Records, VSL.

"The Darkest Abode 2
of Man"

It's dark as a dungeon and damp as the dew,
Where danger is double and pleasures are few,
Where the rain never falls and the sun never shines,
It's dark as a dungeon way down in the mine. . . .

I hope when I'm gone and the ages shall roll,
My body will blacken and turn into coal.
Then I'll look from the door of my heavenly home,
And pity the miner a-diggin' my bones.
                    —*"Dark as a Dungeon"*

Slaves constituted a vital source of labor in southern coal mines as well as in the iron industry. Because of the difficulty in locating manuscript records and correspondence, however, historians generally have ignored the topic. Although a comprehensive overview of the entire industry must await future detailed studies, sufficient materials exist to permit an accurate assessment of slavery in the eastern Virginia coal field, the most important coal-producing center in the South until after the Civil War.

Like the iron industry, southern coal mining consisted of several regional industries dependent upon local economies, governed in turn by geographic considerations. Most of the vast Great Alleghany Coal Field deposits lay buried beneath the western watershed of the Appalachian Mountains. The states of Tennessee, Kentucky, and western Virginia represented a distinctive region unified by geography and a common water transportation system which distributed coal among the towns and cities along the banks of the Ohio River and its tributaries. Similarly, northwestern Alabama constituted another distinct field. Located in the southernmost extension of the Great Alleghany Coal Field, most of the bituminous coal was shipped down the Warrior River to Mobile on the Gulf Coast. Additional deposits existed in Missouri and North Carolina, but they remained undeveloped during the slave era. In fact, until the 1840s, the eastern Virginia coal district alone played a significant role in the economy of the South. Remoteness from urban markets, the small and scattered population, and inadequate transportation facilities all coalesced to inhibit extensive development of other regional coal industries until the late antebellum period. Not until the late 1830s did Kentucky and Tennessee even begin to produce a noteworthy amount of coal. Even though Alabama became one of the most important coal-producing centers in the nation by the end of the nineteenth century and spawned a powerful steel industry as a result, the state's coal deposits essentially remained underdeveloped during the slave era.[1]

While the South's coal fields developed and operated independently, available evidence reveals employment patterns similar to those found in the regional iron industries. In nearly all cases, the use and extent of slaves depended upon a variety of considerations, including the availability of white laborers. The significance of this factor is illustrated by the dramatic differences between employment patterns in western Virginia and Alabama. A steady stream of European immigrants had flooded the bituminous fields of the northern and border states for more than a half century by the 1820s. In the border states, these immigrants had successfully blocked or eliminated competition with slave and frequently free-black labor. The general reluctance of European immigrants and other white miners to settle in the South with its huge reservoir of black labor was not overcome until the late nineteenth century when blacks had been excluded from many traditional occupations.[2]

The most important stimulus to coal mining in western Virginia first came in the southern part of the state along the Kanawha River with the introduction of salt manufacture. Between 1810 and 1860, western Virginia salt furnaces spawned the rapid expansion of auxiliary industries such as coal mining. Although black bondsmen labored in these early mines, the exact number remains uncertain. By 1850, however, coal miners represented a large percentage of the 3,140 slaves who labored in the Kanawha saltworks. Professor William Barton Rogers, the renowned geologist of the University of Virginia, published a study in 1836 which indicated that 995 miners were employed in the pits which produced the 200,000 tons of coal consumed by the Kanawha saltworks that year.[3] Exactly how many coal miners labored inside the slopes of independent western Virginia pits remains difficult to ascertain. The census of 1850 indicated that only 1,044 workmen were employed at the mines in the entire state. The census data conflict with other evidence, however, which demonstrates that eastern Virginia pits alone utilized that many slave hands. An educated estimate of bonded workers in the western part of Virginia comes closer to two thousand slaves in both coal mines operated by salt companies as well as pits run by independent coal companies.[4]

By 1860, twenty-five independent coal company mines had been incorporated in western Virginia. One of the largest, the Virginia Cannel Coal

Company, which operated mines along the tributaries of the Big Coal and
Little Coal rivers, above Charleston, shipped its product down the river by
barge to Charleston, Cincinnati, and occasionally to New Orleans. In 1851,
the company had twenty flatboats manned by ten hands each.[5] The coal
companies of the region apparently could not get enough slave hands to
meet their needs, since they advertised for all classes of labor during the
1850s. That many of the miners and boat-hands consisted of slaves was
corroborated by the labor policy of the companies in the region. An
editorial in the *Kanawha Valley Star* expressed the concern of some local
leaders regarding the wisdom of permitting outside (northeastern) capital
to develop slave-operated mines and questioned whether such a policy
served the best interests of the community.[6]

When the state constitutional convention met in 1862, slaves represented
only 12,771 of the 347,696 total population in the state. Many of these
slaves were concentrated in the mining district along the Kanawha River,
and, while small in number, the issue of their future in the state caused
enough controversy at the convention that, as a compromise, the delegates
decided to exclude any mention of them in the state's new constitution.[7]

Broader social and economic forces shaped different labor patterns in
Maryland. Entrepreneurs in the state had been, and continued to be,
pioneers in the rising iron industry. But with the expansion of the state's
industrial base, European immigrants filled the new occupations created.
Consequently, the percentage of slave industrial workers contracted. Unlike the changes in labor practices of the iron industry evolved over the
course of a century, the development of Maryland's extensive coal deposits came late in the slave era. Moreover, established and evolving
demographic characteristics of the coal region militated against the
employment of slave labor at these new mines and favored immigrant
labor.

Settlers began to occupy western Maryland before the American Revolution, and by 1790 Fort Cumberland had developed into a dispersed
community of about four thousand people. Coal was probably discovered
and mined for domestic purposes by the early settlers, for a map produced
in 1782 indicates a *mine de carbon,* or coal mine, located at the mouth of
George's Creek. Not until 1804, however, was coal discovered in the more
accessible area of Frostburg. Available transportation rendered the
Frostburg coal more favorably situated for commercial exploitation since a
nearby road connected Frostburg with the cities of Frederick and Baltimore. By 1818, the improved road became part of the famous National
Highway which connected the seaboard with the Ohio Valley at Wheeling
in western Virginia.[8]

The distance of the coal from the eastern markets dampened any immediate flush of excitement among potential entrepreneurs. Farmers as

well as town dwellers still relied on wood for domestic heating, and iron-masters only grudgingly began to accept new techniques which utilized bituminous fuel. All of these factors discouraged the commercial development of the region's coal deposits, and as late as 1841, the *Baltimore Sun* observed that the "coal region is at present one of the most unproductive regions in the state."[9]

During the early years, before the field came under commercial exploitation, little systematic mining took place. Before the arrival of the railroad in 1842, the coming of winter signaled the beginning of a short-lived coal trade. During their off-season, from March until May, farmers became part-time miners who dug and wagoned their coal from the outcrops in the hills to the banks of the Potomac River near Cumberland. The miners heaped the coal upon the banks and awaited weather conditions which promised an adequate "boating stage" in the river level. Constructed of wooden planks, Potomac flatboats, or "coal-arks," were usually eighty feet long, thirteen feet wide, and three feet deep. Each ark contained between 1,500 and 1,800 bushels of coal. The boat was manned by four men: two of the men operated one side oar each, the third an oar which extended over the bow, and the fourth acted as "steersman" handling an oar at the stern. The steersman generally directed the work of the other three. Although the average number was much smaller, as many as forty coal-arks occasionally departed in one fleet from Cumberland for down-river cities. A festive occasion, the departure of the boats generally brought out local residents to watch the fleet begin its swift and treacherous voyage down the rock-filled Potomac. Almost every season, numerous boats were dashed upon the rocks and several crewmen drowned. When the coal reached its destination at the tidal basin, the steersman sold the ark for the highest offer, and the crew began its trek back up the river to Cumberland.[10] No records have survived which reveal the volume of coal transported down the river from the Cumberland field by this means. The Baltimore Association of Commerce estimated that the average annual total of coal shipped down the Potomac by ark amounted to several thousand tons. After the Baltimore and Ohio Railroad reached Cumberland in 1842, shipments gradually decreased, and when the Chesapeake and Ohio Canal also connected Cumberland with the Atlantic tidal basin, river shipments ceased completely.[11]

Between 1828 and 1850, the Maryland legislature passed acts incorporating thirty companies to mine coal in the Cumberland field. Although political squabbling between the Baltimore and Ohio Railroad and the Chesapeake and Ohio Canal hindered development of the two construction projects, both would eventually reach western Maryland. The canal promoters justified their project on the grounds that the canal would help develop the coal fields, while the railroad would carry only passengers.

Both enterprises augured well for the eventual expansion of the western Maryland coal trade to a level of national importance. Experts testified in 1854 that the entire field contained four billion tons. Without a satisfactory means for transporting the coal to market, however, the field remained only a potentially rich source of coal.[12] English businessmen invested heavily in some of the first commercial mines. For example, the George's Creek Coal and Iron Company was launched in 1835 by a London and Baltimore financial syndicate, and Englishmen continued to hold much of the company's stock as late as 1882. Many of the original commercial mines either failed or ultimately were absorbed by the Consolidation Coal Company. Established in 1864, Consolidation eventually became the largest bituminous coal company in the United States. At the same time, Maryland became one of the principal coal producers in the nation.[13]

The expansion of the Cumberland coal field came as a direct result of two internal improvements, both of which were financed by Baltimore syndicates. On July 4, 1828, both the Chesapeake and Ohio Canal and the Baltimore and Ohio Railroad Company broke ground for their respective undertakings and began a race for the industrial Ohio Valley. Even though large-scale mining still lay in the distant future (it took fourteen years for the railroad and twenty-two years for the canal to reach Cumberland), speculators and coal entrepreneurs anticipated the potential for profits and immediately began to purchase the mineral rights in the Cumberland region.[14]

In addition to these two major links with the eastern markets, numerous small, crudely constructed lines began to appear during the interval between 1828 and 1850. The construction of these intra-field rail facilities revealed a pattern of investment which probably helps to explain, at least in part, why the Cumberland coal field differed so radically from other southern fields with regard to its labor force. While southern mines usually were capitalized and operated by local southern entrepreneurs, Maryland's coal reserves were developed by foreign and northeastern financiers. The Maryland and New York Iron and Coal Company, for example, was organized by a group of New York businessmen who began to purchase all available coal properties in the district. Even if coal did not exist under its land, the company planned to build a series of small railroad lines which would link the major production sites with the main trunk line of the Baltimore and Ohio and assure the company a rich source of revenue. The firm's acquisitiveness and long-range planning led it into the manufacture of rolled iron for its railroads, and in 1844, the company's Mount Savage Iron Works manufactured the first "T" railroad track in the United States. By 1845, the company's tracks connected most of the mines with the city of Cumberland. Financial difficulties soon forced the company into a reorganization out of which emerged the Cumberland and Pennsylvania Rail-

road. As one fish is swallowed by a still larger fish, the new company was almost immediately absorbed by the Consolidation Coal Company, chartered in 1860. According to one authority, Consolidation Coal was "a creature of Boston and New York financiers," including Jay Aspinwall, one of the leading tycoons of nineteenth-century enterprise. The company reflected the broader economic ties which bound many border state entrepreneurs to northeastern financial moguls rather than to pillars of the slavocracy.[15]

Although it cannot easily be reduced to measurement, the influence of close northern ties probably dampened any real enthusiasm for slave labor. For one thing, northern industrialists were not necessarily repelled by the use of slaves, but when a labor scarcity occurred, social conditioning did not automatically incline them to think of slaves as the obvious remedy. Moreover, none of the mines in the Cumberland field was located more than thirty miles from the "freedom line" of Pennsylvania. Unquestionably, slaveowners hesitated to send their property so close to a free state because of the very real possibility that the slave would slip across the border overnight. This was particularly so during the 1850s as the sectional strife increased and the "abolitionist menace" grew ever more threatening. Most importantly, however, western Maryland had been settled by small free-holders. Following the American Revolution, many ex-soldiers migrated into the Cumberland district to claim their land bounties, which produced a demographic settlement pattern of independent small farmers engaged in traditional agrarian pursuits. Although large staple-producing plantations did not develop in the Cumberland area, slaves nevertheless lived there. In 1840, eight hundred of the county's sixteen thousand inhabitants consisted of black bondsmen. Exactly how they were deployed remains unknown, but most of them probably labored as servants, farm laborers, or in the small craft shops. No doubt, some slaves worked in the mines, but they must have been few in number, for until the 1850s the census recorded only 150 miners in the entire county.[16]

When the mines began to produce a significant volume of coal during the late 1840s and early 1850s, that section of the state had been settled by people who had no economic interest in the institution of slavery. In short, slaveowners never represented a large percentage of the population, and the total number of coal miners remained relatively small until a few years prior to the Civil War. Moreover, as the field's importance expanded during the 1850s, European immigrants filled the newly created mining jobs. By then, American mining technology had become sophisticated, and the development of well-financed large-scale mines forced the operators to seek the most skilled miners available. Consequently, the companies recruited mine supervisors in Wales, Scotland, and England rather than train slaves through on-the-job experience. As European miners departed from their homes abroad, they were followed by relatives, friends, and others who heard of the new opportunities by word of mouth. Since slavery did not have a firm hold in the Cumberland district, European workers had no reason to fear the wage-depressing effects of competition with slave labor. Therefore, by the 1850s, a conspicuous influx of miners from Great Britain and Germany swelled the work crews at Cumberland mines. Of course, this development in turn further retarded any potential designs regarding the use of slave labor. In addition, many of the mines readily drew on the surplus of workers at nearby Pottstown, Pennsylvania, a well-established coal town.[17]

Consequently, the employment patterns which evolved in the Cumberland coal field took a sharp turn from the established practices in southern industry as a whole. Although free labor prevailed in both the iron and coal industries of antebellum Maryland, the course followed to that end differed significantly. While Maryland iron producers utilized slave labor almost exclusively during the eighteenth century, waves of immigrants found their way into the state through the port of Baltimore in the nineteenth century and gradually thrust blacks out of that traditional employment. Neighboring southern states with larger concentrations of slaves remained essentially hostile to immigrant labor, while at the same time slavery itself repelled European ironworkers who refused to compete with slave labor for starvation wages. Robert Starobin's assertion that Maryland constituted the third largest employer of slave miners notwithstanding, the Maryland coal industry never relied on slave labor.[18] In fact, from the beginning, its white immigrants provided the chief source of mine labor in the state. That, however, was not the case in Virginia.

Buried in the past and ignored by historians, the now forgotten coal mines in eastern Virginia played a crucial role in the industrial development of the rising towns and cities along the Atlantic seaboard. The increasing scarcity of wood, a growing market for home-heating coal which resulted from a multiplying urban population and improvements in furnaces and grates, the application of steam power for manufacturing and transportation, and new iron-smelting techniques—all coalesced during the antebellum years to create a greater demand for coal than had existed previously. Consequently, between about 1820 and the Civil War, bituminous coal rose from an unimportant overall source of energy to a position of vital significance. It became the chief means for keeping the home fires burning, and it lit the furnaces of industry as well.

Discovered early in the eighteenth century, coal was being mined regularly in eastern Virginia before the American Revolution. In 1760, Andrew Burnaby, the Swedish minister from Delaware, noted that, among other infant industries near Richmond, "some coal mines have also been opened upon the James river [sic]." Six years later, Thomas Jefferson also recorded that numerous mines had been opened along the James.[19] While statistics for the early trade are scanty, Virginia coal was distributed among the cities of the Atlantic Coast from Charleston to Boston before the War of 1812 and for many years supplied most of America's domestic consumption.[20] Although the eastern Virginia field had been utilized extensively on a local basis even before the American Revolution, the eastern Virginia field, known as the Richmond Basin, provided the first commercially developed source of domestic coal in the United States. As early as 1789, Virginia coastal vessels supplied Philadelphia, New York, and Boston with the bituminous coal which those young cities required.[21]

One reason for the consistently high demand for Virginia bituminous lay in its excellent heating characteristics. Between 1800 and 1822, Black Heath Pits was the largest single producer of Virginia coal for coastal trade. The papers of its owner, Harry Heth, are replete with praise for the quality of his coal. For example, in 1800 Atway Byrd of Norfolk wrote Heth that he was "so well satisfied with this coal that I shall always apply to you for my supplies, if you will be pointed in furnishing it of like quality."[22] Black Heath coal continued to enjoy a high reputation after Heth's death. In 1837, a U.S. Navy purchasing agent who advertised for coal in the *Richmond Enquirer* stipulated that "the quality must be equal to the 'Black Heath Company of Colliers' coal."[23] By the 1840s, other mining companies were also doing well in the coastal trade. In 1846, the editor of the *Richmond Enquirer* declared that Virginia coal still ranked very favorably with the "mineral treasures" of the neighboring states. Referring to the rapidly developing Cumberland coal field, he observed that even "in the city of Baltimore, the Richmond [coal] out-sells the Cumberland Coal by one dollar per ton."[24]

One of the most important sources of demand for Virginia coal was for the manufacture of illuminating gas used to light thousands of domestic and public lamps in Atlantic Coast cities.[25] As late as 1848, the famous English geologist Sir Charles Lyell wrote: "The cities of New York and Philadelphia have for many years supplied themselves with coal from the Blackheath mines, for the manufacture of gas for lighting their streets and houses. The annual quantity taken by Philadelphia alone has of late years amounted to 10,000 tons."[26]

As early as 1798, the English inventor William Murdoch had demonstrated the uses of illuminating gas, and by the 1830s the streets of London were lit by thousands of gas lamps. Another Englishman, Benjamin Henfrey, had emigrated to America and in 1802 presented the gas-making process to the cities of Richmond, Baltimore, and Philadelphia. Although Henfrey's "thermo-lamp" failed to persuade the city fathers of its practicality, the device triggered further experimentation.[27] The first urban gasworks in the United States was built in Baltimore by the Baltimore Gas

Light Company, chartered in 1816. Initially, the company used tar as the raw material, but gradually, because of the smell, filth, and expense of tar, it converted to the use of bituminous coal. By the early 1830s, Baltimore consumed large amounts of coal, most of which came from Virginia, to manufacture illuminating gas.[28] Following Baltimore's lead, New York and Boston chartered their own gas light companies. Finally, in 1833, and against the protests of residents, Philadelphia established a committee to study the possibility for illuminating the city's streets. Although Pennsylvania bituminous was preferred, high transportation costs accrued from shipping the raw material eastward across the mountains remained prohibitive. Consequently, like New York, Boston, and Baltimore, Philadelphia became heavily dependent upon eastern Virginia for its supply of raw materials used in the production of gas light.[29]

The great demand for all available bituminous coal among the towns and cities of the eastern seaboard partially explains the success of the Virginia coal trade. Because of the disjuncture of supply and demand in the marketplace, neither Virginia nor imported English coal could satisfy the insatiable demand for the mineral fuel. Virginia occupied a strategic position in this market because the mines near Richmond produced the only domestic coal easily accessible to Atlantic coastal vessels. As Albert Gallatin suggested in his *Report on Roads and Canals,* published in 1808, "the only place where. . . [coal] production is now found near the Atlantic waters as to be capable of immediate transport is on James river [sic]."[30] Although Pennsylvania anthracite was mined close to eastern markets, it required a few decades for industrial technology to adapt to the efficient use of anthracite. During the War of 1812, Virginia bituminous became very scarce. A Philadelphia manufacturer whose supply of bituminous began to run low bought a cartload of "black stone" found in abundance at the headwaters of the Schuylkill River. After that initial supply had been wasted without getting up the requisite heat, another load of anthracite was obtained. After an entire night had been lost in a vain attempt to burn it, the hands closed the furnace door and left the works in frustration. One of the hands had forgotten his jacket, however, and upon returning discovered the coal had become a white-hot mass. Anthracite had been applied to industrial use for the first time, but several decades were still to pass before the fuel and the technology became efficiently interdependent.[31]

Even though huge quantities of bituminous were being mined in the Great Appalachian field, especially in western Pennsylvania, during the first half of the nineteenth century coal could not be shipped to the eastern cities at a feasible cost. Most Appalachian bituminous was consumed locally in the burgeoning mill city of Pittsburgh or the growing industrial towns along the Ohio River, to which coal could be transported cheaply. Not until the 1850s, when western Pennsylvania's vast reserves were made available by a network of railroad lines connecting the Appalachian field with the eastern seaboard, was the demand even barely met on the Atlantic Coast.[32] The connection of Pennsylvania's western supply with its eastern markets signaled the doom of Virginia's dominance of the coastal coal trade. The Keystone state's vast reserves of easily mined coal soon overshadowed all opposition in the marketplace (see Appendix 7). As early as 1800, Pennsylvania produced 87,000 tons of bituminous compared to Virginia's 18,000 tons, and by 1820 the disparity had grown to 225,000 tons for Pennsylvania and 62,000 tons for Virginia. By 1850, when the eastern cities had been connected with the Appalachian supply, Pennsylvania's production completely dwarfed Virginia's production of 138,017 tons, with an astounding 2,147,500 tons of bituminous. By the beginning of the Civil War, the gap yawned even wider to 4,710,400 tons for Pennsylvania and 112,473 tons for Virginia.[33] The dramatic expansion of coal production in the Keystone state was matched only by the growth of its iron industry, and their symbiotic relationship was vividly revealed in their parallel development. It also reflected the rapid evolution of a distinctively industrial North committed to a dynamic industrial expansion, as opposed to a South committed to the agrarian ideals of Thomas Jefferson. These two conflicting conceptions of a "good society" suggested the opposition encountered by industrial entrepreneurs in the antebellum South.

The eastern Virginia coal field provided the first commercial source of domestic coal in the United States. While other states, such as Pennsylvania, had more extensive supplies, Virginia provided the only coal easily accessible to coastal vessels through the ports of Richmond and Petersburg. Between the American Revolution and the mid-nineteenth century, Virginia remained the major supplier of domestic coal on the Atlantic Coast.[34] About twenty-six miles long and four to twelve miles wide, the field ran north and south, with the James River flowing through its middle and the Appomattox River across its southern tip. Prior to the Civil War, the city of Richmond lay about thirteen miles to the east. The bed itself resembled a highly irregular basin, with the coal seams inclined westward, often at a steep angle, and then upward toward the surface at the western edge. Gaseous and "troubled" by geological deformations, most mines were constructed at the outcrops on the outer edges where even there it required vertical shafts from four hundred to eight hundred feet deep to reach the bottom seam.[35]

This was the case of Black Heath Pits, founded on an unspecified date between 1785 and 1790 after a fallen tree uprooted a rich seam of coal. Miners knew little of the underground characteristics of the field, however, until Sir Charles Lyell conducted the first systematic investigation of the region's strata and published the results in 1847. Lyell used the Black Heath workings as one of the bases for his study. Within a quarter mile of the pits, Lyell found two important seams of coal. The upper seam was most important since "the magnitude and persistency of this seam," which measured from thirty to forty feet in thickness, consisted of "as pure a mass of rich bituminous coal as can perhaps be found in the world." The geologist expressed surprise when he first arrived at Black Heath

> and descended a shaft 800 feet deep, to find myself in a chamber more than 40 feet high, caused by the removal of the coal. Timber props of great strength are required to support the roof, and although the use of wood is lavish here as everywhere in the United States, the props are seen to bend under the incumbent weight.[36]

Lyell confirmed what many coal miners already knew when he observed that the strata contained exaggerated disturbances. As a consequence,

> the manner in which, these *troubles* as they are called, the coal is squeezed out at one point and made to swell and thicken at another, . . . must be referred to movements of the rocks and the forcing of the granite against the coal, the distinct layers of which are often cut off abruptly one after the other by the granite in contact. The dips of the strata of coal in the neighborhood of these sudden thickenings and swellings of the seams vary from 20° to 70° and at one point attained an angle of 84°.[37]

The bottom of the basin remained unexplored during the period before the Civil War, and Lyell reported that there had been "no borings for coal in the central parts of the coal-field." On the western side of the Richmond field, the same irregularities existed as those observed in the eastern rim. Thus, at Dover Pits, located on the opposite side of the same seam mined by Black Heath, the coal pitched at no less than fifty degrees east. Only about a mile south of Dover, on the other hand, Lyell observed that the strata near the granite was almost horizontal. In short, "the disturbances have been so great that although the general structure of the coal-field is that of a basin or trough, . . . the deviations from this form are numerous."[38] The general characteristics of the Richmond field may be seen in the cross section illustrated in Figure 3, while the significance of these "troubles" are discussed in Chapter 6.

In the Richmond Basin, one of the first methods of mining coal to the surface was by open quarry, or "trenching." Miners simply removed the mineral until it became impractical to continue. According to one experienced mining engineer, "in the Richmond coal-field numerous excavations of this kind are found along the outcrops of the seams, and, in some cases, immense quantities of earth have been removed to obtain a small amount of coal.''[39] As early as December 1783, Johann David Schoepf, a doctor with the Hessian troops, journeyed through the southern states and stopped to visit the coal mines of the Richmond field. Schoepf recorded:

> There has been discovered a bed of pitcoals 12 miles from here, on the south side of the James River and above the falls, the occasion of. . . . Trenches are dug straight down, and at 26-30 ft. the bed is not yet gone through; these trenches soon filling with water, new ones are continually opened up, although this labor might be avoided. The coals, however are not the best; all Richmond smells of them.[40]

3. Cross Section of the Richmond Coal Field. *Reprinted from Samuel Harries Daddow and Benjamin Bannan*, Coal, Iron, and Oil *(Philadelphia: J. B. Lippincott & Co., 1886), p. 396.*

When trenching was no longer practicable and underground operations became a necessity, more sophisticated technology had to be applied. Deep-shaft mining conducted several hundred feet beneath the earth's surface required an infinitely more complex mode of operations than the mere brute labor of trenching. Given the rudimentary mining technology of the late eighteenth and early nineteenth centuries, and the irregularities of the strata itself, sinking a shaft represented a minor engineering marvel.

The usual method for determining the depth and underground location of the coal consisted of a primitive process known as boring. Performed mostly by hand, boring through several hundred feet of rock was exacting labor, for early tools consisted of chisel bits fastened to the end of a metal pole. As the boring progressed, additional lengths were added. Until steam power became available later in the century, two men turned the long drill-like shaft. The bit "augered" out the ground rock through the two-to-five-inch hole created by the drill. Pressure was applied to the extended bit by means of a long wooden pole manned by two additional men who applied the leverage, while the first two turned the bit.[41]

Having ascertained the location and condition of the coal, the "sinkers" then began to dig the shaft. The depth of the coal dictated the size of the opening, with the deeper shafts measuring ten or twelve feet at the mouth. The opening was then divided into two or four chambers by board partitions in order to prevent cave-ins. With smaller shafts, the operators frequently ignored the partitions. The sinking operation commenced by the removal of the top soil. Under the direction of experienced sinkers, the workmen (usually slaves) suffered few accidents during routine digging and hoisting operations. The work became very dangerous, however, when blasting became necessary. Then, a thirty-by-two-inch hole was chiseled into the rock and packed with a metal casing of gunpowder. The powder had to be tamped with a special device, and if great caution was not exercised, a spark might produce an untimely explosion and tragic death.[42] When sinking had progressed to a level too deep to empty the pit of debris by shovelling, or to be served by a windlass, a "gin" was erected over the pit. Prior to the widespread accessibility of steam engines, the horse-powered gin provided the major source for movement of men and materials up and down Virginia's coal shafts. The gin consisted of a four- or five-foot horizontal drum. Around the drum a long cable wound as a mule turned the gin first one way and then the other, raising or lowering the attached "corves." Resembling baskets with sled-like iron runners, each loaded corve was hooked to one end of the rope and the mule drew it up, while simultaneously an empty corve descended at the other end of the rope.[43]

The process of digging, "cribbing" the sides, and hoisting debris progressed until the sinkers reached the coal, whereupon the shaft was continued another thirty feet beyond the seam. That part of the pit became a sump which facilitated underground water drainage and helped to keep the mines dry. An unusual amount of subsurface water plagued the mines of eastern Virginia, and if left idle for any length of time, the deeper workings quickly filled with water. Aside from the danger involved, pumping water represented a constant source of unproductive work and expense for early mine owners. In a letter to one of his white overseers at Oxford Iron Works, David Ross described how miners at the turn of the nineteenth century freed their deep pits of water:

> When I workt the Deep Run Coal pits I imagine there was fifty times more water collected there than can be at the Iron mines. There was a large old Workings, some of them more than an acre. At the Christmas holidays when the hired negroes went home and before we hired others, the whole of those workings were filled with water. It required constant work for ten days to get it out. Afterwards we could keep it under in two hours every day or less. The bucket we used held an hundred gallons, and was raised by a horse. The Engine stood between the two Shafts & served for both. The engine would not cost more than 50 or 60 if made by hired hands, except the rope. There is no occasion for one to get wet. The buckets are hung in such a manner as to fill themselves and can be empty [*sic*] by a hand on the Bank with one

of his hands only. There is another method of raising water which is probably better. Tis on the same principles as a chain pump which is the method of raising water on board the ships of War.[44]

Harry Heth, the owner of Black Heath Pits, probably erected the first steam-powered hydraulic pump in America to replace the horse-drawn tub device. In November 1811, he agreed with Daniel French of New York to pay for the construction of such an engine with sufficient power "to raise from a pit of the depth of two hundred and fifty feet, one hundred and fifty gallons of water per minute by pumps attached to the Engine" and likewise to raise coal from the same shaft.[45] By the Civil War, further improvements had greatly increased the efficiency of pumping. Apparently, only the largest concerns in the Richmond field utilized the more efficient hydraulic pumps, for according to one contemporary engineer, "most of the proprietors insist on the bucket being the best and cheapest mode of drainage, and keep on *raising water instead of coal.*"[46]

Throughout the nineteenth century, knowledgeable miners everywhere used the same basic plan for "winning" the coal, known as the "pillar and breast" or "post and stall" system (see Figure 4). It was devised to get as much coal as possible while leaving just enough uncut coal at strategic points to pillar, or support, the above strata. From the shaft, two main entries or "drifts" were begun. These became the main working areas. The miners laid small tracks to convey the mule-drawn "buggies" from the working "face" to the shaft, where the coal was then lifted to the surface. At various intervals, tunnels, called "sections," were excavated into the coal at right angles off the main entry. Operators took precautions, however, to ensure that thick walls, or "breasts," remained between the section workings to support the roof. When oxygen failed to reach the face of each section, right angle cuts through the breasts connected adjacent sections and facilitated the circulation of fresh air. Prior to the Civil War, miners used a pick-ax to chip a groove at the bottom of the seam in order to provide a cleavage line and then to bore holes at strategic spots in the coal, packed a charge into them, and blasted the coal loose. After extensive working, the entire mine came to resemble a labyrinth of tunnels and pillars.[47]

Contemporary descriptions of antebellum Virginia mines are rare, but several personal accounts have been preserved which reveal some interesting impressions of coal mines in the field. Henry Howe, the Virginia historian and genealogist, visited the Midlothian mines in 1845. Prior to his descent into the pits, Howe observed that two steam engines hoisted the coal over seven hundred feet up the perpendicular shaft. Once at the top, the corves were placed on small railroad cars, "pushed by the negroes a few rods to where it is emptied, screened, and shovelled into the large cars on the railroad," and carried to the Richmond coal yards.[48] Outside opera-

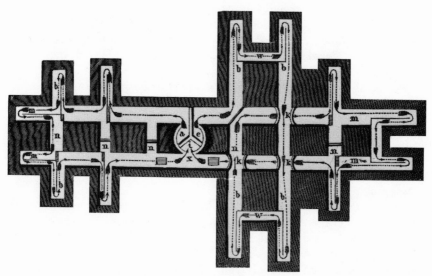

4. The Pillar and Breast System. *Reprinted from John Holland,* The History and Description of Fossil Fuel, the Collieries, and Coal Trade of Great Britain *(London: Whittaker & Co., 1841), p.220.*

tions at Dover Pits differed slightly. Edmund Ruffin, editor of the *Farmers' Register,* noted in 1837 that a narrow railway ran from the shafts directly to the canal along a six hundred yard incline. The railway ran on large beams which extended out over the canal, at the end of which two iron bars prevented the coal car from going over the edge. As the car hit the iron stops, inertia caused the car to tilt and empty the coal directly into the canal boat. One or two slaves handled a rope attached to the rear of the car to prevent it from tilting over completely. A mule then pulled the empty vehicle back up the incline. A slave rode the car to the bottom and manned a hand-brake to prevent the vehicle from running free. The danger associated with this particular occupation was exemplified by Ruffin's account of one rider who had become alarmed and jumped off the car. Without any drag on its downward motion, the vehicle gained such velocity that it broke through the iron stops and "leaped across the canal, without touching the water, and stuck into the bank."[49]

Descending the shaft provided a breathtaking experience for the novice. The Reverend J. B. Jeter, a Baptist minister from Richmond, visited the Midlothian mines in 1843 and shared his adventure with the readers of the *Richmond Daily Whig.* He reported that "no one has any conception of the apparently perilous attempt in going down these shafts, until he has experienced it. The distance and the view descending are truely frightful."[50] Henry Howe experienced a similar feeling of "trepidation" as he descended the same pit for his subterranean tour:

> My friend, guide, and self, each with a lighted lamp, sprang
> into a basket suspended by ropes over pulleys and frame-
> work, above a yawning abyss seven hundred and seventy-
> five feet deep. The signal was given — puff! puff! went the
> steam-engine and down, down, went we. I endeavored to
> joke to conceal my trepidation. It was stale business. Rapidly
> glided past the wooden sides of the shaft — I became dizzy.[51]

Not all miners descended a "yawning abyss" to reach the coal workings.
Edmund Ruffin entered Dover Pits through a steep sloping tunnel cut for a
footway. Geared up by stout timbers, the slope inclined at about a thirty-
degree angle, and the low ceiling required the spectator to walk in a
"stooping posture."[52]

However spectators arrived at the bottom, their awe was heightened by
what they encountered in the underground maze of tunnels. At Midlothian,
Henry Howe was led "through many a labyrinth." He compared the drifts
to the streets, and the pillars to the squares of a "city in miniature." The
main drifts averaged about sixteen feet and the smaller about ten feet in
width, with large intervening pillars of "about sixty feet square." Only the
surrealistic flicker of the wall lamps penetrated the darkness and dis-
oriented the novice.[53] When John Smith visited the Midlothian pits in 1846,
he revealed the effects of this disorientation when he remarked that his
"imagination had very often partially prepared me for the state of things in
coal mines, which I saw there; but a real and an imaginary state of things are
totally different." Smith declared that when "passing along the various
channels and routes . . . you experience a natural restraint on your feelings, and a sincere awe," which he found unpleasant. "The gloominess of
the place and the dread silence of the scene make one sometimes feel truly
his helplessness."[54] The appearance of the "gearing," or reinforcement
timbers, also induced a feeling of helplessness among visitors. As drifts
were dug, miners placed a green piece of timber on each side of the opening
at two-foot intervals. They then lodged a cross-timber between the ceiling
and the two perpendicular side-timbers. The uprights and the cross-pieces
were then framed in by boards connected to the cross-timbers in order to
keep rock from breaking loose from the ceiling. The sight of older timber-
work in Dover Pits, which appeared to be breaking, left Ruffin visibly
shaken:

> As we groped along the drifts, I noticed one of the uprights
> bent to an angle, and splintered, in yielding to the pressure;
> and remarked to the overseer who acted as our guide, that his
> timber there was too small. He answered, as cooly as if we
> were in day light, "No, it is only the creeping of the metals
> above our heads." I soon saw plenty of such cases of shi-
> vered and yielding timbers, and was surprised to learn that it

was not a partial and particular effect, but a general and continued, though usually very slow and gradual sinking of the roof.[55]

If left entirely unattended, the timbers eventually would give way and the drift openings would collapse from the constant downward pressure.

Operations in the newer working sections were also unlikely to arouse confidence in the hesitant novice. Howe witnessed several blasts at the working face in one of the Midlothian mines. He noted that "the match was put, we retreated a short distance,—then came the explosion, echoing and re-echoing among the caverns,—momentary noise of falling coal, like a sudden shower of hail, succeeded, and then all was silence."[56] Workmen shoveled the coal into corves, which were then drawn out of the sections to the main entry, placed on a small car, pulled up the inclined tramway to the bottom of the shaft, and finally lifted to the surface.[57] The mules which pulled the corves from the sections to the main drift were maintained, according to Howe, in "well-arranged stables" and "all requisite attention paid them. Some of the animals remain below for years, and when carried to the strong light of day, gambol like wild horses."[58] The Reverend Jeter corroborated Howe's observation and asserted that the mule stable was "as comfortable and convenient as any in the city of Richmond."[59] Not all mines used mules to drag the corves from the working sections to the main entry. At Dover Pits, for example, Ruffin witnessed "trainers" performing that task:

The dragging of the loaded corves seemed to be heavy and oppressive labor. Each man, has a chain fastened by straps around his breast, which he hooks to the corve, and thus harnessed, and in a stooping posture, he drags his heavy load over the floor of rock. Every digger and trainer has his lamp—and their appearance well accords with the gloomy scene of their labors.[60]

For the safety of the workers, the importance of a mining system was exceeded only by the requirements for adequate ventilation. Without a proper current of fresh air, a coal mine became quite literally a deadly place in which to work. Before the development of high velocity forced-air fans, Virginia mine operators generally employed the same basic two-shaft system of ventilation, illustrated in Figure 5. As specially constructed furnaces (f) heated the inside air causing it to rise up one shaft (a), fresh air from outside was drawn down and through the mine before it too ascended the rise shaft and returned to the atmosphere. The cycle continued as long as the furnace operated, but the system became more complicated as the workings expanded. Since the air tended to flow by the nearest openings in the upcast shaft, most of the drifts would not receive air if it were not

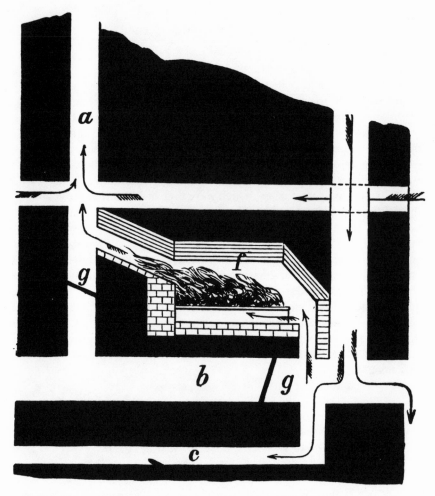

5. The Furnace Ventilation System. *Reprinted from Samuel Harries Daddow and Benjamin Bannan,* Coal, Iron, and Oil *(Philadelphia: J. B. Lippincott & Co., 1886), p.436.*

compelled to traverse the entire mine. Consequently, a series of barriers, or "doors," which usually consisted of canvas, wood, or brick, was erected to cover certain passages so that the air coursed where the miners labored and then to the upcast shaft and out.[61]

By the 1840s, the Midlothian mines utilized this same basic ventilation system. The atmospheric air entered the mines through the deepest shaft, and after "coursing the entire drifts," as Henry Howe characterized it, the air ascended the main entry to the more elevated workings, and up the shaft carrying with it the methane gas emitted by the coal.[62] The Midlothian pits produced great quantities of methane gas, the presence of which made a firm impression upon most visitors. Howe "heard the gas escaping from the coal make a hissing noise" and saw it "set on fire in crevices of the walls by the lamp of our conductor."[63] And the Reverend Jeter "saw the gas bubbling through the small streams which were flowing in some of the drifts, and saw it from the contiguity of a lamp ignite and blaze for a considerable time, on the wall."[64] A.S. Wooldridge, the president of Midlothian, also recognized that "large quantities of inflammable gas are thrown out from the coal in the mines constantly," and any interruption in the ventilation could result in disastrous consequences from an explosion. Wooldridge reminded his readers, however, that the most efficient ventilation system was utilized and fresh air coursed the whole mine.[65] Indeed, according to Reverend Jeter, the air circulated freely in every section of the mine, and in some places the current was almost "too strong for comfort."[66]

Ventilation has always been vital to the operation of coal mines and the safety of the workers. In the Virginia field, where most sound theories were thwarted by the irregularity of its seams and a well-deserved reputation for gaseousness, proper ventilation became at once imperative and nearly impossible. When the fire in the furnace was neglected, or trap doors carelessly left open, death might well be the result. Wherever the air failed to circulate, stagnations occurred and methane gas given off by the coal, sometimes called "fire-damp," might accidentally be ignited. When that happened, the entire mine was illuminated by

> A roaring whirlwind of flaming air, which tears up everything
> in its progress, scorching some of the miners to a cinder,
> burying others under enormous heaps of ruins shaken from
> the roof; and, thundering to the shaft, wastes its volcanic fury
> in a discharge of thick clouds of coal, dust, stones, timber,
> and not infrequently limbs of horses.[67]

At Dover Pits, methane gas was channeled into metal pipes. Once lit, it burned continually and helped reduce the danger of accumulation. If the gas was permitted to collect along the ceilings, an unwitting miner could easily ignite a violent explosion with his lamp.[68]

As destructive and spectacular as the mine explosion was, most of the miners worked in sections off the main entries and frequently escaped the blast itself. With all the ventilation barriers blown down by the concussion, however, and the atmospheric current entirely excluded from the mine, workers who survived the explosion itself instantly suffocated from "after-damp" (carbonic acid), which immediately filled the vacuum caused by the explosion. When the mines are properly ventilated, after-damp, the heaviest of mine gases, lies near the floor. When the explosion of methane above it creates a vacuum, after-damp then rises and suffocates miners working in its presence.[69] Although eastern Virginia mines suffered many such explosions, those catastrophes were never as numerous as the dead left in their wake.

On June 20, 1796, the French nobleman Duc de la Rochefoucauld left Richmond, Virginia, for Monticello to visit Thomas Jefferson. On the way, he stopped to examine several coal mines at Dover belonging to Messrs. Graham and Havans, "mernhants of Richmond." La Rochefoucauld observed that while the mine operators had discovered coals of superior quality, they were "content to grope their way without applying for advice to more enlightened men; for there is not one person throughout America versed in the art of working mines." La Rochefoucauld also noted that the mine shafts were located on a farm composed of three hundred and fifty acres of land, and like the farm, they were run "very badly." Most significantly, the French traveler noted that Graham and Havans employed about "five hundred negroes in this mine, and the business of the farm."[70] Although La Rochefoucauld may have exaggerated the case, he nevertheless touched on the most striking characteristic of southern coal mining. From the very beginning, mines in the South depended upon the sinew and sweat of black bondsmen.

In the September 20, 1780, issue of the *Virginia Gazette*, Samuel DuVal gave notice that he desired to sell his "valuable coal pits" in Henrico County, twenty miles from Richmond. The vein of coal extended "2 miles in length, and as to its width and depth, the labor of 10 hands ever since the year 1760 has proved insufficient for discovery." "Hands" in this case probably meant slaves, for a subsequent notice in another Richmond newspaper announced the sale of several bondsmen who had worked for "many years at the Deep Run coal pits for Samuel DuVal."[71] In 1798, a Goochland County mine owner employed twenty-one water hands to float his coal to Richmond and forty-one hands for the pits. Judging from the amount of money expended for Negro hire, most of these workmen must have been slaves.[72]

Among the earliest mines along the James River, Black Heath Pits were located in Chesterfield County near the town of Manchester. Founded in 1788 and operated for the next three decades by Henry (Harry) Heth (1760?-1821), Black Heath became synonymous with high-quality coal.[73] Harry Heth was probably born in Frederick County, Virginia, sometime during the 1760s. His parents emigrated from either Ireland or England (that too remains uncertain) during the 1740s. During the Revolutionary War, Heth served as a captain in the Continental Army and became a charter member of the Virginia Society of the Cincinnati. Following the Revolution, Captain Heth became the U.S. commissioner of loans for Virginia and until his death resided about twelve miles southwest of Rich-

mond at the family estate of Blackheath. During the War of 1812, Heth
served as a major in the Virginia militia. After several years of illness, he
died in 1821 at Savannah, Georgia, upon returning from a trip to England.
As the oldest male of Harry Heth's eight children, John Heth (1798-1842)
became heir to the coal business his father had pioneered and, like his
father, became one of the leading colliers of the region. John was the father
of Confederate General Henry Heth (1825-1899), the most famous of the
Heth family.[74]

Although Harry Heth owned many hands, he probably hired a majority
of his slave force. In March 1810, he advertised that he wished to hire for
"the balance of the year, 30 or 40 able bodied Negro Men, for whom a
liberal price will be given."[75] Slaves also formed the vast majority of the
170 full- and part-time workers employed at Heth's coal yards during the
summer of 1813.[76] The owner of considerable coal land, Heth leased a
number of pits to other operators in exchange for a production royalty. As a
means of control, Heth usually stipulated that the lessee had to employ a
specific number of full-time workmen underground. Thus, when two small
local operators leased seventy-five acres of coal land from Heth in 1819,
they agreed to work not less than twenty-five hands nor more than fifty per
year, while on another parcel they agreed to work not less than fifteen, nor
more than thirty hands, "should there appear to be coal sufficient."[77]

Not only did Heth employ large numbers of slave miners, but he also
worked them in every occupation associated with the business, including
the most highly skilled. For example, after his first steam engine failed to
work efficiently in 1813, a Philadelphia manufacturer, Oliver Evans,
negotiated with the operator to build and install a more powerful engine.
For his efforts, Evans required $6,000. In addition, for $3 per day in wages,
an engineer would install the engine and teach a local mechanic how to
operate and maintain it. Heth responded that $3 per day for an engineer was
too high. The collier intimated that his own hands could take care of the
engine as well as any Philadelphia engineer and cost Heth much less.[78] In a
scoffing reply, Evans told Heth that a good engineer would not accept less,
and added:

> I fear you have wrong Ideas if you think Slaves can keep a
> steam engine in order. A man must be free before his mind
> will expand so much. They might soon learn to keep the
> engine going as long as it will go without the piston being
> pushed, or anything else requiring to be put to rights. Slaves
> cannot keep a saw mill or flour mill at work without the
> millwright not even a plow without the assistance of the plow
> maker. So that you must think of engaging some mechanical
> Man always about the place.[79]

Although Heth purchased the engine, he did not follow the Philadelphian's advice about the engineer, for in 1817 Heth informed a neighboring operator, A.S. Wooldridge, that he "had two young negro men to hire out, & one or two machine boys—one of the men has generally been employed at the pitts [*sic*] for the last ten years the other for two or three. both [*sic*] the boys have been employed as machine drivers."[80] Heth's bondsmen also labored in such diverse occupations as blacksmithing and numerous other tasks both skilled and unskilled.[81] When Heth leased his Stonehenge coal property in 1819, he agreed to furnish the company with "fifty Negroe Men, a Smith & Striker, with Obey the Cork Maker, with Billy Griffen & Gilbert to attend the Engines."[82] By 1819, Heth had been ill for several

Table 4

HARRY HETH'S SLAVE TAXABLES, 1800–1820

Year	Number of Slaves	Year	Number of Slaves
1800	7	1811	68
1801	21	1812	114
1802	7	1813	80
1803	40	1814	38
1804	52	1815	3
1805	52	1816	57
1806	70	1817	46
1807	47	1818	81
1808	—	1819	45
1809	102	1820	30
1810	100		

Source: Personal Property Tax Books, Chesterfield County, Virginia State Library. Reference is to both personal and company slaves, but which group worked strictly in the coal mines cannot be determined. The 1808 records were destroyed by fire.

years and apparently contemplated giving up the business, for that year he drew up a "List of Negroes which the proprietor will sell all together." Heth enumerated fifty-two men and women, among which he included Phill Cox, "a tolerable cooper," as well as a blacksmith, striker, carpenter, bricklayer, and ten laborers.[83] At the time of his death in 1821, Heth owned forty-one slaves who had been hired to the company and upon whom the remaining partners had to pay hiring fees to the estate. They calculated that a fair hire for the slaves "belonging to the Estate of Mr. Harry Heth—Dec [d] for nine months ending the twenty-fifth December 1821," totaled $11,855 for thirty-four males, three females, and four children.[84] The number of slave taxables for which Heth was assessed between 1800 and 1820 may be seen in Table 4.

In his memoirs, the Confederate general, Henry Heth, grandson of the mine promoter, recalled his childhood at Blackheath, the family estate. Among the general's earliest recollections were the family coal mines and the childhood curiosity which led him to descend into the pits even though his father (John Heth) had forbidden it.

> The desire to do what was forbidden, combined with the curiosity, was too strong, so I saved what money was given me for several weeks; with this and some cake that I got from my mother's storeroom I bribed a foreman of the mine, an old "darkey," to take me down the mine seven hundred feet deep. Remaining in the pit some two hours, I asked the old "darkey" to take me out. The illusion of a coal pit was dispelled from that day.[85]

Whether slave or free, this black foreman must have had considerable experience in coal mines to acquire the knowledge mandatory for underground supervision. His position suggests just how far Heth carried his commitment to black labor.

Following the death of Harry Heth in 1821, John Heth and his brother-in-law Beverly Randolph reorganized Black Heath Pits into the Black Heath Company of Colliers. Heth and Randolph continued to rely on slave labor. When they entered a temporary partnership with David Hancock in 1831, the articles of agreement stipulated that Hancock would furnish "twenty five good hands & Randolph & Heth twenty five more" to raise the coal and to cut timber for the mine. Although Hancock became the underground foreman, John Heth remained the general superintendent "as to working hands etc."[86] After an explosion in 1836 which killed forty-five blacks and two white overseers, the company was reorganized into the Maidenhead Pits.[87] In an effort to get back into production, Heth and Randolph immediately began to purchase new hands. In December 1836, the colliers acquired a slave blacksmith along with his wife and child for $2,260. The following year the partners spent an additional $11,345 for slave workers. Between the reclaimed workings and an adjoining mine, over one hundred blacks toiled by the end of 1837, "including those at top and bottom and cartsmen."[88] The Maidenhead Pits never recovered the losses sustained from the explosion, and in 1840 all of its stock was sold to a group of English capitalists organized into the Chesterfield Coal and Iron Mining Company.[89] Unlike most coal mines in the region, however, the Chesterfield Company employed 130 free blacks rather than slaves. Why the company followed this policy remains unclear. Slaveowners probably feared the loss of their human property in another explosion and temporarily refused to hire bondsmen to the company.

By the late 1830s and early 1840s, numerous coal companies operated in the eastern Virginia field. One of the largest of them was the famous Midlothian Mining Company, chartered in 1836. According to the president of the company, A.S.Wooldridge, the capital was divided into three thousand shares of a hundred dollars each; and one third, being one thousand shares, was sold to some thirty shareholders, in and around Richmond—generally, of "the most respectable and wealthy class." By 1841, two of the prospective four shafts were in production, and according to Wooldridge, "the whole effective force at these mines, including the coal yard hands, and top and bottom hands, is one hundred and fifty men and boys, with some twenty five mules."[90] Two years later, in 1843, the informed visitor Henry Howe confirmed that these were black workers when he observed that the Midlothian mines employed in all their operations "some 150 negroes."[91] Many of these Negroes must have been slaves, for John Smith, who visited Midlothian in 1846, noted that these pits are of "incalculable benefit" to the nearby farmers who hired those excess slaves to the pits "who would otherwise be idle and a burthen on their hands."[92] Midlothian did hire several free blacks in addition to slaves. An 1846 advertisement for slave hirelings notified owners that the company employed "several free coloured men," but assured squeamish owners that the free blacks were well-disciplined.[93]

During the 1850s, the Midlothian Company continued to rely on hired slave labor. The 1850 census recorded 123 male bondsmen at the mines, only 7 of whom the company owned.[94] By 1860, the Midlothian had increased its labor force to two hundred workers, at least one hundred of whom belonged to the company.[95] If traditional patterns prevailed, the remainder consisted largely of hired bondsmen and a sprinkling of free blacks and whites. Following the Civil War, the Midlothian mines made the transition from slavery to freedom by continuing to employ as many ex-slaves as possible rather than to replace them with whites. According to the superintendent engineer of Midlothian, Oswald J. Heinrich, as late as 1871, "most of our labor here is colored labor, although we have a few good white miners amongst us. The men have faced great danger and undergone much hardship bravely."[96]

By the 1830s and 1840s, numerous additional pits had been sunk in the Richmond Basin. As president of the Midlothian Mining Company for two decades after its founding in 1837, A. S. Wooldridge headed one of the largest mining operations in the antebellum South. A pioneer in the industry and an extremely knowledgeable observer, in 1841 he published a description of the coal mines currently operating in the field. That document remains one of the few sources still available regarding the scope of mine activity during the period. According to Wooldridge, at least twelve companies raised coal from the field in 1841 from about thirty or forty individual pits; most of them employed slave labor. Immediately adjoining the

Maidenhead Pits were the mines owned by Murchie, Mosely, and Brander known as Gowrie Pits. At the two shafts then in operation, forty hands labored on the top and bottom, and the nearby Duval and Company pits utilized about fifty hands.[97] The Creek Company of Colliers, organized in 1837, also represented a fairly extensive operation which employed the labor of seventy hands. Apparently, most of the men were hirelings, for Wooldridge noted that this company owned all the necessary machinery and about thirty men. Two of the largest operators in the neighborhood were Crouches and Sneed, who employed about one hundred and fifty hands and raised four hundred thousand bushels of coal in 1841. Several other operators employed numerous bondsmen, such as the Tuckahoe Coal Company which utilized about twenty hands, the Edge Hill Pits about thirty, Townes and Powell about twenty, and the Deep Run Pits, still in operation after half a century, forty miners. At the southern extreme of the field, along the Appomattox River, Clover Hill Company utilized a work force of twenty hands at one pit and another twelve at an adjoining mine.[98] The 1850 census revealed that two-thirds of the 120 males employed at Clover Hill were slaves, and most of the 140 men who labored on the railroad which connected the mines with the Petersburg coal yards consisted of bondsmen as well.[99] By 1860, the Clover Hill mines had contracted its scope of operations. Nevertheless, sixty-six of the ninety workmen employed by the company were slaves. Similarly, the company railroad now employed 133 men, 109 of them bondsmen.[100]

Still other mining companies operated in the Richmond field by the 1850s. One of the most important among them, Carbon Hill, also employed a large number of slave workmen. In January 1855, agent John Werth advertised his desire for "40 or 50 good Coal Pit Hands" during the ensuing year. Similarly, in 1858 Carbon Hill again advertised for fifty Negro men to work in the company's pits, and the following year for "Sixty Able Negro Men."[101] Also like most other mines in the area, Carbon Hill employed slave labor in all facets of the operation, not just those designated as routine, for in 1860 the company required slaves to work "on the surface at the Mines on the railroad, in the canal boats, and at the coal yards in the city."[102] In addition to these occupations, the company needed fifty slave hirelings, "among them, a first-rate Carpenter, two Track Layers, and Engine Runners."[103]

Ranked among the earliest mines in the eastern Virginia field, Dover Pits depended on slave labor from the beginning. While journeying to Monticello, La Rochefoucauld stopped at Dover Pits in 1796 and noticed that the owners employed "about five hundred negroes" at the mines and the attached farm.[104] Little is known about Dover Pits during the ensuing decades, but apparently they continued to utilize slave labor in every capacity. When Edmund Ruffin visited Graham's Coal Pits (Dover) in

1837, he remarked that "Graham's mining operations had been superintended and directed entirely by a confidential slave of his own, (whom he afterwards emancipated, and then paid $200 a year wages,) and the laborers were also slaves; and they, only, knew anything of the condition of the coal." Ruffin considered this just one of the "several remarkable cases of ignorance" that existed in the coal industry of eastern Virginia.[105] A supervisor at Dover Pits recorded his knowledge of the mine's history in an 1860 ledger book. Most of the information available about Dover Pits between the 1790s and the 1850s comes from this account. Unfortunately, it consists primarily of technical mining descriptions and contains no mention of the labor force. The supervisor touched on the difficulty in any attempt to reconstruct the early history of these mines when he declared that "there are no records on Sinkings of the underground works at Dover. If made they have been lost or destroyed." Little else can be gathered about the works during the antebellum era, for "the fact is, these pits have been owned & leased by so many different persons, that they have been injured & gutted just so far as the cupidity and ignorance of the colliers might carry them."[106]

During the 1850s, Christopher Quarles Tompkins began to organize several mines, including the original mine, into what became known as the Dover Coal Mining Company. A graduate of West Point (Class of 1836), Tompkins had campaigned in the Second Seminole War as well as the Mexican War. Apparently, he saw a brighter future for himself as a civilian, for he retired from the U.S. Army in 1847. He then entered upon a career as an iron manufacturer and coal mine operator in the Kanawha Valley of western Virginia. Although he opposed secession, Tompkins accepted a colonel's commission when the Civil War began and raised a regiment of Virginia Volunteers during the summer of 1861. Following a dispute with a superior officer, Tompkins promptly resigned his commission and returned to Richmond where he maintained a home and numerous business interests, the most important of which was the Dover Coal Mining Company.[107] Like most mine operators in the field, Tompkins employed numerous slaves in the newly reorganized Dover Pits. A Richmond newspaper reported an excursion in January 1855 by "a number of ladies and gentlemen" who descended into the mine, which was 1,030 feet deep. Fascinated by the subterranean maze, one of the visitors was prompted to characterize the workings as "the darkest abode of man." The spectators found that Tompkins employed slave labor in these pits as well, forty of whom were industriously engaged as the party toured the chambers.[108] Several other mines in Goochland County which were absorbed by the Dover Company had also been operated "generally by Slave labor."[109]

By the outbreak of the Civil War, Dover mines consisted of some fifteen or twenty shafts sunk at "irregular intervals" along the western margin of the outcrop of the field, about seventeen miles from Richmond on the James River and Kanawha Canal. Once the Civil War began in earnest, shipments of Pennsylvania anthracite (crucial for gun production) were halted, and the crucial Tredegar Iron Works became short of coal to fire several of its furnaces. Consequently, the company installed coking furnaces to produce coke fuel from the nearby bituminous coal. Still, the coal supplied by the two largest operators in 1860, the Midlothian and the Clover Hill mines, failed to produce enough coal on a regular basis to insure integrated operation with the huge Tredegar Works. Therefore, in October 1862 the Tredegar partners purchased the Dover coal mines for $90,000, and in January 1863 took a five-year lease on the Tuckahoe Pits, located a few miles from Dover in Henrico County. The various mines gathered into the company's holdings, usually identified as the Dover and Tuckahoe, or Trent's Pits, fell under the general supervision of Christopher Quarles Tompkins.[110]

In 1863-1864, the Dover and Tuckahoe Pits employed about 150 blacks. Of these hands, Dover employed 103 and Tuckahoe 38; the remaining nine hands worked the farm connected with the mines. The company owned a few, but hired the majority of these black miners by the year and did not restrict them from any occupation. Table 5 identifies their occupations and hiring prices.

Of the 150 black hands at work at the Dover and Tuckahoe Pits in 1863-1864, there were 24 free blacks. Their occupations and rate of pay, where it was possible to determine, are given in Table 6. Between 1864 and 1865, whites represented only twenty-one of the total number of workmen at Dover and Tuckahoe. Since only two of them were "boss men," and since such a large force, working in two-shift relays, probably required six or eight supervisors, it is highly likely that blacks filled some of those positions as well.[111]

The figures presented in Tables 5 and 6 provide some valuable clues to the prevailing labor patterns at slave-operated coal mines. They also may constitute the only actual analysis of exactly what jobs slaves, free blacks, and whites held at these pits, and the percentage of the total represented by each. If the Dover and Tuckahoe Pits provide a reasonably accurate picture, slaves made up the vast majority of the work force, with whites comprising about 12 percent, free blacks about 14 percent, and slaves 67 percent of the total labor force of 171 men from 1863 through 1865. Seven percent of the hands are unaccounted for by race. The tables also reflect the long tradition of reliance on slave labor without restriction by race from occupation or place of work. Thus, bondsmen toiled not only in the dangerous underground operations, but also on the surface where it was relatively safe, and practiced the skilled trades as well as unskilled. These patterns prevailed throughout the industry until by 1861, the twenty-two

Table 5

NUMBER AND OCCUPATION OF SLAVES AT DOVER AND
TUCKAHOE PITS, 1863–1864

Occupation	Number of Hands	Approximate Annual Hiring Rate of Each	Annual Hiring Costs Per Occupation
Teamster	3	$ 345	$ 1,035
Trainer [a]	5	300	1,500
Fireman	3	250	750
Coal digger	8	700	5,600
Carpenter	3	625	1,875
Laborer	28	325	9,100
Top hands	24	325	7,800
Miner	10	350	3,500
Bricklayer	1	500	500
Engineer	7	350	2,450
Wood chopper	1	300	300
Boy	4	150	600
Blacksmith	2	1,000 [b]	2,000
Slater	3	125	375
Farmer	6	275	1,650
Miller	5	150	750
Bottom hand	2	350	700
TOTAL	115		$40,485

[a] A "trainer" pulled a basket-like vehicle with iron runners, called a "corve," filled with coal from the working face to the main drift, where it was hauled to the bottom of the shaft and then to the surface. He was probably being trained by the miner, or the workman who actually "dug" coal. This was a skilled and sensitive occupation which required specialized knowledge and experience.

[b] No price was given for the hire of the blacksmiths or the wood chopper. The figures given are conservative estimates.

Source: "Commonplace Book of Christopher Quarles Tompkins, 1863–1867" Tompkins Family Papers, Virginia Historical Society. Compiled and arranged by the author.

Table 6

FREE BLACK OCCUPATIONS AT DOVER AND
TUCKAHOE PITS, 1863–1864

Occupation	Number	Rate of Pay
Trainer	4	—
Laborer	1	—
Driver	1	—
Engineer	3	$3. per day
Sinker	1	$3. per day + bd.
Miner	5	$3-4. per day + bd.
Bottom hands	2	"By the day on trial"
Top hands	3	$2-3. per day
Blacksmith	1	—
Bricklayer	1	$500 per year
Unspecified	2	—
TOTAL	24	

Source: "Commonplace Book of Christopher Quarles Tompkins, 1863–1867,"
Tompkins Family Papers, Virginia Historical Society.

leading Virginia coal companies employed 1,847 slave miners.[112] By late 1863, the Tredegar Company became desperate for workmen. In December, Joseph Anderson wrote to his hiring agents: "It is of infinite importance that we obtain hands for our blast furnace and Coal pits, now so important to the Confederacy in her struggle."[113] By 1864, it became nearly impossible for Tredegar to secure even the most crucial laborers from the army. In August 1864, Anderson personally urged Lee to intervene in order to solve the problem of a shortage of coal miners. The ironmaster requested that at least six experienced miners be detailed to the pits in order to maintain a continuous supply of coal for the furnaces. Lee refused, for every available man was vital to the struggle against armies of the North.[114] Finally, in 1864, the Confederacy issued orders which exempted certain slave workers, particularly those whose impressment might result in the disruption of important industrial facilities. When the Tredegar partners applied for exemptions for their slave furnacemen, the government complied with their wish. Unfortunately, the partners failed to include slave miners in the exemption request, and the military confiscated Tuckahoe pit slaves in January 1865.[115]

Following the war, Anderson was forced to sell his antiquated ironworks in the Valley along with the Dover coal tract. The Dover mines represented the company's most valuable property aside from the Tredegar plant in Richmond. After several unsuccessful attempts to negotiate a sale with prominent northeastern capitalists, Anderson finally succeeded in writing an equitable agreement with the famous entrepreneur William H. Aspinwall of New York. Aspinwall offered to buy 40 percent interest in the Dover property for $80,000 and, along with a group of New England entrepreneurs, subscribed $100,000 in Dover Company stock in February and March 1866. The Dover enterprise was doomed to failure, however, for the speculators had hoped to mine coal for the manufacture of illuminating gas. When that proved impractical, the company collapsed from insolvency in 1870.[116]

The Virginia coal industry had expanded enormously by 1861. Although several important mines had been founded in the western part of the state, the Richmond Coal Basin of eastern Virginia remained the most significant field in the South. Throughout the slave era, black bondsmen, both owned and hired, constituted the chief source of mine labor, and many coal companies invested significant amounts of capital in acquiring the services of their slave workers. When the Civil War began, Virginia's twenty-two leading coal mine companies employed 1,847 slaves.[117] In fact, most operators would have agreed in principle with one prominent Alabama mine owner who declared in 1859 that every day's experience confirmed his opinion "that it is next to impossible to prosecute my mining interest successfully with free labor. . . . No reliance whatever can be placed upon it. . . . I have now not a white man on my work force. . . . I must have a negro force or give up my business."[118]

NOTES

1. See Appendix 7; Phil Conley, "Early Coal Development in the Kanawha Valley," *West Virginia History* 8 (January 1947) : 207–15; James T. Laing, "The Development of the Coal Industry in the Western Counties of Virginia, 1800–1865," *West Virginia History* 27 (January 1966) :144–55. "Reports," of the Virginia Cannel Coal Company for 1851, 1853, and 1865, Virginia State Library, hereafter cited as VSL.

2. Sterling D. Spero and Abram L. Harris, *The Black Worker: The Negro and the Labor Movement* (New York: Atheneum, 1972, originally 1931), pp. 208–209.

3. Laing, "Development of the Coal Industry," pp. 145–46; John Edmund Stealey III, "Slavery and the Western Virginia Salt Industry," *Journal of Negro History* 59 (April 1974): 105–31; William B. Rogers, *Report of the Geological Reconnaissance of the State of Virginia* (Philadelphia: Desilver, Thomas & Co., 1836), p. 123; Edna Chappell McKenzie, "Self-Hire Among Slaves, 1820–1860.

Institutional Variation or Aberration?'' (Ph.D. dissertation, University of Pittsburgh, 1973), pp. 52–76.

4. Seventh Census of the United States, 1850, National Archives Microfilm Publications, hereafter cited as NA; Laing, "Development of the Coal Industry," p. 152.

5. Ibid. During the 1840s, experiments in Scotland led to a new process of producing light and lubricating oil from coal. Some claim that the Scots said it burned like a candle (cannel), and thus the origin of the term. Conley, "Early Coal Development in the Kanawha Valley," p. 213.

6. James Morton Callahan, *Semi-Centennial History of West Virginia* (Charleston: Semi-Centennial Commission of West Virginia, 1913), p. 87; *Kanawha Valley Star* (Charleston), October 10, 1859.

7. Callahan, *Semi-Centennial History*, pp. 149n, 150.

8. W. L. Fairbanks and W. S. Hamill, *The Coal-Mining Industry of Maryland* (Baltimore: Maryland Development Bureau of the Baltimore Association of Commerce, 1932), p. 35.

9. Frederick Gutheim, *The Potomac* (New York: Rinehart & Co., 1949), p. 219.

10. Ibid., pp. 219–20; James W. Thomas and T.J.C. Williams, *History of Allegany County*, Vol. 2 (Baltimore: Regional Publishing Co., 1969), pp. 451–52; Katherine A. Harvey, *The Best-Dressed Miners: Life and Labor in the Maryland Coal Region, 1835–1910* (Ithaca, N.Y.: Cornell University Press, 1969), p. 5.

11. Fairbanks and Hamill, *Coal-Mining Industry of Maryland*, p. 36.

12. Harvey, *Best-Dressed Miners*, p. 8.

13. Ibid., pp. 9, 15.

14. Fairbanks and Hamill, *Coal-Mining Industry of Maryland*, p. 38.

15. Gutheim, *The Potomac*, p. 226.

16. Harvey, *Best-Dressed Miners*, pp. 17–18.

17. Ibid., pp. 16–22.

18. Robert Starobin, *Industrial Slavery in the Old South* (New York: Oxford University Press, 1970), p. 23.

19. Andrew Burnaby, *Travels Through the Middle Settlements in North America in the Years 1759 and 1760 with Observations upon the State of the Colonies* (London: T. Payne, at Mews-Gate, 1775), p. 16; Thomas Jefferson, "Notes on Virginia," in Albert Ellery Bergh (ed.), *The Writings of Thomas Jefferson*, Vol. 2 (Washington, D.C.: Thomas Jefferson Memorial Association of the United States, 1907), p. 26.

20. Victor S. Clark, *History of Manufactures in the United States, 1607–1860*, Vol. 1 (New York: Peter Smith, 1949, originally 1929), p. 331. Also see numerous letters scattered throughout the Heth Family Papers, University of Virginia, hereafter cited as U Va., for references to the cities receiving coal from Black Heath Pits, the leading producer of Virginia coal during the period before 1820.

21. Samuel Harries Daddow and Benjamin Bannan, *Coal, Iron, and Oil; or, the Practical American Miner* (Philadelphia: J. B. Lippincott & Co., 1866), p. 108.

22. Atway Byrd to Harry Heth, February 18, 1800, Heth Family Papers, UVa.

23. *Richmond Enquirer*, March 23, 1837.

24. Ibid., June 2, 1846.

25. Frederick Moore Binder, *Coal Age Empire: Pennsylvania Coal and Its*

Utilization to 1860 (Harrisburg: Pennsylvania Historical and Museum Commission, 1974), p. 27.

26. Sir Charles Lyell, *On the Structure and Probable Age of the Coal-Field of the James River, near Richmond, Virginia* (London: By the Author, 1847), p. 269, photostat copy at VSL.

27. George T. Brown, *The Gas Light Company of Baltimore: A Study of Natural Monopoly* (Baltimore: Johns Hopkins University Press, 1936), pp. 10–12; Binder, *Coal Age Empire,* pp. 27–28; *Niles' Weekly Register* 6 (May 2, 1814): 198–99.

28. Brown, *Gas Light Company*, pp. 12–20.

29. Binder, *Coal Age Empire*, pp. 30–31, 34–35.

30. For examples of this demand, see the following letters to Harry Heth from agents in various coastal cities: George Plumsted (Philadelphia), May 11, 1800; John Davidson (Washington, D.C.), September 22, October 19, 1801, and September 12, 1803; J. Steward (Norfolk), November 3, 1803; Henry Thompson (Baltimore), March 7, 1807; William Heth (New York), April 2, 1815; Richard Hughes, October 3, 1819, all in the Heth Family Papers, UVa.; Albert Gallatin, *Report on Roads and Canals* to the Senate, April 6, 1808, 10th Cong., 1st Sess., American State Papers, Vol. 37, Misc. 1, p. 760.

31. Erskine Hazard, "History of the Introduction of Anthracite Coal into Philadelphia," in *Memoirs* of the Historical Society of Pennsylvania, Vol. 2 (Philadelphia: Carey, Lea & Carey, 1927), pp. 158–60.

32. Clark, *History of Manufactures*, Vol. 1, pp. 331–32; Binder, *Coal Age Empire*, pp. 2–3, Chap. VI.

33. See Appendix 7. For a discussion of the discovery of coal in Pennsylvania, see William J. Buck, "History of the Early Discovery of Coal," *Potter's American Monthly* 4 (January 1875) :180–82.

34. Clark, *History of Manufactures*, Vol. 1, pp. 331–32, 520; Daddow and Bannan, *Coal, Iron, and Oil*, p. 108; Binder, *Coal Age Empire*, pp. 34–35.

35. Lydell, *On the Structure of the Coal-Field of the James River*, pp. 262–63.

36. Ibid., p. 265; "An Account of the Coal Mines in the Vicinity of Richmond, Virginia, Communicated to the Editor in a Letter from Mr. John Grammar Jun.," *American Journal of Science* 1 (1819) :126.

37. Lyell, *On the Structure of the Coal-Field of the James River*, pp. 265–66.

38. Ibid., p. 267.

39. Daddow and Bannan, *Coal, Iron, and Oil*, pp. 411–12.

40. A. D. Schoepf, *Travels in the Confederation, 1783–84*, Alfred J. Morrison (ed.), Vol. 2 (Philadelphia: University of Pennsylvania Press, 1911, originally 1785), p. 67.

41. John Holland, *The History and Description of Fossil Fuel, the Collieries, and Coal Trade of Great Britain* (London: Whittaker & Co., 1841), pp. 176–78.

42. Ibid., pp. 179–84; A. S. Wooldridge, "Geological and Statistical Notice of the Coal Mines in the Vicinity of Richmond, Va.," *American Journal of Science and Arts* 43 (October 1842) :7.

43. Edmund Ruffin, "Visit to Graham's Coal Pits," *Farmers' Register* 5 (August 1, 1837) :315.

44. David Ross to William Dunn, September 16, 1813, Ross Letterbook, Virginia

Historical Society, hereafter cited as VHS.

45. Agreement between Harry Heth and Daniel French, November 30, 1811, and anonymous to Messrs. Fenton, Murray and Wood, November 26, 1818, Heth Family Papers, UVa.

46. Daddow and Bannan, *Coal, Iron and Oil*, p. 402.

47. Ibid., pp. 429–36, 440, 411–27; Holland, *History and Description of Fossil Fuel*, pp. 211–25; Ruffin, "Visit to Graham's Coal Pits," p. 135.

48. Henry Howe, *Historical Collections of Virginia; Containing a Collection of the Most Interesting Facts, Traditions, Biographical Sketches, Anecdotes, etc., Relating to its History and Antiquities* (Charleston, S.C.: Babcock & Co., 1845), p. 230.

49. Ruffin, "Visit to Graham's Coal Pits," pp. 317–18.

50. *Richmond Daily Whig and Public Advertiser*, June 26, 1846.

51. Howe, *Historical Collections of Virginia*, p. 230.

52. Ruffin, "Visit to Graham's Coal Pits," p. 316.

53. Howe, *Historical Collections of Virginia*, p. 231.

54. *Richmond Whig and Public Advertiser*, June 26, 1846.

55. Ruffin, "Visit to Graham's Coal Pits," p. 316.

56. Howe, *Historical Collections of Virginia*, p. 231.

57. Wooldridge, "Coal Mines in the Vicinity of Richmond," pp. 6–9.

58. Howe, *Historical Collections of Virginia*, p. 231.

59. *Niles' Weekly Register* 65 (1843):108–109. Mules were lowered into the pits through the shaft. After their feet were tied and their eyes blindfolded, miners lowered the animals down the shaft in a large water tub and released them below.

60. Ruffin, "Visit to Graham's Coal Pits," p. 317.

61. Daddow and Bannan, *Coal, Iron, and Oil*, pp. 434–42; Holland, *History and Description of Fossil Fuel*, pp. 417–22.

62. *Niles' Weekly Register* 65 (1843):108–109. According to one Midlothian visitor, the furnace consumed fifty bushels of coal every twenty-four hours (*Richmond Whig and Public Advertiser*, June 26, 1846).

63. Howe, *Historical Collections of Virginia*, p. 231.

64. *Niles' Weekly Register* 65 (1843):108–109.

65. Wooldridge, "Coal Mines in the Vicinity of Richmond," p. 9.

66. *Niles' Weekly Register* 65 (1843):108–109.

67. Holland, *History and Description of Fossil Fuel*, pp. 225–26.

68. Ruffin, "Visit to Graham's Coal Pits," p. 317.

69. Holland, *History and Description of Fossil Fuel*, pp. 225–26; Daddow and Bannan, *Coal, Iron, and Oil*, pp. 440–41.

70. Duc de La Rochefoucauld-Liancourt, *Travels Through the United States of North America, the Country of the Iroquois, and Upper Canada, in the Years 1795, 1796, and 1797; with an Authentic Account of Lower Canada*, Vol. 3 (London: R. Phillips, 1799), pp. 122–25.

71. *Virginia Independent Chronicle*, March 4, 1789.

72. Memorandum Account, 1798, reproduced in Howard N. Eavenson, *The First Century and a Quarter of American Coal Industry* (Pittsburgh: By the Author, 1942), pp. 60–62.

73. "An Account of the Coal Mines in the Vicinity of Richmond, Virginia, Communicated to the Editor in a Letter from Mr. John Grammar Jun.," *American Journal of Science* 1 (1819) : 126–27. Manchester has been incorporated into the city of Richmond; Ida J. Lee, "The Heth Family," *Virginia Magazine of History and Biography* 42 (July 1934) :273–82. Henry Heth used the name "Harry" both officially and informally. Some idea of his pioneering leadership in coal mining may be inferred from his proposal to establish an institute to train American youths in the technical aspects of mining. "Coal Mines Seminary," in Harry Heth's hand, October 10, 1819, Heth Family Papers, UVa. Harry's most famous descendant was his grandson and namesake, the Confederate General Henry Heth (1825–1899).

74. Ibid. During the first few decades of operation, the pits and the family residence of Blackheath were spelled the same. By the 1830s, the spelling "Black Heath" became most frequently used with reference to the mines. I have maintained the different spellings for purposes of clarity.

75. *Richmond Enquirer,* March 2, 1810.

76. William Pennock to Harry Heth, July 10, 1813, Heth Papers, UVa.

77. Agreement, C. & R. Railey and Harry Heth, n.d., 1819, and Harry Heth to David Street, January 12, 1819, Heth Family Papers, UVa.

78. Agreement, Harry Heth and Daniel French, November 30, 1811, Oliver Evans to Harry Heth, June 15, 1813, and Harry Heth to Oliver Evans, July 8, 1813, Heth Family Papers, UVa.

79. Oliver Evans to Harry Heth, July 14, 1813, Heth Family Papers, UVa.

80. Harry Heth to A. S. Wooldridge, December 28, 1817, Heth Family Papers, UVa.

81. William Pennock to Harry Heth, July 10, 1813, Agreement, Wiley Jackson, Harry Heth, S. Adams, and Beverly Randolph, December 21, 1814, anonymous to Harry Heth, July 20, 1815, Benjamin Sheppard to Harry Heth, December 15, 1815, all in Heth Family Papers, UVa.

82. Agreement, Harry Heth with James and John Bavid [*sic*], December 8, 1818, Heth Family Papers, UVa.

83. "List of Negroes which the proprietor will sell all together," n.d., 1819, Heth Family Papers, UVa. Apparently, Heth continued the traditional pattern among early industrialists in the region of owning highly skilled slaves in order to assure stability at key production posts.

84. "Accounts & Receipts," 1821, Heth Family Papers, UVa.

85. James L. Morrison, Jr. (ed.), *The Memoirs of Henry Heth* (Westport, Conn.: Greenwood Press, 1974), p. 11.

86. "Memo Agreement Between Beverly Randolph and John Heth with David Hancock," February 10, 1831, Heth Family Papers, UVa.

87. *Richmond Enquirer,* March 23, 1839.

88. James Lyons to John Heth, December 30, 1836, and "Accounts & Receipts," 1837, Heth Family Papers, UVa.

89. Oswald J. Heinrich, "The Midlothian, Virginia, Colliery in 1876," *Transactions* of the American Institute of Mining Engineers, hereafter cited as AIME., 4 (May 1875–February 1876):309.

90. Wooldridge, "Coal Mines in the Vicinity of Richmond," pp. 6, 8.

91. Howe, *Historical Collections of Virginia*, p. 232.

92. *Richmond Whig and Public Advertiser*, July 15, 1846.

93. Ibid., January 2, 1846.

94. Manuscript Industrial and Slave Schedules, Chesterfield County, Virginia, Seventh Census of the United States, 1850, National Archives Microfilm Publications.

95. Ibid., Eighth Census of the United States, 1860.

96. Oswald J. Heinrich, "The Midlothian Colliery, Virginia," *Transactions* of the AIME, 1 (May 1871–February 1873) :356.

97. Wooldridge, "Coal Mines in the Vicinity of Richmond," p. 4; "Report on Gowrie Colliery," December 29, 1850, by A. F. Hopper and John Steele for Christopher Q. Tompkins, Tompkins Family Papers, VHS.

98. Wooldridge, "Coal Mines in the Vicinity of Richmond," pp. 5, 11, 12; Tuomey, "Notice of the Appomattox Coal Pits," *Farmers' Register* 10 (September 30, 1842) :449.

99. Seventh Census of the United States, 1850, Products of Industry, Virginia, Chesterfield County, Schedule 4.

100. Eighth Census of the United States, 1860, Products of Industry, Virginia, Chesterfield County, Schedule 5; Ms. Slave Schedules 1860, Virginia, Chesterfield County, NA.

101. *Richmond Daily Dispatch*, January 11, 1855, January 11, 1858, December 31, 1859.

102. Ibid., December 31, 1859.

103. Ibid., January 5, 1861.

104. La Rochefoucauld, *Travels Through the United States*, Vol. 3, p. 123. Traditionally, Dover has been regarded as the oldest commercial coal mine in the South. Kathleen Bruce, *Virginia Iron Manufacture in the Slave Era* (New York: Augustus M. Kelley, 1960, originally 1930), p. 88. This does not appear to be accurate, for the *New York Mercury*, July 22, 1765, carried an advertisement by Garrard Ellyson for the sale of coal from his "bank of Coal in Chesterfield county." Clipping in the Archibald Cary Papers, VHS.

105. Ruffin, "Visit to Graham's Coal Pits," p. 315.

106. "History of the Pits," the Commonplace Book of Christopher Quarles Tompkins, 1863–1867, hereafter cited as Tompkins Commonplace Book, Tompkins Family Papers, VHS.

107. Ibid.; William M.E. Rachal (ed.), "The Occupation of Richmond, April 1865: The Memorandum of Events of Colonel Christopher Q. Tompkins," *Virginia Magazine of History and Biography* 73 (April 1965) :189; Ellen Wilkins Tompkins (ed.), "The Colonel's Lady: Some Letters of Ellen Wilkins Tompkins, July-December 1861," *Virginia Magazine of History and Biography* 69 (October 1961): 387.

108. Lease of John James Flournoy, May 28, 1847, Tompkins Family Papers, VHS, represented the first notice of his use of slave miners (*Richmond Daily Dispatch*, January 11, 1855).

109. Report by Richard Smethurst and Sampson Vivian, December 22, 1858, Tompkins Family Papers, VHS.

110. Charles B. Dew, *Ironmaker to the Confederacy: Joseph R. Anderson and the Tredegar Iron Works* (New Haven, Conn.: Yale University Press, 1966), pp.

34, 99, 149–50; "Corporate Holdings, 1866," and Tredegar Journals, December 1862, Tredegar Company Records, VSL; Bruce, *Virginia Iron Manufacture*, p. 88; Rachal (ed.), "Occupation of Richmond," pp. 189–93; Tompkins Commonplace Book, Tompkins Family Papers, VHS.

111. "List of White Persons at Dover Pits—1864," and "List of White Hands at Trent's Pits—1865," in Tompkins Commonplace Book, Tompkins Family Papers, VHS.

112. Clement Eaton, *The Growth of Southern Civilization, 1790–1860* (New York: Harper & Row, Publishers, 1961), p. 231.

113. Anderson & Co. to E. R. Pullen, December 23, 1863, and to William A. Bibb, December 24, 1863, Tredegar Letterbooks, VSL.

114. Anderson & Co. to Robert E. Lee, August 24, 25, 1864, to I. M. St. John, August 31, September 7, 1864, to Joseph Marston, September 16, 1864, and to J. L. Kemper, January 26, 1865, Tredegar Letterbooks, Tredegar Company Records, VSL; Dew, *Ironmaker to the Confederacy*, p. 237.

115. Dew, *Ironmaker to the Confederacy*, p. 257; Anderson & Co. to Alexander Stevens, March 1, 15, 1864, to William A. Glasgow, October 26, 1864, and to General J. L. Kemper, February 7, 1865, Tredegar Letterbooks, VSL; "Tompkins Commonplace Book, 1863–67," Tompkins Family Papers, VHS.

116. Dew, *Ironmaker to the Confederacy*, pp. 305–307. The affairs of the reconstructed Dover Company can be examined in the Dover Company Records, UVa. According to a report prepared by Meriweather Jones, an authority on local mines, the Dover Company was placed under the management of retired U.S. Army General Charles P. Stone who abandoned the old shafts because they were too small for modern mining, and sunk new shafts of nine hundred feet and three hundred feet, neither of which reached the coal. The company folded, however, according to Meriweather Jones, when "General Stone was offered a position as Minister of War in the new Egyptian government, and resigned, and the Dover Coal Company abandoned their operations, not due to lack of coal." Meriweather Jones, *A Report on the Richmond Coal Field* (Richmond: By the Author, April 1916), p. 5, photostat at VSL.

117. Starobin, *Industrial Slavery in the Old South*, pp. 22–23; Eaton, *Growth of Southern Civilization*, Chap. 10.

118. W. P. Browne to A. Saltmarsh, September 24, 1859, Browne Papers, Alabama Archives, Montgomery, cited in Starobin, *Industrial Slavery in the Old South*, p. 23.

"Playing Both Ends   3 Toward the Middle"

Many a northern manager has seen the contradiction when, facing the apparent laziness of Negro hands, he has attempted to drive them and found out that he could not and at the same time has afterward seen someone used to Negro labor get a tremendous amount of work out of the same gangs. The explanation of all this is clear and simple: the Negro laborer has not been trained in modern organized industry but rather in a quite different school.
      —W. E. B. Du Bois, *The Gift of Black Folk*

American historians have frequently argued that slave-hiring was a particularly brutal mechanism for the allocation of industrial slave labor. Many agree with Charles S. Sydnor, who contended that the "common hired slave was liable to be driven hard." Since the slave's employer "had no permanent interest in his well-being" and was concerned only with "the amount of labor he could extort for a limited period of time," the hireling was not "treated as well as he would have been by his own master."[1] Kenneth M. Stampp shares this bleak view of the hiring-out system and notes that the practice helped spawn conditions of "ruthless exploitation." Moreover, "the overworking of hired slaves by employers with only a temporary interest in their welfare was as notorious as the harsh practices of overseers." Life was much worse for blacks hired to industries, for "slaves hired to mine owners or railroad contractors were fortunate if they were not driven to the point where their health was impaired."[2] Others, Robert S. Starobin and S. Sydney Bradford among them, view hiring-out to industrial employers as a harsh system where the slaves' humanity was generally ignored by industrialists concerned only with the maximization of production.[3]

Historian Clement Eaton takes a different view of the hiring practice. According to Eaton, many examples of overwork and cruelty can be found in the records. Yet, he found "considerable evidence" indicating that "many of the plantation slaves of the Upper South desired to be hired in the cities and industries to secure the privileges, social opportunities, rewards, and freedoms which they could not enjoy on the plantation."[4] Richard B. Morris argues that during the antebellum era hiring-out represented a "trend toward upgrading slaves into a shadowland of quasi-freedom."[5] Richard C. Wade agrees with this assessment as it related to the cities. "The urban slave enjoyed considerable advantages over his country counterparts," for life in the city could "mitigate the harshness of slavery." Partially because of hiring-out and the greater flexibility required for nonagricultural occupations, Wade believes that by 1860, "the institution of slavery was in great disarray in every Southern city. . . .The network of restraint so essential to bondage no longer seemed to control the blacks."[6]

Even though the implication that the existence of slavery was threatened by the hiring-out system has been overdrawn, the interpretation presented by Eaton, Morris, and Wade contains considerable merit. An in-depth study of the daily operation of slavery in the iron and coal industries discloses a system founded less on brute force than on forced compromise. Slaves in these industries, of course, still labored as bondsmen, and masters had ultimate authority which, if necessary, they maintained by physical coercion. As long as blacks did not challenge the industrialist's authority or the institution itself, however, employers of industrial slaves usually found an accommodative approach less fraught with difficulties than reliance on mere intimidation. As Robert Fogel and Stanley Engerman have observed, "force" provided the crucial element in the maintenance of slavery. But rather than "perfect" submission, which manifested itself in cruelty, masters sought only "optimal" submission, for crushed men made poor workers.[7] Whatever the merits of Fogel and Engerman's thesis concerning slave treatment on southern plantations, the model portrays blacks as mere recipients of white-initiated action and therefore does not apply to the industrial setting. It fails to consider the influence slaves exerted on their own behalf in compelling whites to adjust their labor policies accordingly. This process involved a three-way relationship: slaves pushed just hushed just hard enough to win additional advantages, gain some life-space, and yet remain within acceptable (if unspoken) bounds. On the other hand, employers yielded without losing ultimate control, while slaveowners attempted to protect and profit from their property at the same time. By initiating, and then manipulating, this triangular push-and-pull of self-interest, blacks gained a degree of influence over the nature of their daily existence.

The first ironmasters owned most of their slaves, so the problems of hiring blacks to labor at ironworks were not pressing. By the mid-eighteenth century, however, rising prices had already produced a squeeze on slave purchasing and a solid trend began toward hiring slave workers, especially common laborers. For example, in 1721 the Principio Company purchased nine unskilled slaves for £22, seven others for £20, and one for £27.[8] In 1737, unskilled slave ironworkers at the Baltimore Iron Works were selling at about £30. There was a steady increase over the years until by 1783, when the Swedish scientist Samuel Hermelin visited the area, the price for a skilled black ironworker was about £80 to £100 "but others, 50 to 60 pounds sterling."[9] When laborers could be hired for about £15 to £16 per year, it is easy to see why an ironmaster, pinched for ready capital, would favor hiring rather than purchasing slave workers.[10] Even skilled slaves could be hired with considerably less capital than if purchased. Although ironmasters usually owned a core of skilled hands vital to production, that did not fully satisfy their needs. After the Revolution, Chesapeake iron-masters on the whole increasingly depended on the hiring system in order to gain some capital flexibility rather than invest heavily in labor pur-chases. Although the coal industry developed a half century later, it fol-lowed the same pattern as the iron industry in the conversion to hiring slave labor. Early colliers showed a strong preference for slaveownership. For example, in 1813 Harry Heth planned to operate six different mines. In the lease, Heth reiterated that, "as I have all along stated to you, I go upon the presumtion [*sic*] that the Stock put in shall be sufficient to purchase our own Negroes."[11] Numerous other purchases attest to Heth's preference for owning his own slaves.[12] But conversion to the hiring system came quickly. As the economy expanded and diversified, slave prices escalated steadily, and like ironmasters, colliers sought the capital flexibility associ-ated with hiring.

Leased slaves often came from the immediate area of the coal mine or ironworks. Jordan and Irvine rented a number of hands from owners living in nearby counties, and Graham's Iron Works also hired most of their black laborers from local planters.[13] Similarly, the vast majority of the hirelings at Black Heath Pits came from the same neighborhood. Not all leasees came from plantations. For example, Washington College (now Washington and Lee University) owned several slaves which it hired to ironmasters in Rockbridge County between 1829 and 1839.[14]

Many slaves in the Valley of Virginia came from east of the Blue Ridge Mountains; the eastern counties of Pittsylvania, Louisa, Spotsylvania, Orange, Albemarle, Amherst, Nelson, and Fauquier were all important sources for rented slaves.[15] Hiring usually occurred around Christmas and took about a month to complete. When possible, ironmasters themselves supervised the business of hiring. The owner of Black Heath Pits wrote in 1815 that his son's "exertions to obtain hands on hire for the prosicution [*sic*] of my coal business will be absolutely necessary."[16] Cyrus H. McCormick, partner and manager of Cotopaxi Furnace, crossed the Blue Ridge Mountains during the winter of 1836 to hire black workers for his furnace.[17] William Cash of Jane Furnace crossed the Blue Ridge Mountains in December 1849 to hire slaves for the following year.[18] If the industrial employer could not attend to the hiring himself, he usually appointed an agent to handle the business for him. In return, the agent received a fee. Thus, Harry Heth's hiring agent informed the collier that several hands had been procured for 1816 and that he, the agent, expected "a commission of five Dollars for Each hand I send you."[19] And in 1849, Colonel L. Partlow earned one dollar per hired hand procured for Catawba Furnace.[20] Even though prices had risen dramatically during the intervening years, the significant differential between the amounts paid by the collier and the ironmaster vividly illustrate the difficulties in procuring slave hirelings for coal mine labor. The agent usually kept the industrialist informed of prevailing market prices and regulated his hiring bonds according to the number of hands required and the maximum price he could pay. The typical hiring bond covered the period between the first of January to the following Christmas.[21]

Slave renting posed hazards for everyone involved. Periodically, the employer was at the mercy of the market. For example, in 1805 agent Richard Brooke wrote to Harry Heth that it was not "possible to procure hands here at this season, harvest being near at hand."[22] Also, severe weather frequently accompanied hiring-time and delayed the departure of much-needed hands for their respective assignments. Nearly one month after he was hired in January 1807, slave Booker had not reported for work at Black Heath Pits. Upon inquiry from the employer, Booker's owner wrote that "the wetness of the Roads" prevented the slave's "geting [sic] to the works as soon as he out [sic] to do. This I mention to prevent your thinking Negligence was used & to prevent blame being attached to the Negroe."[23] In 1817, another hand reported late for work at Black Heath Pits, and his master explained that he was "sorry" but "the winter has prevented me from sending him upon the first of the month."[24] One owner wrote to Jordan and Irvine in January 1831 that "in consequence of the very heavy rains and badness of the weather I have delayed starting any hands."[25] An agent for William Weaver wrote to him in February 1836 that there "has been & is still so much snow with us & the weather so intensely cold that not many have sent their hands over the mountains."[26] This, of course, disturbed ironmasters who had to delay getting their operations underway for weeks because of the lack of hands. Then again, workers sent out during bad weather might fall ill before arriving at the ironworks, which happened to one group of hands who trudged across the Blue Ridge Mountains during bad weather and became so ill that they lost even more time than the thirty days consumed in travel.[27] If hands were too late, employers were particularly incensed, especially if the weather provided no excuse. One ironmaster wrote to an owner that "all hands, but yours, have been in 2 weeks and I certainly cannot pay full price for boys, that get here so much beyond the time & I shall certainly expect a deduction for the lost time." If the owner objected to the deduction, the ironmaster told him that he would be "happy to let you keep them."[28] When an employer did not send a slave back to his owner at the end of the hiring period, the reverse problem arose. An owner wrote to William Weaver that "my fellow Harry was not yet over the Mountains." It was February 5, and "he would have been sent home at least by the 3rd day of January the day of my Hiring." Three other hands had not returned to their master "untill some time after the Hiring on acct. of which I (the owner) lost thirty dollars." The owner demanded Harry's immediate return because the slave was already late getting to his next employer.[29]

At times, the divorce of management and ownership in slave-hiring produced serious conflicts between masters and employers, and the system invited sharp business practices among the parties involved. In 1811, Harry Heth leased several hands to John Cunliffe, a neighboring mine operator, who in turn subleased the slaves at night after work was finished in the mines. When Heth received word of this practice, he wrote what must have been an indignant note to Cunliffe. The employer responded that after inquiring among his managers about Heth's complaints, Cunliffe found that "some of my people was [*sic*] at work. . . . on Tuesday Night," but it was without "my consent & knowledge & it has uniformly been my directions to the Men & Overseers not to suffer any of my Men to work for any person in the Night."[30] Heth responded to Cunliffe's message that same day. He informed his neighbor that if the "men have been working for those people without your consent, you have been grieviously deceived." Actually, "many of them were found there last week as well as this," and Cunliffe's manager had notified Heth that "he had *your* permission to hire your hands at night." Heth informed Cunliffe in no uncertain terms that, friendship aside, the practice must cease.[31] Heth was not always the ideal client either. In 1811, his long-time friend and agent Richard Brooke complained to the collier: "You still stand indebted to me for the last years hire of Negroes . . . beyond all doubt upon this subject I have before written you."[32] Another master-employer conflict occurred when an owner hired two hands to William Weaver of Buffalo Forge for the year 1828. Weaver hired one slave for a stipulated $50, while the price of the second was left to the discretion of the ironmaster. When Weaver named $25 as a fair price, the owner promptly complained: "I do not know when I have felt more mortified and disappointed, than when I examined the note which you inclosed me for the hire of my two men Dennis & Manuel." Angered at first, the owner concluded his letter on the philosophical note that this encounter would serve as a "warning to me hereafter, to trust to the liberality of no man, or . . . place myself in the power of any man, to fix his own price upon my property."[33] At the first of the following year, the owner had even more cause for outrage when he received a doctor's bill from Weaver. "The Doctors Bill for attending Dennis was also rec'd and I could (not) but feel indignant at the manner in which you treated me after my placing such implicit confidence in you as a high minded, liberal gentleman," complained the master to Weaver. "I put it to you as a man of good sense whether or not $25 was a fair & just equivalent for the services of Dennis for twelve months, and then to bring in a medical bill reducing his hire to the pitiful sum of $15—'Shame where is thy blush!'"[34] Perhaps one ironmaster's agent felt some of the same frustration when he failed to hire a hand because someone else had acquired the slave's services by bribing not only the owner but the slave as well. Another agent lamented in 1855 that "you have no idea of the trouble there is in hiring hands, . . . there is all sorts of trickery and management."[35]

All sorts of "trickery and management" in the hiring market were small problems for ironmasters and colliers compared with the scarcity of labor. Labor shortages in the eighteenth century had escalated the purchasing price for slaves so dramatically that it produced a conversion to the hiring system. The problem persisted into the nineteenth century, and the greater demand relative to supply continued to inflate prices. The major reason for this constant upward pressure lay in the vigorous competition among various industrial and agricultural interests for slave labor. Canal building, turnpike construction, and gold mining interests offered strong inducements to slaveowners for hired hands throughout the 1820s and 1830s. The railroads also entered the hiring markets during the 1840s and 1850s. Meanwhile, agents for urban tobacco factories, textile mills, and various other industries all actively competed with the operators of coal mines and ironworks for black labor.[36]

During the first two decades of the nineteenth century, prices remained relatively stable. There were variations, however. In early 1812, David Ross exclaimed that "the price of slaves seems steadily to advance in this part of the country." He found a "man of 55 years who was unwilling to go up to the Iron Works and hired him for 120$," which Ross believed to be much too high.[37] Local scarcities existed, too. For example, in 1806 ironmaster Francis Preston found "hands exceedingly scarce" and wondered if his brother could "spare any for the blast."[38] Nevertheless, stable prices for hired hands persisted for the most part. Between 1805 and 1809, Ridwell Furnace paid the average price of about $55 per year for hired slave hands.[39] Fifty dollars a year represented William Weaver's maximum outlay for black workers during the 1820s.[40] As late as 1830, Clifton Forge and Lucy Selina Furnace paid an average of $50 to $60 per hand.[41]

Competition from tobacco factories, coal fields, cotton mills, and other industries for slave hands began in earnest during the 1830s. Tuyman Wayt, agent for Jordan and Irvine, explained to the partners that he "could not get the quantity you wanted, as it was not in my power to go into the Country to attend the different hirings."[42] Another iron company's agent lamented that "the price of labor is increased" as a consequence of the "many branches of internal improvements together with the gold mining (who give Eight dollars per month)."[43] By 1836, the price of slave hands nearly doubled to about $110 to $120 per year for laborers. Although the Panic of 1837 probably forced a decline during the late 1830s and early 1840s, prices once again burgeoned until by the 1850s they had risen to an all-time high.[44] William Weaver's hiring agent reported to the ironmaster in December 1855 that the slaveowners "are asking $135 to $150 for good hands, no one can tell what the price will be, untill new years day." Even at those prices, however, the agent told Weaver that he did not "expect to be able to hire more than thirty or forty hands, we may get fifty; but I can assure you, the prospect is very gloomy."[45]

The railroads were still in the market competing for slave hands. John Bibb, agent for the Virginia and Tennessee Railroad, notified a large slaveowner in 1853 that he wished "to hire a lot of hands for the ensueing [*sic*] year to work upon the Rail Road," and promised "to give you a good hire" and to "feed and clothe well and treat hands with the utmost degree of humanity in every other respect, Give me a trial and I will Warrant Satisfaction."[46] Even when the railroad men had no chance of getting an owner's hands, the fees offered to owners drove prices upward. One owner informed an ironmaster that he wanted to hire his hands to the ironworks, as he had for many years, "provided I can get my price which is one hundred & fifty dollars apiece. This price is now being offered for hands to work on the Central Railroad."[47] James C. Davis of Gibraltar Forge in Rockbridge County, Virginia, also had difficulties hiring hands and believed that "the cause of it is the high price of the produce of farms & the consequent demand for their labor in that direction."[48] A few days later, Davis noted that "there are not so many Iron & no more railroad men in the field, but the farmers make a formidable phalanx of opposition. Some of them are giving $140 & $150 for men, & $70 to $90 for women. Women are higher than ever known before."[49] One letter in particular demonstrated the iron men's frustration over the scarcity and high prices for slave hands:

> Mr. Brady & Charles Gorgas [William Weaver's nephews] passed through here yesterday, on their return from negro hiring. they were the worst used up and the most disconsolate looking persons you can imagine. Although they used every exertion in their power they only succeeded in hiring 15 hands. They dreaded meeting Mr. Weaver, they feared that he would become excited, & that it might have a bad effect upon him.
>
> I understand that Sam Jordan & (Frank) Anderson succeeded no better than Brady & Gorgas. I heard someone say that Anderson had returned, without hiring any hands at all.

> Gorgas says that none of the iron men obtained more than a
> half force. The Tobacco Factories & rail road contractors
> monopolized the market.[50]

If anything, the financial pinch affected colliers more than it did ironmasters, for the dangers inherent in coal mining forced prices even higher than they were normally. In 1836, the colliers memorialized Congress for an increase in the protective tariff. "That a great increase in the price of labor has taken place, is universally known," exclaimed the colliers, "and the price of labor in the coal-pits (by no means a favorite occupation) has perhaps risen more than in any other pursuit, from the competition for laborers in public and private works, most of which have the preference as employments."[51]

The great difficulties encountered by ironmasters and colliers in hiring enough hands to operate their furnaces and mines made it vital to their interests to avoid a reputation for harsh treatment of slave workers. Moreover, given the heavy demand and short supply of slaves, owners enjoyed a relatively favorable market position and could force employers to avoid excessively harsh treatment or lose their labor supply. In turn, this enabled slaves to ply a certain amount of leverage between the interests of the master and the owner. The result was a system not of absolute power, but one which involved a complex interplay between the ironmaster, the slaveowner, and the slave himself. How this relationship operated during the colonial period is difficult to establish with certainty. Nevertheless, it is clear that at least some compromise with economic realities existed during the eighteenth century as well. In 1732, Dr. Carroll stated his conviction that "none here are to be trusted without a watchful Eye & Strict hand."[52] The tendency of both indentured whites and black slaves to run away from the Baltimore Iron Works may have been in part the result of the harsh conditions of life and labor. The company's "Strict hand" labor policy was illustrated in several letters written by Stephen Onion, who was manager during the 1730s. In response to instructions, Onion assured the partners on July 1, 1734, that he would "give Correction" to those who misbehaved and would permit "none of the Hands to go abroad on Sundays."[53]

Several months later, "Negro Cesar" returned to the works after an unexcused absence with a note from his master stating that Cesar must not be beaten and that he was to work under the overseer of the wood choppers, James Flanigan. Nevertheless, Onion reported that he planned to "put a Collar" on Cesar as a corrective measure, otherwise "youl have by Turns most of the negroos [*sic*] running to Annapolis to Know Where they must work and Overseers will be of little use, as I conceive Flanigan is." Onion's complaint against Flanigan was based on the fact that he was considered too lenient with the hands.[54] It is unclear whether this "Strict hand" policy ever gained the company anything more than a serious rash of runaways and general labor unrest.[55]

Most eighteenth-century ironmasters utilized more sophisticated methods of slave discipline than brute force or the "Strict hand." For example, the brother of a slaveowner who had hired several of his bondsmen to work at Ridgely's Northampton Furnace wrote:

> My brother's two Hands have returned complaining of the Beef being rotten—I have sent them back and informed them that you will inquire into it & if really so will not give it to them—But I am afraid that they will not want to stay there & make that as an excuse to get away. They are five plantation Negroes, perhaps it may [behoove] you to [go along with them]. If not please let them know I have hired them & there [sic] master has determined that they must be governed by your direction or go into the mine banks.[56]

The letter demonstrates several important points. First, the slaves left the ironworks and returned to their owners without permission, and there was no indication that they ever received any punishment. On the contrary, there is the suggestion that the ironmaster "go along with them," for the owner feared that they might take the initiative again and run away from the works using the bad beef as an excuse "to get away." Moreover, to influence the conditions of their bondage, the slaves themselves sought to parlay the interests of their owner, who naturally wanted to keep his property healthy, against those of the ironmaster. Of course, if the slaves did not respond positively or at least acquiesce to the ironmaster's leniency, then sanctions would follow; that is, they would be sent to the mine bank. Significantly, punitive measures were invoked only if the positive ones had failed.

When hiring, employers also had to consider the owner's reluctance to send bondsmen where they did not want to work. Singular as it may appear, some bondsmen preferred to work in the coal mines. Tony's master rehired the slave to Black Heath because "he has been formerly at the Coal pits & was anxious to go back again."[57] Adam also preferred the pits and "opposed going any where else."[58] One owner informed Harry Heth that an agreement had been reached between Heth's overseer and the owner which stipulated that his hirelings would work only on the farm, not in the pits. Nevertheless, "as the boys went up they came by my House, and told me they were on the way to the pits." The master "ordered them back to Curles Heth's farm," but they "plainly told me they coud [sic] not Stand this and would prefer going" to the pits. The owner decided that he would reconsider since "they are young & fine boys," and he did not want them "to get in [the] habit of Runing [sic] away."[59]

Normally, however, problems arose not from slave demands to work in the mines so much as from their refusal to do so. One agent notified Harry Heth in 1813 that two slaves refused to work in the pits, but their master had ordered them to report to the mine anyway. Both Anderson and Robin were "greatly opposed to going to the pits," for one of them claimed that he had been "twice in danger of losing his life."[60] A few years later, an agent informed Heth that it would be impossible to hire any black miners. A slaveowner who had promised to lease six hands changed his mind and now "positively objects to their working in the coal pits . . . & the negroes themselves also positively object to going to the pits." To emphasize his point, the agent attached to a letter an enclosure from the master which stated that he had based his decision on the fact that "the negroes positively refuse to work" in the mines.[61] Just as frequently, owners refused to hire their hands to work in the coal mines, usually out of fear for their safety. In 1813, Heth's agent Richard Brooke informed the collier that it was "impossible to hire hands here for the Coal Pits. There [*sic*] owners are generally indisposed to the labor, on acct of the danger as they imagine."[62] Still another owner wrote to Heth in 1815 that he would hire hands to the collier, but it must be "expressly understood" that "neither of these fellows are to work in the C. Pitts."[63]

The refusal to permit slave hirelings to work in coal mines was not an aberration confined to the eastern Virginia field. In his study of the western Virginia salt industry, Edmund Stealey found that because coal mining represented "the most dangerous of all nineteenth century employments," some slave-hirers stipulated that a hireling could not work in the pits attached to saltworks.[64] Stealey discovered, however, that hired hands did, nevertheless, toil underground despite prohibitive contractual stipulations. For example, one owner sued a saltworks operator in 1832 because the owner's slave had been "suffocated, crushed, and killed" in a coal mine, even though the hiring-bond had emphatically restricted the slave from pit labor. On that ground, the slaveowner won a judgment against the saltworks operator.[65] No strong evidence exists to prove that this practice was widespread, but when colliers failed to hire enough slaves to labor in the pits, they undoubtedly resorted to any means necessary rather than hinder production.

The difficulty of obtaining an adequate supply of slave hirelings for coal mines was seriously aggravated by the adverse working conditions and outright dangers associated with underground labor. Early coal pits generally, and those in the eastern Virginia coal field specifically, justified the old refrain of being "dark as a dungeon and damp as the dew/Where danger is double and pleasures are few." In fact, miners conducted a perennial courtship with danger; accidents plagued slaves physically and masters financially. Rock falls were one of the most persistent threats to life and limb. Harry Heth wrote to a neighboring miner in 1812 that present operations had become "very dangerous" and that the coal and rock had "tumbled so much last week, as to oblige us to abandon it for many days."[66] A few months later, Heth's foreman informed the operator that several of the men were injured. Toby had recovered since a visit by Dr. Turpin and should be able to work soon. "Shadrack & Chester Brown got . . . hurt with a piece of coal that fell from the roof though Shadrack is working & Chester will in a few days."[67] Others were not so fortunate. For example, Ned was "Nearly Killed" and had been incapacitated since his accident.[68] Another slaveowner demanded compensation from Heth "for the. . .man who was killed by accident in your coal pits."[69] The same Petersburg lawyer wrote Heth again five months later concerning compensation for "the old Lady whose servant was unfortunately killed in your coal pits."[70]

Flooding provided another constant irritant to miners and helped make their work, according to one contemporary, a "gloomy avocation."[71] Most of the deep pits of the eastern Virginia field were worked day and night in relay shifts, except on Sunday when the water was pumped most of the day "to keep the works below from being flooded."[72] More than an unpleasant working condition, however, flooding represented a source of grave danger. In 1835, miners at Dover Pits suffered from such an accident. After sinking a shaft near the James River, the operator began drifting with the pitch of the seam, which led his excavations under the river itself. The drift nearly spanned the width of the stream, about two hundred yards at that point, when the pillars gave way and permitted water from above to overflow the workings. Whether or not any miners died remains uncertain, but the incident certainly rendered the entire effort profitless.[73] Most of the coal excavated from the first mines came from the seams closest to the surface. Once worked out or abandoned, these excavations quickly filled with water. Since few records were maintained regarding their underground location, the old water-filled workings presented a constant source of peril to miners working in the deeper pits of the late antebellum period.[74] One Friday afternoon in 1856, for example, Midlothian miners found the water rising rapidly in the "deep shaft" which acted as a sump. Upon investigation, the supervisor found that the water had risen about forty feet above the bottom of the shaft. He and the general supervisors attempted to reach the men trapped below by descending the "rise shaft," by which the coal was brought to the surface, but found that the water had cut all communications in the passage which connected the two shafts. After rescuing two white men, the relief party "failed to find another human being, leaving but little doubt on the mind of any one connected with the work, that they had all perished in the deluge." The next morning, the relief party rescued two unconscious whites. The remainder did not share such good fortune; the list of casualties included one white man, three company slaves, and four slave hirelings. According to the account reported by the *Richmond Daily Dispatch,* "the cause of the accident was by one of the working drifts intersecting the old works of the White Chimney Pits, which had been abandoned many years ago, and stood full of water. Similar accidents have occurred . . . notwithstanding the great precaution taken in boring ahead of the working."[75] At Midlothian one problem led to another. In 1858, the company purchased a five hundred horsepower Cornish pump, the best then available for deep shafts, to draw off the hundreds, and sometimes thousands, of gallons of water which accumulated in the mines every day. Just as the bottom of the shaft had been cleared of water, the coal took fire, probably by spontaneous combustion, and sent the miners up the shaft in a "hasty retreat." The works had to be sealed off in 1861, permitting the water to reclaim the subterranean chambers.[76]

In 1873, Oswald J. Heinrich, one of the leading mine engineers in the United States and superintendent of Midlothian, presented a paper before the American Institute of Mining Engineers in an attempt to explain the frequency of devastating fires in the eastern Virginia coal field. Heinrich observed that the field had a "well-founded bad reputation" because of the coal's unusually high content of volatile matter. He maintained that "many lamentable disasters, causing great loss of life and property, could have been avoided if a suitable system of mining had been pursued." Sometimes no system had existed at all, and pillars left to support the roof often failed to bear the weight of the above strata and were crushed from top pressure. Ultimately, the heat which resulted from the constant pressure on the supporting pillars, along with the presence of gas, and the loose coal and slate which littered the floors, rendered spontaneous combustion an ever-present possibility.[77]

As early as 1788, fire forced the closing of some sections of Black Heath Pits. Although these sections were sealed off, that initial fire continued to smolder for at least thirty years. It presented an omen of the future, for Heth's pits were plagued by fires thereafter.[78] Heth's partner, Beverly Randolph, wrote to him on the morning of August 24, 1810, that it was "now certain that we shall have the fire in the river pits, the day before yesterday they [the hands] were driven out by the smoke, which was very abundant all day." Even as Randolph wrote, the workmen had been "driven out of the Pit" again, and the fire and smoke had turned one of the shafts into a huge chimney.[79] The following day, Randolph informed his partner that conditions had worsened. Upon inspection, Randolph had discovered, "not very much to my surprise, that the fire had taken possession."

> This morning I went again to the pit after receiving your letter
> to see if anything could possibly be done and took three or
> four hands with me, but had not been down five minutes

before the hands began to stagger & fall from the effects of the Sulphur, which is intolerably strong. It was with great difficulty that we could get Jim Warren out, and I was very doubtful for some considerable time whether he would recover. I fear there is no chance of our ever being able to do anything more in that pit, for the fire has increased smartly since yesterday evening.[80]

The underground overseer, David Street, also wrote to Heth and further explained how the fire had driven the worker out entirely. The "old works," which continued to smolder, had not been responsible, however, for the fire had begun "amongst the tumble Coal and Slate." Apparently, Heth suffocated the fire by sealing the shafts and permitting the lower pits to fill with water.[81]

The most frightful of all mine disasters, the explosion, has always produced both horror and fascination. Its suddenness and unpredictability, even when elaborate precautions have been undertaken, and the enormity of its destructive power have always left an indelible impression on both experts and novices alike. Generally caused by improper ventilation, explosions rocked the eastern Virginia coal field with alarming regularity. The first explosion shook Black Heath Pits in 1817; it remains unknown how many men met their death in that accident.[82] Throughout its existence, Black Heath Pits periodically suffered explosions. In 1839, the combustion of methane gas resulted in the death of forty-five Negroes and two white overseers. Unlike many such disasters, the men were killed by the explosion itself rather than by the "after-damp" (carbolic acid) which inevitably followed to suffocate those who remained alive.[83] According to one interested contemporary:

Some years since, when ventilation was less understood than at present, an explosion took place in a neighboring mine of the most fearful character. Of the fifty-four men in the mine, only two, who happened to be in some crevices near the mouth of the shaft, escaped with life. Nearly all the internal works of the mine were blown to atoms. Such was the force of the explosion, that a basket then descending, containing three men, was blown nearly one hundred feet into the air. Two fell out, and were crushed to death, and the third remained in, and with the basket was thrown some seventy or eighty feet from the shaft, breaking both his legs and arms. He recovered, and is now living. It is believed, from the number of bodies found grouped together in the higher parts of the mine, that many survived the explosion of the inflammable gas, and were destroyed by inhaling the carbolic acid gas which succeeds it. This death is said to be very pleasant; fairy visions float around the sufferer, and he drops into the sleep of eternity like one passing into delightful dreams.[84]

Even though the "most approved methods of ventilating the mines had been introduced" in the interim, another explosion occurred in 1844 at Black Heath Pits which resulted from "the leaking out of gas from some deserted works, which had been ineffectually dammed off from the new galleries."[85] That explosion claimed the lives of eleven persons.[86] Another explosion in the same mines "killed three men" in 1855.[87] Still another explosion rocked Black Heath Pits in 1857. Nothing is known of this mishap, except that one slave, Garland, never returned to his owner. In 1857, Garland's owner, Brickerton Lyle Winston, of Hanover County, Virginia, recorded the simple epitaph: "Garland came to his end in an explosion in the Black Heath Pits."[88] The Midlothian Company, perhaps the most professionally operated mine in the field, also had its share of explosions. Thus, in 1842, Maidenhead Pits suffered a tremendous concussion. A.S. Wooldridge, company president, described the disaster as follows:

> A terrific explosion occurred . . . by which thirty-four persons were instantly killed, and a number of others so badly burned that little or no hopes are entertained of their recovery. . . .
> Mr. Atkins (who descended a shaft with a rescue party) describes the scene as heart-rendering in the extreme. Some of the dead men, the flesh charred on their bones, held their shovels in their hands. . . . and Samuel Hunt, a small boy, who had been deprived of reason for the time, by the concussion, was calling loudly to the mule he had been driving to go along. Those who were not dead . . . begged earnestly not to be left, and then prayed loudly for a few drops of cold water to quench their burning thirsts.[89]

A serious explosion killed about fifty-five of the slave force at Midlothian in 1855. Before the pits were closed in the 1870s, several additional eruptions killed an unspecified number of blacks who had continued to work in the mines after the war.[90]

Because slaveowners were reluctant to expose their human property to such dangerous working conditions, colliers waged an advertising and editorial campaign in the local newspapers to convince owners that mines were, on the whole, safe places in which to work. For example, in January 1846, the Midlothian Company posted notice for "able-bodied, healthy, well disposed Negro Men." The company tried to assure the owners that "there is no work in which slaves are better satisfied and contented than coal-mining; . . . There have been fewer deaths amongst the Company's hands from disease or casualties, since its organization 12 years ago, than will be found in a like number of men any where."[91] Similarly, in 1858 an article appeared in the *Richmond Daily Dispatch* entitled "The Coal Pits of Chesterfield County," which attempted to assuage the fears of owners of slave hirelings. In a newspaper article written by Jacob Atkins, the manager of Black Heath Pits, current problems encountered at the mines were assessed, especially the recent flooding of the lower works. Then Atkins observed:

> This has not been the only source of difficulty with which we have had to contend; slave owners, apprehending danger, have more than once removed their hands, at times when their services would have been of the greatest importance to the Company, which has subjected us to great inconvenience and loss. . . . The apprehension of danger from water which has hitherto been an objection to hands working at this place, being now removed, I can now recommend our pits as perfectly free from any disaster of that nature, notwithstanding the doubts which many have had of our ultimate success.
>
> I am fully aware that time has not erased from the minds of a large portion of this community the fearful results which attend colliery foundations, and would simply say, for the information of the public, that as regards any objection to our mines on this subject, that the point of supposed danger is now passed.[92]

That same month, the Carbon Hill mines advertised for fifty slave hirelings and felt compelled to assure the public that "the location is very healthy, and the employment as safe as any ordinary labor, as we have not had during the past five years, a single case of serious injury to any one engaged in our mining operations."[93] The next year the same company advertised for hands, adding that "*no accident from any cause involving life or limb* has occurred therein for the past Seven Years."[94]

Insurance was one means by which owners and employers alike tried to minimize the possible loss of human property. As early as 1815, one owner wrote to Harry Heth that he had been "informed that you [Heth] are now anxious to hire hands to work in your coal pits and that you will insure them against accidents which might happen."[95] Another owner informed Heth: "My Man Cey has again consented to return to you to work," but the slave had "to be Insured against the danger of the Pits."[96] By the 1840s, insurance for slave miners was commonplace. A representative example of Midlothian advertisements asserted in 1846 that "the lives of Slaves hired to the Midlothian Company can be insured at a reasonable premium, if desired by the owners."[97] By the late 1850s, however, insurance companies had become wary of insuring slaves who worked in coal pits with a reputation for accidents. This development further complicated the recruitment of an adequate labor force. In 1858, the manager of Black Heath Pits, where several slaves had recently drowned, observed that, "from the impending danger they supposed to exist, slave-owners could not be induced to engage their hands without first effecting an insurance upon them." Yet, because "accidents from similar causes have of late occurred" in which "life has been sacrificed," the insurance companies had become "greatly intimidated" and reluctant to take "risks on hands similarly circumstanced as those who have suffered on previous occasion."[98] Consequently, the very operation of a mine might be affected by this series of interlocking circumstances unique to coal pits.

Although ironmasters did not encounter the same degree of difficulty in acquiring a slave force, they did share a variety of additional problems with colliers when they entered the hiring market. Like some pit hands, numerous slaves also preferred to labor at ironworks rather than in the fields. The ironmasters of Lebanon Forge, near Lexington, wrote to owner Samuel McDowell Reid that "your two Boys say they want to live with us another year and we are anxious to hire them."[99] Another owner told Jordan and Davis to keep his five hands; for he was informed that "they all, except Jemmy, preferred staying & he seemed to be indifferent about returning" to work at the forge.[100] Also like the collier, however, the ironmaster was more likely to encounter problems when hands did not want to work at an ironworks. "Our agreement," wrote one owner in 1829, "was if Brandus was not willing to go to you, I should not force him and on seeing Mr. Brawly, who says the boy is anxious to remain with him," the owner could not think of "compelling him to go any where it is not his wish, as that has always been my rule."[101] In 1854, a hiring agent informed William Weaver: "I am wiling [*sic*] to hire for you," but that would make little difference "as persons let their hands go pretty much where they please."[102] One owner believed it unnecessary for his slave Jefferson to come home "if he can be satisfied up there & you want him for the next year."[103] John Chew hired "a negro man named Fielding" and told the ironmaster that he "would have sent another man, but he refused to go."[104] "Winston would not consent to go back (to the works), having as I understand taken a wife," Tuyman Wayt informed Jordan and Irvine.[105] Some slaves refused to be hired because of their geographic preferences. Thus, one agent complained that he had "not been able to get any Boatmen. Those immediately in our neighborhood are unwilling to work from above the ridge and their Masters (are) not disposed to compel them."[106]

Sometimes slaves exercised a degree of control over who would purchase them. For example, William Weaver informed David Garland that he wished to purchase a valuable slave f. .m him. Garland replied that "it being Holliday times the fellow has Concluded to Visit his friends owned by you and to see you also, in order th . he may make up his mind how far he would be pleased with an Exchange of residence." This statement implies that the slave, Billy Goochland, would evaluate the ironmaster and his works before consenting to be purchased by the ironmaster.[107] Another owner offered to sell Weaver his "negro man Stephen" if Weaver wanted to purchase him "and he is willing to remain with you."[108] One owner was willing to take a loss of "a few hundred less" than his slave was worth: "From the number of years Danniel has been with you and the anxiety he has to stay with you induces me to believe he had rather stay with you than come back. Feeling a desire to gratify him I have concluded I would sell him to you."[109] Slave Jim Turner had a difficult decision to make, for he had to choose whether he would go with his wife and four children to Roanoke, where she was being sent to serve the owner's daughter, or be sold to a man in the neighborhood. The owner gave him several days to make his decision, and although the owner was "decidedly of the opinion that Jim should go with his wife," Jim chose to remain in the neighborhood, "consequences be what they may."[110] One slave ironworker was able to make his preference known in writing: "Mr. Davidson I take this pleasure to write to you that I am not willing to live with mister [Frank] Anderson and I don't want you to sell me to him if you please." The slave told Davidson that if Anderson came for him, "don't let him have me."[111]

The hiring system was further complicated for both owners and employers by the fact that dissatisfied bondsmen frequently ran away. While this possibility caused employers to be more accomodative toward black hirelings, it also prompted owners to be cautious about sending bondsmen where they did not wish to work. For example, one owner had hired a slave to Jordan and Irvine in January 1830 and then reversed his decision:

> The reasons which have influenced this cours [sic] is the previous bad character of the fellow, in Connection with the recent declarations of his. Has left no doubt on my Mind, but he wou'd make an effort to reach the State of Ohio, and by being placed at your Works it wou'd greatly facilatate [sic] his Object.
>
> Was I to send him I am persuaded that he wou'd render you no services, and it might be the means of my loosing [sic] the fellow entierly [sic].[112]

In another case, an owner wrote to the ironmaster that "I am sorry to inform you that one of the Men I hired you (Isaac) has expressed such an unwillingness to return to you, that I feared should I send him over he would run away, and perhaps be of little or no service to you during the year." Apologetically, the owner explained: "When I hired him I was under the impression he would be willing to serve you,—but I find he is not."[113] The same master agreed to hire another of his black hands to Weaver only if the ironmaster complied with the slave's request. The owner told Weaver that "Sam has requested me to ask the favor of you, to permit him to stay at the establishment at which you live. . . .He was also unwilling to return; but says he would have no objection, provided, he could live at your own establishment."[114] Whether or not Weaver accepted the arrangement is unknown, but the slaveowner's terms provide significant commentary on the actual functioning of the hiring system.

Employers could find themselves short of hands if they did not proceed carefully with hired slaves and their owners. When William Weaver took advantage of an owner named Dickinson by paying only half the current market value for hands, the irate owner informed Weaver that "if you ever get another gentleman in your power as I have been [I want] to caution you how you treat him," and "I sincerely hope it may terminate all intercourse between us."[115] Apparently, Weaver replied to Dickinson's letter, and Dickinson responded that Weaver's antics were ungentlemanly; "this letter however will close (I hope forever) any correspondence with you."[116] And so ended a vital source of black hands for Weaver at a time when slaves were becoming more scarce and expensive. An unsavory reputation could also create difficulties for an ironmaster at hiring-time among slave hands themselves, as Weaver found out in January 1830 when his agent R. Crutchfield informed him: "I have not been able to get you any hands. . . . You will not take it unfriendly when I say to you in candour that some of the hands (I know not whom) have made somewhat an unfavourable impression on the negroes in the neighborhood as to the treatment at the place [the ironworks]."[117] Hired slave ironworkers who felt mistreated sometimes returned to their masters. Such was the case of Ben who "has come home this morning and complains of being very unwell also of his work at your Iron Works," as well as "other harsh treatment." The owner informed the ironmaster that he would "take him back," for Ben was "not willing to stay with you."[118]

Owners were usually interested in the treatment their slaves received at the hands of employers and often interceded on the slaves' behalf. Harry Heth hired a hand to a neighboring collier in 1802 and informed him that, "in case I should be so fortunate as to regain my Negroe Man Daniel, he will be no longer hired to you, either by the month or otherwise. The life of the Fellow as well as my own feelings and interest forbid it."[119] In 1807, an owner complained to Heth that a hand hired to the collier had returned home badly clothed and refused to return to the pits because of bad treatment. While the owner reassured Heth that *his* "humanity" was not questioned, the owner expected an "account of your Overseer."[120] Speaking for several owners, an agent notified Heth in 1819 that his clients wanted to know why their slaves ran away. Although they "have never had any Idea that you could be capable of treating them in any other manner" than humanity dictated, the owners resented harsh treatment of their property.[121] Slaves knew and often used to their own advantage the conflicting interests of owner and employer. A number of hands left Black Heath Pits in 1815 when the regular overseer, Mr. Marsett, left for Kentucky. Since he would not return for two months, a temporary overseer, Mr. Hughes, was employed to supervise the pit hands during the interim. Hughes' heavy-handed treatment of the slaves created such discontent among the workmen that they took the initiative and exploited the natural tension between owner and employer in order to protect themselves. Robert Perkins wrote to Heth about the situation:

> Bookker has been detained one day on account of Rain &
> also on account of Rheuben & Ben leaving the Pits, who have
> come to Mr. Watson owner & me agent [sic]. I have Sam, Mr.
> Shermans' Hubert, & Wm. Christians' Frank, who came
> with Bookker Ben & Rheuben as to the discontent which
> prevails at the pits on acct. of Mr. Hughes your overseer.
> They also state Mr. Burton & he does not agree. I saw
> Marrsett the day before he went to Kentucky & I heard no
> complaint of him whom all the Boys agree they are pleas [sic]
> with. He told me he would return in two months when I have
> no doubt they will all again be pleas'd. They state 9 or 10 on
> acct. of Hughes have left the pits. If this be correct there must
> be some grounds of Objection to him & will operate very
> much against your Hiring the next year. . . . I will be up on
> Sunday or Monday evening next, when all as above I hope
> will be better understood & every thing arranged to the
> Satisfaction of all parties. I will be glad when I come up you
> will ride with me to the Pits where Hughes lives in order that
> the whole truth may be known with respect to the charges, &
> if these Boys have told what is not correct, they ought to be
> made to know better. Ben & Rheuben will be up with me.[122]

Rheuben came in after a few days, and Perkins informed Heth that the slave would be back at the pits in a few days. For punishment, Perkins suggested that "Rheuben's Hollidays will make good the time lost."[123]

Slave ironworkers were equally adept at manipulating to their own advantage the conflict between the two groups of masters. Abram did just that in April 1829 with his owner W. Dickinson and the employer, William Weaver of Buffalo Forge:

You perhaps may think a little strange of my not returning
Abram to you before this time. When I returned from your
side of the mountain he was then in the woods and did not
come in until last Saturday morning. . . .His conduct towards
your uncle I know & almost was unpardonable but as I have
chastised him severely for it myself, if you will pass it over in
silence I will esteem it as a favor as long as I live. —As his
principle [sic] complaint seemed to be lodged against your
Overseer I will thank you if convenient with your arrangements to put him to cutting wood.[124]

The master of another slave hired to a furnace in Rockbridge County wrote
to the ironmaster: "My boy Edmond . . . got here the eight of this month
[November 1849], he says that your overseer is so cruel that he could not
stand him." The owner explained that he had hired Edmond for the past
three years without any complaints, and "I know he will do his work as well
as any negroe unless the person that overlooks him is barbourse." Furthermore, the owner had started Edmond back and admonished, "if you
thrash him do not be too rough and I know he will do his work as well as any
other negroe at your furnice [sic]."[125]

Significantly, Edmond, as well as Abram in the previous incident, knew
that if they complained of maltreatment at the ironworks their masters
would intercede for them. Even one of William Weaver's hiring agents was
upset when he notified the ironmaster that he had "received a letter from
some one with no name to it saying that Robert [a slave hired by the agent
for Weaver] had left you and the reason assigned was that your manager
wished him to work in the Ore Bank and it was so dangerous that all your
white hands had quit on that account." If this was so, he continued, "I am
surprised for I had always thought you a different man and had always
represented you as being one of the safest men to hire to as regards to
treatment."[126] Weaver immediately inquired into the validity of the
charges, and the furnace manager replied in a detailed explanation that
"there is not one word of truth" in the "tale."[127]

Clearly then, employers were constantly aware that they could not
afford to ignore owners' instructions about working conditions or charges
that they abused slave hands. Ever present was the underlying three-way
conflict of interests, which often yielded advantages for the slave who
manipulated the interests of owner and ironmaster for his own benefit and
protection. Slave hands also pitted the owner and hirer against each other
in order to influence working conditions. In January 1825, owner R. Brooks
told Weaver that "Davy does not wish to blow Rock and I promised him
that he Should not."[128] Once again, in 1829 Brooks hired Davy, this time to
Jordan and Irvine. Brooks interceded again: "Davy Says that Working in
the furnace is ruinous to his Eyes therefore I do not Wish him to work there

against his will.''[129] Another owner wrote to Jordan and Irvine in January 1931 about ''my man phill,'' saying that it was ''necessary to inform you that I am very unwilling for him to work in the ore or blowing Rock as he has been so much injured by it and he is very dissattesfied at it—but he is willing to work at anything that thear is not so much danger [*sic*].''[130] In January 1858, Joseph Gibbs agreed to hire ''my boy George for the present year to work at the blacksmith trade.'' The owner made the point strongly, however, that ''I want you to understand me fully, I do not want him to work at the ore Banks.''[131]

Several letters clearly illustrate that the interaction among slaves, owners, and employers was initiated by bondsmen on their own behalf. Most significant perhaps was the elaborate charade employers and owners felt compelled to act out in dealing with slave ironworkers. ''This is to inform [you] that my negro man Tom run off from my plantation . . . with a view as I suppose to get . . . in this neighborhood of your Iron Works,'' wrote a slaveowner to William Weaver in May 1831. ''I wish you to set him to work as though you had hired him, he may intend to dodge through your neighborhood,'' continued the owner. ''In that case I think if you would proclaim among your hands that long Tom has run away from his master . . . in consequence of which you have hired for the balance of the year he would come forthwith & if he should get safe . . . remain with you the balance of the year.'' The owner implored Weaver to ''use any scheme you may think proper to save em.''[132] Another letter from the manager of an ironworks to its owner, F. T. Anderson, suggested how the intricate maneuvering went on when it involved only members of the ironworks:

> Bob came here this morning, and I told him you said he must go to the Furnace he said he would not go there, that he would go home first. I then told him to go to Fincastle and see you. No he said he did not like to do that, and intimated very clearly that he meant to run away, so I concluded the best plan would be to let him go to the Kilns with Moses, where you could find him and advise you you had better go and see him yourself I think.[133]

One letter plainly revealed the web of interpersonal dynamics involved in the hiring system. The letter described the difficulties faced in 1856 by the son of Gibraltar Forge ironmaster, James C. Davis, who tried to rehire a group of slave hands from east of the Blue Ridge Mountains. On January 5, 1856, in a detailed letter to his father at the forge, he discussed his trials with this group of hands:

> There is some difficulty about Dickinson's hands & I hardly know how to act. When they came from over the mountain they wished to go back: & under the impression that they still

wished so I hired them of Dickinson at the Ct House Tuesday. Shortly after I hired them he came & told me that Elick
did not wish to go, that a railroad man had offered him five
dollars cash in his hands to go with him & that tickled his
fancy, but says he "I believe he will get over that & be willing
to go with you & if he does not I will not ask him any odds but
send them (the other hands) on," & the subject dropped. But
yesterday I received a letter from him saying that his boys
had come to him & avowed they would not go, & if they did
they would run off after they got there. Now I believe that
this is nothing but an empty threat for the purpose of scaring
their master & that it only requires decisive measures to bring
them straight. But if they were in earnest they would be apt to
run before they got there & not after they crossed the blue
Ridge Mountains, for they know that they dont understand
the country well enough to start when so far from home.
Should they do this they will come down in Dickinson's
neighborhood & he will be perfectly willing to take them back
& so no harm will result in that case But should they on the
other hand run off after they get there, which I dont believe
they will do, not being used to the country, nor skilled in the
wiles of running away, will be taken before they get far. All
this is on the hypothesis that Elick goes with them. If he is
cooled down & kept in Jail until I choose to let him off & the
others sent on I dont apprehend any difficulty whatever:
because he is the ringleader and has persuaded the
other's . . . who were willing to go back up at last Monday
when I saw them at the Ct. House. Should I let these hands
off it is now too late to get others in their places, for the hands
through the country are hired: else I would not care so much
to let them off. Moreover I got them cheaper than I could get
hands again even if I could find any for hire. In consideration
of all these things I wrote to Mr. Dickinson by this morning's
mail that I could not let them off, but for him to take them to
the Ct House Monday Morning, put Elick in Jail before the
eyes of the others without saying a word as to the meaning of
it, then take the others & send them on the cars for Staunton
with a pass to Gibraltar: and after they are gone to take Elick
out of Jail & hire him out there at the Ct House by the day,
letting on to him that he (Dickinson) will hire him where he
wishes to go when he finds a place, which he might do if I
found I could make it suit to let him off: if not, I would take
him over when I went. I think this plan will work.[134]

Davis closed this letter in a tirade against Elick, whom he compared to a dog. "Of all those five Negroes," Davis fumed, "he was the only one that escaped the lash [the previous year]; & frequently received favors that I would have denied the others. Now he not only turns from me but tries to lead them away likewise."[135] Despite Davis's anger and delicate maneuvering, the owner hired the slaves elsewhere. Davis urged his father to file suit against the owner for the damages, if the owner refused to deliver the hired slaves, for no other hands were available and "consequently we cannot prosecute our business."[136]

This incident deserves special attention, for it synthesizes the problems which confronted the industrialist in hiring slaves and the complexities in the hiring system itself. The ironmaster was compelled not only to convince the owner that he should rehire his slaves to the works for another year, but Davis also had to persuade the blacks themselves that they should return. Even though all the hands but Elick had received the lash, initially they were willing to return to the forge for another year. This would have been an unlikely possibility if harsh treatment was the normal fare at the forge. More importantly, the agent was forced to play what Charles B. Dew has aptly called a "psychological game" with Elick and the other slave hands. Although Davis needed these slaves, their owner refused to compel them to go where they were unwilling to work. Consequently, the ironmaster planned an "elaborate charade" to separate the trouble-maker Elick from the others and transport them west of the Blue Ridge Mountains close to the forge, which made it unlikely that they could easily return home. The whole affair illustrates the triangular dynamics which operated between owner, slave, and employer. It reveals a subtle system in which blacks played an active role in deciding, always within institutional limits, of course, the physical conditions of their daily lives in bondage.[137]

NOTES

1. Charles Sackett Sydnor, *Slavery in Mississippi* (Gloucester, Mass.: Peter Smith, 1965, originally 1933), p. 179.

2. Kenneth M. Stampp, *The Peculiar Institution: Slavery in the Ante-Bellum South* (New York: Alfred A. Knopf, 1956), p. 84.

3. Robert S. Starobin, *Industrial Slavery in the Old South* (New York: Oxford University Press, 1970), Chaps. 3 and 4; Samuel Sydney Bradford, "The Ante-Bellum Charcoal Iron Industry of Virginia" (Ph.D. dissertation, Columbia University, 1958), Chaps. 4 and 5, and his article, "The Negro Ironworker in Ante Bellum Virginia," *Journal of Southern History* 25 (May 1959): 201–204.

4. Clement Eaton, "Slave-Hiring in the Upper South: A Step Toward Freedom," *Mississippi Valley Historical Review* 46 (March 1960) :668–69.

5. Richard B. Morris, "The Measure of Bondage in the Slave States," *Mississippi Valley Historical Review* 41 (September 1954) :239.

6. Richard C. Wade, *Slavery in the Cities: The South, 1820–1860* (New York: Oxford University Press, 1964), pp. 142, 208, 243.

7. Charles B. Dew, "Disciplining Slave Ironworkers in the Antebellum South: Coercion, Conciliation, and Accommodation," *American Historical Review* 79 (April 1974) :394. Robert William Fogel and Stanley L. Engerman, *Time on the Cross: The Economics of American Negro Slavery* (Boston: Little, Brown & Co., 1974), p. 232.

8. "Acct of Negroes," Principio Company Papers, 1723–1730, Maryland Historical Society, hereafter cited as MHS.

9. Samuel G. Hermelin, *Report About the Mines in the United States of America*, trans. by Amandus Johnson (Philadelphia: John Morton Memorial Museum, 1931), p. 52.

10. Journal A & B, 1767–1794, Patuxent Iron Works, Maryland Hall of Records, hereafter cited as HR.

11. Articles of Agreement, Harry Heth and Thomas Taylor, January 31, 1813, Heth Family Papers, University of Virginia, hereafter cited as UVa.

12. For examples, see letters to Harry Heth from James Cocke, April 11, 1815, Erasmus Reamus, June 21, 1810, Peter Farrar, August 6, 1810, Edward Diggs, January 9, 1812, all in Heth Family Papers, UVa.

13. Bonds of Hire, throughout the Jordan and Irvine Papers, State Historical Society of Wisconsin, hereafter cited as SHSW; Ledger, Paramount Furnace; Negro Time Book. 1833–1839; and Negro Time Book, 1839–1852, Graham Ledgers, UVa.

14. Miscellaneous items, Reid-White Papers, Washington and Lee University.

15. Bradford, "Charcoal Iron Industry of Virginia," pp. 101–102.

16. Harry Heth to Henry Heth (son), February 26, 1815, Heth Family Papers, UVa.

17. James McDowell to Thomas W. Gilmer, December 20, 1836, Cyrus H. McCormick Papers, SHSW.

18. W.G.T. Nelson to W. W. Davis, December 30, 1839, Jordan and Davis Papers, SHSW.

19. Th. L. Booth to Harry Heth, November 30, 1815, Heth Family Papers, UVa.

20. F. F. Tanner (for J. R. Anderson) to Colonel L. Partlow, December 15, 1848, Tredegar Letterbook, Tredegar Company Records, Virginia State Library, hereafter cited as VSL.

21. Lester J. Cappon, "History of the Southern Iron Industry to the Close of the Civil War" (Ph.D. dissertation, Harvard University, 1928 [microfilm copy of earlier draft, UVa. Library]), pp. 151–52; for examples, see the various Bonds of Hire scattered throughout the Jordan and Irvine Papers, SHSW, and the Heth Family Papers, UVa.

22. Richard Brooke to Harry Heth, June 7, 1805, Heth Family Papers, UVa.

23. Nat Perkins to Harry Heth, March 1, 1807, Heth Family Papers, UVa.

24. W. G. Weaver to Harry Heth, March 7, 1817, Heth Family Papers, UVa.

25. John W. Smith to Jordan and Irvine, January 3, 1831, Jordan and Irvine Papers, SHSW.

26. James Coleman to W. Weaver, February 19, 1836, William Weaver Papers, Duke University, hereafter cited as Duke.

27. S. Forrer to W. W. Davis, January 10 and 29, 1850, Jordan and Davis Papers, SHSW.

28. Daniel Brady to Capt. Gabrial Long, January 24, 1861, Day Book and Letterbook, Bath Iron Works, Weaver-Brady Papers, UVa.

29. John Dillon to W. Weaver, February 5, 1831, William Weaver Papers, Duke.

30. John Cunliffe to Harry Heth, August 29, 1811, Heth Family Papers, UVa.

31. Harry Heth to John Cunliffe, April 29, 1811, Heth Family Papers, UVa.

32. Richard Brooke to Harry Heth, December 11, 1811, Heth Family Papers, UVa.

33. F. Dickinson to W. Weaver, March 8, 1828, William Weaver Papers, Duke.

34. F. Dickinson to W. Weaver, January 15, 1829, William Weaver Papers, Duke. Slave masters obviously knew their Shakespeare; "Shame where is thy blush!" is from *Hamlet*, Act III, Scene IV.

35. Bradford, "Negro Ironworker in Ante Bellum Virginia," p. 197.

36. John Chew to W. Weaver, December 5, 1830, James Coleman to W. Weaver, February 5 and 19, 1856, William Weaver Papers, Duke; Tuyman Wayt to Jordan and Irvine, January 6, 1830, and Pallison Boxley to Jordan and Irvine, January 13, 1831, Jordan and Irvine Papers, SHSW; Joseph Clarke Robert, *The Tobacco Kingdom: Plantation, Market, and Factory in Virginia and North Carolina, 1800–1860* (Gloucester, Mass.: Peter Smith, 1965, originally 1938), Chap. 10. Also see the *Richmond Dispatch* throughout the 1850s. For the same phenomenon in the Valley of Virginia during the 1850s, see numerous advertisements in the *Lexington Gazette*. The Virginian and Tennessee Railroad Company alone advertised for "400 able-bodied Negroes" in 1856 (*Richmond Daily Dispatch*, December 15, 1856). Also see Claudia Dale Goldin, *Urban Slavery in the American South, 1820–1860: A Quantitative History* (Chicago: University of Chicago Press, 1976), Chaps. 4 and 5.

37. D. Ross to Edmond Sherman, February 9, 1812, David Ross Letterbook 1812–1813, Virginia Historical Society, hereafter cited as VHS.

38. Francis Preston to his brother, July 27, 1806, Preston Family Papers, VHS.

39. Ridwell Furnace, Ledger, 1805–1809, University of North Carolina, hereafter cited as UNC.

40. James C. Dickinson to W. Weaver, January 2, 1828, Weaver-Brady Papers, UVa.

41. "A Register of the Black Hands at C. Forge for 1830," and "Register of Furnace for 1830," Jordan and Irvine Papers, SHSW.

42. Tuyman Wayt to Jordan and Irvine, January 6, 1830, Jordan and Irvine Papers, SHSW.

43. Pallison Boxley to Jordan and Irvine, January 13, 1831, Jordan and Irvine Papers, SHSW.

44. Bradford, "Negro Ironworker in Ante Bellum Virginia," p. 196.

45. Henry A. McCormick to W. Weaver, December 29, 1855, Weaver-Brady Papers, UVa.

46. John Bibb to Mr. Jefferson Turner, November 3, 1853, William Weaver Papers, Duke.

47. James Coleman to W. Weaver, February 5, 1856, William Weaver Papers, Duke.

48. James C. Davis to W. W. Davis, January 5, 1856, William W. Davis Papers, UVa.

49. James C. Davis to W. W. Davis, January 7, 1856, Jordan and Davis Papers, SHSW. According to Fogel and Engerman, *Time on the Cross*, pp. 102, 235, in the rural areas demand for slaves was quite "inelastic," or not easily substituted by alternative forms of labor. This factor no doubt provided a constant upward pressure on prices. They also observe that demand for slave labor in urban areas was generally more "elastic," or readily substituted with white workers. Whatever the case with urban industries, the production of iron remained primarily a rural endeavor, and demand for slave labor throughout the slave era seems to have been quite inelastic as well.

50. Greenlee Davidson to James D. Davidson, January 9, 1859, James D. Davidson Papers, SHSW.

51. "Coal Trade — Richmond," 24th Cong., 2nd Sess., House Document 93, 1837.

52. Dr. Carroll to Charles Carroll, November 9, 1732, Carroll-Maccubbin Papers, MHS.

53. Stephen Onion to Charles Carroll and Company, July 1, 1734, Carroll-Maccubbin Papers, MHS.

54. Stephen Onion to Charles Carroll, September 29, 1734, Carroll-Maccubbin Papers, MHS.

55. Keach Doyel Johnson, "Establishment of the Baltimore Iron Company: A Study of the American Iron Industry in the Eighteenth Century" (Ph.D. dissertation, State University of Iowa, 1949), pp. 74–78.

56. B. Nicholson to Capt. Charles Ridgely, n.d., probably ca. 1780, Ridgely Family Papers, MHS.

57. James Henderson to Nicolson and Heth, March 28, 1818, Heth Family Papers, UVa.

58. Robert Perkins to Mr. Hughes (Mgr.), March 9, 1819, Heth Family Papers, UVa.

59. J. Binford to Harry Heth, May 24, 1819, Heth Family Papers, UVa.

60. Richard Brooke to Harry Heth, January 6, 1813, Heth Family Papers, UVa.

61. Robert Gaines to Harry Heth, December 20, 1815, Heth Family Papers, UVa.

62. Richard Brooke to Harry Heth, January 6, 1813, Heth Family Papers, UVa.

63. W. G. Warner to Harry Heth, March 9, 1817, Heth Family Papers, UVa.

64. John Edmund Stealey III, "Slavery and the Western Virginia Salt Industry," *Journal of Negro History* 59 (April 1974) :116.

65. Ibid., pp. 116–17.

66. Harry Heth to Thomas Railey, July 7, 1812, Heth Family Papers, UVa.

67. N. Sanders to Harry Heth, September 16, 1812, Heth Family Papers, UVa.

68. Robert Brooke to Harry Heth, February 22, 1801, Heth Family Papers, UVa.

69. W. B. Pillsborough to Harry Heth, February 6, 1819, Heth Family Papers, UVa.

70. Ibid., June 26, 1819.

71. John Holland, *The History and Description of Fossil Fuel, the Collieries, and Coal Trade of Great Britain* (London: Whittaker & Co., 1841), p. 247.

72. Joseph Martin, *New and Comprehensive Gazetteer of Virginia* (Charlottesville, Va., 1835), p. 152; Frederick Law Olmsted, *A Journey in the Seaboard Slave States, with Remarks on Their Economy* (New York: Mason Brothers, 1859, originally 1856), p. 48.

73. Edmund Ruffin, "Visit to Graham's Coal Pits," *Farmers' Register* 5 (August 1, 1837) :317.

74. Samuel Harries Daddow and Benjamin Bannan, *Coal, Iron, and Oil; or, the Practical American Miner* (Philadelphia: J. B. Lippincott & Co., 1866), p. 402; Oswald J. Heinrich, "The Midlothian, Virginia, Colliery in 1876," *Transactions* of the AIME, 1 (May 1875–February 1876) :310.

75. *Richmond Daily Dispatch*, December 15, 16, 1856.

76. Heinrich, "Midlothian, Virginia, Colliery," p. 310.

77. Oswald J. Heinrich, "The Midlothian Colliery, Virginia," *Transactions* of the AIME, 1 (May 1871–February 1873):346–49, 356, 360, 364.

78. "An Account of the Coal Mines in the Vicinity of Richmond, Virginia," Communicated to the Editor in a Letter from Mr. John Grammar, Jun., *American Journal of Science* 17 (July 1834) :126–28; David Street to Harry Heth, August 10, 1810, Heth Family Papers, UVa.

79. Beverly Randolph to Harry Heth, August 24, 1810, Heth Family Papers, UVa.

80. Ibid., August 25, 1810. Randolph was Heth's son-in-law as well as his partner.

81. David Street to Harry Heth, August 25, 1810, and Beverly Randolph to Harry Heth, n.d., 1818, Heth Family Papers, UVa.

82. Wooldridge, "Notice of the Coal Mines in the Vicinity of Richmond," p. 129.

83. Sir Charles Lyell, *On the Structure and Probable Age of the Coal-Field of the James River, near Richmond, Virginia* (London: By the Author, 1847), p. 270; *Richmond Enquirer*, March 23, 1839.

84. Henry Howe, *Historical Collections of Virginia; Containing a Collection of the Most Interesting Facts, Traditions, Biographical Sketches, Anecdotes, etc. Relating to Its History and Antiquities* (Charleston, S.C.: Babcock & Co., 1845), pp. 231–32.

85. Lyell, *On the Structure of the Coal-Field of the James River*, p. 270.

86. *Richmond Times and Compiler*, November 21, 1844.

87. *Richmond Whig and Public Advertiser*, November 28, 1854, November 30, 1855.

88. Bickerton Lyle Winston Manuscript Slave Account Book, VHS.

89. Wooldridge, "Notice of Coal Mines in the Vicinity of Richmond," p. 2; also see *Mining Magazine* 4 (1855) :316–17.

90. Heinrich, "Midlothian, Virginia, Colliery," p. 310; Oswald J. Heinrich, "An Account of an Explosion of Fire-Damp at the Midlothian Colliery, Chesterfield County, Virginia," *Transactions* of the AIME, 5 (May 1876–February 1877):148–61.

91. *Richmond Whig and Public Advertiser*, January 2, 1846.

92. *Richmond Daily Dispatch*, January 29, 1858.

93. Ibid., January 11, 1858.

94. Ibid., December 31, 1859, January 1860.

95. B. Dandridge to Harry Heth, April 1, 1815, Heth Family Papers, UVa.

96. H. B. Christian to Harry Heth, March 1, 1819, Heth Family Papers, UVa.

97. *Richmond Whig and Public Advertiser*, January 2, 1846.

98. *Richmond Daily Dispatch*, January 29, 1858.

99. Bryan & Shaw to Co. Saml. McD. Reid, December 19, 1834, Reid-White Papers, Washington and Lee University.

100. Samuel Jordan to William Davis, July 10, 1840, Jordan and Davis Papers, SHSW.

101. C. Wiglesworth to W. Weaver, December 31, 1828, William Weaver Papers, Duke.

102. T. R. Towles to W. Weaver, November 27, 1854, William Weaver Papers, Duke.

103. John Wiglesworth to W. Weaver, December 7, 1829, William Weaver Papers, Duke.

104. John Chew to W. Weaver, January 2, 1830, William Weaver Papers, Duke.

105. Tuyman Wayt to Jordan and Irvine, January 6, 1830, Jordan and Irvine Papers, SHSW.

106. John Schoolfield to W. Weaver, January 5, 1832, William Weaver Papers, Duke.

107. David Garland to W. Weaver, May 23, 1828, William Weaver Papers, Duke.

108. Thomas Duke to W. Weaver, July 13, 1830, William Weaver Papers, Duke.

109. J. H. Coleman to F. T. Anderson, January 24, 1852, F. T. Anderson Papers, Duke.

110. James H. Paxton to James Davidson, December 23, 1859, and M. H. Parry to James Davidson, December 24, 1859, James D. Davidson Papers, SHSW.

111. John Luckes letter not to sell him, December 12, 1859, James D. Davidson Papers, SHSW.

112. Ro. Garland to Jordan and Irvine, January 3, 1830, Jordan and Irvine Papers, SHSW.

113. William Staples to W. Weaver, January 4, 1830, Weaver-Brady Papers, UVa.

114. Ibid.

115. F. Dickinson to W. Weaver, January 15, 1829, William Weaver Papers, Duke.

116. F. Dickinson to W. Weaver, February 2, 1829, Weaver-Brady Papers, UVa.

117. R. Crutchfield to W. Weaver, January 10, 1830, William Weaver Papers, Duke.

118. Elizabeth Mathews to W. Weaver, March 29, 1830, William Weaver Papers, Duke.

119. Harry Heth to Thomas Wooldridge, August 3, 1802, Heth Family Papers, UVa.

120. William Smith to Harry Heth, January 3, 1807, Heth Family Papers, UVa.

121. G. Savage to Harry Heth, May 26, 1819, Heth Family Papers, UVa.

122. Robert Perkins to Harry Heth, May 18, 1815, Heth Family Papers, UVa.

123. Ibid., June 5, 1815.

124. W. Dickinson to W. Weaver, April 19, 1829, Heth Family Papers, UVa.

125. John T. Day to Shanks, Anderson & Anderson, November 9, 1849, Anderson Family Papers, UVa.

126. Thomas R. Towles to W. Weaver, November 11, 1857, William Weaver Papers, Duke.

127. Charles K. Gorgas to W. Weaver, November 17, 1857, William Weaver Papers, Duke; William Rex was Weaver's nephew, who, along with Charles Gorgas, another of Weaver's nephews, managed Etna Furnace.

128. R. Brooks to Weaver, January 3, 1825, William Weaver Papers, Duke.

129. R. Brooks to Jordan and Irvine, January 2, 1829, Jordan and Irvine Papers, SHSW.

130. Nancy Matthews to Jordan and Irvine, January 18, 1831, Jordan and Irvine Papers, SHSW.

131. Joseph Gibbs to F. T. Anderson, January 23, 1858, F. T. Anderson Papers, Duke.

132. Stephen Nicholls to William Weaver, May 3, 1831, William Weaver Papers, Duke.

133. John Wilson to F. T. Anderson, January 14, 1851, Anderson Family Papers, UVa.

134. James C. Davis to William W. Davis, January 5, 1856, William Davis Papers, UVa.

135. Ibid.

136. James C. Davis to William W. Davis, January 9, 1856, Cyrus H. McCormick Papers, SHSW.

137. See also Dew, "Disciplining Slave Ironworkers," pp. 403–404.

"The Carrot and the   4
Stick": Discipline and
Motivation of Slave
Workers

We Wear the mask that grins and lies,
It hides our cheeks and shades our eyes,
This debt we pay to human guile;
With torn and bleeding hearts we smile,
And mouth with myriad subtleties.

Why should the world be over-wise,
In counting all our tears and sighs?
Nay, let them only see us, while
    We wear the mask.

We smile, but, O great Christ, our cries
To thee from tortured souls arise.
We sing, but oh the day is vile
Beneath our feet, and long the mile;
But let the world dream otherwise,
    We wear the mask.
                —Paul Lawrence Dunbar,
                "We Wear the Mask"

Once ironmasters and colliers had secured an adequate slave labor force, their major concern was with labor efficiency and productivity. Industrialists who employed slaves on a large scale faced the difficult problem of attempting simultaneously to motivate and discipline them. Productivity, discipline, and motivation were interrelated objectives which demanded constant attention if industrialists expected to stay in business. While employers had the power to inflict physical punishment on troublesome slave workers, excessive brutality created difficult labor problems among the hands. Too much coercion could demoralize them, lead to an outbreak of runaways, and increase the incidence of slave abuse of draft animals, theft, arson, and acts of industrial sabotage, or even self-inflicted physical damage. Even if slaves limited their resistance to relatively mild forms such as slowdowns or careless work habits, normal operations could be seriously hindered. In short, industrial slaves, and especially skilled craftsmen, were in a position to render financial damage to the industrialist's interest.[1] Accordingly, most employers during the eighteenth and nineteenth centuries utilized more sophisticated methods of slave discipline than brute force.

Although Robert Fogel and Stanley Engerman are in basic agreement with the U. B. Phillips interpretation of a benevolent regard for slaves in the Old South, they do not agree that this regard was fostered by the paternalism of a unique civilization. Instead, Fogel and Engerman recast the southern slaveowner into the role of "homo economicus." For pure economic men governed by rational economic decisions, cruelty to slave property was obviously out of the question since damaged goods produced deflated values in the marketplace. In fact, Fogel and Engerman believe that slaveowners came close to resembling a sort of bourgeoisie who manipulated slaves with the calculated shrewdness of efficiency experts or personnel managers. More than this, they maintain that by responding to a variety of work incentives (discussed below) which fused their interests with those of their masters, the slaves themselves reflected rational economic men. In short, according to Fogel and Engerman, slaves, like their masters, became part of a bourgeois order infused with the "Protestant work ethic."[2] To the extent that industrial slavery reflected the operation of this model, both the Phillips and Fogel/Engerman interpretations appear to be at least partially correct regarding the general treatment of slave workers, but their explanations of that behavior are wholly inadequate.

Industrial employers of slave labor followed a general policy of compromise toward bondsmen for reasons which had little to do with humanitarian sentiments. Bondsmen were already "troublesome property," and when further disgruntled, they might become even more inefficient and unproductive. This consideration, in turn, created a whole new round of discipline problems for industrialists, problems that were complicated by the fact that employers could demand the services of hired slaves for only a limited time. If hired hands were constantly unproductive, employers might lose substantial sums of money. Moreover, owners worried about the treatment of their hired hands, for slaves who felt abused were much more likely to run away and damaged workers declined in value. Black bondsmen were well aware of their economic value and used it to good advantage. In a reported conversation with a white employer of bonded labor, Frederick Law Olmsted summed up this subtle form of slave power:

The Slave, if he is indisposed to work, and especially if he is not treated well, or does not like the master who has hired him, will sham sickness—even make himself sick or lame—that he need not work. But a more serious loss frequently arises, when the slave, thinking he is worked too hard, or being angered by punishment or unkind treatment, "getting the sulks," takes to "the swamp," and comes back when he has a mind to. Often this will not be till the year is up for which he is engaged, when he will return to his owner, who, glad to find his property safe, and that it has not died in the swamp, or gone to Canada, forgets to punish him, and immediately sends him for another year to a new master.[3]

Industrialists were acutely aware that slaves could not be forced to labor beyond certain limits. For example, David Ross had to abandon the richest vein of iron ore at Oxford Iron Works when his slaves refused to go back into the pit after three black miners were killed in a rockfall.[4]

Although employers could not rely strictly on physical force, a range of negative incentives played an integral role in the discipline and motivation of slave workers. Verbal chastisement provided the most common, and mildest, form of coercion. While slave hands went about their daily jobs, white and black supervisors reprimanded them for laziness or careless workmanship. In 1812, David Ross of Oxford Iron Works informed his white managers: "Tis an essential part of duty never to withhold censure from bad workmanship," and "there ought to be no indulgence on this point (for) 'tis injurious to the workmen and disgraceful to the business."[5] Another form of coercion involved transfer of a troublesome slave to a more difficult task. For example, in 1813, Ross censured one of his slave weavers by sending her to the mine banks, one of the most arduous jobs at the works: "Susan . . . who has for Sometime promised to improve took retrograde course & fell off I sent her to the mines by way of an agreeable change & improvement—I understand she has returned and that the digging of iron ore & raking it, has greatly enlightened her weaving talents."[6]

Whipping was probably the harshest common form of physical punishment administered to slaves. Whether by negligence or sabotage, three of Ross's boatmen at Oxford Iron Works lost a valuable cargo of slave clothing in 1813. "I must confess I never before experienced such infidelity even in the worst of our Black Servants as you . . . have represented to me of Peter, Aaron, and Lewis," Ross complained to his clerk. "I presume Peter will not make his appearance any more at Oxford," but, Ross ordered his clerk, "if he does you must inflict the law upon him—39 lashes on his bare back." Ross's white manager was to take "some of the respectable" blacks and "seize upon Aaron & Lewis, carry them with ropes round their necks to the boat landing where the load was lost & there have them Stript naked & 39 stripes inflicted well placed on the bare backs of each of those Scoundrels.'' Ross warned his clerk to proceed swiftly, but cautiously, for ''if they get notice of your intention they will abscond & merit double punishment.'' The outraged ironmaster added that ''you are to give some of my trusty servants half a dollar for whipping each of those rascals provided they do their duty.''[7] In September 1829, Sam, a slave hand at Paramount Furnace, got into an argument with another slave over a card game that ended in a brawl. As punishment he was whipped and ''laid up'' the following day.[8] In another incident, Bryce was struck so hard on the arm by one of the whites at Paramount Furnace that he was unable to work for a week.[9] One slaveowner who hired a hand to Shanks, Anderson and Anderson at Glenwood Furnace complained in 1849 that ''my boy Edmond'' ran away from the ironworks because ''your overseer is so cruel that he could not stand him.''[10] The manager of the works replied that he had ''never Struck him (Edmond) one lick on account of his work.'' The furnace manager ''gave him a good dressing,'' however, for causing ''a continual uproar and fighting with other negroes'' at a neighborhood plantation.[11] In February 1858, two slaves were whipped at Glenwood Furnace because they had made a dagger. But the manager was hopeful that the number of whippings could be cut down: ''If the managers do their duty they certainly ought hereafter to get along with very little whipping.''[12]

Slaves were reluctant to return to ironworks where they were treated harshly. For example, as mentioned earlier, four slaves and Elick, their leader, refused to go back to Gibraltar Forge in 1856. After fuming about Elick, the ironmaster, without realizing it, probably touched upon the reason for this reluctance when he noted that ''of all those five negroes he [Elick] was the only one that escaped the lash & frequently received favors that I would have denied the others. Now he not only turns from me but tries to lead them away likewise.''[13] At the Tredegar Iron Works, however, only seven bondsmen were whipped between 1843 and 1865, probably because Joseph Anderson accepted only slaves who wanted to work at Tredegar.[14]

Coal mine operators whipped refractory slaves as well. One of Harry Heth's hands whom the collier had hired to a neighboring miner received a whipping in 1807 for shirking his work. When Heth remonstrated against this kind of treatment of his bondsmen, the employer responded that not only did the hand deserve his punishment, but also he had run away with two other slaves who were not but ''ought to have been whiped [sic].''[15] Another slave ran away from Black Heath Pits in 1812 because he did not want to work in the mines. The hand's owner wrote to the employer that ''if Jeffery should come back I beg you will have one hundred lashes given for less than that number does him no good. I will endeavour to find him and make an example of him.''[16] And in 1815 the troublesome Ben was finally subdued and administered his punishment at Black Heath. News of the fracas reached his owner who wrote to the mine operator that "Simon yesterday told me Ben was with you & was well flogged" and otherwise "much beaten."[17] While some owners intervened on their slaves' behalf when punishment was delivered, other owners actually hired their slaves to Black Heath in order to have them disciplined. Consequently, in 1804 one owner hired several waggoners to Harry Heth and was "extreemly obliged" to Heth "for the attention already paid to some" of his slaves, "and will thank you in future to take Notice of them, and if you think they conduct themselves Imperfectly please to request your overseer to give them such correction as you may think they deserve."[18] Nine years later, another master hired a hand to Heth whom the owner considered "a very valuable Servant" but in need of "proper management." "If you will take him you will confer a particular favor on me by being very Strict with him as by that means he may loose [*sic*] Some bad habits to which he is addicted— gambling &c.—You may take him for one two or three years for what you think his value."[19]

Discipline at Black Heath was often harsh. One slave workman caught stealing in December 1815 received a trial and was sentenced "to be burnt in the hand" and given "39 lashes" upon his back.[20] In 1819, one of Heth's Scotch foremen became overly zealous in the administration of discipline and killed a slave miner. In a half-literate letter from his jail cell, the miner pleaded for Heth's compassion:

> Sir I write you with my hart full of greefe in consequence of this unfortunate accident and I thank God that I had not the smallest intention to hurt the Boy that I am now in this dredful place for can any Man think for a moment that I had the smallest interest in punishin this boy or any other one. no far from it, and that supreme bene that has all Mens harts in his hands knows it & came to Chesterfield when the accident happened. . . . ? late the same of you as I all ways thought that you were my friend and I can vow to god that I have don every thing as one Man for the good of your company and it will appear to you by that I am the best collier in this country at preasant. all who write my self the Shaft & that I had of at Deep Run was Right & this last one is wrong which I could explane to you if you will belive a nufe & call and see poor unfortunate me and mine in a strange land—my Dear and all moas hart broken wife.[21]

Nothing is known of the foreman's fate, or if his employer posted bail, but certainly his fate was more secure than that of slaves who fell under the management of such a man.

Another negative incentive used by employers was to threaten to sell a slave south for recalcitrant behavior. David Ross complained angrily about his watermen, "the most unfaithful people attached to the estate," who took a boat down the James River to Richmond half-loaded and double-manned and it took them twenty days instead of the necessary five days. "Let them know I am acquainted with their rascally behavior—I shall be pleased to sell them both to the Carolina Hogg drivers—Such scoundrels are not fit companions for honest servants," Ross fumed.[22] One of the most refractory hands with whom Harry Heth ever had to deal caused such an uproar at the mines that it was finally "reduced to a certainty," an agent wrote to Heth in September 1815, that "Ben is to be Sold & as you once told me" for his rebellious behavior.[23]

Ironmasters frequently used the whip or the threat of physical punishment to discipline slave workers. Most iron men, however, clearly recognized that such means might stifle motivation and, indeed, might very well reduce labor efficiency, discipline, and iron production. Accordingly, ironmasters relied on a range of positive incentives to maintain a high level of work performance for slave hands. One such positive incentive used at ironworks throughout the slave era provided slave hands with free time on holidays, especially the week or ten days traditionally granted to slaves at Christmas. No doubt, Frederick Douglass's observation was correct when the black abolitionist wrote that holidays kept bondsmen "occupied with prospective pleasure within the limits of slavery. . . . These holidays were also used as conductors or safety-valves to carry off the explosive elements inseparable from the human mind when reduced to the condition of slavery."[24] Reuben left his employment at Black Heath Pits in 1815 and hid for several days before reappearing at his owner's house one morning. The owner's agent wrote to Heth that the hand would "be up in a few days" and that "if no other punishment" is administered, "his master wishes his Hollidays taken from him."[25] Thomas Jefferson spurned the use of the whip to motivate hands working in his nail factory. In January 1801, he wrote to Thomas Mann Randolph, "to ask the favor of you to speak to Lilly as to the treatment of the nailers. It would destroy their value in my estimation to degrade them in their own eyes by the whip." Jefferson believed that the lash "therefore must not be resorted to but in extremities. as they will be again under my government, I would chuse they should retain the stimulus of character."[26]

Another kind of reward provided slave hands with rations of rum and whiskey, or extra provisions of food and clothing. While these extras comprised a small part of the incentive system, slave hands seeking to make their lives a little more comfortable prized them. Not only were extra rations or provisions used as rewards for behavior that industrialists considered productive, but also, when curtailed, they constituted punishment for unproductive labor. Accordingly, any threat to withdraw them often served to spur favorable behavior and productivity.

Most ironmasters distributed, both by rationing and sale, large quantities of rum and whiskey. With characteristic wit, William Byrd of Westover noted in his 1732 journal that ironworkers required a great deal of "strong drink to recruit their spirits."[27] The rum ration was a very important element in the incentive system employed during the colonial era. The account book of John Tayloe for Neabsco Furnace for 1740 and 1741 contains many references to rum that was given to slave hands.[28] All ironworks stores for which records survive indicate that they regularly stocked alcoholic beverages. For example, the Dorseys' store at Elk Ridge Furnace purchased cider, whiskey, and rum by the hundreds of gallons each year during the 1750s and 1760s. In addition, alcohol was stocked as part of an iron company's routine provisions. The Bush River Iron Works, for example, on October 18, 1763, ordered six barrels of rum, each containing 31¼ gallons.[29] At Elk Ridge Furnace, Bush Town Iron Works, and many other furnaces and forges, slaves not only received alcohol as part of their provisions but also sometimes consumed a large part of their overwork pay in alcoholic beverages.[30] All laborers at ironworks appreciated their liquor, and to have it taken away was punishment indeed. Some owners of hired hands were leery of the practice of providing liquor to blacks. One owner wrote to William Weaver to "request of you not to leting [*sic*] negroes have much spirits. . .for there are some of them who are very fond of it, and would no doubt before the end of the year be of but little service to yourself, and render them a great deal less valuable to their owners."[31] Both owners and hirers apparently ignored the fact that giving liquor to slaves was illegal.

Ironmasters frequently manipulated their food and clothing provisions as well as their liquor rations in order to control and motivate slaves. In 1783, the Swedish scientist Samuel Hermelin recorded that the yearly allowance for food and clothing provided to each slave in the region varied according to their skills. For food, skilled slave forgemen received twenty bushels of corn meal and three hundred pounds of pork. They received no more in the way of food except what they could grow in the small garden patches allotted to slaves. For clothing, skilled slaves were rationed seven yards of "coarse cloth," one hat, four pairs of shoes, twelve yards of "Osnabrygg" for shirts, and one summer suit. Unskilled hands at ironworks did not fare so well in the necessities of life. Hermelin observed that "for ordinary negroe laborers at the works," thirteen bushels of corn meal, 225 pounds of pork, seven yards of osnaburg, one or two pairs of boots, and a single pair of socks had to suffice. In terms of costs, the skilled slaves' provisions amounted to twice the £1 to £10 for the unskilled workers' provisions.[32]

Thomas Jefferson also manipulated the food and clothing provisions of the approximately twenty slaves who worked at the nailery he operated at

Monticello between 1794 and 1823. When the French nobleman La Rochefoucauld visited Jefferson in the late 1790s, he noted that Jefferson's nailery was run by blacks and "yields already a considerable profit," and that "he animates them [the slaves] by rewards and distinctions."[33] Isaac Jefferson, a slave blacksmith at the shop, noted in his memoirs that Jefferson "gave the boys in the nail factory a pound of meat a week, a dozen herrings, a quart of molasses & a peck of meal. Give them that wukked the best a suit of red or blue: encouraged them mightily."[34]

Similarly, at Ross's Oxford Iron Works, "the male laborers are allowed a double Quantity of Bread and an equal quantity of meat as the Common rations allowed to a Soldier or a Sailor," and the women were provisioned "in due proportion" to the work they performed.[35] Again in 1813, Ross told his managers that "you may be assured that nothing will be lost by feeding the people well."[36] Ross also attempted to motivate, or discipline, his slave workers by manipulating the clothing issue:

> I direct the distribution as followeth—I shall begin with infants—each infant is allowed by me 1½ yds white Flannel, the same may be given to pregnant women and where the infants are advanced some months give them 2 yds—I direct to all females, a jacket of cotton with long sleeves, to shelter their arms from cold & frost—The Waggoners are to have coats, vests and pantaloons of cotton—all of the Colliers & Miners the same—The blue cloth is of good quality and I allot it to the furnace people first & potters, Smiths next & forgemen next—a coat of blue cloth & waistcoat of scarlet flannel with sleeves—Edmund (a potter) to be particularly attended to—give him pantalloons also of blue cloth—as to the distribution of the Blankets, the first object is to supply women with young children and next such cases as you may think proper. . . . So far as I am able to judge the Watermen are the most unfaithful people attached to the estate—you'll give them nothing.[37]

One of the most important incentives in the discipline-by-reward system employed by ironmasters was monetary remuneration for performance beyond the required task or quota. This incentive could take a variety of forms. One technique was the "bonus" which was designed to encourage slave furnacemen and forgemen to produce more than their quota. A related kind of incentive was the "production allowance" or "wage" which was geared to the quantity of iron produced. Perhaps more than any other motivational device, the production allowance recognized that skilled slave ironworkers were in a position to impair the ironmaster's economic interests if they became sufficiently disgruntled. Thus, a slave forgeman at the Principio works received a wage of one shilling per ton of bar iron. Although the white forgeman's pay was twenty shillings per ton,[38] he had to pay out most of his earnings for food and shelter. Considering that the slave forgeman did not have to meet these same expenses, he could earn what was a significant amount of money for *any* man of that era, let alone a slave. Another slave hand hired to work at John Blair's foundry in Grayson County, Virginia, received a bonus of four shillings in 1797, probably while working as an iron founder.[39] Likewise, at William Weaver's Etna Furnace, Joshua Crews received an allowance of $60 per year, apparently as a founder who supervised the furnacemen under him.[40]

Normally confined to a few skilled black hands, the wage did not have as wide an impact on the slave work force as some other incentive devices. Perhaps the most important monetary measure for stimulating slave hands was the payment of cash, or credits at the company store, to slaves skilled and unskilled who worked extra hours beyond those normally required of them. This was the "overwork" system, the key motivational device employed at ironworks throughout the slave era.

The overwork system attempted to make the industrial slave a disciplined and productive worker by merging his physical and economic interests with those of his employer. In turn, this system would reduce the need for physical coercion, which might do more harm than good to the ironmaster's production goals. Although the slaves who responded positively to the overwork system accepted the ironmaster's wishes, nonetheless they themselves decided whether or not to take advantage of the incentive offered. In that sense, they exercised at least some measure of discretion. If slaves decided to spend their extra time at work rather than leisure, the sums they earned were their own to do with as they pleased and provided them with an even greater degree of choice.[41] When an ironmaster utilized this system extensively, as most did, slaves could acquire a considerable measure of control over the nature of their bondage—always within the limits of the institution, of course.

The dearth of surviving business papers for pre-Civil War coal companies prevents any detailed analysis of the manner and extent to which overwork was employed as a labor incentive. Although the Heth papers are relatively complete between 1800 and 1820, the financial accounts are not in good order. Nevertheless, colliers seem to have followed the general pattern of reliance on overwork to motivate the slave hands. Thus, in December 1800, Harry Heth paid his hands £29 5s. 8d. for overwork. Billy received £1 11s. for two months' extra work, while fifteen other hands received a nominal 6s. each. The rest was distributed for undisclosed work.[42] It is not known how Heth distributed the money, but this ledger entry represents the earliest known evidence of overwork being paid at a slave-operated coal mine. In December 1811, Heth's overseer at Black Heath wrote that "there is [sic] about 5 hundred bushels of coal raised by the hands. . . . There is [sic] ten hands that has a claime in it.'' The overseer listed the hands, nine of whom were hired and one of whom belonged to Heth, and rated the overwork pay due each hand at five cents per bushel. The total overwork received was $25.00 to be split among the hands at $2.50 each.[43] In the company receipt filed for 1831, John Heth recorded considerable amounts of cash distributed among the hands. Among the fifty-six slave hands hired at Black Heath that year, the operator recorded payment of $59.17 "cash to hands at sundry times" in one entry and $67.44 in another.[44]

By the 1830s, the practice was utilized extensively at the mines in the Richmond field. Edmund Ruffin, editor of the *Farmers' Register,* visited Graham's Coal Pits in 1837 and observed that

> the laborers are permitted to do extra work for their own gain, and that they do earn money in that manner. I even saw afterwards where they had opened two (not very deep,) shafts to the coal, for their own private working—though their proceedings had been stopped, and certainly should not have been permitted to be commenced, on so distinct and independent a footing.[45]

The Midlothian Company also used cash payments to entice slaves into extra work. Although no company records have survived to provide detailed evidence about how well the system worked, according to a January 1846 advertisement for hirelings, "There is no work in which slaves . . . have an equal chance of making money for themselves."[46] That some hands did earn significant sums of money at extra work was corroborated six months later by a visitor to the Midlothian mines. Writing about his sojourn into those pits, John Smith informed the readers of the *Richmond Whig and Public Advertiser* that "many of the slaves lay up $50 per annum for work done out of the regular hours."[47] Similarly, in 1849 the James River Coal Pits paid its hands $298 for extra work between January 30 and August 1 of that year. And, in December 1864, before closing down for Christmas, seventy pit hands at the Dover mines received a total of $595 for overwork, along with extra issues of pants, shirts, socks, shoes, coats, and blankets which amounted to $1,086 for the year. Sixteen farm hands connected with the mines earned $314 in cash and extra clothing. Including cash and extra clothing, Dover Pits expended a total of $1,400 in overwork benefits to eighty-six hands in 1864.[48]

Any thorough analysis of the overwork system must focus on the iron industry for which the surviving correspondence and company records for both the eighteenth and nineteenth centuries are much more substantial. Caleb Dorsey's Elk Ridge Furnace in Maryland provides an excellent illustration of the early application of discipline-by-reward on a wide scale.

Any slave so motivated to earn extra money by chopping wood at two shillings per cord could earn as much overwork pay as he was physically capable of at Elk Ridge. Many slaves took advantage of the system at Elk Ridge, although generally the sums earned were small because life was hard enough without excessive additional exertion.[49] Nonetheless, some did earn substantial sums of money. In June 1764, "Thomas Dorsey's Joe" earned £7 12s. for cutting seventy-six cords, and "Selman's Jack" earned £3 1s. for cutting thirty and a half cords of wood.[50] Slaves often accumulated overwork pay for making charcoal and carting it to storage bins near the furnace. Since most iron plantations tried to grow much of their own food, slaves also earned overwork pay by doing farmwork or by selling vegetables which they grew on their own plots.[51]

At Elk Ridge Furnace, as at most ironworks, skilled slaves were best able to earn extra pay. "Boy Jack," a founder at Elk Ridge, earned substantial amounts of money throughout the 1760s and 1770s for practicing his craft beyond his regular work assignments. For example, on July 9, 1770, he earned £4 12s. 9d. on his own time for making castings at the furnace.[52] Although skilled slaves had the greatest opportunity for taking advantage of the overwork system, any slave could work overtime at Elk Ridge and earn the same rate of pay as a white man who performed the identical task. In October 1766, Dorsey compiled a "List of Debts due from the Company." Among the 316 separate entries, 45 were for money owed to the slave hands for extra work.[53]

The same general emphasis was placed on overwork at most other ironworks, and large numbers of slave hands took advantage of the incentive to acquire the extra cash or provisions that made life a little less wearisome. At Patuxent Iron Works, not far from Elk Ridge, both skilled and unskilled workers earned substantial sums for overwork (Table 7). The company's account book contains many entries such as the "£1-4-3 For the Labour of sundry Negroes in their own time" recorded in July 1767.[54] Among these laborers were "Negro Abram" who earned £1 "For 10 days Labour. . . in his own time" and "Negro Scipio" who earned 12s. for working overtime. Similarly, in September 1780 "Negro Dick," a laborer, performed enough extra labor to receive £52 10s. in Continental currency. The following month two black laborers, "Negro Nacy" and "Negro Yarrow," were paid £65 5s. and £9, respectively. Although paid in inflated Continental currency, Yarrow at least received the differential in value between that currency and specie, for on December 4, 1781, he acquired £20 15 s. "For making Continental Money equal with Specie."[55] Apparently, these slave hands were engaged in the wide variety of unskilled labor always needed at ironworks, such as wood chopping and carting ore and charcoal. But slave hands at Patuxent also worked extra time at skilled jobs for overwork pay. In July 1767, the ironworks paid 10 s. "For the Labour of

Sam & Sampson Powell in making [7 tons of] . . . Bloom Iron'' in February 1768, ''Olde Negroe Forge Nedd'' earned 16s. 3d., and ''Negro Nedd'' was paid 14s. 3d. ''for making 9½ [tons of] Bar Iron''; in March 1779,£2 12s. 6d. was ''paid Negroes for making . . . Blooms''; and the following month, ''negro Harry'' earned 15s. ''for making 5 blooms.'' On April 23, 1779, the Patuxent Company extended £5 to ''Negro Sam for Intelligence,'' presumably concerning the maneuvers of British troops.[56]

Table 7

OVERWORK PAYMENTS TO SLAVE HANDS AT
PATUXENT IRONWORKS MADE DECEMBER 24, 1780

Slave	Occupation	Earnings in Continental Currency (£)
Reardin	?	19 10s.
Will Tuttle	?	43 6d.
Absolam	forgeman	39
Ned	forgeman	33 12s. 6d.
Harry	forgeman & founder	12
Yarrow	laborer	14 15s.
Dick	laborer	40 10s.
Cupid	founder & filler	46 10s.
Nacy	laborer	6
Primus	blacksmith	?

Source: Journal A & B, 1767–1794, Patuxent Iron Works, Maryland Hall of Records.

All too often, the entries in the account books of early ironworks did not explain anything about the slaves, their occupations, whether they were owned or hired, or even how they earned their overwork pay. Unfortunately, the entries normally referred only to the name of the slave and to how much he or she received. For example, the account books for Cumberland Forge of Maryland contain numerous entries for overwork payments but lack detailed indications of what slaves did to earn them. Still, extant descriptive entries support the conclusion that these hands did similar work carried on by slaves at other works. In 1802, ''Negro Jack Gilbert'' received his pay ''for picking baskets of coal,'' while ''Negro Bill Rigbie'' earned his £1 ''for 5 days work. . . at Fences & garden posts.'' Most of the hands appear to have earned their overwork for chopping wood for the charcoal makers, such as ''Negro Jacob Wallace'' who received £9 13s. 6d. in March 1802 for chopping sixty-four and a half cords of wood.[57] ''Negro

Tom," a carpenter, earned £5 10s. during the three months between July 6, 1796, and September 17, 1796.[58]

Although the Ridwell Furnace account book does not describe the kinds of labor performed for overwork, it is clear that Ridwell followed the general practice when it "Paid Daniel (Green's Negro) for Extra Labor— £1-18-3."[59] At nearby Pine Forge, however, blacks were paid for performing the complete variety of jobs connected with an ironworks. "Negro Reuben picked many tubs of coal," and several of the hands earned money chopping wood, while others received overwork pay for reaping, coaling, and working at the furnace. "Negro Reuben" acquired more extra pay than any other hand at the furnace. Reuben was not only a strong worker, but he was also completely trustworthy, for in 1812 he delivered "a load of Bar Iron" and returned to the forge with the £54 3s. 9d. payment for the load.[60]

From the 1780s, when Charles Ridgely's Northampton Furnace was converted from indentured and convict labor to a black force, slaves frequently received significant sums of overwork pay. Once again, most of the account book entries are nondescriptive, such as one for April 18, 1811: "Negro Dan—to cash—$5.63."[61] Although most hands received cash, some entries were for goods, such as that for December 27, 1782: "To 2 Shirts to Negro Frazier— £1-2-0."[62] The example in Table 8, which is taken from a Northampton ledger book, was not unusual. In addition to wood chopping, slaves at Northampton seemed to earn overwork in the same variety of ways that they did at other ironworks. "Ester's Jem Setting Wood over task" warranted $41.25; three hands sold to the company store three bushels of potatoes at $0.50 each; while on December 31, 1816, "Negro Vachel" received $10.00 overwork for "raising Stone For Furnace. . .on his own time."[63]

Table 8

ACCOUNT "CORDWOOD," NORTHAMPTON FURNACE, 1811

November 20, 1811		
to Zach. Hencock for cutting 34 cords		15.87
to Negro Tony with Hirelings	3.50	
to Negro Tony with Task Wood	4.20	7.70
to Negro Dan with Hirelings		7.63
to Negro Anthony Ent.ᵈ with Task Wood		5.36
to Negro Aaron Ent.ᵈ with ditto		87½
		$37.43½
to Negro Tony Provisions at Sundry		
Times acct. cutting wood		5.44

Source: Ledger B–3, 1810–1815, Box 3, Ridgely Account Books, Maryland Historical Society.

Most individual accounts for extra work involved relatively modest sums of money, usually about $10 or less annually. Yet, at a time when white workmen received wages of not much more than $1 per day, these small overwork payments were more significant than they might otherwise appear. Spotty bookkeeping practices and the incomplete nature of surviving records make it difficult to accurately determine how much individual hands earned over an extended period. Table 9 indicates to some extent the amount of goods and money received by slave hands at one furnace.

The overwork incentive could be a double-edged sword. Those motivated by the device performed extra work and got their rewards. Conversely, when slaves produced less than their quotas, the value of their unfinished labor sometimes was deducted from the amount of the credit they had acquired. When this deduction occurred, overwork acted as a disciplinary tool. For example, in 1858 two hired wood choppers at Etna Furnace fell short of their quotas. Accordingly, their accumulated credits were debited at the rate of forty cents per cord. Although several other slave hands at Weaver's ironworks had similar deductions made against their accounts, these cases occurred infrequently and they could easily regain the sums by extra work.[64]

By the late antebellum period, the iron industry had employed overwork as a motivational device for over a century. Ample time had elapsed to test the outer limits of the system and to achieve that critical balance between positive and negative motivation. The records show that few slaves failed to meet their required tasks or quotas. After all, overwork limits set too high would have provided no incentive at all. Rather, the quotas that were set permitted a large number of slave hands to meet their normal tasks and thereafter perform enough overwork to accumulate some quantity of cash or credit. A few examples will illustrate how slaves earned significant amounts by overwork. At Union Forge in 1825, Aaron, a forgeman, drew over 171 tons of bar iron and earned $198.32, and Solomon, another slave forgeman at the ironworks, was paid $59.30 for drawing iron.[65] At Graham's Iron Works, Trial once earned $88.53 for moulding 19,831 pounds of casting.[66] Those who earned large sums of money were not always skilled hands. At F. T. Anderson's Glenwood Furnace, David Henry cut 248-½ cords over his quota and made 36 charcoal measuring baskets during his spare time on Sundays. This slave's overwork earnings for 1847 and 1848 totaled $127.66.[67] Henry Towles, a skilled black at Buffalo Forge, earned $93.53 for extra work in 1856.[68] In April or May 1850, Page, a hired slave hand at Union Forge, ran away. His owner wrote to Jacob Lantz, the ironmaster, that he had no doubt that Page would "try to get to a Free State." He concluded, however, by requesting that "if Page left any Money in your Care or with any one you will please retain it and inform me by the 1st mail."[69]

Table 9

OVERWORK PAYMENTS AT CLOVERDALE FURNACE,
DECEMBER 1854

Slave Worker	Cash	Total
Harrison Queens	10.00	23.75
Harrison Baisley	10.50	10.61
Harry Tolls	4.55	5.03
Washington Wright	4.00	5.03
John Gatewood	2.10	16.75
George Mosley	6.00	5.53
Jackson	3.56	8.44
Willis	5.00	8.21
Tom Chuck	6.52	5.48
Washington	9.46	4.54
Joshua	2.42	4.95
Anthony	9.12	4.43
Toby Gatewood	9.21	8.90
Frank Buckner	14.00	7.41
Tom Anderson	6.00	4.53
Miner Colman	4.25	3.00
Ambrose	2.40	2.60
Bob Carter	1.47	2.28
Absolem	1.28	6.28
Sam Jusing (?)	2.48	2.27
Dick Blacksmith	3.00	1.80
Edmund Gray	9.47	1.87
Horace Jusing (?)	2.08	4.42
Warner	1.00	3.80
Billy Wilson	4.46	7.54
Ed Wright	2.50	3.75
Billy wood leg	3.81	2.18
Carter	3.37	1.63
Jesse	5.00	23.37
Dabny	5.00	11.00
TOTAL	$142.94	$193.18

Source: Unsigned Memo dated December 1854, F. T. Anderson Papers, Duke University.

The overwork account of another black at Union Forge, Absalom Rinker, is impressive both for the amount of cash he earned at overwork and for the variety of labor he performed during the year 1853. From April 30 to the end of May, Absalom earned $26.65 hauling iron, making new collars for the hounds, and repairing a wagon. In September, he was paid $6.62 for making butter; on November 4, he earned $10.00 for hauling iron; four days later he received $5.88 for dressing 107 pounds of beef; and on November 10, he received $1.50 "for ironing 2 shingle trees." Absalom was also farming during the year, for on November 16 he earned $2.50 "for hauling corn," and at the end of the month, he was paid $120.00 for raising "4 Head of Beef Cattle." By the end of 1853, he earned another $45.00 for hauling coal. His total earnings during the year, although the cattle raising required a longer period of time, reached the considerable amount of $217.16.[70]

Much of the overwork money Absalom earned probably went for goods at the company store. No doubt, however, this industrious and talented slave saved part of his hard-earned money in the same way as Sam Williams, a skilled forgeman at Weaver's Buffalo Forge. Like most slave artisans permanently attached to an ironworks, Williams had a plot of ground that he could use for growing crops and raising livestock. In addition, he earned $5 per ton of iron produced.[71] Aside from the various purchases of food and clothing Sam made at the store, by 1855 he had a savings account at a nearby Lexington bank. John Rex, a white worker at the forge, wrote to J. D. Davidson, a lawyer and bank trustee in Lexington:

> I wish to ask you one question whether Sam Williams can draw his money from the Savings Bank or if he cannot, As Sam and Henry Nash [a free black who lived in the vicinity] has got a bet his Watch against the said Nash watch. It is my opinion that he can draw his money if he gives the Directors of the Bank 10 days notice. After he receives the money he wishes to show it to Henry Nash, and then he will return the said money back to the Bank again. As I was witness to the said bargain.[72]

The lot of the industrial slaves was not easy, and only a few had enough money to open savings accounts at nearby banks. Nevertheless, the motivational techniques, plus the employer's need for cooperation from slaves and owners, clearly went a long way toward mitigating at least the overt brutality inherent in the institution of human bondage. This is evident in the large number of slaves who used incentives to maintain some manner of private life and individuality for themselves and their families.

On the other hand, as Fogel and Engerman have pointed out, incentives constituted "a powerful instrument of economic and social control."[73] But the numerous slaves who earned extra cash and also ran away calls into question their notion that slaves were infused with a "Protestant work ethic" and became coparticipants in a rational economic order. Moreover,

industrial employers of bonded labor, who more closely resembled a
bourgeoisie than did planters, were capable of fits of rage against intractable or inefficient slaves. At times, these temper tantrums resulted in violent
recriminations which were decidedly unlike the rational behavior of
"homo economicus."

All the accommodative measures and motivational incentives notwithstanding, many slave ironworkers never adjusted psychologically to
permanent bondage. Like their counterparts in agriculture, slaves on iron
plantations often repudiated the master's control in subtle actions against
the system, such as abuse of draft animals, theft, arson, industrial sabotage, self-inflicted damage, slowdowns, or careless work habits.[74] Slaves
carefully masked their real personality traits from whites by adopting
"sham" characteristics such as "bowing and scraping" and by feigning
docility and ignorance.[75] According to ex-slave Lucy Ann Delaney, slaves
lived behind an "impenetrable mask . . . how much joy, or sorrow, or
misery and anguish have they hidden from their tormentors."[76] The hostility and anger suppressed behind the mask would sometimes surface. Some
slaves tried to drown their hostilities and frustration with liquor. The
considerable quantities always available at ironworks to both whites and
blacks made this an easy outlet, especially around Christmas time when the
hands owned by the company took their traditional two weeks "vacation"
and the hired hands had gone home. On December 24, 1764, for example,
fourteen blacks at Elk Ridge Furnace purchased ten and three-quarters
quarts of rum.[77] Sometimes slaves were drunk on the job, such as Daniel
Forrer at Pine Forge who was penalized $16.66 "for being in a State of
intoxication" in consequence of which the ironmaster "sustained damages" to his property.[78] In 1856, the manager of Etna Furnace recorded
that on June 20 "Moses stole corn," then apparently got drunk and went
into hiding. On June 23, when Moses was next seen, he was "still on a
Tight." Two days later, the manager underscored the notation that Moses
must be *"whipped this Day—if we Catch him."* Whether or not he was
apprehended is unclear, but on June 29, Moses was "Still off on a Tight."[79]

If the anger within the slave was not drowned by liquor, it might be
projected toward his fellows in bondage. In April 1815, for example, Harry
Heth received a message informing him that "the Negroe hired of Denny
was seen in Richmond yesterday evening, having rec'd a severe blow on
the head which was near terminating his existance [*sic*] in a fracus he had
with some other Negroe."[80] Another case in which the anger was directed
against fellow slaves occurred at Etna Furnace ore banks in October 1860:

> Quite a serious affrey took place at the Ore Bank yesterday.
> Bill Carmaskey struck John Sims in the head with a Wheel
> Barrow handle. They sent John down on the cars but he got
> so sick that he had to get off & Spott took him to G. Olphius

where he is now lying & I suppose I will have to send a
wagoner after him. I have heard all that I know about it from
the negroes. I will go up to see John R. & if it is as they say he
desearves [*sic*] a good thrashing. Which I will give him. He is
a self will stuberon [*sic*] the Nigger & nothing but the lash or
feer [*sic*] of being sold has kep [*sic*] him straight during the
years. If John is as bad as Spott say's I do not know but what
the authorities would consider it their duty to arrest him.[81]

Slaves often resorted to theft in order to gain something from a regime
designed to deny them the benefit of their own labor. Harry Heth hired one
hand whose master requested that the collier "keep the money in your
hands till I come after it in Richmond." The owner could not trust the slave,
for "I hired the same fellow in Richmond last fall and when his time was out
the man paid him the money to bring to me and I lost it." The owner knew
that the slave had lied when he claimed to have "lost my money," but there
was nothing to be done but whip the man, even though "that never was
known to return lost goods."[82] As an experienced master, he no doubt
realized that slaves generally regarded anything that they might steal from
their owners as a prize of war. A more blatant case occurred in 1801 and
involved one of Harry Heth's trusted coal boat-hands. In October 1801,
Heth's sales agent in Washington, D. C., wrote to the collier about the
boatman:

> Several circumstances have prevented me from receiving
> payment for the coal delivered. . . . Lawson, with the Coal
> for the President has just arrived—it is a charming load
> indeed. *Green sold his load in Alexandria and has run off.*
> You must keep a good look out for him as I expect he has
> gone back to your River. I hope you may catch, & punish the
> Rascal as he deserves—for his conduct has been a great
> disappointment to me & to others.[83]

In 1847, John Flournoy leased some coal property for himself and his silent
partner Christopher Q. Tompkins. The lease contained the stipulation that
"every precaution" had to be taken by "Flournoy or his agents" in order
"to prevent his hands from committing deprecations [*sic*] on the property" of the owner, Edward Scott, Sr.[84] And in 1857, when the Old Dominion
and Kanawha Coal Company released the hired hands, between the pits
and their homes the hirelings "lost" the extra clothing distributed to them.
When the owners complained that the hands had not come back with the
usual annual clothing issue, the company insisted that *"Every hand, when
they* were discharged from *the Depot,* had been furnished 'with customary
clothing hat or cap and Blanket' and if they did not have them when they
reached their homes it was because they had been disposed of."[85]

When ironmasters attempted to deprive slaves of their traditional days off, such as Christmas and Sunday, slaves went to great lengths to defend their free time. In 1830, the managers of Etna Furnace reported: "We had thought [about] blowing through Christmas holy days and going on as long as possible." The managers found this impossible, however, "as our white hands are few and the most part of the blacks will be going and the few remaining not willing to be closely confined we have concluded to stop up for a short time during Christmas."[86] Similarly, when Anthony, a slave at Etna Furnace, was told to go to Buffalo Forge on a Sunday morning, he refused to do so. The furnace manager told Weaver that

> I waited till about 10 oclock [*sic*] and finding that he had not started I asked him the reason. He said it was Sunday and that he was not going till tomarrow [*sic*]—with some other impudence to me. I collared him and he resisted & struck me—I struck him on the head with a rock. You please will see about the matter. . . . He said that this was Sunday and his day and that he was not going [to] take it up in going to your place.[87]

The following incident illustrates the concealed, but potentially explosive, rage some blacks felt toward the master class. It also reveals the fear of black retaliation which whites harbored but seldom acknowledged. George Junkin, agent for Francis T. Anderson, wrote to the ironmaster in the spring of 1859 regarding Billy, one of Anderson's black hands. Billy apparently tried to use poison as a means of retribution against his white tormentors, but was thwarted in his attempt by another slave, Fanny, who informed on Billy. Junkin told Anderson that he would not confess, since the lawyer might save him from the death sentence, but "will permit him, if he chooses to tell his accomplices if he has any & especially if he proposes to reveal any secret as to the source of the poison." The only hope to save Billy was to have the trial moved to another town, for

> the public feeling is strong vs him & it may be difficult to get an impartial jury—it cant [*sic*] be done from among the town [probably Lexington] people. The impression prevails, that the perils of the times calls for a victim, & I think the disposition is strong to full justice & a little more to Billy.[88]

The story of one slave who was hired to work at Northampton Furnace in 1744 provides an excellent example of the limits to which a slave could be driven by bondage and at the same time render himself of no value to the ironmaster. "Abraham Patterns Man" came to work at the furnace on March 18, 1774. It was not long before he fell into a series of "sicke" spells, missing many days of work. Then on a day when he was supposed to be ill,

"Abraham Patterns Man Ranaway from the [mine] Bank." After eluding capture for several days, the hired slave was returned to the ironworks, whereupon he promptly "cut his Throat." He survived, and shortly thereafter "Abraham Patterns Man [was taken] home by his Master."[89] Aside from the fact that he either tried to commit suicide, or commited self-sabotage at least, Pattern's man only worked forty-eight days out of the more than three months that the ironmaster paid for his hire. Needless to say, had many slave ironworkers been as demoralized as "Abraham Patterns Man," few iron men could have continued to operated for as long as many did.

The ultimate, although apparently least common, mode of resistance among iron and coal slave workers was outright insurrection. Almost no evidence which directly ties any Chesapeake slave with an insurrection has survived, and only a few illusory hints even suggest that the possibility existed. One instance involved the Oxford Iron Works, when a confession was obtained from Gilbert, a slave presumably involved in Gabriel's Revolt in 1800. According to his confession, another slave, Sam Byrd, Jr., had informed Gilbert of the insurrection. A black mail carrier who traveled between Richmond and Charlottesville had told Byrd "that he had conveyed the intelligence respecting the Insurrection as far as Mr. Ross's Iron Works."[90] No evidence has survived which indicates that any of Ross's slaves participated in that revolt or any other. Nor do there appear to have been any specific cases involving ironworkers in the Chesapeake or other iron districts of the South, except the Cumberland iron region of Tennessee and Kentucky. In 1856, a year of rumored as well as genuine slave unrest, panic swept the Cumberland, fanned by an alleged conspiracy among slave ironworkers. The outburst of vigilante activity against the slaves at work at the furnaces and forges in order to crush the supposed plot resulted in the whipping, lynching, and shooting of hundreds of blacks. Many scholars have accepted contemporary white opinion that a true insurrection was indeed in the offing, but according to Charles B. Dew, the most recent student of that episode, the revolt was only rumor and seemed "to have existed only in the panic-stricken minds of white southerners in 1856."[91]

No evidence exists of either a planned or an actual insurrection among slave coal miners, although there were several scares. While the details remain nebulous, the operators must have been frightened of such a possibility in 1807, for in that year they attempted to establish a cooperative response in the case of the event and they agreed to "put a stop to it provided the other colliers would do the same." The correspondent who contacted Harry Heth, however, believed that, despite the rumors, the colliers would not "have any Insurrection."[92] Another oblique reference to a revolt in the area appears in a petition of 1820 which sought permission for an ex-slave to remain in Virginia. Moses had purchasedhis freedom in that year, and his former master's son, a Mr. Peers, supported the petition with the written observation that the former slave was hard working, self-supporting, and had "made communications. . .concerning insurrection." As Peers explained:

> In times when there were frequent alarms of insurrections of the Blacks, in the neighborhood, where there [sic] number was great being near large estates and extensive coal mines your Petitioner has more than once secretly made known to his Mistress the whispers of such Plots being agitated and concerning them he was always distressed and anxious to make discoveries.[93]

But "whispers" and "Plots" were a general characteristic of slave quarters, and few, if any, slave ironworkers or miners took the ultimate step toward group insurrection. Individually, many rejected the institution of slavery by flight.

An inestimable number of slaves attempted to escape from bondage. As Gerald Mullin has shown in his study *Flight and Rebellion: Slave Resistance in Eighteenth-Century Virginia,* among the occupational groups, slave ironworkers were one of the most highly prone to run away during this era. The reason does not appear to be ironmaster brutality so much as the fact that industrial slaves generally were better able to comprehend the white world because of their daily contact with it. As a result, they were more skillful in conducting the subterfuges required for manipulating whites to their own advantage—a consideration of prime importance if a slave were to run away and successfully deal with suspicious whites he encountered along the way.[94]

When Mr. Chiswell of Fredericksville Furnace told William Byrd that from 100 to 125 slaves were needed to operate a furnace, and "the more Virginians amongst them the better,"[95] he was implying that it was too difficult for American ironmasters to communicate with recently arrived Africans, who were then numerous in the region, and that their more communal traditions worked at odds with American individualism.

Colonial newspapers serving the Chesapeake area suggest the magnitude of the runaway problem faced by all slave masters, including those of iron plantations. The advertisements for runaways show that there were many runaways and that they were often quite accomplished in coping with the white slaveowners' world. The *Maryland Gazette*, for example, carried a number of advertisements such as one for "Negro Tom," who ran away from Elk Ridge Furnace in 1759 and spoke English and French.[96] "Negro Dick" ran away from Tayloe's iron ore bank and was considered "lusty" and "clever."[97] "Negro Peter" ran away from Bush River Furnace, and the public was warned to beware for "he will almost deceive anyone by his crafty lies."[98] At times, the overwork system may have had the opposite effect from what ironmasters anticipated. As the *Maryland Journal and Baltimore Advertiser* reported, when Dick ran away from Elk Ridge in 1781, he had "a plenty of money with him" and "may attempt to get to the enemy."[99] "A Negro Man named George" ran away from Patuxent Iron Works in 1787 and headed for Calvert County, "where it is probable he will endeavor to get harboured by the Negroes of the Neighborhood, or endeavor to pass for a free man, and try to get to Pennsylvania."[100] The *Virginia Gazette* also carried many advertisements for runaway slave ironworkers. "David and Aaron" escaped from the mines of Buckingham Furnace and were "lurking about" their old home.[101] One of John Tayloe's slaves named "Billie" ran away from the Neabsco works and was headed for South Carolina, his original home. Billie could be identified by the violin he played and had taken with him.[102] Billie was captured, but the following year he again ran away. This time Billie took "Scipio" with him.[103] "Cooper" ran away from Providence Forge and was thought to be heading toward "Colonel Grymes's Forge, where he once lived, and has a wife."[104] One slave who ran away had served John Tayloe of Neabsco Furnace since childhood and left for "parts unknown."[105] Some slaves apparently never gave up trying to escape. One black was "a notorious run-away," and although he had an iron collar about his neck for his troubles, he ran away again from the Marlboro Iron Works.[106] Caleb Dorsey of Elk Ridge Furnace charged to general expenses one shilling "for putting a collar on Joe."[107] Slave runaways could be expensive, especially when they had to be pursued or retrieved from jail. For example, in the single year 1777, Westham Foundry, which had a relatively small black force of about fifteen, expended £39 9s. 16½d. to retrieve fugitive slaves who fled the works.[108]

Runaway slave hands continued to present problems for nineteenth-century ironmasters. In 1805, Pine Forge paid £3 "for taking Glasgoe from Prison."[109] One ironmaster complained to his brother in 1806 that

> I came here last night to bring home Soloman who has been run away three weeks and was only taken 2 or 3 days ago, Such has been the indulgence given by myself and others to the Negroes for transgressions that they are grown insuffera- bly bad. I am now making and mean to make this fellow an example to the rest by severe and continued punishments.[110]

The irate furnaceman then unwittingly provided the probable reason for his "indulgence" when he added, "I find hands exceedingly scarce, could you spare any for the blast."[111] Despite the fact that slaves were sometimes made "an example to the rest," black ironworkers persisted in running away, such as the hand who ran off from Catawba in 1838 and cost the ironmaster $4 for expenses "in pursuit of [a] runaway."[112]

Some slaves left work for a short time and reappeared, apparently not ready to attempt the extended effort to get to freedom. Thus, a slave at Paramount Furnace "Ranaway [and] lost ½ day." Another slave at the same furnace was more determined. On July 6, 1836, "Brice Run Away." Brice returned on the twelfth only to run away again one month later. This time Brice's efforts were apparently successful, for his name disappeared from the company records.[113] One slave at Paramount, it appears, only wanted an extended break from the work routine. Thus, on July 8, 1830, "Charles Ran Away," but exactly one month later he returned and "commenced work." There is no indication that he was punished for his absence.[114]

Some masters in eastern Virginia were reluctant to hire their slaves to ironmasters across the Blue Ridge Mountains. One such slaveowner balked at hiring a hand to Jordan and Irvine in 1830 because his slave "left no doubt on my Mind, but he would make an effort to reach the State of Ohio, and by being placed at your Works it would greatly facilletate [*sic*] his Object."[115] Two other slave hands did effect their escape from Jordan and Irvine's ironworks and apparently headed for Richmond where they were caught. Upon investigation, the owner found his hireling "in the corporation gaol with another Negro Named James . . . he says you hired." The owner assured the ironmasters that "they are both at present well . . . [and] the sooner they are put to work the better."[116] Between 1829 and the Civil War, only thirteen slaves ran away from William Weaver's ironworks. Most of these were hired hands who returned to their owners east of the Blue Ridge Mountains and complained about poor living conditions, or "lurked about" their home neighborhoods.[117]

As with their counterparts in the iron industry, flight constituted the most frequent direct action taken by coal-pit slaves. Thus, in 1800 Sam ran off from Black Heath Pits. Apparently, someone tried to capture Sam, for "soon after he came away, a man met him in the road & tryed [*sic*] to Take him but could not, that is all I ever heard of him."[118] The following year, James ran away from the same mine and was thought to be lurking about in Richmond.[119] A few years later, another owner wrote to Heth that he had "made all exertions to get possession" of an escaped pit-hand, but so far he failed.[120] In 1819, a master informed Heth that a $10 reward had been offered for the capture of a fugitive miner, without success, but expressed the hope that the hand would soon be caught since "I have got an old man to get him in a situation to be caught by a bribe."[121] That same year, the owner of another runaway from the mines informed Heth that he had "Cyrus safely lodged in jail and have determined to sell him" since "I find that he will not be worth any thing to you or myself in employment at the pitts [*sic*]."[122] One master who decided to sell a slave to Black Heath Pits felt compelled to put "the fellow" in the "Penitentiary a few weeks ago, least as he was a verse [*sic*] to being sold, he should put himself out of the way.''[123] One captured runaway put up such a struggle when cornered that it took considerable effort to subdue the man. In May 1815, the agent who hired the hand to Black Heath wrote to the owner that "Simon yesterday told me Ben was with you & was well flogged much beaten otherwise & . . . pierced with a bayonett. This [I] expect was probably done in subduing [him]. If so I hope he has only got what he likely deserved.''[124]

Heth also owned a saltworks along the Kanawha River in western Virginia. Since salt furnaces required large quantities of coal, and because few slaves resided in the transmontane region, Heth occasionally sent some of his Black Heath slaves across the mountains to work in the western mines as well. One of Heth's overseers, David Street, attempted to march a coffle of these pit-hands to western Virginia in 1819.[125] As the coffle progressed into the dense forests of the Blue Ridge Mountains, several bondsmen struck out for freedom. The escape produced a revealing series of letters from the driver to Harry Heth which reflected the determination of some slave miners to gain their liberty. Just prior to this incident, Street had written to his employer that he had reached Buckingham County with all "going very well." Street felt confident that none "of my men will have it in their power to give me the slip," for he maintained "a strict watch over them and three of them I chained and shall be untill I git [sic] several hundred miles from this place," even though they had begun to get "very leg wery [sic].''[126] The driver's confidence proved to be misplaced, for six days later, on April 16, 1819, Street wrote to Heth that

> I have met with very bad luck. the three negroes Billey and the 2 Johns that I had chained to gether—Escaped the night of the 13 Instant—they went on apparantly [sic] well Satisfied. So much so that I intended taking off their Irons as soon as I got over the ridge which would have been some time the next day. I got to a house near the ridge that the [sic] man objected to the Negroes cussing in his yard to stay all night—I set a camp some little distance from the house. I was with them until Eleven Oclock. My seting [sic] up the night before with them I felt very much fatigued—I went to the house to take a nap but after I got to the house I felt uneasy and sent John Marrasett to see how all things was, that was near midnight—at about 2 Oclock old Shadrick came to the house and told me that thay [sic] was gone.[127]

The slaves chose their moment carefully and gained a head-start of several hours on their pursuers, for "it being Such a Mountainous Place" it was "impossible to find them" that night. Since the area was surrounded by mountains and dense forests, Street considered it "the completest den for villians that I ever saw." The driver tracked the slaves to a location near

Lynchburg "60 miles Below where they left me" and had "been for 2 days and nights under Whip and Crack after them." Street suggested that the collier post a notice in the Richmond newspapers in case the runaways made it that far, but the driver still hoped to capture them "before I leave this neighbourhood," for "if they dont come across some villian of a smith the Irons is not Easely [*sic*] got off."[128] Two days later, Street informed his employer of the most recent developments in the case:

> One of my fellows—Yellow John was Caught yesterday be-twixt this and new London—they was all three to gether [*sic*] and if the old man [and] a young lad had of acted with Prudance [*sic*] they might have took them all—but in Sted [*sic*] of their giting Surfisant [*sic*] close they attacted [*sic*] them just them two—John not being so Expert as the other two they took him—Billey finding that they had took John he came back to rescue John with a club and if it had not been that a man hearing the alarm runing [*sic*] that way with a gun . . . Billey would have Surtainly [*sic*] releast John—they are now about in the mountains. . . . I got a parsel of men to take a stand last night—just below where they are on the road—as their ame [*sic*] is to lye by the day and travel of nights—monday morning I am now wating [*sic*] fer [*sic*] their return—to fetch me the nurse. . . . John informs me that Billey's intention was to Kill me if he had it in his power.[129]

Street believed that the escapees intended to cross the James River above Richmond and "make their ways" to Fredericksburg and Gloucester where they had friends to hide them. After an exhausting week with every attempt to apprehend the runaways frustrated, Street's optimism faded as he sought to make "the best I can with a bad bargain."[130] What happened to the slaves remains a mystery, for all trace of them disappeared from the Heth correspondence. Ironically, Street also disappeared and a search of several months presumably failed to locate the man. Finally, in November 1819, Heth's friend C. L. Stevenson informed the collier that he had not "been able, after the most diligent enquiries, to hear any thing of David Street, who has fled so much in your debt; he has a relation in this town, who has been engaged in the negroe trade" and Stevenson thought that Street might be "lurking about him."[131] Unfortunately, that hunch proved false, and as with the slaves, all references to Street abruptly cease in the Heth papers. Street probably sold the remainder of the coffle, pocketed the money, and, like so many other scoundrels, disappeared into the western frontier.

The problem of runaway pit-hands was not confined to Black Heath. Replete with advertisements for runaways, contemporary newspapers re-

vealed the problem as a constant source of aggravation for most eastern
Virginia mine operators. Thus, Gabriel left the pits of Crouches & Sneed
and hid himself in the back alleys of Richmond.[132] In 1837, Sam and Daniel
"ran away from the Coal Mines of Murchie, Brandt & Brooks, in Chesterfield County" and were believed to be heading out of the state.[133] "A
Negro Man named William" ran away in 1845. When last heard of, he was
"running a boat from Winter Pock Pits, in Chesterfield county, to
Petersburg." William probably escaped in the boat for parts unknown, and
a $100 reward was offered to whoever apprehended him.[134] Another es-
capee must have been involved in a mine incident, for when Isaac fled from
W. T. Mosley's pits in 1858, an advertisement identified him as having been
badly burned.[135]

Many fugitives became "outlying" slaves who hid in the forests and
pillaged at night, while others seemed to desire little more than a respite
from the routine drudgery of bondage. Mystery surrounds the ultimate
destination or fate of those slave ironworkers and miners who disappeared
from the records entirely. Some evidence exists to support the hypothesis
that runaway slaves from Maryland and Virginia found employment in the
iron communities of southeastern Pennsylvania and a refuge from slave-
chasers. Some blacks had always labored at these ironworks and probably
offered sanctuary to slaves in flight. One predominantly black community
which developed in a secluded valley between Hopewell Furnace, Joanna
Furnace, and Birdsborough Forges was founded by escaped slaves who
worked at the nearby ironworks.[136] Joseph Walker, the best available
authority on black ironworkers in pre-Civil War Pennsylvania, believes
that the theory that fugitive slaves from the South "found friends and
employment in the charcoal iron industry of southeastern Pennsylvania is
perhaps based more upon a feeling one gets from what records say, and do
not say, than documentable historical fact."[137]

The fugitive slave laws discouraged the Pennsylvania ironmasters from
keeping any written record of runaways employed at their works. Enough
antislavery sentiment existed in the district, however, to prompt George
Washington to comment on November 20, 1786, that once a runaway
reached southeastern Pennsylvania, it became nearly impossible to recover the slave because so many people in the district would "facilitate the
escape."[138] The infamous Christiana Riot of 1851 occurred in the heart of
the iron district when a slaveowner attempted to recapture a fugitive
bondsman being harbored by a free black family. The resultant furor
underscored Washington's earlier observation regarding the fervor of
abolitionist sentiment among the black and white residents of that area.

The best evidence that runaway slaves found refuge at these ironworks
appears in the furnace account books. Walker examined the Hopewell
Furnace records and found that numerous blacks arrived at the iron com-

munity, worked a few days, and then disappeared. Thus, "Black Frank began work at the furnace" on October 1, 1802, and after getting paid for his work on November 2, 1802, Black Frank "Left the Furnace." Similarly, on June 22, 1803, "Black Dine Came," but three weeks and two days later, "Black Dine went away." No record of these workers' origin or destination was kept, but there is a distinct probability that northbound fugitives from slavery found both temporary and permanent safety, sympathy, and employment at southeastern Pennsylvania ironworks.[139] Word of these furnaces and forges just across the Mason-Dixon line surely reached the ears of experienced slave ironworkers in Maryland and Virginia by way of the skilled white ironworkers who drifted or were imported into camp from Pennsylvania by Chesapeake ironmasters. No evidence has been found which suggests that slave coal miners found similar opportunities in the mines of free states.

When the Civil War reached Virginia, runaway slaves became a major concern among colliers and ironmasters alike, for many slave miners took advantage of the occasion to gain their freedom. The superintendent of Trent's Pits added a postscript to a "List of Coloured Hands" for 1864, which noted that the list contained all the hirelings for that year "except the Runaway Billy Jordan."[140] Similarly, the manager of Dover Pits noted that Andrew ran away on January 16, 1864, and Abner, a trainer, "deserted to [the] Yankees March 1st, 1864." Abner took a friend with him, for another trainer, Phill, also "deserted to [the] Yankees" on that same date.[141] According to the operator of Dover Pits, Christopher Q. Tompkins, as the Union forces occupied the Confederate capital in April 1865, "All the negroes" went "quick for Richmond" and desertion became the "order of the day." In a remarkably dispassionate memorandum of the events which surrounded the occupation, Tompkins observed:

> Of the 108 slaves at these pits only four or five left Monday evening, but the next evening there was 30 or 40, the provisions were not entirely issued & some held back to get their weekly allowance of meat &c. The negroes were slow to realize the fact that they were free. Many disclaimed any disposition to be so, particularly Alfred, Phil &c. &c. But by Tuesday evening the fever was so high that every soul who had legs to walk was running to Richmond.

Although most of the free black miners stayed on the job, desertion among the slaves became so complete that Tompkins finally "concluded to stop the pits."[142]

The war produced a similar response among slave ironworkers in the border states, although not so dramatic as that at Dover Pits. In June 1864, Union General David Hunter campaigned in the Valley of Virginia, and five slaves from Buffalo Forge escaped to freedom with Hunter's troops. Daniel Brady wrote to one owner that "your boy Beverly went off with the enemy" during a raid on June 12. Brady further reported that he had lost three of his hands to the Yankees during the same raid and was himself lucky to escape.[143] No doubt, other slaves at the forge would have escaped with the Union troops if they had not been evacuated when the federal army temporarily occupied nearby Lexington. The drama of the episode is obviously lost in the company's journal, which merely carries the notation that "Warder, Beverly, Sport, Benny, Scipio went to the federals."[144] Joseph Anderson's Tredegar Iron Works suffered a greater loss from slave hands who ran off to the enemy during the war. In June 1863, the company wrote to one slaveowner whose hired hands had escaped that "the demoralization among the negroes here and at our furnace is a source of much disquietude to us who have contracts with the government for iron [upon which] the fate of the country may depend."[145] In the same month, a company letter sent to Tredegar furnace managers in the Valley of Virginia lamented what appeared to be "almost a stampede among your hands."[146] In June 1864, during the same raid that freed five of the slaves at Buffalo Forge, Hunter's cavalry freed an undetermined number of blacks from the Tredegar's Cloverdale, Grace, and Mount Torry furnaces in the Valley of Virginia.[147] By December 1864, Anderson had to acknowledge that "this has been a rather disasterous [*sic*] year for the hirers and owners of slaves, so many having run off to Yankees."[148]

Until the Civil War, runaway slaves presented a constant problem but never a major calamity which threatened to close down an ironworks or coal mine. In the absence of a reasonably good opportunity to escape, slaves appear to have adjusted to a life of industrial bondage. They did not accept bondage as a desirable, permanent condition, but lacking other feasible alternatives, psychologically they attempted to make the best of their oppression. They sought solace within their families; in the quarters, blacks removed the masks that protected their inner selves from white scrutiny and, resuming their particular individual identities, became their own men and women. In the mid-1780s, Irish traveler Isaac Weld grasped the essence of bondage, accommodation notwithstanding. Weld noted that slaves were treated well in Maryland and Virginia:

> Still, however, let the condition of a slave be made ever so comfortable, as long as he is conscious of being the property of another man, who has it in his power to dispose of him according to the dictates of caprice; as long as he hears people around him talking of the blessings of liberty, and considers that he is in a state of bondage, it is not to be supposed that he can feel equally happy with the freeman. It is immaterial under what form slavery presents itself,

whenever it appears there is ample cause for humanity to weep at the sight, and to lament that men can be found so forgetful of their own situations, as to live regardless of the feelings of their fellow creatures.[149]

Like most blacks who resisted slavery, rebellious ironworkers and coal miners did so not because they were treated more or less humanely. They resisted out of a sense of injustice based upon the larger realization that as blacks they were destined to perpetual bondage. They did so, as Jermain Loguen reported, from the refusal to shape their lives "upon the absurdity of white supremacy."[150]

NOTES

1. The following are examples of studies dealing with the whole range of slave reactions during the antebellum era: Eugene D. Genovese, *The Political Economy of Slavery: Studies in the Economy and Society of the Slave South* (New York: Random House, 1965), especially Chap. 2; Robert S. Starobin, *Industrial Slavery in the Old South* (New York: Oxford University Press, 1970), Chap. 3, and his article "Disciplining Industrial Slaves in the Old South," *Journal of Negro History* 53 (April 1968): 111-28; Raymond A. and Alice H. Bauer, "Day to Day Resistance to Slavery," *Journal of Negro History* 27 (October 1942): 388-419; Charles B. Dew, "Disciplining Slave Ironworkers in the Antebellum South: Coercion, Conciliation, and Accommodation," *American Historical Review* 79 (April 1974): 393-418.

2. Robert William Fogel and Stanley L. Engerman, *Time on the Cross: The Economics of American Negro Slavery* (Boston: Little, Brown & Co., 1974), Vol. 1, p. 147.

3. Frederick Law Olmsted, *Journey in the Seaboard Slave States, with Remarks on Their Economy* (New York: Mason Brothers, 1859), p. 100.

4. D. Ross to John Staples, June 3, 1813, Ross Letterbook, Virginia Historical Society, herafter cited as VHS.

5. D. Ross to Robert Richardson, n.d., probably December 1812, Ross Letterbook, VHS.

6. D. Ross to John Duffield, January 9, 1813, Ross Letterbook, VHS.

7. D. Ross to Robert Richardson, January 14, 1813, Ross Letterbook, VHS.

8. Furnace Account Book, 1829–1832, Graham Ledgers, University of Virginia, hereafter cited as UVa.

9. Negro Time Book, 1833–1839, Graham Ledgers, UVa.

10. John Day to Shanks, Anderson & Anderson, November 9, 1849, Anderson Family Papers, UVa.

11. Burns, agent, for Shanks, Anderson & Anderson to John Day, December 18, 1849, Anderson Family Papers, UVa.

12. R. A. Glasgow to F. T. Anderson (uncle), February 16, 1858, F. T. Anderson Papers, Duke University, hereafter cited as Duke.

13. James C. Davis to William W. Davis, January 5, 1856, William Davis Papers, UVa.

14. Kathleen Bruce, *Virginia Iron Manufacture in the Slave Era* (New York: Augustus M. Kelley, 1960, originally 1930), pp. 242, 254–55.

15. John Harris to Harry Heth, April 19, 1807, Heth Family Papers, UVa.

16. Harry Randolph to Harry Heth, June 11, 1812, Heth Family Papers, UVa.

17. Robert Perkins to Harry Heth, May 28, 1815, Heth Family Papers, UVa.

18. Robert Mimms to Harry Heth, April 11, 1804, Heth Family Papers, UVa.

19. Robert Nichols to Harry Heth, August 24, 1813, Heth Family Papers, UVa.

20. H. Lawrence to Harry Heth, December 12, 1815, Heth Family Papers, UVa.

21. Thomas Lauther (Richmond Jail) to Harry Heth, October 12, 1819, Heth Family Papers, UVa.

22. D. Ross to William Dunn, January 1813, Ross Letterbook, VHS.

23. Robert Perkins to Harry Heth, September 18, 1815, Heth Family Papers, UVa.

24. Frederick Douglass, *Life and Times of Frederick Douglass Written by Himself: His Early Life as a Slave, His Escape from Bondage, and His Complete History* (London: Collier-MacMillan Ltd., 1962, originally 1892), p. 147.

25. Robert Perkins to Harry Heth, May 28, 1815, Heth Family Papers, UVa.

26. Thomas Jefferson to Thomas Mann Randolph, January 23, 1801, as reproduced in Edwin Morris Betts (ed.), *Thomas Jefferson's Farm Book with Commentary and Relevant Extracts from Other Writings* (Princeton, N.J.: Princeton University Press, 1953), p. 442.

27. William Byrd, "Progress to the Mines," as reproduced in Louis B. Wright (ed.), *The Prose Works of William Byrd of Westover: Narratives of a Colonial Virginian* (Cambridge, Mass.: Belknap Press of Harvard University Press, 1966), p. 354.

28. John Tayloe Account Book, 1740–1741, Box 1, Tayloe Family Papers, VHS.

29. Miscellaneous item in the Bond Family Papers, Maryland Historical Society, hereafter cited as MHS.

30. Journal CC, 1764–1772, Elk Ridge Furnace, Maryland Hall of Records, hereafter cited as HR: Bush Town (Md.) Store Ledger, 1765–1766, and Journal, 1747–1773, Library of Congress, hereafter cited as LC.

31. Dennison Rose to W. Weaver, March 25, 1838, William Weaver Papers, Duke.

32. Samuel G. Hermelin, *Report About the Mines in the United States of America,* trans. by Amandus Johnson (Philadelphia: John Morton Memorial Museum, 1931), pp. 52–53.

33. Duc de La Rochefoucauld-Liancourt, Francois Alexandre Frederick, *Travels Through the United States of North America, the Country of the Iroquois, and Upper Canada, in the Years 1795, 1796, and 1797; with an Authentic Account of Lower Canada* (London: R. Phillips, 1799), 3:157–58.

34. Isaac Jefferson, "Life of Isaac Jefferson of Petersburg, Virginia Blacksmith Containing a Full and Faithful Account of Monticello & the Family There, with Notices of Many of the Distinguished Characters that Visited There, with His Revolutionary Experiences & Travels, Adventures, Observations, & Opinions, the Whole Taken Down from His Own Words," ed. with commentary by Rayford W. Logan, *William and Mary Quarterly* 8 (October 1951):561–82.

35. Ross advertisement to lease Oxford Iron Works, September 3, 1811, William Bolling Papers, Duke.

36. D. Ross to William Dunn, August 1813, Ross Letterbook, VHS.

37. Ibid., January 1813.

38. Ledger of North East Forge for 1754, cited in William G. Whitely, "The Principio Company: A Historical Sketch of the First Iron-Works in Maryland," *Pennsylvania Magazine of History and Biography* 11 (1887):192.

39. Ledger of John Blair, 1795–1797, College of William and Mary.

40. Negro Books, 1854–1861, and 1857–1860, Etna Furnace, Weaver-Brady Papers, UVa.

41. Also see Dew, "Disciplining Slave Ironworkers," p. 407. Professor Dew has studied several southern ironworks and has found the same prevailing patterns.

42. Account Book, 1800, Heth Family Papers, UVa.

43. David Street to Harry Heth, December 24, 1811, Heth Family Papers, UVa.

44. Accounts and Receipts, 1831, Heth Family Papers, UVa.

45. Edmund Ruffin, "Visit to Graham's Coal Pits," *Farmers' Register* 5 (August 1, 1837):317.

46. *Richmond Whig and Public Advertiser,* January 1846.

47. Ibid., June 26, 1846.

48. McCaw Journal, James River Coal Pits, 1849–1851, UVa.; "Cash and Clothing Issued to hands at Dover Mines—Farm Decr. 24th, 1844," Tompkins Family Papers, VHS.

49. Journal of Ledger C, 1758–1761, and Journal AA, 1761–1762, Elk Ridge Furnace, HR.

50. Journal BB, 1762–1764, Elk Ridge Furnace, HR.

51. Ibid.

52. Journal CC, 1764–1772, Elk Ridge Furnace, HR.

53. Ibid.

54. Journal A & B, 1767–1794, Patuxent Iron Works, HR.

55. Ibid.

56. Ibid.

57. Cumberland Forge Day Book, 1802, LC.

58. Cumberland Forge Account Book, 1796–1797, LC.

59. Ridwell Furnace Account Book, University of North Carolina, hereafter cited as UNC.

60. Pine Forge Ledger, Vol. 5, UNC.

61. Ledger B-3, 1810–1815, Box 3, Ridgely Account Books, MHS.

62. Ledger B-1, 1782–1785, Box 2, Ridgely Account Books, MHS.

63. Daybook, b–19, 1815–1821, Box 9, Northampton Furnace, Ridgely Account Books, MHS.

64. Negro Book, 1857–1860, Etna Furnace, Weaver-Brady Papers, UVa.

65. Union Forge Ledger, Rinker-Lantz Daybooks and Ledgers, Duke.

66. Negro Time Book, 1837–1852, Paramount Furnace, Graham Family Ledgers and Papers, UVa.

67. Negro Book, 1847–1849, Glenwood Furnace, Anderson Family Papers, UVa.

68. Negro Book, 1850–1858, Buffalo Forge, Weaver-Brady Papers, UVa.

69. Wm. Dulany to Jacob Lantz, May 13, 1850, Rinker-Lantz Papers, UVa.

70. I. P. Rinker & Co. Journal, 1853–1857, Rinker-Lantz Papers, UVa.

71. Daniel C. E. Brady, Home Journal, 1860–1865, State Historical Society of Wisconsin, hereafter cited as SHSW.

72. John Rex to James D. Davidson, February 25, 1855, James D. Davidson Papers, SHSW.

73. Fogel and Engerman, *Time on the Cross,* Vol. 1, pp. 40–41.

74. Genovese, *Political Economy of Slavery,* especially Chap. 2; Starobin, *Industrial Slavery in the Old South,* Chap. 3; Bauer and Bauer, "Day to Day Resistance to Slavery," pp. 388–419; Dew, "Disciplining Slave Ironworkers," pp. 412–14. For example, William Weaver's furnace manager, William Rex, reported that he "had a notion of Comeing down tomorrow evening, . . . but I am afraid if I leave there they will steal the place. They come very near it while I am here." W. Rex to D. Brady, March 15, 1861, Weaver-Brady Papers, UVa.

75. Blassingame, *The Slave Community: Plantation Life in the Antebellum South* (New York: Oxford University Press, 1972), p. 207.

76. Lucy Ann Delaney, *From the Darkness Cometh the Light: Or Struggles for Freedom* (St. Louis, n.d.), p. 18, cited in Blassingame, *The Slave Community,* p. 208. Reference to the "mask" is found throughout Afro-American thought and writing.

77. Journal CC, 1764–1772, Elk Ridge Furnace, HR.

78. Pine Forge Ledgers, Vol. 3, UNC.

79. Time Book, 1854–1858, Etna Furnace, Weaver-Brady Papers, UVa.

80. Robert Hughes to Harry Heth, April 10, 1815, Heth Family Papers, UVa.

81. W. Rex to D. Brady, October 26, 1860, William Weaver Papers, Duke.

82. William Chandler to Harry Heth, September 7, 1815, Heth Family Papers, UVa.

83. John Davidson to Harry Heth, October 22, 1801, Heth Family Papers, UVa.

84. Lease of Edward Scott, Sr., to John James Flournoy, May 28, 1847, Tompkins Family Papers, VHS.

85. Robert T. Brooke to Edmund Taylor Morris, March 16, 1857, Woolfolk Family Papers, VHS.

86. Jordan Davis & Co. to W. Weaver, November 24, 1830, William Weaver Papers, Duke.

87. John K. Watkins to W. Weaver, July 30, 1854, William Weaver Papers, Duke.

88. George Junkin to F. T. Anderson, March 31, 1859, Anderson Family Papers, UVa.

89. Charles Ridgely & Company Account Book, 1774–1780, LC.

90. Gerald W. Mullin, *Flight and Rebellion: Slave Resistance in Eighteenth-Century Virginia* (New York: Oxford University Press, 1972), p. 143; "Information from Jno. Foster respecting the intended Insurrection, Sept. 23rd, 1800," Executive Papers, Virginia State Library, hereafter cited as VSL.

91. Charles B. Dew, "Black Ironworkers and the Slave Insurrection Panic of 1856," *Journal of Southern History* 16 (August 1975):338. For those who believe that a plot actually existed, see Harvey Wish, "The Slave Insurrection Panic of 1856," *Journal of Southern History* 5 (May 1939):222; Herbert Aptheker, *Ameri-*

can Negro Slave Revolts (New York: International Publishers, 1943), pp. 347–49; Kenneth M. Stampp, *The Peculiar Institution: Slavery in the Ante-Bellum South* (New York: Alfred Knopf, 1956), p. 138; Starobin, *Industrial Slavery in the Old South*, pp. 89–90.

92. Edward Mosely to Mr. John Cunliff or Cpt. Heth, July 8, 1807, Heth Family Papers, UVa. Cunliff was Heth's partner for a short time.

93. Quoted in Aptheker, *American Negro Slave Revolts*, p. 273, n. 26.

94. Mullin, *Flight and Rebellion*, Chaps. 2 and 3. According to Mullin, "More slaves ran off from iron foundries than from any other non-agricultural industry" during the colonial era. It should be noted, however, that only 2 percent of these runaways were skilled workers; most were semiskilled or common laborers (Mullin, *Flight and Rebellion*, p. 185).

95. William Byrd, "Progress to the Mines," p. 348.

96. *Maryland Gazette*, August 30, 1759.

97. Ibid., September 6, 1759.

98. Ibid., November 18, 1762. For other advertisements in the same paper, see the following issues: March 31, 1747, December 1, 1768, October 22, 1779, November 7, 1754, September 9, 1784, February 19, 1795, and July 19, 1798.

99. *Maryland Journal and Baltimore Advertiser*, May 29, 1781.

100. Ibid., August 3, 1787. Also see issues for June 24, 1777, August 11, 1778, July 27, 1779, August 7, 1781, October 3, 1782, June 22, 1784, and August 1, 1788.

101. *Virginia Gazette* (Rind), April 21, 1768.

102. Ibid., August 4, 1768.

103. Ibid., February 9, 1769.

104. Ibid. (Purdie & Dixon), November 21, 1771.

105. Ibid., July 15, 1773.

106. Ibid. (Pinkney), November 23, 1775.

107. Journal BB, 1762–1764, Elk Ridge Furnace, HR.

108. Public Foundry, Westham Ledger, 1776–1779 (1788), VSL.

109. Pine Forge Ledger, Vol. 3, UNC.

110. Francis Preston to his Brother, July 27, 1806, Preston Family Papers, VHS.

111. Ibid.

112. Account Book, 1838, Edmundson Family Papers, VHS.

113. Negro Time Book, 1833–1839, Paramount Furnace, Graham Family Ledgers, UVa.

114. Negro Time Book, 1830–1831, Graham Family Ledgers, UVa.

115. R. Garland to Jordan and Irvine, January 3, 1830, Jordan and Irvine Papers, SHSW.

116. Balard Smith to Jordan and Irvine, November 3, 1831, Jordan and Irvine Papers, SHSW.

117. Wm. Watson for Joel W. Brown, Jailor (Charlottesville, Virginia), to Post Master, Lexington, Virginia, April 19, 1829; W. E. Dickinson to Abraham Davis, April 19, 1829; James C. Dickinson to W. Weaver, May 10, 1830; Elizabeth Mathews to W. Weaver, March 29, 1830; Lewis Rawlings to W. Weaver, August 22, 1832; Charles Perrow to W. Weaver, September 17, October 26, 1833; and John A. Turpin to W. Weaver, August 28, 1854, all in the William Weaver Papers, Duke; Henry A. McCormick to W. Weaver, December 29, 1855, Weaver-Brady Papers,

UVa. Also see entries under "Lawson," in Negro Book, 1857–1860, Etna Furnace, Weaver-Brady Papers, UVa; and Dew, "Disciplining Slave Ironworkers," p. 413.

118. Jesse Cole to Harry Heth, August 4, 1800, Heth Family Papers, UVa.

119. William Kimbrough to Harry Heth, June 3, 1801, Heth Family Papers, UVa.

120. David Paterson to Harry Heth, March 2, 1803, Heth Family Papers, UVa.

121. John E. Browne to Harry Heth, June 28, 1819, Heth Family Papers, UVa.

122. R. Tankersley to Harry Heth, August 28, 1819, Heth Family Papers, UVa.

123. James P. Cocke to Harry Heth, April 11, 1815, Heth Family Papers, UVa.

124. Robert Perkins to Harry Heth, May 28, 1815, Heth Family Papers, UVa.

125. Numbers of letters during 1815 refer to Heth's venture into mining and salt manufacture in western Virginia. For example, see Harry Heth to Beverly Randolph, January 24, 1815, and J. Barhu to Harry Heth, February 15, 1815, Heth Family Papers, UVa.

126. David Street to Harry Heth, April 9, 1819, Heth Family Papers, UVa.

127. Ibid., April 16, 1819.

128. Ibid.

129. Ibid., April 19, 1819.

130. Ibid.

131. C. L. Stevenson to Harry Heth, November 5, 1819, Heth Family Papers, UVa.

132. *Richmond Daily Courier,* September 21, 1836.

133. *Richmond Enquirer,* May 23, June 6, 1837.

134. Ibid., June 17, 1845.

135. *Richmond Daily Dispatch,* May 5, 1858.

136. Wayne Homan, "The Underground Railroad," *Historical Review of Berks County* 23 (1958):112–18.

137. Joseph E. Walker, "Negro Labor in the Charcoal Iron Industry of Southeastern Pennsylvania," *Pennsylvania Magazine of History and Biography* 93 (October 1969):483.

138. John C. Fitzpatrick (ed.), *The Writings of George Washington* (Washington, D.C.: U.S. Government Printing Office, 1939), Vol. 29, pp. 78–79.

139. Walker, "Negro Labor in the Charcoal Iron Industry," pp. 484–86.

140. "List of Coloured Hands at Trent's Pits, 1864," Tompkins Family Papers, VHS.

141. Tompkins Commonplace Book, Tompkins Family Papers, VHS.

142. William M. E. Rachal (ed.), "The Occupation of Richmond, April 1865: The Memorandum of Events of Colonel Christopher Q. Tompkins," *Virginia Magazine of History and Biography* 73 (April 1965): 192–93.

143. Daniel C. E. Brady to James Stewart, July 7, 1864, Daybook and Letterbook, 1844–1847, 1861–1865, Bath Iron Works and Buffalo Forge, Weaver-Brady Papers, UVa. On June 12, 1864, Brady also noted that Yankees had captured Mr. Rex, manager of sister works Etna Furnace, and that the Union troops had destroyed Jordan's furnace and other property. Ibid., and Daniel C. E. Brady Home Journals, SHSW.

144. Daniel C. E. Brady Home Journals, SHSW.

145. Anderson & Co. to R. C. Dabney, June 24, 1863, Tredegar Letterbooks, Tredegar Company Records, VSL.

146. Anderson & Co. to Benjamin Holladay, June 23, 1863, and to F. Glasgow, June 25, 1863, Tredegar Letterbooks, Tredegar Company Records, VSL.

147. Anderson & Co. to James Whitfield, October 12, 1864, Tredegar Company Records, VSL.

148. Anderson & Co. to (?) Forbes, December 16, 1864, Tredegar Company Records, VSL. For other slave runaways, see "List of Negroes at Catawba, 1863," Tredegar Company Records, VSL; also see Charles B. Dew, *Ironmaker to the Confederacy: Joseph R. Anderson and the Tredegar Iron Works* (New Haven, Conn.: Yale University Press, 1966), pp. 255–56, 260–61.

149. Isaac Weld, Jr., *Travels Through the States of North America and the Provinces of Upper and Lower Canada During the Years 1795, 1796, and 1797* (London: John Stockdale, Piccadilly, 1800), p. 115.

150. Jermain Wesley Loguen, *The Rev. J. W. Loguen, as a Slave and as a Freeman. A Narrative of Real Life* (Syracuse: J. G. K. Truair & Co., Printers, 1859), p. 165.

Daily Life   5

Can a people . . . live and develop over 300 years by simply
reacting? Are American Negroes simply the creation of white
men, or have they at least helped create themselves out of
what they found around them? Men have made a way of life in
caves and upon cliffs, why can not Negroes have made a way
of life upon the horns of the white man's dilemma?
                                    —Ralph Ellison, *Shadow and Act*

When Frederick Law Olmsted, the well-known northern journalist, made
his famous journeys throughout the South during the 1850s, he observed
that slaveowners were sometimes reluctant to hire slaves to ironworks
because they were worked hard, had too much liberty, and acquired bad
habits. They earned money by overwork, spent it on whiskey, and got into
a habit of roaming about and taking care of themselves, because when they
were not at work in the furnace, nobody looked out for them.[1] Olmsted
touched on nearly every important aspect of the black ironworkers' daily
lives. Slaves who stopped short of threatening either the plantation regime
or the institution of slavery itself generally were not harassed by ironmasters because too much of the "Strict hand" could lead slaves into either
overt or covert retaliation against their masters' interests. Consequently,
"when they were not at work in the furnace, nobody looked out for them."
In short, ironmasters did not control free time, home life, or leisure activities in the slave quarters. Compromise necessitated reliance on motivational techniques other than overt forms of oppression, unless, of course,
ironmasters found their authority jeopardized. In the planter's view, this
reliance provided slave ironworkers with "too much liberty," and they
"got in the habit of roaming about" during leisure hours.
   This relative freedom of movement during off-work hours was significant in preventing industrial slavery from becoming what Stanley Elkins[2]
identifies as a "closed system" of "absolute power" which stripped the
slave of his individual personality, or which "brutalized" blacks, as historians such as Kenneth Stampp have asserted.[3] Overwork played an equally
significant role in mitigating the debasement of the individual slave worker

and affected the most fundamental aspects of the daily life of the slave community. As Olmsted noted, slaves "earned money by overwork," and although some "spent it on whiskey," many others improved their standard of living by purchasing extra articles of clothing and larger provisions of the food they liked best. The ability of the male slaves to purchase extra necessities for themselves and for their wives and children greatly enhanced their self-esteem in the family and in the quarters. In the quarters, where the slave was rarely under the direct surveillance of his master, he could be a man. According to John Blassingame, the slave could express his true feelings and gain respect and sympathy in his family circle. Friendship, love, sexual gratification, fun, and values which differed from those of the master were all found in the quarters.[4]

Owners of bondsmen hired to industrialists frequently worried about the treatment of their slaves. Aside from humanitarian considerations, owners feared that ill treatment would prompt hirelings to run away or would make them unwilling to work thereafter for a particular ironmaster or collier. Consequently, employers tempered their treatment of slave hands for the same reasons. Similarly, both owners and hirers concerned themselves about the clothing and food provided to bondsmen, for slaves who did not have enough of these basic necessities could not labor productively and could more easily become ill from improper diets or exposure.

Owners attempted to insure that their hired slaves would receive sufficient clothing to protect them from the weather. One master wrote to ironmaster William Davis that his "fellow Bob," whom Davis had hired for the year 1840, had "failed to get his clothes from the man that hired him last year, & it was too late when I learned the fact, to buy them." The master wanted Davis to "give him on his arrival . . . a coat & pantaloons such as negroes generally have for the winter" and to charge them to the *owner*.[5] Another master wrote to ironmaster William Weaver, asking if he would "be so good [as] to go to Mr. Moore and buy the boy 2 good Blankets and cloth to make him a coat . . . and charge it to me."[6] The surviving papers of ironmasters are replete with similar requests. Slave masters usually tried to protect their leased bondsmen by stipulating in the hiring bonds what black workers should receive as provisions. For example:

> On the 25th day of December 1850 we promise to pay George W. Morris the Sum of Eighty three Dollars the Same being for the hire of his boy Charles from this date up to that time. the Said Morris to furnish the Said boy in a Comfortable Winter Suit, Shoes Hat & Blanket for the Present year & we bind Ourselves to furnish the Customary Clothing Allowed hirelings Pay his Taxes & Return him Comfortably Clad in Winter Suit Shoes Hat & Blanket at the expiration of the time

Say 25th Decr 1850. to the true performance of which we bind
Ourselves given under Our hands this 13th day of Nov 1849.

[signed]
Shanks & Andersons
by James L. Patton[7]

Slaves themselves sought to insure that they would not go without the
traditional garments due to them. One owner hired a slave hand to William
Weaver in 1830, who was "to be returned well Clothed as usual," and
"would have sent another man, but he refused to go, because his clothing,
Blanket etc. were at Laura [a plantation near Fredericksburg, Virginia] &
he could not do without them."[8]

Even with such precautions, however, slaves sometimes went without
the proper clothing. David Ross of Oxford Iron Works was always concerned about how his hands were attired. On at least one occasion, even
Ross lamented that "many of the Oxford servants are suffering from
cloaths."[9] In 1840, Jordan wrote to his partner inquiring: "Did you engage
any Shoes in Louisa—My hands [at Jane Furnace] are badly off for
shoes."[10] During the winter of 1859, William Weaver also was troubled by
clothing shortages. The manager of the furnace, William Rex, complained
that "our Sole leather is . . . [exhausted] & a good many boys barefooted. I
will have to give them new shoes," unless leather arrived to repair the old
ones.[11] Throughout the year 1860, Rex pleaded for shoes for his hands. In
April, the manager reported:

> Some four or five of our Blk hands are entirely out of shoes. I
> will be obliged to buy 4 par in town. Spott is laying up at Bank
> for the want of a par. The bank is very wet, it is so rough they
> cannot work without them. There was only 2 par of the last
> lot that would fit the negroes—they went to the bank. Two of
> the Car's boys is barefooted, they will be layed up if they are
> not shod.[12]

During the entire summer of 1860, Rex continued to lament, "What are we
to do for shoes?"[13] By September, "three of the Blk & some of the white
hands at the [ore] bank" were "entirely out" of shoes, and when several
pairs did arrive they did not fit.[14] Black workers suffered from want of
shoes and, although the lack obviously affected him differently, so did the
master. Slaves who had no shoes were "layed up" and unproductive for
the entire period. The presence of shoeless men did not indicate that the
managers of Weaver's ironworks brutalized black workers by trying to cut
clothing costs. That kind of cost-cutting was illusory, for slaves did not
work when barefoot. Rather, the case illustrated either poor management

or the more general southern problem of a scarcity of consumer goods, or both. Moreover, a manager deliberately trying to reduce clothing expenses would not have pleaded so incessantly for those same essentials.

Ironworks periodically suffered from food shortages as well. The correspondence between Clement Brooke, manager of the Baltimore Iron Works during the 1770s, and Robert Carter of Nomini Hall, a partner in the company, is filled with a constant lament for food. Unlike most ironworks in the Chesapeake region, the Baltimore Iron Works did not attempt to be self-sufficient because the partners provided specific quotas to the works as provisions were needed. Because of the company's organization, however, poor management was almost assured; the partners were nearly always at odds, and each seemed determined to provide the company with as little as possible.[15] As a result, the works constantly faced shortages of provisions for the hands, at least during the late 1760s and early 1770s. For example, Clement Brooke wrote to Robert Carter that "I saw your orders . . . to purchase Beef for the Works, but that will not do in place of pork . . . [we] have plenty of that article & want pork for the Workmen."[16] Several years later, in 1777, Brooke wrote to Carter again that "the works is much in want of your proportion of corn due. The people and Stock are starving almost."[17]

Apparently, another ironmaster just north of the Baltimore works also had some trouble with his food supply, for in 1780 two hands hired by Charles Ridgely to work at Northampton Furnace returned to their owner "complaining of the Beef being rotten."[18] By 1813, David Ross of Oxford Iron Works had to admit that "by bad management [the slaves] had had a short half allowance of meat."[19] At William Weaver's works, slave hands lacked meat, flour, and corn during the winter of 1828. The flour that did arrive was returned because it was "very bad."[20] During the following year, the manager repeatedly requested the delivery of flour, but three months passed and soon the hands were "living on corn pones at present."[21] That winter he complained again, "We want about six Bbls Flour, our Hands have not had any for some time past."[22]

Weaver's ironworks once again suffered from shortages of food during the spring of 1859. When food supplies failed to arrive by April, the manager reported that the blacks were very dissatisfied, and "it is taking all our management to get off that beef and to keep them in good humor . . . John Purely sent us word yesterday that the hands at the bank would leave if they did not get bacon—they are sending it back as fast as we send it to them."[23] In July 1859, the manager reported that "we are out of Bacon . . . last week & this. there is a good deal of complaint about bad meat."[24] During the following spring of 1860, the slaves became so disgruntled over the shortages that the manager wrote: "Our hands are here wanting flour coffee & tobacco. I have for the past month been putting them off—I am afraid they will leave in a body & throw us behind. We by all means should have something to satisfy them if we wish to keep them."[25]

Some historians, such as Robert S. Starobin and S. Sydney Bradford,[26] have interpreted these unfortunate sufferings for lack of food and clothing as part of the general brutalization of slave labor in an industrial setting where hirers of bondsmen were interested only in getting as much work for as little as possible. A closer look at the correspondence of ironmasters suggests that this view is superficial. In the first place, by emphasizing the obvious hardship experienced by slaves when shortages in the basic necessities of life occurred, it is easy to forget the constant pleading of the managers of these works for food and clothing for their slave hands. Without reducing the fact that blacks suffered at Oxford Iron Works from being placed on a "short half allowance of meat," it is easy to ignore the fact that Ross generally provided his hands with ample provisions and instructed his manager that "you may be assured that nothing will be lost by feeding the people well."[27] Moreover, there was no advantage to Weaver at all in having his hands hungry, for as one contemporary writer suggested, "Time and experience have fully proved the error of a stinted policy" on food;[28] or as another observer noted, "The master cannot expect full work from one who is but partially fed."[29] In addition, the nature of the evidence itself suggests that such circumstances occurred sporadically. Thus, at Weaver's ironworks, one period of shortage arose in the late 1820s and early 1830s, and the next shortage appeared in the late 1850s. Most importantly, however, it is erroneous to exaggerate the power that ironmasters held over their slave hands. Black ironworkers were not docile. Untenable living and working conditions could prompt slaves to "leave in a body" and forced ironmasters to do "something to satisfy them if we wish to keep them."[30]

Forces beyond the control of the ironmasters must not be disregarded either. In 1830, Samuel F. Jordan inquired of William Weaver, "What do you think of Pork at $4.50?" Jordan continued by saying "it is thought that it will be high in consequence of the drought in the west, and consequently the scarcity of corn there will not be a half crop in this Co., and west of this I believe it is no better."[31] While scarcity was a problem, the size of a work force itself presented a feeding problem. For example, in November 1853 Buffalo Forge alone slaughtered 130 hogs and the following month 78 more, in addition to at least 52 beeves killed for meat. Still, this was not always enough to feed Weaver's workmen.[32] That Weaver's manager, Charles Gorgas, feared the slaves would leave "in a body" itself suggests that blacks did not passively submit to starvation.[33] It does not suggest that slave hands at ironworks were used to such scarcities. In fact, their constant complaints and their threats to leave indicate precisely the opposite—that black hands were hardly willing to put up with such conditions. It also shows that slaves had nothing to fear from their masters if they did leave the works for home because of poor food and clothing. Even on economic grounds, the argument that the basic needs of slaves were intentionally neglected by ironmasters is unfounded, for it rests on the assumption that ironmasters were all-powerful, while their black hands had no way to affect the conditions of their daily lives; that simply was not the case. Technically, slaves had no such power, but hirelings exhibited considerable ability in manipulating power relationships which resulted in an informal exercise of influence, whether masters chose to recognize it or not. Even though the manuscript data for the coal industry are less extensive, available evidence suggests that the same interpersonal behavioral patterns were also operative among slave miners.

Just before the Civil War, a coal mining engineer from Scotland, James M'Killop, visited the Virginia coal field. Like most foreign miners, M'Killop loathed the institution of slavery. He expressed the conviction that "nothing could be more wretched than the condition of this cheap system of labour, which was compelled to be wrought by the whip, and rewarded with the coarsest of food—corn meal and bacon—and the meanest of clothing."[34] Although slave miners probably did not fare significantly better than other bondsmen with regard to food and clothing, neither did they receive significantly less than other industrial slaves.

Most hiring bonds, for example, stipulated that employers of slave miners had to furnish them with the traditional issue of clothing. Thus, Harry Heth's hands, "four negroe men named George, Lewis, Dick & Charles," whom he leased to a neighboring mine company, had to be furnished with a "coat & pantaloons of stout color'd cloth 2 shirts of german osnabg a pr. of shoes, & stockings & a Hatt, or the value of the above if not furnished."[35] Owners of hired slave miners monitored the actions of employers in this regard. In response to inquiries from one owner, agent Robert Perkins wrote to Heth in 1817 that "I have told him I believed your custom was to give what ever they stood in need [of]."[36] For an industrial employer, issuance of clothing represented a significant expense. In 1815, Heth issued a "shirt, pantaloons, shoes, etc." to thirty-five hired slave miners.[37] Eighteen years later, Heth's heirs paid "one hundred & eight dollars and 25 cents in full for making 111 suits of clothes for [the] coal pits & Norwood [a plantation] hands."[38] Moreover, pit work, which was always dirty and wet, necessitated special clothing provisions. A sensitive sojourner who visited the Midlothian pits in 1843 described the peculiar clothing worn by miners:

> Through the kindness of the president of the company, I was allowed to descend into the mines. I was first conducted to a building where I put on a coarse suit, which is perhaps worthy of description. Firstly, imagine a figure about five

feet . . . incased in a pair of pants of the coarsest "hard-times" cloth, coming up nearly to his shoulders, with legs as large as the wearer's body. Throw over these a coat of the same material, with a very short skirt, and over its collar place a shirtcollar of sail-cloth [waterproof], turned over "a la Byron," being the upper termination of a garment operating most unmercifully as a flesh-brush upon the tender skin of its wearer. Mount this interesting figure in a pair of negro shoes, crown him with a low black wool hat, stuck just on the top of his head.[39]

Little is known about shelter at slave-operated coal mines, except what can be learned from inference. For example, in an agreement to lease a coal tract along the James River, a landowner granted Harry Heth the "liberty to cut and use such timber . . . from his River Estate as may be necessary for props in the pits, and for Huts for the negroes."[40] At least some slaves lived in barracks similar to those occupied by unmarried bondsmen who labored in urban factories. Robert Hughes, the coal yard foreman in Manchester, informed Harry Heth that upon hearing the cry of "fire," Hughes had run out of the office and to his "astonishment saw the House occupied by the negroes at the Coal yd. in flames" caused by too many hot ashes in the fireplace.[41]

The mainstay of the slave miner's diet consisted of much the same provisions as were provided elsewhere in the slave regime. Heth ordered huge quantities of pork over the years. For example, in 1804 he noted receipt of a barrel of pork and two hundred pounds of bacon.[42] In 1833, John Heth distributed 2,652 pounds of pork among the hands.[43] Fish provided another important source of protein, and over the years Heth purchased many barrels of fish for consumption by the slave miners.[44] Corn provided much of the starch in the slave diet, and in 1815 Heth utilized "400 barrels of good corn." Between August 1816 and May 1817, the collier purchased five thousand bushels of grain from neighborhood farmers, and a year later he ordered another six hundred barrels of corn.[45] More than likely, slave hands also received a daily dram of whiskey to ward off the chill of working in knee-deep water, for in 1815 a merchant notified Heth that "I shall send up Barrels of Whiskey with Simon."[46] Slaves at other mines probably received traditional slave victuals. At the James River Coal Pits, from March 7 to April 7, 1849, the company distributed among its forty or so hands, one barrel of flour, two barrels of molasses, fifty pounds of coffee, one hundred pounds of sugar, three barrels of oil, and one hogshead of bacon.[47] Like their counterparts elsewhere in the southern economy, slave miners supplemented their diets during appropriate seasons with produce which they grew themselves. One observer remarked in 1846 that at Midlothian mines "many of the laborers have their gardens which they work for the purpose of raising vegetables for themselves and to carry to market.—This is not confined solely to the whites and free blacks, but the slaves enjoy this benefit'' as well.[48]

Lack of manuscript data also hampers an examination of the frequency of illness among black miners. Illness must have been recurrent enough, however, to warrant the insertion of contingency clauses into hiring contracts. In April 1812, for example, Harry Heth and two other colliers formed a partnership to operate Falling-Creek Coal Mine. In the agreement, it was "expressly understood and agreed, that the said Gordon & Currie shall always keep on the said estate . . . at least four negro fellows & the said Heth at least eight," so that in case of continued sickness among the hands, their positions could be easily filled.[49] In many cases, dampness and "foul air" was the root cause of illness among miners. Toby and several other slaves became "very sick," and it was believed that "working in the warter [*sic*] is the cause of it."[50] Damp working conditions did not represent the only source of illness among the miners. At least one slave at Black Heath contracted venereal disease, for Dr. Phil Turpin directed Heth,

> Please to give the Boy the salts to day. A Teaspoonful of the Solution . . . is to be added to two Tablespoonful of water, of which about a Teaspoonful is to be injected in the penis four times . . . [each] day. He should eat nothing Salt, and flaxseed Tea will be proper for his common Drink.[51]

Dr. Turpin treated Black Heath miners for many years, and his itemized bills provide some insight into daily ailments at the pits. Turpin's invoice for services rendered between 1810 and 1811 totaled $48.15 for thirty-one visits. On many occasions he treated women, at least one of whom was "Expectful," while he prescribed remedies for several slaves who complained of stomach ailments. On another occasion, Turpin presented a bill for "vaccinating little negroes."[52] The operators of Cunliffe's Pits paid the doctor $156 in 1816, primarily for tending to Phill, Isaac, and Herbert. The doctor examined Phill on January 6, 1816, and the hand apparently recovered by August when he received his last treatment. Considering the nature of the cure, his recovery was remarkable, for Phill was bled seven times, "purged" once, and received the application of ointment on several other occasions. Similarly, when Isaac contracted pneumonia, he required four bleedings, three purges, and numerous blister packs. The more fortunate Herbert required only applications of "ointment mediums" for his skin burns.[53]

Occasionally, contagious diseases affected the operation of a coal mine. Harry Heth received a letter from a friend in 1817 expressing regret "to hear of the sickness which has prevailed among your Negroes, & consequently that you had not commenced business at Stone Henge Pit, but hope as they recover you will commence your operations there.''[54] The slaves apparently recovered, for a few months later Stone Henge once again was "raising coal rapidly."[55] Two years later, disease among the miners hindered operations at another Heth mine. In March 1819, the collier received word from a worried friend who had been informed by a third party that "at your pits there was some very bad feaver [*sic*] & that as many as 10 had died of a day. I hope he has been wrongly informed."[56] Unfortunately, the accuracy of this third-hand story remains uncertain. Like their predecessor, the heirs to Black Heath Pits paid numerous medical bills as well, such as that in 1832 which totaled $86.75 for fifty-two calls.[57]

The exact kind of facilities colliers made available for slaves in need of medical treatment remains obscure. By 1843, however, Midlothian had constructed a "comfortable hospital" for sick or injured slaves which was "under the care of a steward, and daily attended by physicians."[58] The Midlothian Company did not intend to bear the entire financial burden for maintaining the health of slave hirelings. An 1846 advertisement informed slaveowners: "A well conducted Hospital, . . . daily attended by three Physicians, is provided at the Mines, and owners of slaves may have them secured from all Medical and Surgical charges, by the payment of three dollars each per annum."[59] The company continued to offer the same health care nine years later, for in 1855 Midlothian advertised that "two physicians" attended the hospital at the mines and that slaves could be insured for their possible treatment at $3 per hand.[60] According to Richard C. Wade, among southern cities "Richmond was best equipped with industrial hospitals." The Tredegar Iron Works operated a complete medical facility, to accompany that at nearby Midlothian which continued to function as late as March 1860.[61]

Some slaves placed a high priority on spiritual comfort as well as physical cure, and religiously inclined miners were provided the opportunity to practice their faith. The slaves of the Richmond coal field were never more than a few miles from an active black congregation. The history of the black church in Virginia falls into three general phases: 1750–1790, 1790–1830, and 1830–1860. During the first period, the new revivalistic denominations of the Great Awakening, especially the Baptists and Methodists, welcomed Virginia slaves with enthusiasm. Because the new churches advocated the abolition of slavery, blacks naturally reciprocated with equal enthusiasm. By 1790, therefore, thousands of blacks, both slave and free, became members of these churches.

During the middle phase, from 1790 to 1830, the Awakening lost much of its energy in Virginia. Masters gradually became convinced that the egalitarian message spread by the new churches, not to mention their outright abolitionist teachings, represented a grave threat to the established order. If proof that more control over bondsmen was required, it came in the form of the Haitian Revolt in 1793 and Gabriel's Revolt of 1800, hatched only a few miles from Richmond, in Henrico County. Masters now began to restrict slave religious meetings and required them to be monitored by whites.

But while control was exerted in the more remote areas, blacks in or near the cities continued to enjoy a significant degree of religious independence. Especially in Richmond and Petersburg, churches attracted not only urban bondsmen, but also slaves from the surrounding rural counties. Masters of the coal field area apparently had no desire to prohibit hands from going into Richmond or Petersburg to hear the Sunday sermon and to socialize with relatives and friends. Blacks did not actually control their own churches at this time, but they did exercise a considerable degree of freedom. Because they represented such a large percentage of the congregation at the First Baptist Church of Richmond, for example, slaves were permitted to preach and otherwise involve themselves in church affairs.[62]

The last phase, from 1830 to 1860, was of particular importance in the development of independent black churches near the coal field. During this period, the abolitionist movement reached maturity, and the era was characterized by an increasingly strident antislavery posture in the North, while the South became aggressively defensive about its "peculiar institution." Religion was an integral part of this heightening antagonism, as each section appealed to the Bible for moral authority to condemn or condone the ownership of human property. Intensive abolitionist pressures during this phase forced the slavocracy to develop an elaborate justification for its way of life. In order to counter the charge that they were insensitive to the spiritual needs of their slaves, and to control the kind of spiritual guidance to be received, southerners began a vigorous campaign to evangelize and gather slaves into churches controlled by the masters. On the contrary, abolitionists within the northern churches opposed the use of religion as a mechanism for slave control. This growing division over slavery and the role of religion in society produced the schisms within the Baptist and Methodist national organizations in 1844 and led to the foundation of the northern and southern departments of those two denominations.

Unlike slaveowners in the South generally, those near the Richmond coal field during this period continued to follow the established practice of permitting slaves to belong to the church of their own choice. In fact, bondsmen gained more religious independence than they had previously experienced. Blacks overwhelmingly preferred the Baptist, although a significant minority joined the Methodist Church. The Baptists' emphasis on local self-rule and a ministry that was "called" rather than educated to preach, as well as their direct appeal to the lower classes, attracted blacks in massive numbers.[63]

By the 1850s, the independence of black churches in the surrounding area of Richmond and Petersburg, but especially those within the cities, was a fact in practice, if not in law. These independent African churches, as they were called, generally grew out of severe overcrowding in the white churches. As a result, four African Baptist churches were established in Richmond, and three in Petersburg. These African churches were usually founded near the white "parent" churches out of which they evolved. While the white parent minister supposedly controlled the black church, normally his presence was only a formality, and the African congregations conducted their own affairs. By 1860, the black churches in Richmond numbered 4,633 members, and in Petersburg 3,563.[64]

Not all slave coal miners who sought religion were forced to make the trip into the city on Sunday, for in some cases the churches came to them. The Reverend J. B. Jeter, a Baptist minister, must have experienced one of the rarer moments of his religious career when he visited the Midlothian mines in 1843. While making his tour, the underground foreman "kindly offered to collect the hands" if the pastor would preach to them. Jeter "readily acceded" to this proposal, for it "accorded well with the stillness and solemnity of the place." After a difficult "journey" to the ascribed meeting place, which included "vigorous exertions" such as crawling on hands and knees, climbing steep inclines, and an examination of the underground furnace and blacksmith shop, the minister finally reached "the place appointed for worship, covered with sweat and not a little fatigued." A curious group it must have been, gathered at the bottom of a deepshaft and seated upon logs and boxes. All the miners were in attendance, and several hands from outside joined the "congregation." Some "ladies and their attendants," tourists as well, also joined the group and sat in a small chamber cut out of the solid coal. "The small brilliant lamps of which every collier has one, were suspended along the walls of our chapel, creating a dazzling light. The congregation consisted of about 90 persons; 80 colored, and 10 white." Jeter was unimpressed by the vocal aptitude of his black congregation, and he characterized their singing of the hymns as "greatly inferior to that of their brethren in the tobacco factories in Richmond." Still, Reverend Jeter found the "circumstances were impressive and awful," and under such conditions there could be no doubt that "God was present."

> The colored friends sang another song. I was desirous to know how many professors of religion there were among them, and first having all seated, I requested those who were professing christians to rise. Thirty rose—they are all, or nearly all, members of the Baptist church. I was gratified to learn from the managers, that many of them are orderly and consistent in their deportment, and that generally, there is marked difference between the conduct of those who profess and those who do not profess religion.

The sermon ended, the congregation dispersed, and the underground superintendent, who had spent his entire working life in the coal mines of England and America, informed Jeter that he had "frequently heard social prayer" in the pits but never a sermon. The novelty of preaching a sermon eight hundred feet "beneath the sleeping place of the dead" left a vivid impression on Reverend Jeter which he was unlikely to forget.[65]

In 1846, an African church was founded in Manchester, at the edge of the coal field and the terminal point for Virginia bituminous destined for coastal cities. That same year, another African church was established in Midlothian, the community which developed near the mines bearing that name, to serve the numerous slave and free blacks who toiled in the pits and on the surrounding farms.[66] The establishment of the Midlothian African Church had a significant impact on the black community, for one white visitor to the mines in 1846 observed that:

> The President of the Company, Maj. Wooldridge, is not annoyed and harassed for a "respectable minister" to preach the gospel to his people, . . . for he has three or four of them. The colored operatives have a meeting house and a Church organized here. On Sabbath last three professed to have "new hearts and new hopes," and are soon to be "buried in baptism." The place is in a high degree moral and orderly.[67]

Although they may have given polite attention to white ministers, slaves preferred their own preachers. Realizing that most whites were agents of the slavocracy, bondsmen responded accordingly. An ex-slave from Virginia recalled when Uncle Silas, a man nearly one hundred years old, rose during a sermon and halted the white minister. "Is us slaves gonna be free in Heaven?" Uncle Silas asked. When the minister tried to ignore the old man, Uncle Silas repeatedly interrupted: "Gonna give us freedom 'long wid salvation?"[68] Black preachers understood, even if their white counterparts did not, that a people trapped in bondage did not care to hear that the same fate awaited them in the hereafter. Eugene Genovese's observation regarding the black preacher comes close to the essential truth of his position: "The black preacher faced a problem analogous to that of the early Christian preachers: they had to speak a language defiant enough to hold the high-spirited among their flock, but neither so inflammatory as to rouse them to battles they could not win nor so ominous as to the rouse the ire of ruling powers."[69]

Most black preachers simply emerged from the masses upon receiving the "call" and became local figures preaching to local folks. Tom Knight, for example, was a prized blacksmith from Fredericksburg who was "moved" to preach. Whenever a few souls gathered around the blacksmith shop, Knight would climb upon a box and deliver his favorite sermon, "My gog an' gog,'' which, incidentally, no one ever understood. They listened to him, however, because he had "style." [70] This quality seems to have been the one universal requirement of all black preachers. Few rivaled Richmond's John Jasper in rhetorical skill and popularity. According to his own account, in 1826 Jasper "was hired out in the county of Chesterfield to Dr. Wo[o]ldridge, where he worked for one year in the coal pits, and during this year the first railroad was laid from the coal pits to the city of Richmond." After leaving the mines, Jasper worked in the Richmond tobacco factories until the fall of that city in 1865. Although a slave, Jasper apparently enjoyed considerable freedom of movement, for when he began preaching, popular demand called him to various places throughout eastern Virginia. Both blacks and whites came to hear Jasper preach and to be bound by his spell. [71]

The foundation of the separate black church resulted from the Negroes' insistence upon independence of spiritual expression. The church provided coal miners, farm hands, and every other class of bondsman with a sense of autonomous community with leaders of their own choosing. The black church was an institution devised to fire its members with a feeling of self-worth and acted as a defensive barrier against the racism which daily pressed in upon them from the outside world. [72]

Since most furnaces and forges existed in relatively isolated areas where there seemed to be little need to establish a church, slave ironworkers, unlike miners, encountered restricted opportunities to participate in organized religion. This very isolation which hampered the founding of churches at ironworks, however, accentuated the importance of another vital institution—the company store. While the coal mines operated close to nearby Richmond and other smaller towns where conventional mercantile services could be found, iron companies were forced to provide this service for themselves.

Traditionally, the company store was stocked with nearly everything necessary in the daily life of the iron community. For example, as early as the 1730s the Baltimore Iron Works company store carried items from coffee and sugar to salt petre, razors, saddles, stationery, and "west indies goods." The total inventory of the Baltimore company store in 1736 amounted to the very considerable sum of £656 9s. $2^2/_3$d. [73] Indeed, the company store was often the supplier of goods for the people of the surrounding countryside, and not just for the iron community itself. Most of the overwork earnings acquired by slave ironworkers was spent at the company store. Normally, the store maintained a record of the slave's credits built up over the accounting period, usually a year or six months, as well as his purchases over the same period, and the account was balanced. On the whole, the slaves came out ahead by building up enough credits while carefully dispensing small sums for extra rations of coffee or sugar.

Slaveowners frequently requested or permitted their hands to secure a few items at the store, and the purchases were charged to the owners' accounts. At Bath Iron Works, the total charged to eight individual owners for provisions distributed to the same number of slaves in 1829 amounted to $17.04.[74] Occasionally, however, an ironmaster encountered difficulties with the hireling's owner if the hand ran up an account at the store without building enough credits in overwork to cover his account. In 1859, William Weaver attempted to charge one master for slave John's account. The owner curtly informed Weaver that he had "no business trading with John or any of my negroes without permission. In the eyes of the law you are liable to a heavy fine . . . if you buy or sell six and one fourth cents from a negro without an order from his master." The irate owner told Weaver that "you ought not to have sold John the boots without my permission. In the 2nd you had no right to trade with him for corn without my permission."[75]

Although the overwork system was designed primarily to motivate slaves, it also provided the employer with means to discipline blacks. If a slave spent more at the company store than he earned, he was forced to do extra work. For example, one slave at Etna Furnace spent his overwork faster than he earned it and finished the year 1858 owing the company store $6.84. The following year, the slave had to work several extra Sundays to pay off his debt.[76] In addition, ironmasters sometimes deducted the value of uncompleted work from the accounts of slaves who did not produce their quotas. When two hired hands at Etna Furnace were short of their wood chopping in August 1858, their accounts were debited at the normal rate for chopping extra wood.[77] At F. T. Anderson's Paramount Furnace, Moses, a slave waggoner, ran up a store account of $22.44 in 1849. By December 22, Moses had only earned $19.50 in overwork credits. In order to pay his account at the store, Moses had to stay at the furnace and work after the other hands had left until he earned enough to balance his account at the store.[78] In such cases, black workers generally were able to remove their debts in a relatively short time and to resume normal purchases at the company store.

Most black ironworkers escaped the disciplinary edge of the overwork system and improved their standard of living. Although slaves frequently earned just enough to purchase what they wanted at the store, some blacks had an insatiable appetite for consumer goods. For example, at Paramount Furnace from April 1847 to October 1848, Daniel Henry purchased food and clothing to the amount of $126.95. By chopping wood, making coal baskets, and working in the ore banks, Daniel Henry earned $127.66, or just about broke even.[79] Harry Lewis's account at Paramount Furnace was more within the average amount of credits and debits, although Lewis appears to have worked only enough to supply himself with a few extras during the year. In 1849, Lewis purchased items such as coffee and shoes which at the end of the year totaled $32.32.[80] The same was true of Jim Allen, another slave at Paramount Furnace, who purchased $19.25 worth of goods in 1849 and performed just enough extra labor to earn $19.25 to cover his debts.[81]

Even unskilled slave hands frequently made large sums of money at overwork, especially the wood choppers. The 1820 overwork account of "Negro Enoch," for example, shows how Enoch greatly improved the daily fare for himself and his family. During 1820, Enoch purchased an extra 120 pounds of pork and 5¼ bushels of meal, for a total debit of $21.20.[82] A more striking example can be seen in the 1820 account of "Negro Jem Aires" (Table 10), another slave hand at Northampton Furnace. In addition to the normal supplies provided by the ironmaster, between January 5 and November 14, 1820, Jem Aires spent a little over $65 on 20¾ bushels of meal, 247 pounds of pork, and 141 pounds of extra beef.[83]

Table 10

STORE ACCOUNT OF "NEGRO JEM AIRES" FOR 1820

Date	Goods Purchased			Cost
January 5	22 lbs pork,	141	lbs beef,	
		3	lbs meal	$ 7.60½
February 28	25 lbs pork,	2¼	bushels meal	6.00
March 31	22 "	"	"	5.62½
April 12	14 "	1½	"	3.60
May 31	45½ "	6	"	12.82½
June 30	32½ "	3¾	"	8.62½
	13 "	1½	"	3.45
September 30	37½ "	3¾	"	8.87½
October 31	25½ "	2¼	"	6.07½
November 14	12½ "	½	"	
	½ lbs rye flour			2.93½
			(debit)	$65.61½

Source: Daybook B19, 1815–1821, Box 9, Northampton Furnace, Ridgely Account Books, Maryland Historical Society.

Skilled slaves were normally in the best position to earn overwork pay. They also had the most money to spend at the company store and were able to improve the material quality of their lives by purchasing extra provisions plus a few luxury items. In December 1760, "Caleb Dorsey's Jack" purchased for himself a felt hat, a linen hanky, and one penknife. But he also purchased for his wife nine yards of Irish linen, two yards of check linen, three and a ninth yards of striped linen, and one and a quarter yards of ribbon.[84] Likewise, in July 1770 "Boy Jack" spent four shillings at the company store "for Diahna's petticoat."[85] Cato apparently acquired a few possessions with which he did not wish to part, for in December 1760 he bought a pair of stockings, a pair of buckles, and "1 padlock."[86] Similarly, at Buffalo Forge skilled craftsmen used their $3 to $5 per ton for extra work at the forge to accumulate significant credit balances at the company store. Sam Williams, for example, maintained a large credit balance in 1856 and 1857. After purchasing a number of items such as bed ticking, a barrel of flour, coffee, and sugar, his account totaled $155.87.[87] Obviously, then, skilled hands like Sam Williams improved the physical conditions of their families to a significant degree.

It can only be assumed that slave miners followed the same pattern of behavior in purchasing extra goods for themselves and their families when the opportunity arose. Because the coal fields were located so close to town, however, the collier did not need to maintain a company store and both owned and hired slaves spent their earnings elsewhere.

The iron and coal industries provide a valuable point-counterpoint for highlighting the effect of different industrial environments on slave family life. Placing these families in historical perspective, however, is a tenuous enterprise at best. Aside from the scant data base available, the task is further complicated by a complex, sometimes racist, but always controversial, historiography of the topic in general. Because the industrial environment varied considerably from that of the plantation regime, employment patterns of slave-hiring and slaveownership also varied, and this difference in environment had a significant impact on the family lives of bonded workers. Clear examples can be seen in the contrast between the iron industry, where an important percentage of workers was owned by the employer, and the coal industry, where employers usually hired slave workers. Among owned ironworkers, "stable" primary kin units were common, and among hired hands who had left immediate family behind, a clear quasi-kin network emerged alongside loyalty to the original primary kin unit. Undeniably, the male's position in his role as husband and father, whether hired or owned, was precarious. In countless ways, the black male was frustrated in asserting authority over the ultimate destiny of his loved ones. Beyond those universal limitations of bondage, however, practical economic requirements of the industrial employer made it easier for many bondsmen to assert themselves in strengthening the family and bolstering their position within it. Extra work represented one of the most important means by which this could be done.

For over a century, both skilled and unskilled slave ironworkers used overwork to help elevate their own and their families' quality of life. One of

Ben Tasker's skilled hands at the Baltimore Iron Works used his overwork in the 1730s to purchase a bed, two blankets, and a rug totaling £2 10s. for his wife "Negro Flora & Children."[88] At John Blair's foundry in May 1797, "Negro Phil" purchased for his wife shoe leather and "7½ yards of ribbon."[89] At Patuxent Iron Works, "Negro Harry" had his account charged with several payments of cash: to his wife Nan, £9 12s. 6d. in March 1796; to son Jacob, £1 2s. 6d. in March 1797; and another £3 15s. "cash paid son Joe" in July 1797. In 1801, Forge Harry's account was charged £3 15s. for "cash paid Son Harry," and £3 15s. 11d. was "paid Son Dick" that same year.[90] At Cumberland Forge in Maryland, "Negro Dick Snowden" purchased "1 pair Shoes for his wife" for 11s. 3d.[91] Abraham was charged $1.75 in 1825 for "1 pr. shoes for Eliza."[92] In 1850, Toller, a skilled hand at Buffalo Forge, drew $5 for his wife, and at Etna Furnace Bill Jones acquired "1 pair Brogans for his wife" for $2 and "Daniel Dumb Boy" was debited several times for "cash for Louisa."[93]

If historian Herbert Gutman's calculations are correct, about one in six (or seven) slave marriages was ended by force or sale.[94] Exactly what percentage applied to the iron and coal industries is impossible to assess, especially since employers hired so many of their hands. Normally, the industrialist was unable to control these events, unsettling as they were to his current and future hired labor force. Slaveowner J. C. Dickinson, for example, wrote to Weaver in October 1830 informing him "of the death of my mother" and stating that Dickinson was making preparation for the "division of the negroes which is to take place Xmas." "I will be extremely glad," wrote Dickinson, "if you will give all & every one of my negroes a pass & send them home." The owner realized that these circumstances were troubling to Weaver's operation and added that "I will aid you much as possible in geting [*sic*] hands for another year."[95]

Slaves hired to employers who were too far from home to enable the hands to get home at night or on weekends suffered from lengthy separations. Owners recognized the tensions this absence created in the family. Planters who hired their bondsmen to ironmasters went to great lengths to insure that their slave men would be permitted to go home at least once or twice a year to visit their wives; masters often inserted that clause into the hiring bond or stipulated the proviso in their letters to ironmasters. One owner wrote to Jordan and Irvine in 1829 that they must permit a slave hired to them to "come home once in the course of the year to see his wife."[96]

Another master wrote to Weaver that he was going to Tennessee, and "I will be much obliged to you if you will ascertain of my man Nelson whether he is wiling [*sic*] to go or not if Nelson is willing to go with me to Tennessee I shall hire him out the next year untill the first day of September but if he has a wife and is not willing to part with her to go with me I am willing to sell him."[97] "I hope you will buy Paris as I would not like her to get into hands who would separate the children from the mother," wrote another slaveowner to an ironmaster.[98] The master of a hired slave wrote to ironmaster F. T. Anderson that he was going to "sell out this spring & Moove [*sic*]," and continued, "My Girl Evoline is anxious to be as near George as she can I am disposed to sell her . . . to you and as she and George both wants you to buy her I am willing to accomadate [*sic*] them."[99] A few days later, the owner wrote once again, "George is here and insists on Me to Send you a few lines as he is very anxious for Me to sell you Evoline." He offered Evoline to Anderson for $800. He could "do better than that but it would not please them (the negroes). this is all I can or will do If you do not want her I can have her in this county at a place that Geo can get to as easy as this."[100]

Other slave ironworkers actively participated in matters concerning their wives. Tuyman Wayt, agent for Jordan & Irvine, wrote to the ironmasters in 1830 about a slave hand they wanted to hire, "Mr. Jones requested me to say to you," wrote the agent, that "Winston would not consent to go back [to the works] having as I understand taken a wife."[101] Another slave being transferred to F. T. Anderson's works made certain that his wife did not have to trudge all the way on foot. Frank Glasgow, manager of one of Anderson's works, wrote to Anderson that he "paid a baggage waggon that Reuben had employed to take his wife & baggage to the Depot $1.50." The slave informed Glasgow that "there was to be some arrangement made to send his wife by Packet from Lynchburg [to the furnace] and having no doubt you so intended I have advanced him $2.00 to pay fare."[102]

Several blacks at Buffalo Forge, such as "Garland," had wives who resided near the forge, and these hands regularly spent the remainder of the weekend with them when work stopped on Saturday.[103] Difficulties sometimes arose with slave men who could not readily see their wives. For example, Weaver's manager at Etna Furnace described the problems he had with a hand in 1862:

> You ask me about Griffen. I consider him a triffling [*sic*] hand. he laid up here very often & for long periods—but it was only when we worked him about the Furnace he laid up so often that we had finally to take him away. . . . Tell him that you will put him in the wood chopping when he gets well & I will guarantee he will soon be out—that is his object now in laying up. I found that he laid up very seldom when he could get a chance to run to his wife.[104]

A complete reconstruction of the daily lives and family patterns of slave ironworkers is not possible because adequate manuscript material simply does not exist. Two particularly valuable sources, however, provide exceptional glimpses of family life at Ross's Oxford Iron Works. Because of their importance, the documents deserve to be reproduced at length. The first is a detailed slave enumeration listing Oxford's black work force by family units, with the father, mother, children, and sometimes superannuary relatives grouped together. Since Oxford was operated by a slave force of 220 and constituted one of the largest ironworks in the new nation, the list carries special significance. It is summarized in Table 11.

The second document which illuminates some of the hidden recesses of slave family life at southern ironworks is a letter contained in David Ross's letterbook for 1812–1813. In 1812, an unmarried slave woman named Fanny, out of an apparent religious conviction, attempted to destroy her newly born infant. The incident provoked Ross to vent his feelings at length concerning slave marriage, slave parenthood, and slave family life in general. Because it is one of the rare glimpses we have into an ironmaster's attitudes regarding slave family life, the letter merits full quotation:

> I cannot lose a minute in expressing my surprise and indignation at the extravagant conduct of little Fanny. Tis happy for her and pleasing to me, that the infant has been preserved, 'tis particularly pleasing, because had the innocent child perished I would have prosecuted her unto the ignominious [*sic*] death of the Gallow, the laws of humanity and the laws of the land must not be prosterated [*sic*] to the wild ravings of fanatisism [*sic*]. Tis well known that I demand moderate labour from the servants, as a compensation for my benevolence toward them (you know how small the compensation I have received) in other respects, I have (in a great measure) left them free only under such controul [*sic*] as was most congenial to their happiness. I have never laid any restrictions on their worshipping the deity agreeably to their own minds (so far as rational) in any manner they please—as to their amorous connections (perfectly natural) I have not been merely passive, but have upon more occasion than one or two declared my sentiments, that the young people might connect themselves in marriage, to their own liking, with consent of their parents who were the best judges. 'tis true I have discouraged connections out of the estate and particularly with free people of colour, because I was certain, 'twould be injurious to my people, but I have violence to prevent those connections for tis well known that now they exist upon my estate and have not been expelled but no longer attend—tis very much my wish that my servants should connect themselves in a decent manner and behave as a religious people ought to do—human nature is frail and apt to err—Fanny was under no restraint as to a husband whom

Table 11

SLAVES AT OXFORD IRONWORKS IN FAMILIES AND OCCUPATIONS

Family Unit	Mother	Father	Children	Grand-parents	No. Children at Jobs Same or Different from Parents		Too Young to Work [a]	Other [b]
					Same	Different		
1	1	1	6	0			6	
2	1	1	1	0				1
3	1	1	4	0	2		2	
4	0	1	3	0			3	
5	0	1	3	0			3	
6	1	1	4	0	2	2		
7	1	1	3	0	2		1	
8	1	1	2	0				2
9	1	1	5	0	1		4	
10	1	1	3	0	1	1	1	
11	1	1	0					
12	1	0	2	0			2	
13	1	1	3	0		3		
14	1	1	0	0				
15	1	1	8	0				8
16	1	1	13	0	4	3	5	1
17	1	1	3	0			2	1
18	1	0	8	0			5	3
19	1	1	5	0	2	1	2	
20	1	1	7	0		2	5	
21	1	1	8	1	1	6		1
22	0	1	6	0			6	
23	0	1	3	0			3	
24	1	1	7	0	1	1	5	
25	1	1	8	0	2		4	
26	1	1	8	1	1	1	6	
27	1	1	5	0	2	3		
28	1	1	5	0				5
29	0	1	3	0			3	
30	1	1	3	0	1	1		1

[a] Includes children between the ages of ten and fourteen who were "nurses" and took care of the children but did not work full time.

[b] Includes those slaves who cannot be associated with an occupation because it was not listed.

Source: "List of Slaves at the Oxford Iron Works in Families & Their Employment, taken January 15, 1811," Bolling Family Papers, Duke University. Compiled by the author.

so ever she might choose—What then could induce her to such an inhuman act. She had little to fear from heaven—two wrongs can never make any point right—because when united the two makes it a much worse matter—her going astray was most certainly wrong, but an attempt to destroy the most innocent infant was horrid damnable—as to Fannys tale of being delivered in the woods, it is not to be credited. My conduct to pregnant women requires no comment, you know that no pregnant woman is put to labour within some weeks of her delivery, and as long afterwards—Tis not my desire to make this poor woman unhappy quite otherwise but 'tis my earnest wish that this hapless innocent may be taken the utmost care of and that nothing may be wanting to the preservation of this exposed child that my estate can furnish.

PS You will please me and I hope to be pleased yourself in exposing such an abominable conduct the disgrace of all religion and most abominable to me as the master.[105]

Taken together, these two documents provide valuable insights into how at least one leading ironmaster viewed slave family life. The documents also indicate that black slave parents at Oxford took much more responsibility for the lives of their children than has been assumed. Normally, slave offspring remained within the family unit, and Ross encouraged parents to approve or disapprove any prospective marriage. The Oxford list reveals several patterns with important social implications for slave families. For example, the list shows that members of family units not only lived together, but that slave artisans also taught craft secrets to their sons. Thus, several of the children and a grandchild of collier Big Adam also worked in some phase of charcoal production. The same relationship existed in four other colliers' families and throughout the skilled crafts generally.[106] No doubt Ross believed that a strong slave family structure was morally proper and humane. Beyond this, he recognized that a viable slave family helped insure the growth of his slave force and a continuation of the skills vital to iron production. Moreover, stable family arrangements helped maintain discipline and deterred runaways. That Ross fully appreciated the implications of marriage can be seen in the example of Solomon, who ran off to rejoin his wife after Ross had acquired him. Recognizing the inevitable problems that would result from forcing Solomon to remain at Oxford, Ross sold him to a planter in the vicinity of his wife's home and commented that "my intention was to leave the man where he seemed desirous of living."[107]

Perhaps the most significant observation which can be made from the Oxford slave list is that, of the thirty individual family units cited, twenty-three had both mother and father present, and two units contained one grandparent. Remarkably, in only two families was the father absent, while in five there was no mother. Thus, 77 percent of the Oxford families were headed by both parents, and among the 23 percent of the units where only one parent presided, the tendency was for the *father* to head the family, not the mother. Although it was a clear exception to the norm, family organization at Oxford Iron Works indicates the dramatic differences which might occur in the industrial setting.

It would be invaluable to know the character of slave family life at other ironworks, but lack of surnames and the repeated use of common slave names present almost insurmountable barriers. Still, Ross was not unique in recognizing the importance of a stable slave family structure for the operation of an ironworks. From the 1760s until the 1790s, for example, there was at Patuxent Iron Works a consistently stable group of skilled and semiskilled workers and women, which probably reflected a stable family system. Patuxent slaves exhibited a similar male to female ratio over time as that which prevailed at Oxford. The same was true at most ironworks, where skilled blacks, along with their wives and children, provided the steady core of the work force, while unskilled hands tended more often to be hired and, consequently, relatively transient. Table 12 summarizes the sex ratio at Patuxent during 1769–1784.

Table 12

SLAVES AT PATUXENT IRONWORKS, 1769–1784

Number of Slaves	Years at the Works															
	1	2	3	4	5	6	7	8	9	10	11	12	13	14	15	16
Skilled/male (45)	3	4		2	1			6	4	1	3	1	1	1	1	5
Women (30)	5	4	2		2	2	1	2	2	1	3	1	1	1		3
Unskilled/male (57)	26	11	8	4	1	2	2	1	2							

Source: Journal A & B, 1767–1794, Patuxent Iron Works, Maryland Hall of Records. Compiled by the author.

At least one slave family at Patuxent remained intact for thirty years. "Negro Forge Harry" first appeared in the company ledgers during the late 1760s. The same was true for his wife Nann. By the late 1790s and in 1801, Forge Harry's account was debited for giving sums of money to his wife and his sons Joe, Jacob, Harry, and Dick.[108] The same outward characteristics of iron communities remained throughout the antebellum era until the Civil War when the Tredegar Company advertised that it would hire entire slave families and place the women and children on farms near the ironworks where the husband was employed.[109] At ironworks where a skilled black labor force existed, which included most, the conditions for a relatively stable family structure prevailed, and incentive systems such as overwork helped to strengthen its foundations.

Gutman's thesis regarding the slave practice of naming children after the father in order to maintain familial continuity over time seems to be supported by the fragmentary evidence available for early iron communities. For example, Forge Harry and his wife Nann, mentioned above, named one of their sons at Patuxent Iron Works "Harry," after the father.[110] The best illustration is the 1811 slave family list for Oxford Iron Works. At that iron community, Big Abram and his wife Jeany named two of their five male children "Young Abram" and "Little Abram," after the father; Woodhauler Jim also dubbed his son "Jim"; three of the male children born to Big Fanny and Briton were named "Joe Briton," "Jim Briton," and "Little Briton"; Aaron, the hammerman at the Oxford forge, christened one of his three boys after himself; Arthur, the waggoner, had a son known as "Little Arthur"; and Forge Charles had a son named "Charley."[111] Such evidence is, of course, too fragmentary for confident generalizations, but the requisite physical conditions and outward appearances suggest that Gutman's thesis probably held true at most stable iron establishments.

For a variety of reasons, family relationships differed among slave coal miners. For one thing, most mine operators apparently did not follow the practice typical among ironmasters of owning skilled hands to insure stability within the production process. Coal mining differed from iron production in that most skilled tasks at ironworks were relatively less dangerous than any underground occupation, whereas *all* occupations within the pits presented dangers, and rockfalls or explosions killed indiscriminately. Thus, the economics of slaveownership differed for the collier. Furthermore, by the time mining became widespread during the 1820s, slave prices had already begun to take their second dramatic rise since the founding of the nation, and colliers with limited capital could not easily enter into the business because of the large investment required to purchase a work force. However, the prospective mine operator might easily have afforded a force hired by the year. Thus, coal miners never had the female component frequently found at ironworks. Mine operators hired their hands almost exclusively, and if the men had families, they resided elsewhere. The disruptive potential must have been considerably greater with hiring for pit work since such a vast majority of bondsmen were drawn away from their families. On the other hand, the Richmond coal field was close to the city of Richmond and also was nearly surrounded by a dense population of plantation slaves who, if hired to work at the mines, were not far from their families.

Both slaves and their owners, however, attempted to mitigate some of
the disruptiveness inherent in the system. In 1807, Heth's slave miner Phil,
who had a wife at Mr. Jordin Flournoy's nearby plantation, attempted to
persuade the planter to purchase him so that he could be closer to his
wife.[112] Another hired slave had worked at Heth's pits previously and
desired to return. The owner informed Heth that the hand could be hired
"in this neighbourhood for $110 as a Ditcher, but as he is Desireous [sic] to
live with you & is convenient to his wife I wish to indulge him."[113] Two
hands were hired to Black Heath in 1817 with the proviso that they work as
top hands only. The owner added that "Ned has no wife, Charles has and of
course he will be allowed time to see her."[114] That same year, Heth
informed a neighboring operator that he, Heth, had two hands for hire, both
of whom were generally employed at the pits. One of the men was not
married, but the other had "a wife in about nine miles of the Pitts [sic]."[115]

Some slave miners used visiting their wives as an excuse to gain more
physical mobility. After receiving a pass to spend the weekend with his
wife, one hand failed to report for work on Monday morning. Heth checked
with the slave's master, who responded that he had not seen "Bob until
Saturday night." The following Thursday, the owner had inquired about
Bob at his wife's quarters and was informed that the Slave "had sett [sic]
off to the coal pits."[116] Still other slave miners used visiting their wives as a
pretext for activities other than maintaining conjugal relations:

> Daniel who is said to belong to you, has been coming up to my
> house for some time past, under the pretext of seeing a wife.
> There is a mere pretext, in as much as he does not remain
> with her when he comes—I have lately formed a deter-
> mination, to recommend a discontinuance of his visits, for
> several reasons, particularly as I desire to have no communi-
> cation between my negroes and those in the vicinity of
> Richmond—I have thought it proper to advise you by letter,
> of the determination herein expressed, supposing it will be
> greatly to your Interest, that he should form a connexion
> more convenient to him. it will conduce very much to my
> satisfaction for him to do so.[117]

From the employer's position, married hirelings could present still other
problems. For example, in 1814 Heth informed a friend who sought to lease
several hands that "hired boys from this part of the Country I fear would be
of little use to you. they would be apt to run away or be too often applying
for liberty to come down to see their connections."[118] A slave who belonged to Heth persisted in running off to see his wife, owned by planter

William Browne. Heth received a letter from Browne in June 1819 expressing his chagrin over the slave's misconduct. The problem did not reside in
maltreatment at the pits, Browne wrote, for the hand "was with a kind and
humane master, as he often acknowledged to me; but having his wife who
has been an unusually faithful and kind nurse to my children I feel that it is
the only return I can make her for such services" to buy Heth's slave for his
servant and that would put a stop to the running away.[119]

In such cases, the family provided sanctuary from the harsh realities of
life, especially for young men who did not want to break the bond with their
parents. In 1807, a young man ran off from his owner at a plantation several
miles from the pits. The master explained that his "Boy Adam . . . is a Son
of Charlotte's," one of Heth's servants at Black Heath, "and I have good
reasons to believe he is gone up with his mother" once again. Rather than
undergo repeated incidents of misconduct, the young slave's new owner
offered to "hire or sell him" to Heth permanently.[120] Similarly, a young
hand who fled the pits in 1811 probably ran back to his parents:

> I am satisfied that Squire had not bin [*sic*] to my house since
> he absconded. It is probably that he may be at Maj. Clarks
> plantation near Richmond whare [*sic*] his father & mother is;
> Squire is not 19 years old & I expect not able to bare [*sic*] the
> hard labour in the pitts. Mr. Edwd. had consulted me be four
> [*sic*] he hired him he should never went in the pitts.[121]

Olmsted visited the Midlothian mines in the mid-1850s. Later, when he
recorded his recollections of that experience, he had the distinct "impression" that "it was customary to give the slaves a certain allowance of
money and let them find their own board" rather than have it provided by
the company.[122] If this indeed was the practice, it would have had a direct
effect on family practices among Midlothian slaves. The census for 1860
listed all males at Midlothian and no females at all. The roster of slave
hands at Clover Hill Coal Mining Company, near Petersburg, contained
only one female among the 66 hands employed; there were no women
among the 109 slaves who worked on the company's railroad. Furthermore, over 80 percent of the slaves hired by both companies were clustered
in the age range between twenty and forty-nine, when they were most likely
to be married. This fact strongly suggests that Olmsted's observation
contains some merit, at least for Midlothian and Clover Hill, which were
the two largest mines in operation at the time.[123] Many of these men
undoubtedly had wives who worked on nearby company-owned farms. An
advertisement posted by the Tredegar Iron Works in November 1863, for
example, called for one thousand hands to hire: "Parties having families of

negroes, consisting of men, women and boys, may make arrangements with us for the whole, provided the classes are not disproportioned, as there are farms attached to some of the furnaces and collieries, on which the women and boys can be employed."[124] Still other slaves miners no doubt had wives at surrounding plantations or in the cities of Richmond and Petersburg. Also, the proper sex ratio existed among the bonded population of Chesterfield County to support a family system, with 2,605 male and 2,659 female slave residents in 1850. Olmsted was probably correct in his recollection that, by the 1850s at least, mining companies did not maintain slaves in families but rather permitted their hired hands to find homes for themselves.[125]

Strong family attachments continued to affect the operation of southern industries which relied upon black labor during the post-Civil War era. For example, in 1886 Alfred F. Brainerd, a man of "considerable practical experience in the management of colored mining labor in the South," shared his thoughts on the topic with colleagues of the American Institute of Mining Engineers. In southern mining, he observed in an Institute publication, black labor was "largely in excess of any other." A "trying time" for the mine manager occurred during the holiday season, he declared, "when nearly every man on the place wants to go home—and does go." The exodus usually began about the first of the year. The majority of the absentees remained at home from one to three months, during which time there was a partial or total suspension of mining. According to this supervisor, the only "remedy" was to induce the men "to bring their families to the place where they work and to provide suitable quarters for them."[126] Being absent from their families had never rested well with black miners. As slaves, there was little they could do to alter these circumstances, but as free men, black colliers displayed a determination to improve their family ties as best they could within an increasingly rigid industrial system. That determination was not a result of emancipation, however. It came as the natural outgrowth of a tradition that had deep roots in slavery, a tradition of resistance to the dehumanization and destruction of the black family unit.

NOTES

1. Frederick Law Olmsted, *A Journey in the Seaboard Slave States, with Remarks on Their Economy* (New York: Mason Brothers, 1859), p. 58.

2. Stanley M. Elkins, *Slavery: A Problem in American Institutional and Intellectual Life* (Chicago: University of Chicago Press, 1959), Chap. 3.

3. Kenneth M. Stampp, *The Peculiar Institution: Slavery in the Ante-Bellum South* (New York: Alfred A. Knopf, 1956), p. 84.

4. John W. Blassingame, *The Slave Community: Plantation Life in the Antebellum South* (New York: Oxford University Press, 1972), pp. 206–207.

5. Benjamin Spindle to W. W. Davis, January 13, 1840, Jordan and Davis Papers, State Historical Society of Wisconsin, hereafter cited as SHSW.

6. George Salling to William Weaver, January 5, 1859, Weaver-Brady Papers, University of Virginia, hereafter cited as UVa.

7. A typical Bond of Hire, Shanks, Anderson & Anderson by James L. Patton, November 13, 1849, Anderson Family Papers, UVa.

8. Joshua Chew to W. Weaver, January 2, 1830, William Weaver Papers, Duke University, hereafter cited as Duke.

9. David Ross to R. Richardson, January 1813, Ross Letterbook, Virginia Historical Society, hereafter cited as VHS.

10. Samuel Jordan to William Davis, March 7, 1840, Jordan and Davis Papers, SHSW.

11. W. W. Rex to D. Brady, February 25, 1859, Weaver-Brady Papers, UVa.

12. C. K. Gorgas to D. Brady, April 2, 1860, William Weaver Papers, Duke.

13. W. W. Rex to D. Brady, May 29, June 19, July 6, 1860, William Weaver Papers, Duke.

14. Ibid., September 2 and 26, 1860.

15. See the Carter-Brooke correspondence series in the Robert Carter Papers, Maryland Historical Society, hereafter cited as MHS.

16. Clement Brooke to Robert Carter, June 24, 1772, Robert Carter Papers, MHS.

17. Ibid., March 3, 1777.

18. B. Nicholson to Charles Ridgely, n.d., probably 1780, Ridgely Family Papers, MHS.

19. D. Ross to T. Hopkins, August 25, 1813, Ross Letterbook, VHS.

20. J. Doyle to A. W. Davis, December 1, 1828, Weaver-Brady Papers, UVa.

21. Jordan, Davis & Co., to A. W. Davis, August 11, 1830, William Weaver Papers, Duke.

22. S. F. Jordan to W. Weaver, December 7, 1830, William Weaver Papers, Duke.

23. C. K. Gorgas to W. Weaver, April 6 and 11, 1859, Weaver-Brady Papers, UVa.

24. W. W. Rex to D. Brady, July 26, 1859, Weaver-Brady Papers, UVa.

25. C. K. Gorgas to W. Weaver, April 2, 1860, William Weaver Papers, Duke.

26. Robert S. Starobin, *Industrial Slavery in the Old South* (New York: Oxford University Press, 1970), especially Chaps. 2 and 3; S. Sydney Bradford, "The Negro Ironworker in Ante Bellum Virginia," *Journal of Southern History* 25 (May 1959): 203–204.

27. D. Ross to William Dunn, August 1813, Ross Letterbook, VHS.

28. James D. B. DeBow (ed.), *DeBow's Review and Industrial Resources, Statistics, etc., of the United States and More Particularly of the Southern & Western States* (New York: Augustus M. Kelley, 1966, originally January 1846 through April 1862) 17 (1854):423.

29. *DeBow's Review* 19 (1855):359.

30. C. K. Gorgas to W. Weaver, April 2, 1860, William Weaver Papers, Duke.

31. Samuel Jordan to W. Weaver, September 29, 1830, Jordan and Irvine Papers, SHSW.

32. Time Book, 1843–1853, Buffalo Forge, Weaver-Brady Papers, UVa.

33. C. K. Gorgas to W. Weaver, April 2, 1860, Weaver-Brady Papers, UVa.

34. Cited in Howard N. Eavenson, *The First Century and a Quarter of American Coal Industry* (Pittsburgh: By the Author, 1942), pp. 129–130.

35. Hire Bond, Johnson & Cunliffe, John Cunliffe, and Needler Robbins with Harry Heth, April 21, 1815, Heth Family Papers, UVa.

36. Robert Perkins to Harry Heth, February 14, 1817, Heth Family Papers, UVa.

37. "Clothes Furnished Hands," Accounts and Receipts, 1815, Heth Family Papers, UVa.

38. Accounts and Receipts, 1833, Heth Family Papers, UVa.

39. Henry Howe, *Historical Collections of Virginia; Containing a Collection of the Most Interesting Facts, Traditions, Biographical Sketches, Anecdotes, etc. Relating to its History and Antiquities* (Charleston, S.C.: Babcock & Co., 1845), p. 230.

40. Lease, Daniel Trabue and Harry Heth, February 4, 1811, Heth Family Papers, UVa.

41. Robert Hughes to Harry Heth, April 10, 1815, Heth Family Papers, UVa.

42. A. Nicolson to Harry Heth, September 22, 1804. Also see Robert Hughes to Harry Heth, June 15, 1815, and John Potts to Harry Heth, June 9, 1815, Heth Family Papers, UVa.

43. Accounts and Receipts, 1833, Heth Family Papers, UVa.

44. A. Nicolson to Harry Heth, September 22, 1804, and John Landy to Harry Heth, November 2, 1817, Heth Family Papers, UVa.

45. B. Randolph to Harry Heth, July 31, 1815, John Tandy to Harry Heth, May 27, 1817, and James Fayre to Harry Heth, November 5, 1817, Heth Family Papers, UVa.

46. John Potts to Harry Heth, June 9, 1815, Heth Family Papers, UVa.

47. McCaw Journal, James River Coal Pits, 1849–1851, UVa.

48. *Daily Whig and Public Advertiser,* June 26, 1846.

49. Articles of Agreement, Robert Gordon, James Currie, and Harry Heth, April 30, 1812, Heth Family Papers, UVa.

50. Edward Mosely to Harry Heth, August 29, 1811, Heth Family Papers, UVa.

51. Phil Turpin to Harry Heth, August 11, 1801, Heth Family Papers, UVa.

52. Accounts and Receipts, 1811, Heth Family Papers, UVa.

53. Ibid., 1816.

54. Dan. Mayo Railey to Harry Heth, March 10, 1817, Heth Family Papers, UVa.

55. Ibid., May 21, 1817.

56. R. Perkins to Harry Heth, March 17, 1819, Heth Family Papers, UVa.

57. Accounts and Receipts, 1832, Heth Family Papers, UVa.

58. Howe, *Historical Collection of Virginia,* p. 231.

59. *Richmond Whig and Public Advertiser,* January 2, 1846.

60. *Richmond Enquirer,* January 2, 1855.

61. Richard C. Wade, *Slavery in the Cities: The South, 1820–1860* (New York: Oxford University Press, 1964), p. 139; *Richmond Enquirer,* March 20, 1860.

62. Luther P. Jackson, "Religious Development of the Negro in Virginia from 1760 to 1860," *Journal of Negro History* 16 (April 1931):168–239.

63. Ibid., pp. 188–99, 211, 216, 218.

64. Ibid., pp. 222, 227–29, 233.

65. *Niles' Weekly Register,* 65 (1843):108–109.

66. Ira Berlin, *Slaves Without Masters: The Free Negro in the Antebellum South* (New York: Vintage Books, 1974), pp. 294–95.

67. *Richmond Whig and Public Advertiser,* June 26, 1846.

68. Charles L. Perdue, Jr., Thomas E. Barden, and Robert K. Phillips (eds.), *Weevils in the Wheat: Interviews with Virginia Ex-Slaves* (Charlottesville: University Press of Virginia, 1976), pp. 184–85.

69. Eugene D. Genovese, *Roll, Jordan, Roll: The World the Slaves Made* (New York: Vintage Books, 1976), p. 266.

70. Perdue, et al., *Weevils in the Wheat,* p. 203.

71. Ibid., pp. 282, 290; Edwin Archer Randolph, *The Life of Rev. John Jasper, Pastor of the Sixth Mt. Zion Baptist Church, Richmond, Virginia: From His Birth to the Present Time, with His Theory on the Rotation of the Sun* (Richmond: R. T. Hill & Co., 1864), p. 6.

72. Genovese, *Roll, Jordan, Roll,* pp. 235, 238, 283.

73. "Baltimore Company—Inventory of Store Goods, Belonging to Benjamin Tasker and Company," November 29, 1736, Box 3, Carroll-Maccubbin Papers, MHS.

74. Ledger, 1828–1830, Bath Iron Works, Weaver-Brady Papers, UVa.

75. D. Rittenhouse to W. Weaver, January 7, 1859, William Weaver Papers, Duke.

76. Negro Book, 1857–1860, Etna Furnace, Weaver-Brady Papers, UVa.

77. Ibid. The normal overwork rate for chopping extra wood was forty cents per cord.

78. Negro Book, 1847–1849, Paramount Furnace, F. T. Anderson Ledgers, UVa.

79. Ibid.

80. Ibid.

81. Ibid.

82. Daybook B–19, 1815–1821, Box 9, Northampton Furnace, Ridgely Account Books, MHS.

83. Ibid.

84. Journal for Ledger C, 1758–1861, Elk Ridge Furnace, Maryland Hall of Records, hereafter cited as HR.

85. Journal CC, 1764–1772, Elk Ridge Furnace, HR.

86. Journal for Ledger C, 1758–1761, Elk Ridge Furnace, HR.

87. Negro Book, 1850–1858, Buffalo Forge, Weaver-Brady Papers, UVa.

88. "Inventory of Ben Tasker at Baltimore Co.—1737," Box 3, Carroll-Maccubbin Papers, MHS.

89. Ledger of John Blair, Iron Founder, 1795–1797, College of William and Mary.

90. Ledger of the Executors of Thomas Snowden, December 24, 1775–January 2, 1801, Patuxent Iron Works, HR.

91. Cumberland Forge Day Book, 1802, Library of Congress, hereafter cited as LC.

92. Daybook, 1825–1836, Union Forge, Rinker-Lantz Papers, Duke.

93. Negro Book, 1850–1858, Buffalo Forge, and Negro Book, 1857–1860, Etna Furnace, Weaver-Brady Papers, UVa.

94. Herbert G. Gutman. *The Black Family in Slavery and Freedom, 1750–1925* (New York: Pantheon Books, 1976), p. 318.

95. J. C. Dickinson to W. Weaver, October 21, 1830, Weaver-Brady Papers, UVa.

96. R. Brooks to Jordan & Irvine, January 2, 1829, Jordan and Irvine Papers, SHSW.

97. R. Dickinson to W. Weaver, November 15, 1829, William Weaver Papers, Duke.

98. Pendleton Adams to James W. Harrison, October 31, 1850, William Weaver Papers, Duke.

99. John Huff to F. T. Anderson, March 20, 1856, Anderson Family Papers, UVa.

100. Ibid., March 24, 1856.

101. Tuyman Wayt to Jordan and Irvine, January 6, 1830, Jordan and Irvine Papers, SHSW.

102. F. Glasgow to F. T. Anderson, January 1, 1858, Anderson Family Papers, UVa.

103. Daniel C. Brady Home Journals, SHSW.

104. W. Rex to D. Brady, March 22, 1862, Weaver-Brady Papers, UVa.

105. D. Ross to Robert Richardson (manager of the Oxford Works), April 30, 1812, Ross Letterbook, VHS. Reproduced with permission of VHS.

106. Ibid.; and "List of Slaves at Oxford," Bolling Family Papers, Duke.

107. D. Ross to John Cole, November 28, 1812, to Edmond Sherman, August 19, September 8 and 13, 1813, and to Robert Wright, August 22, 1813, all in the Ross Letterbook, VHS. Also see Charles B. Dew, "David Ross and the Oxford Iron Works: A Study of Industrial Slavery in the Early Nineteenth-Century South," *William and Mary Quarterly* 31 (April 1974):213.

108. Ledger of the Executors of the Estate of Thomas Snowden, December 24, 1775–January 2, 1810, Patuxent Iron Works, HR.

109. *Richmond Examiner,* November 14, 1863.

110. Journals A & B, 1767–1794, Patuxent Iron Works, HR.

111. "List of Slaves at Oxford Iron Works 1811," William Bolling Papers, Duke.

112. Peter Duprey to Harry Heth, January 7, 1807, Heth Family Papers, UVa.

113. William Hundley to Harry Heth, January 18, 1817, Heth Family Papers, UVa.

114. W. G. Warner to Harry Heth, March 9, 1817, Heth Family Papers, UVa.

115. Harry Heth to A. S. Wooldridge, December 28, 1817, Heth Family Papers, UVa.

116. A. Cowley to Harry Heth, January 27, 1807, Heth Family Papers, UVa.

117. George Harris to Harry Heth, June 8, 1810, Heth Family Papers, UVa.

118. Harry Heth to Mrs. Eliza Railey, January 19, 1814, Heth Family Papers, UVa.

119. Wm. Browne to Harry Heth, June 2, 1819, Heth Family Papers, UVa.

120. William Banks to Harry Heth, January 27, 1807, Heth Family Papers, UVa.

121. Edward Mosely to Harry Heth, August 29, 1811, Heth Family Papers, UVa.

122. Olmsted, *Journey in the Seaboard Slave States,* p. 47.

123. Eighth Census, 1860, Chesterfield County, Virginia, Slave Schedules and Industrial Schedules, manuscript census on microfilm, Virginia State Library, hereafter cited as VSL.

124. *Richmond Examiner,* November 14, 1863.

125. Seventh Census, 1850, Chesterfield County, Virginia, Slave Schedules and List of Inhabitants, manuscript census on microfilm, VSL.

126. Alfred F. Brainerd, "Colored Mining Labor," *Transactions* of the AIME, 14 (June 1885–May 1886):78, 80.

The Economics of   6
Slave Labor

We live and we love, and our tyrants shall learn
    We are men with passions and might;
We love and we live, and our rough hearts yearn
    For the day that shall follow our night;
When we'll live joyous lives with our children and wives,
    No longer debased by our toil,
When each man shall take what each man shall make
    In the pit, the mill, or the soil
    In the pit, the mill, or the soil.
        —W. H. Utley, "Song of the Miners"

In his pioneering study *Industrial Slavery in the Old South,* Robert S. Starobin synthesizes his research into the business records of numerous antebellum southern enterprises. His study reveals that textile mills which employed slave labor earned annual net profits varying from 10 to 65 percent, and averaged a lucrative 16 percent. Similarly, a Kentucky hemp manufacturer earned annual net profits of 42 percent during the 1840s, and a tannery reported 10 percent annually between 1831 and 1845. Official state reports testify that Louisiana sugar mills yielded profits of over 7 percent in 1830 and nearly 11 percent in 1845. Starobin also estimates that at least one cotton press earned 10 percent during the 1850s, the same dividend earned by southern gas works in 1854. He cites one study of the famous Haxall Flour Mills of Richmond which reportedly "made large fortunes for their owners for over a half a century."[1]

Southern extractive industries also produced significant earnings. Starobin found turpentine enterprises of North Carolina and Georgia which achieved "satisfactory returns" during the 1850s. Likewise, a Louisiana lumber yard earned annual profits ranging between 12.5 and 25 percent between 1846 and 1850. Sizable profits also were realized in the lumber industries of Virginia and North Carolina's Dismal Swamp, as well as in west Florida. Mines employed slaves almost exclusively, and according to

Starobin, these enterprises yielded unspecified but handsome profits.[2] A Missouri lead smelter is quoted, declaring that "a slave, with a *Pick* and *Shovel* is supposed to do nothing, if the net proceeds of his labor, do not amount, annually, to the sum of 400 dollars—the price which his master has probably paid for him." Gold mines also paid handsome dividends, such as those of John C. Calhoun and Samuel J. Tilden, which generated nearly $1 million and $4 million respectively, while in operation.[3]

Starobin cites numerous additional cases of southern enterprises which relied upon slave labor and showed "reasonable," and sometimes substantial, profits. He concludes, therefore, that slave-operated industries were usually profitable. Whether Starobin's generalization applies to the southern iron and coal industries, however, cannot be stated with complete assurance. Actually, Starobin all but ignores southern coal mining, and he does not make a careful assessment of the iron industry. His reasons for not doing so are clear: a definitive study of the profitability of slavery in the coal and iron industries is impossible, for the data simply do not exist to either prove or disprove the hypothesis. Extant business statistics are unreliable indices because many, perhaps most, enterprises failed to maintain records on any systematic basis, and of those which did, only fragmentary accounts remain. Consequently, those records which survive do not constitute anything like a representative sample. Rather, they are special cases generally pertaining to isolated enterprises which might well have prospered *despite* slave labor rather than *because* of it. Data on labor costs and profit rates, where they exist at all, are usually even more unsatisfactory because of the crude and unsystematic accounting methods characteristic of the slave era. Most records reveal the use of simple cash-flow, or receipt-expenditures, accounting techniques which are too imprecise for making that kind of judgment.

Other variables enter into the accounting process and render definitive statements of profitability hazardous. During the late antebellum period, as business organization began to develop into more complex corporate forms, companies frequently attempted to present their financial position in an appealing light for the benefit of prospective stockholders. As a result, expenses tended to be minimized, and profits exaggerated. Census data do not provide much assistance either, since they were collected haphazardly. Finally, unlike the controlled uniformity of modern automated industry, pre-Civil War coal and iron production both were highly personalized, individualistic undertakings. The caliber of management then, although a nebulous economic variable, might well constitute the major determinant of profitability in the slave-based coal and iron industries. Despite the hazards, however, valuable insights into the economic problems and financial rewards of southern industry may be gleaned from an examination of the surviving data on several key enterprises which operated at various periods during the slave era.

Like any manufacturer, early ironmasters had to consider the three factors of production. *Capital* for initial investment was available, considering the relative wealth of the first iron entrepreneurs in the region, and additional capital needs were low. Nor did *land* present a problem since the requisite natural resources of timber and ore abounded in the surrounding wilderness. *Labor* was the most significant production cost in the early iron industry. Because of the scarcity of labor in America, exorbitant by English standards, the high cost of labor could have devastating consequences for the would-be entrepreneur. Hence, whether an employer paid wages to free artisans, acquired indentured servants, or purchased slaves, it became a cost consideration of paramount importance.

On the whole, the price of a male indentured servant varied at the beginning of the eighteenth century from £2 to £4 sterling for each year of service. The value of an indentured servant depended upon the expense of his passage across the ocean. William Matthews, having three years and nine months to serve, was rated in the inventory of his master at £12 sterling. A servant of Robert Leightenhouse, having two years to serve, sold for £19, while a youth bonded to Ralph Groves for seven years brought £10 sterling.[4] The price paid for indentured servants tended to increase gradually during the eighteenth century, until by the 1750s white servants usually sold for about £14 to £16 for four years' service.[5] To this expense must be added the cost of the servant's upkeep in clothing and food, the small stake provided by the master when the servant finished his term of service, and the loss of productivity resulting from turnover. On the other hand, a vigorous male slave could be purchased for £18 to £30 at the beginning of the century. Assuming that the slave gave his master twenty-five years' service, the prorated cost for each year would have been slightly less than £2 sterling (calculated with Present Value Formula at 5 percent interest). In the matter of purchase price, then, the slave was cheaper than the white indentured servant, especially for those entrepreneurs who possessed sufficient capital and the ability to take advantage of the economies of scale.

In 1813, the English traveler Henry Bolingbroke observed that "the great use of selling a man by auction is this, that he is thereby beckoned immediately into the form of employment for which there is the greatest call."[6] Since most slaves in the Chesapeake region were sold by auction, the higher price differential between the plantation slave and the bondsman purchased for an ironworks reflected a constantly higher demand for both skilled and unskilled slave labor in the iron industry. Throughout the eighteenth century, the increase in the market value of slaves for iron manufacturing remained higher than that of slaves for agriculture. The Principio Company purchased eighteen slaves in 1721 at an average price of £22 sterling.[7] At the same time, plantation slaves sold for about £18 to £20 sterling. If the slave happened to be a skilled craftsman, his value reached a

much higher level. As early as 1737, the Baltimore Iron Company owned
two slaves worth £80 each, while two others were valued at £70 each.[8]
Even unskilled slave ironworkers sold for about £30,[9] while tobacco plantation slaves brought £20 or less.[10] When the Swedish scientist Samuel
Hermelin visited eastern Maryland in 1783, he observed that the price paid
for a black ironworker was approximately £80 to £90, "but others 50 to 60
pounds sterling."[11] Even though the price differential varied over time, the
market value of slave ironworkers was consistently higher than that of
agricultural slaves throughout the eighteenth century.

Although ironmasters had to make fixed annual expenditures for the
maintenance of their slave workers and could not pare these costs below an
irreducible minimum, some apparent advantages nonetheless persisted.
Hermelin, a very careful and experienced observer, found as late as 1783
that maintenance costs remained low. Skilled slave ironworkers received
slightly better treatment than did unskilled bondsmen. Hermelin recorded
that the annual food allowance provided to skilled hands cost the ironmaster 115 shillings. The colonial ironmaster spent about 29 shillings for
clothing annually, while miscellaneous expenses came to about 36 shillings. The total annual expense to the ironmaster came to about 180
shillings, or about £3 sterling per slave. Lodging constituted no real expense to the ironmaster, since slaves usually built their own cabins from
wood cut in the surrounding forests.[12] Unskilled ironworkers did not fare
as well in the necessities of life as their skilled counterparts, for according
to Hermelin, the ordinary Negro laborers at the works received food which
cost the ironmaster only 82 shillings per year, while annual clothing expenses totaled only 19 shillings. Thus, the cost of maintaining an unskilled
slave ironworker for one year totaled 101 shillings, or less than £2 sterling
per year.[13] Supervisory costs probably did not increase appreciably with
slave labor because bondsmen worked under the direction of white skilled
artisans who had to be employed at any rate. They had a sort of quasi-
supervisory role, and direct surveillance over slave workmen constituted a
side oenefit.[14] According to Hermelin, ironmasters benefited from the
offspring of their slaves as well:

> The negroes in Virginia . . . increase to such an extent that
> the purchase price for them cannot be regarded as lost when
> they die. But if this should be computed, presuming that one
> negroe, costing 90 pounds sterling, is good for 30 years labor,
> it would make 3 pounds per year (which tkaes care of extra
> loss through death and the like).[15]

Productivity, measured in terms of cost per unit of production, is also
important in measuring the efficiency of employing slave ironworkers.
When Dr. Carroll launched the Baltimore Iron Company, he estimated the

expense of producing and marketing one ton of pig iron at £3 1s. sterling.[16] Although production expenses varied, Dr. Carroll's estimate was confirmed in 1732 when Alexander Spotswood informed William Byrd that per ton cost amounted to £3 sterling. Mr. Chiswell of the Fredericksville ironworks further corroborated that estimate; both ironmasters suggested that slave labor kept expenses low.[17] In his calculations for constructing the Baltimore Iron Works, Dr. Carroll projected that an initial outlay of £5,615 sterling would be necessary to erect and operate the furnace for eighteen months. Of this amount, outlays for full- and part-time white labor amounted to £789 for eighteen months, whereas £780 would purchase twenty-six slaves for life. To offset these initial capital and operating expenditures, Dr. Carroll anticipated that the works would produce five hundred tons of pig iron per year, which in fact was the annual average for the first four years. He concluded that this initial investment would completely pay for itself in two years.[18] By early 1737, the Baltimore partners had invested over £15,000 sterling in capitalization and operating expenses. Exports alone for the first four years amounted to 1,977 tons of pig iron. If the pig iron was sold for £8 per ton, gross receipts would have reached an estimated £15,816.[19] With production and marketing costs at a conservative figure of £4 per ton, net profits would reach £7,808. By Dr. Carroll's calculations, this constituted a handsome profit of about 100 percent if computed against operating costs, or 50 percent against total investment. If Dr. Carroll's estimates were accurate, there was an extraordinary return on investment.

Dr. Carroll's analysis soon proved overly optimistic, however. Unexpected difficulties arose over the poor quality of iron ore which increased operating expenses, while the anticipated high market prices for Baltimore iron failed to materialize. One of the major reasons Chesapeake iron lost preeminence in America by the end of the colonial period was the simultaneous depletion of good quality ore in Maryland and Virginia, and the increasing exploitation of very high grade ores in Pennsylvania. According to Arthur C. Bining, a leading authority on the subject, iron ore was the most important single ingredient in the manufacturing process. Inferior ore reduced furnace production and at the same time strained the bellows and hearth. By the American Revolution, therefore, Chesapeake ironmasters were at a cost disadvantage compared with Pennsylvania and New Jersey ironmasters who tapped rich and accessible iron ore deposits unequaled in Maryland and Virginia.[20] As early as 1734, the manager of the Baltimre Company had complained to part-owner Charles Carroll that it would not be profitable to "use the ore available if there was any other way of obtaining an adequate supply."[21] In 1753, Dr. Carroll informed his son that a growing shortage of both ore and wood existed in the Tidewater region. He stated that Spotswood's Virginia works was exceptional in possessing a fine supply of ore, while the Principio and Bristol companies closed their Virginia installations for lack of ore. The Neabsco Works continued to operate, but it was compelled to import its ore supply.[22]

When Hermelin studied the Middle States iron industry in 1783, iron ore shortages had become even more acute. Nevertheless, Maryland and Virginia continued to compete with Pennsylvania and New Jersey iron. Hermelin reported that in Pennsylvania production costs per ton of pig iron averaged £4 12s. sterling, while in New Jersey the average came to about £6 sterling. Meanwhile, in Maryland and Virginia those same expenses totaled about £4 10s. sterling. The Swedish geologist added that, although processing iron ore was more expensive in Virginia, labor costs were much lower than in New Jersey or Pennsylvania and helped to keep Chesapeake iron competitive in the market.[23]

Marketing also created financial difficulties. Most of the iron produced by the Baltimore Company consisted of unfinished pig and bar iron, for the size and dispersion of the American population restricted the colonial market for iron wares. The manager of the Baltimore Company, Dr. Carroll, explained to a Boston merchant that his company did not make "potts skilletts or such kind," mainly because "we have neither the Industry or number of People to Create it which you have in your Colony."[24] Because the small home market was so easily glutted, American market prices fluctuated wildly. Although Maryland and Virginia ironworks also cast wares for the local economy, the largest Chespeake concerns, such as the Baltimore Company, produced pig iron for British markets where the Industrial Revolution called raw iron into great demand.

In 1742, the Baltimore partners divided the product of the furnaces into equal fifths and sold their portions independently rather than in common as they had in the past. Taken collectively, however, Baltimore and nearby Principio iron comprised a significant portion of the colonial iron in the English market during the 1750s, and the profitability of slavery must ultimately rest on the profitability of the trade itself. Professor Keach Johnson, the leading authority on the Baltimore Company, has analyzed the sales of Charles Carroll's 1750–1751 consignments to his London agent. Johnson calculates that Carroll's fifth-share totaled 376 tons of pig iron and brought in gross receipts of £2324 10s. 2d.[25] From this amount were deducted shipping charges, miscellaneous expenses, and agents' fees which totaled £545 1s. 9d. sterling. On the other hand, production costs on Carroll's pig iron amounted to a relatively modest £3 2s. 3d. sterling per ton, or £1170 6s. for the entire shipment. In breaking down the production costs, two loads of charcoal came to £2; three tons of ore to £1 2s. 6d.; wages of founder and assistants to 8s.; and lime and charge for the furnace to a little over 12s., for a total of £3 2s. 3d. sterling per ton of pig iron. Since the only labor costs to be found in the company's records consisted of wages for a founder and assistant, it is reasonable to assume that slaves working at the furnace were owned by the company and were not considered a cost since they would have been fed, clothed, and sheltered whether they worked on the plantation or at the ironworks. In reality, of course, there was the inevitable cost of agricultural output forgone, but company accounting did not include such calculations and that information is now irretrievable. Johnson computed Carroll's net profit in each of the three English markets to which his iron was shipped:[26]

	London 108 tons	Bristol 193 tons	Bewdley 75 tons
Sales	£640 7s. 11d.	£1182 6s. 8d.	£501 15s. 7d.
Cost	£437 10s. 7d.	£ 852 8s. 2d.	£425 9s. 2d.
	£202 17s. 4d.	£329 18s. 6d.	£76 6s. 5d.
Net profit per ton	£1 17s. 7d.	£1 14s. 2d.	£1 0 4d.

Total production and marketing costs, therefore, came to £1715 7s. 9d., leaving a profit of £609 2s. 5d., or a 35 percent return on investment. The only available profit data relating to the other partners consist of a few passing references in Dr. Carroll's correspondence.[27]

Faced with rising expenses from an inadequate ore supply and with disappointing market prices, Chesapeake ironmasters probably sought to retrench by gradually shifting away from reliance upon relatively expensive and unpredictable white workers, toward a firm commitment to slave labor. No doubt, this change accounted for the increase in Principio's slave force from fewer than 12 in 1721 to at least 101 by 1780. Even though the Baltimore Company continued to acquire numerous indentured servants, hired seasonal laborers for wood cutting, and used convict labor when necessary, throughout the 1760s and 1770s the company came to place a heavy reliance upon a large core of slave ironworkers. Consequently, the company's force of bondsmen grew from 26 in 1733 to over 150 in 1764.[28] The continued operation of these firms for over a half century strongly suggests that slave-produced iron could be a profitable undertaking. In 1764, Carroll informed his son that, while the family plantation (12,700 acres) yielded £250 sterling per year, his fifth-share of the Baltimore Iron Works earned £400 sterling per annum.[29] A French visitor observed in 1765 that the Baltimore Company belonged to "five Gentlemen" and yielded "500 ps. per annum to each altho in its infancy."[30] In 1764, Carroll valued his fifth-share at £10,000 sterling,[31] and Daniel Dulany asserted that a tenth-share was worth "at a moderate Estimate, £7,000 Sterling."[32] While the partners probably exaggerated these estimates, the works were worth a considerable sum of money.

The profitable production and marketing of colonial iron apparently depended less upon whether the labor force was free or slave than upon proper management. When the Baltimore partners began to lay plans for erecting their ironworks, they sought advice from ironmasters who used free labor in Pennsylvania as well as those who used slave labor in Virginia. Clement Plumsted of Philadelphia responded that extreme care must be taken in the prosecution of an iron business, and the prospective operator must beware of the many pitfalls awaiting the inexperienced adventurer. He assured the partners that for this reason enlightened management represented the vital key to success.[33] This same opinion was expressed in 1733 by the Virginia ironmaster Ralph Falkner, owner of the Bristol Iron Works. Falkner believed that production expenses were determined primarily by the quality of management. Falkner informed the partners that at least in one case, proper supervision had reduced the per ton production costs from £4 17s. to £3 10s. sterling. To underscore his point, Falkner reiterated that if the partners managed their ironworks properly, it should be as profitable as any in the colonies.[34] This conviction that management, rather than the status of its labor force, constituted the key to success in the iron industry was voiced even more strongly by David Ross, a Virginian whose career as an ironmaster began to ascend just as the Baltimore Iron Works completed its decline into insolvency during the 1780s. Much as the Baltimore Company became the leading colonial American ironworks, so David Ross's Oxford Iron Works of Campbell County, Virginia, became one of the leading American installations during the New National Era.

Few Chesapeake ironmasters had greater faith in the utilization of slave labor than Ross. As previously noted, by the 1780s he had gradually acquired a fortune and estate through land speculation and numerous mercantile interests, including fur trading, flour milling, and coal mining. By the immediate post-Revolutionary War era, Virginians considered him among "the richest of all planters."[35] When the War for Independence came, Ross found himself in a strategic position to profit from the high wartime demand for iron. By 1776, he constructed the Oxford Iron Works which played a significant role in the entrepreneur's accumulation of wealth.

By 1812, however, Ross's fortunes had slipped considerably, and Oxford, his major holding, faced insolvency. Presumably, the works had been in difficulty for some time, for in November 1812 he informed his nephew and chief clerk, Robert Richardson, that the ironworks had "for many years been a most ruinous business" and numerous unpaid debts now embarrassed the ironmaster.[36] A few months later, the beleaguered ironmaster complained that "we have no credit" because of indebtedness, and indeed "no one ought to trust because we don't pay."[37] By August 1813, financial problems became so acute that the once "richest of all planters" found himself seeking a loan from his daughter-in-law, Juliana, for the paltry sum of $217.12 in order to pay a persistent creditor. However reluctantly, Ross was forced to make the request by the "urgent occasion for money" brought on by the "expenses at the works" being so great.[38] Creditors, such as one artisan who had waited five years for payment, were not the only sufferers. "Witness the poor slaves," Ross lamented, "uncloathed [sic] for two years—the horses half fed."[39] The ironmaster still had confidence in his slave artisans, and he himself lived on a "frugal Scale." How then did it happen, Ross puzzled, "that we are the servants of servants; disgraced, involved in distress & Mortifications. This is the true question. How does this ruinous state of things happen."[40]

Typically, the sources do not permit anything like a complete analysis of the ironmaster's financial "Mortifications." The detailed correspondence contained in a recently restored David Ross letterbook for the period between January 1812 and December 1813, however, does offer a rare insight into one ironmaster's views of his own financial problems, and their relationship to his slave labor force.

Even though Ross never faltered in his commitment to industrial slavery, he believed that at least part of the blame for Oxford's financial ruin lay with his black workers. In a long and detailed letter to his chief clerk at Oxford Iron Works, Ross vented some of his frustrations on that subject. While his black ironworkers were expert craftsmen, they usually worked without regard to waste or expense. These "Swaggering Forge men," he fumed, "care little . . . of the injury they are doing to a benevolent master."[41] Although the "coliers [sic] and teams were capable," when the furnace had to be shut down unnecessarily in the fall of 1812 because the charcoal-makers had not set by a sufficient supply for continued operation, Ross was convinced that his slaves produced more debt than anything else.[42] He also complained bitterly about slaves who pilfered wares made at the ironworks, presumably for sale in the black market. The abuse had been of "long continuance & must be corrected."[43] Therefore, Ross directed his clerk to place all wares under "lock and key," for the potters were "rogues who will also steal with ease, unless you take proper precaustion [sic]."[44]

A more serious problem was the poor quality of slave workmanship. When Ross ordered a shipment of bar iron and castings to sell in Richmond, he felt compelled to remind his clerk that the product would have no value unless of "good workmanship." With traces of envy, the ironmaster informed his manager about a nearby blacksmith shop in Richmond in which every artisan "black & white works twice as much as our Smiths and I really believe the Wheelwrights do three times as much as our people." The difference could not be explained by the status of the Oxford smiths, however, for several of the workmen at the Richmond shop were also bondsmen. Yet, Ross found the quality of their work "astonishing." He remained convinced that "if the smiths are kept at faithful & steady labour," the Oxford blacksmith's shop could be the most profitable department at the works.[45] He enjoined Richardson, his nephew and clerk, that "tis an essential part of duty never to with hold [sic] censure from bad workmanship. There ought to be no indulgence on this point 'tis injurious to the workmen and disgraceful to the business."[46]

Inefficiency and "misconduct" among the hands reflected a far deeper concern for Ross. If slaves failed to meet acceptable standards of production, the fault lay not with the slaves themselves, but with their supervisors. Ross would have agreed with the numerous antebellum exponents of "scientific" slave management who, through the agricultural journals, advised southern planters about proper management and slave efficiency. In an exceptionally detailed series of letters to his Oxford clerks, the ironmaster revealed his views on the topic of mismanagement. In plain terms, Ross informed his chief clerk that the Oxford Iron Works was near insolvency and that he, the owner, believed that "the ruin of the estate is founded in the management of it."[47]

The firm's only hope for arresting its financial decline depended upon correcting the "abuses in the different departments."[48] "Tis not the blure of coals, the sound of the Bellows that makes a Furnace productive"; only "good clean . . . management" could accomplish that goal. Because Robert Richardson and William Dunn drew salaries rather than wages, Ross charged, the clerks worked little more than required since the Oxford managers did not "feel so sensibly where the shoe pinches."[49] The ironmaster complained that, compared with productivity, the expense of employing 150 slaves at the furnace and forges was exorbitant. He cautioned that if each slave lost one hour per day, it would be "equal to the loss of 12 labourers for a whole day. How many hours do they lose & what ruinous loss does it produce?"[50] This low labor productivity resulted directly from inept slave supervision. Ross fully understood that since bondsmen did not receive the fruits of their own labor, they had little interest in the efficiency of the business itself. Although he had devised numerous techniques to motivate his bonded workers, they were to no avail without proper supervision. Ross beseeched his managers to be more attentive to their duties, for the true cause of Oxford's demise must be found in "the want . . . of sobriety in the manager & clerks," which over the last ten years had reduced the estate into "distress & ruin from which it will be difficult, perhaps impossible to relieve it."[51]

The truth of the matter rested on the fact, Ross chided, that "we are a very trifling people and incapable of making use of the means in our power." Oxford possessed all the natural advantages with "Mechanicks & labourers adequate to every purpose," yet it still lost money.[52] After thirty-six years of operation and ten years of experience for Richardson, Oxford "has not improved in the Smallest degree." In fact, for the past year Oxford could "be said to have no manager" at all, Ross scolded. Actually, Oxford's supervision problems had existed for years. The previous manager, a Mr. Gilchrist, had been so uneducated that Ross chose not to plead with the man "because it would be like cutting a block of marble with a razor." But Richardson had no such excuse, his parents had not been poverty striken, and he had received a proper education. For Ross, however, this made Oxford's plight all the more unpardonable. Richardson should have been incensed, his pride stung into activity; but alas, Ross chided his clerk, "those that ought to represent the master are not infrequently inferior to the Servant."[53] Furthermore, the ironmaster expressed little confidence in the business expertise of his Oxford clerks. "It will require little reflection & less penetration," he wrote his chief clerk, to understand that accounts must be settled promptly. For an indebted ironworks the "misfortune" was threefold: (1) "We cannot . . . command the money" for general operations. (2) The works, therefore, had to acquire provisions on credit with iron as security, which placed a lien against future production. (3) A vacuum existed in the market once controlled by Oxford, and other iron companies quickly undercut additional Oxford sales.[54] Thus, the downward spiral continued, with more expenditures than revenues, until by September 1812 "every thing that had been made for the four years before had been spent and $20,000 besides."[55]

By February 1813, Ross was so frustrated with his clerks that he wondered whether it was "most dangerous to employ an active sensible scoundrel or an honest simple indolent man." He had heard that question debated by a group of businessmen, he declared, and they had decided that

> the first character was safest provided the employer was apprized of it, because he was capable of exertions and the employer would be on his guard. As to the other character 'twas more dangerous that confidence was placed in his honesty and be ruined or injured by his apathy and folly.

Ross apparently believed that his clerks conformed to one of these categories, for both lacked "industry and judgement." To be candid, he declared, he had not the least faith left in the ability of his clerks to improve Oxford's performance, for since the aging ironmaster had moved to Richmond, they had been "in a state of stupifaction [sic]."[56]

Ross's conviction that his managers had also overstepped the bounds of their authority and had exercised poor judgment in the financial affairs at Oxford seems justified. For example, in July 1813 he received a letter from George, a trusted slave carpenter at the works, indicating that the assistant clerk, William Dunn, had begun the construction of a new dam for the forge waterwheel.[57] George informed his master that, even though waste plagued the project, the slaves could not presume to instruct their white overseer. The slave carpenter's communication thoroughly incensed Ross, for Dunn had directly contradicted the owner's orders to repair the old one.[58] Moreover, Ross readily accepted George's complaint about inefficiency, for that resembled "our mode of doing business at Oxford." Building a new dam rather than repairing the old one not only was expensive, but also illustrated a lack of business judgment and foresight, given the serious financial straits of the Oxford Iron Works. "Everything is to be accomplished by the Main Strength of the Servants. They are compelled by the folly of their conductors to work up hill constantly, & what little they accomplish is by treble labour."[59] It seemed that Ross held more confidence in his slaves than in their overseers.

By August 1813, Ross had formulated a plan to remove the works from its present location to a site along the James River where water power was more plentiful. He hoped to erect a larger and more modern operation,[60] but continued competition from newer blast furnaces in the Valley, adverse legal judgments, further financial difficulties, and protracted illness prevented the hitherto unsinkable David Ross from realizing his plans to improve Oxford.[61] He died on May 4, 1817. The necessity for settling the debts of the estate, as well as the provisions of his will, which directed that his estate be divided among his two sons and two daughters, accounted for the eventual liquidation of the Oxford slave force by 1819.[62]

The opinion of such an astute businessman as David Ross, that Oxford's financial woes sprang primarily from mismanagement rather than from slave labor itself, provided sound testimony that slave labor could be used with profit. Ross himself cannot escape the final responsibility, however. He *was* the owner of Oxford Iron Works, and if his supervisors failed to perform their duties satisfactorily, then he should have asserted his authority and taken stronger corrective measures. More importantly, the Ross letters reflect a vivid sense of laconic drift at the ironworks. This general lack of initiative seemed to characterize Oxford's operations during its final years.

In one letter, Ross indicted his clerks for failure to keep abreast of technological improvements in the iron industry, which accounted for Oxford's growing inability to compete in the open market. Ironworks in England, Europe, and even in America had made "vast improvements," while "Oxford remains a Sad, Solitary instance of remaining stationary."[63] This sense of drift also pervades Ross's envious description of the high quality work performed by bondsmen at the Richmond wheelwright shop. Ross asked Richardson to read that letter to "old Ned & his Sons," the Oxford wheelwrights. Old Ned and his sons were "good people" but had never "seen any other workmen than at the Oxford estate. They have no chance for improvement. There is no emulation. The father & sons joggs [*sic*] on in the old way. I wonder they do so well.''[64] Even Ross recognized that slavery could only maintain itself within a closed social system. "Tis mortifying," he lamented, "that we remain allways [*sic*] in a State of primitive ignorance and that in thirty years we have not gain'd one week on the Scale of improvement." In response to a letter from a friend regarding the poor state of workmanship at Oxford, Ross responded:

> I dare say you are correct as to my Forgemen, they are as good workmen 20 years ago as they are now. They have had no chance to see other works and the annual improvements and I have taken up a deep predujice [*sic*] against your travelling Iron Works people. I dont [*sic*] permit them to stop. So that my people in every branch have remained as it were stationary. I hope to give them a better chance in a short time.[65]

Like slaveowners generally, Ross was ultimately more concerned with slave *control* than with the economic rationalism underlying the debate over the relative profitability of slave and free labor. The traveling free ironworkers whom Ross so detested might possess updated technological skills, but as carriers of new ideas they also represented a potential threat to the status quo. Ross found himself caught in the characteristic dilemma confronted by southern industrialists: as a southern conservative committed to the slave regime, he sought a closed social and racial system which effectively screened the potentially disruptive notions spawned in a freer society; on the other hand, he keenly felt the need for progressive industrial innovations developed in that same open society from which he hoped to isolate his slave community. This dichotomy plagued southern industrialists until the end of the slave era.

It is generally understood that industrialization in the American South lagged far behind that of the North by the 1830s. Suffice it here to say that by the antebullum period, the North had larger markets, a superior industrial technology, a rapidly expanding transportation network, and the experienced labor force and management personnel to outproduce southern industry. Moreover, the North enjoyed higher grade mineral resources, such as coal and iron ore, and an abundance of investment capital. To make matters worse, northern industry had the ability to ship its products directly into the South and successfully compete with local producers.

In their attempt to overcome these competitive disadvantages, southern industrialists tried to reduce the costs of production with the means most readily at their disposal. Frequently, this attempt was translated into a search for maximum efficiency in the utilization of slave labor. Consequently, slave women and children were employed extensively in southern tobacco, textile, and other factory work. Women also labored at ironworks—for example, the "ole woman" the Reverend Andrew Burnaby observed working in Spotswood's ore mines during the 1750s,[66] and the eleven black women listed as miners at Principio's Lancashire Furnace or banks in 1781.[67] Few ironmasters employed as many women and children as Ross. Among the fifty-five women and children of working age in 1811, a majority of them worked at the charcoal grounds, ore banks, furnace, or at the forges.[68] Although no slave managers of ironworks have been discovered in the records of the Chesapeake iron industry, some trusted black craftsmen did take on managerial functions, thereby reducing supervision costs. Slave founders, for example, frequently became production supervisors at iron furnaces by exclusivity of their skill. For example, the technical judgment of Abram, a founder at Oxford Iron Works, was held in high regard. Most ironworks had at least one such slave artisan whose strategic abilities placed him at the top of the slave force hierarchy, even though he was not considered a "boss man."

Ironmasters also attempted to increase productivity by "coupling" bondsmen with skilled artisans, through either formal apprenticeships or on-the-job training. By teaching youthful hands a skilled trade, ironmasters increased the value of slave property. Therefore, ironmasters trained only that core of bondsmen whom they owned, while hired hands were normally used as laborers. The main intention, of course, was to reduce the expenses inherent in reliance upon expensive hired white or black craftsmen. Between the mid-1840s and early 1850s, therefore, Joseph Anderson hired white artisans to teach slaves the technical skills required to operate the Tredegar rolling mill.[69] More frequently, however, young blacks received their training from other slaves. At Oxford, certain occupations seemed to have been the province of particular families, with the father teaching his skill to at least one of his children. For example, Big Abram, a collier, taught the craft to his son, nineteen-year-old Mickie.[70]

Although the relative efficiency of slave and free labor is impossible to ascertain from the sources, comparative wage scales during the antebellum era provide a rough index. According to Starobin, white wages did not increase substantially between 1800 and 1861, but remained stable at about $310 per year, while the cost of slave-hiring for factory work rose dramatically. Starobin's summary of hiring prices are presented in Table 13.

Although prices fluctuated over the short run, the long-term pattern in the Chesapeake iron industry mirrored this general trend. From about 1800 to 1830, the average price for one year's hire came to about $55. As a result of the stiff competition between established planters and the rising Chesapeake industrialists during the 1830s, slave-hiring increased by 100 percent to about $120 per hand. Prices stabilized at that level until about the mid-1850s, when industrial hiring once again increased substantially to an

Table 13

SUMMARY COST OF SLAVE-HIRING BY SOUTHERN
INDUSTRIES (in dollars)

Period	Daily	Monthly	Annually
1799–1833	0.76	13.14	66.39
1833–1852	0.77	16.51	100.55
1853–1861	1.44	19.68	150.00

Source: Robert S. Starobin, Industrial Slavery in the Old South (New York: Oxford University Press, 1970), p. 274, n. 21.

average of about $150 per annum.[71] This trend no doubt reflected a growing demand in the face of an inadequate supply of slaves. It also suggested that slave labor must have compared favorably with available white labor in order to be preferred in the hiring market.

Some historians have argued that the capitalization of slave labor retarded the development of southern industry because it "froze" investment capital and created an immobile labor force.[72] Starobin contends that this argument did not apply to southern industries, however, for many of them were actually "capitalized by transferring bondsmen from farming or planting to manufacturing, milling, mining, and transportation. And slaveowners themselves, not merchants or bankers, were the chief source of capital for industrial investment."[73] Whatever occurred in other industries, Starobin's analysis does not accurately explain the patterns which prevailed in the iron industry. During the colonial period, several ironworks partially capitalized their facilities with black bondsmen. For example, in 1733 the Baltimore Company began operations with about half its work force composed of slave laborers. The five partners agreed to provide an initial seven slaves each to the company in order to get the works under way.[74] Similarly, other iron companies were at least partially capitalized in this way. But for reasons relating to growing capital availability, the practice became increasingly uncommon by the turn of the nineteenth century, and ironmasters shifted to a primarily hired slave labor force. Antebellum ironmasters owned only that 25 percent of the workmen who were skilled craftsmen. As a result, even though ironmasters bore the unmeasurable costs of interests and depreciation, the huge initial capital investment required for ownership was avoided by hiring. Unlike their colonial counterparts, antebellum ironmasters tended to be first-generation operators rather than well-heeled elites seeking new forms of investment. Like most businessmen without independent means, ironmasters had to borrow money in order to build or purchase their facilities. Consequently, to reduce their total indebtedness, they borrowed enough to hire black workmen rather than to purchase them.[75] Therefore, Starobin's assertion regarding slave capitalization was only partially true for the iron industry. On the other hand, the records do indicate that common slave hands frequently were hired variously to plantations, railroads, ironworks, and other business concerns. In short, the ability to move them from one sector of the economy to another was not diminished by their slave status.

After initial investment, maintenance and supervision costs represented the largest portion of annual expenses for antebellum slave ironworkers. Between 1820 and 1860, annual expenditures generally averaged at the highest about $50 for food, $15 for clothing, $3 for medical services, $7 for housing, and $27 for supervision. Miscellaneous expenses, such as insurance and incentive payments, probably averaged about $5 annually per slave. The average maintenance expense per year, therefore, ranged around $100 for each bondsman, in addition to the typical annual hiring price of $100 to $150. On the other hand, wages for a white common laborer averaged about $3 per day. Between 1800 and 1861, annual white wages remained relatively unchanged at approximately $310 for common laborers and $930 for skilled craftsmen. Like slaves, free whites also incurred supervision costs, but they generally provided their own food, clothing, and shelter. Therefore, on a yearly average, it was about one-third cheaper to employ a common industrial slave than it was to hire a free white laborer.[76] Thus, Starobin contends, "slave hirelings remained between 25 and 40 per cent cheaper to employ than wage laborers."[77] Assuming that the typical ironworks employed a force of about ninety slaves, sixty of them hired hands, and using $112 as the average difference between total hiring and maintenance costs for leased slaves and wages paid white workers, the annual savings for the ironmaster would have totaled $6,720. This cost advantage apparently held true at other southern ironworks as well.

James D. Norris, a close student of Maramec Iron Works (located about seventy-five miles southwest of St. Louis, Missouri, and established in 1826) concludes that at Maramec slaves represented a more economical source of labor than free whites. Most of the workers at Maramec were lured to the western frontier from the iron regions of Pennsylvania, Ohio, Tennessee, Kentucky, and Virginia. Although these "migrants" formed the largest source of skilled labor at Maramec, which was an exception to the norm in the Chesapeake iron industry, owners Thomas James and Samuel Massey resorted to slaves for the routine and unskilled positions. Both ironmasters believed bondsmen were more dependable than free whites who might leave the works as the notion struck them, but they found skilled bondsmen difficult to locate on the frontier. James and Massey themselves owned only a few bondsmen. From 1828 to 1831, during its infancy, Maramec utilized about twenty slaves, mostly at woodchopping. At that time, the annual labor costs for employing a free white male ranged from $180 to $200 per year, or $14 to $16 per month in wages, plus $10 per month for housing. Thus, the expenses for a white workman came to about $300 to $320 per annum. A prime male slave, on the other hand, rented for about $100 per year and required another $80 per year to maintain.[78] Massey calculated that slaves cost less than fifty-four cents per day to hire, feed, clothe, and supervise. The difference between the conservative annual wage estimate of $300 received by white common laborers and $180 for hired slaves came to about $120 per year. Since the works hired an average of twenty hands each year, the company saved a total of $2,400 per year by opting to employ slave laborers rather than free whites.

If the hired slaves worked less efficiently than the more expensive white workers, however, this reduction in expenses did not necessarily result in real savings for James and Massey. The best way to measure this relative efficiency is to compare labor costs per unit of production. Here, too, Maramec slaves were more economical than free white laborers. The assigned daily task of a slave woodchopper at the ironworks was 1½ cords of wood per day, which represented a labor cost of thirty-eight to forty-two cents per cord in 1829. This cost compared favorably with the forty-five cents per unit when chopped by seasonal white workers from nearby farms. Although they were included in Norris's analysis, supervision charges did not represent a significant cost differential since white wood-chooppers also required an overseer to measure, check, and record the wood gathered. In 1829, when the ironmasters calculated their expenses, Maramec used about four thousand cords of wood each year.[79] At that level of production, the total advantage of slave labor amounted to only $200 per year. While this slight edge did not amount to much in actual dollars, the significant point lies in the fact that slave inefficiency had not developed to eliminate the initial employment savings of $2,400. The relative advantage of slave labor at Maramec, then, represented an annual saving for the company of $2,600.

Slaves also achieved higher productivity for the Tredegar Iron Works of Richmond. According to Charles Dew, who has thoroughly examined the extensive collection of Tredegar papers, any analysis of the topic must be confined primarily to the rolling mill.[80] First of all, the most detailed records were maintained for that department. Second, ironmaster Joseph R. Anderson's major effort to reduce operating expenses was to replace free whites in that department with black bondsmen. In 1848, the president of Tredegar observed that slave labor "enables me, of course, to compete with other manufacturers."[81] To assess the accuracy of this contention, Dew has analyzed rolling mill cost records and has concluded that once the slaves had been trained and became experienced, they achieved modest reductions in expenses for the company. According to Dew's reckoning, labor costs in the mill dropped from an estimated $12.02 per ton during the mid-1840s to an average of $10.59 per ton by the early 1850s.[82]

Although the introduction of slave hands into the rolling mill operation at Tredegar eventually reduced labor expenses in the department by 12 percent, the reduction did not sufficiently improve the company's competitive position in the national marketplace. During the 1850s, northern and English iron of equal quality sold well below the price of Richmond iron. In 1860, when Tredegar rolled iron sold for $85 per ton, quality-grade English bar iron brought $75 and common bar iron sold for $65 per ton, a rate between 12 and 25 percent cheaper. In Baltimore that same year, English bar iron sold for $55 and $60 per ton, or 30 to 35 percent lower than Tredegar's, while northern bar iron sold for $60 to $65, or 25 to 30 percent less per ton.[83] Southern iron generally suffered a dramatic competitive disadvantage in the national market, as can be seen in Table 14.

Table 14

BAR, SHEET, AND RAILROAD IRON PRODUCED IN
THE UNITED STATES DURING THE YEAR ENDING
JUNE 1, 1860

Region	Bar Iron (tons)	Railroad Iron (tons)	Boiler Plate (tons)	Average Price per Ton
New England states	17,340	24,350	6,000	$66.44
Middle Atlantic states	154,297	158,577	22,795	57.70
Western states	41,973	40,000	2,100	69.10
Southern states	14,072	12,180	—	91.52

Source: Charles B. Dew, *Ironmaker to the Confederacy: Josept R. Anderson and the Tredegar Iron Works* (New Haven, Conn.: Yale University Press, 1966), p. 30.

Anderson attempted to maintain a hold on the southern iron market in order to offset the lack of competitiveness in northern markets. He did so by stoking sectional pride, urging the establishment of a self-sufficient southern economy, while at the same time assuring his customers that only Virginia's finest charcoal iron went into Tredegar's products. In addition, Tredegar provided credit by accepting promissory notes from southern railroad companies, some of which had such poor financial status that they would not have received credit otherwise. Nevertheless, northern and English iron continued to present formidable competition for the Tredegar Company, even in the South.

Even though Tredegar rolling mills utilized slave labor in order to cut production costs, northern iron manufacturers apparently held an edge even in that department. For example, the Crescent Iron Manufacturing Company of Wheeling, located in the western part of Virginia, produced finished iron with free labor at only $6 per ton in 1855. English iron producers had an even greater labor advantage, according to the Tredegar owner. In fact, in 1858 English iron could be imported at a lower price than Tredegar iron because the company employed "labour that costs three times what it does in Europe."[84] Although Tredegar had intensified its campaign to secure slave hands, the company still had to seek skilled rolling mill workers in the northern cities. Because of the heavy reliance on slave labor in Richmond, however, only high wages could lure free skilled workmen to the city,[85] and that, of course, exerted a very direct pressure on already excessive production costs.

Until the mid-1850s, Tredegar purchased much of its pig iron from the charcoal furnaces in the Valley of Virginia. The construction of the James River and Kanawha Canal, followed by the Virginia and Tennessee, Virginia Central, and the Manassas Gap railroads during the three previous decades, had linked the Valley furnaces directly with the Richmond iron manufacturers. Because Virginia ironworks continued to rely on increasingly outmoded technology, however, their charcoal furnaces simply could not compete with the vastly more efficient anthracite furnaces in Pennsylvania and western Maryland. By the 1850s, the handwriting was on the wall as the gap between the costs to produce charcoal iron and anthracite iron grew increasingly wider. In the face of improved technology, neither connecting railroads nor slave labor could compensate for the market disadvantages suffered by Virginia ironmasters. Virginia iron failed to compete with anthracite-produced metal even in the Richmond market.[86]

The Tredegar experience clearly illustrates that, while slaves offered a cheaper source of labor, they presented no bonanza for southern iron manufacturers. Slave labor might reduce production costs, but not sufficiently to offset the greater technological disadvantages which confronted the southern iron industry in an increasingly national market, a market controlled by the outsiders from the North. A similar fate confronted the region's coal industry.

Like their counterparts in the iron industry, the operators of Virginia's slave-run coal mines also failed to incorporate contemporary technological advancements into their mode of operations. Over time, therefore, productivity declined at southern mines while it rose dramatically at the more "progressive" pits in the North. Slave efficiency represented less of a problem, however, than other serious economic handicaps unique to the South.

One of the main reasons for the relatively high production costs at Virginia mines must be sought in the geological conditions over which the operators had little control. Virginia mines were of the deep shaft variety described in Chapter 2. The burden of sinking these shafts required considerably larger amounts of capital than were necessary in the Maryland and Pennsylvania mines, which entered the horizontal coal seams directly at their outcrops. In 1854, an engineer estimated that it cost between $11 and $16 per perpendicular foot to sink one shaft 10 x 16 feet wide. Frequently, more than one shaft was required. The expense incurred in sinking Virginia shafts is summarized in Table 15.

Table 15

COST FOR SINKING A SHAFT IN VIRGINIA IN 1854

Average Depth of Shaft	Cost Based on an Average of $13.50 per Perpendicular Foot
100	$1,350
200	2,700
300	4,050
400	5,400
500	6,750
600	8,100
700	9,450

Source: "Report by Richard Smethurst and Sampson Vivian, December 22, 1854," Tompkins Family Papers, Virginia Historical Society.

In some cases, costs exceeded the average several times over. For example, by 1843 the Midlothian Company had sunk a shaft which required three years of labor and an excess of $20,000 to reach the coal.[87] This additional expense, disposal of the waste materials, the necessity of hoisting men and equipment up and down the shaft, and the machinery required for the task, all insured significantly larger expenses compared with mines where these were unnecessary. In addition, much time and efficiency were lost in pumping water from the pits, which was a continuous problem in the Richmond coal field. All of these factors contributed to very large expenses and yet produced no coal.

When mines were built at the edge of the Richmond Basin, shafts of one hundred to two hundred feet normally sufficed and required only modest outlays for horse-powered equipment to raise the coal and to pump the mines free of water. Once colliers began to sink five hundred- to eight hundred-feet shafts into the deeper coal seams and the underground workings entered the dips of the strata, however, steam-powered machinery became an additional requirement. As early as 1811, steam engines powerful enough to operate shafts of 250 feet cost $5,000.[88] Thus, as progress

continued costs increased commensurately. By the 1820s, capital investment requirements effectively transformed coal mining from an individual
to a corporate form of enterprise. Some companies required a capitalization of over $300,000.[89]

The irregularity and unpredictability of the seam itself created additional
financial obstacles. While drifting, colliers frequently encountered a hitch
(a buckle in the seam) and attempted to cut straight through to the other
side, only to lose the coal seam entirely. This step entailed great expense
and occasionally forced the complete cessation of operations. For example, Harry Heth informed a colleague in 1812:

> Since writing to you as above, our prospect in the new Shaft
> has been very gloomy. The coal apparently runing [sic] out as
> we proceed to the South, & so extremely Hitchy as to make it
> very dangerous to work it—indeed it tumbled so much last
> week, as to oblige us to abandon it for many days, we have
> however commenced again, with a view to drive through the
> Hitch, if but a Hitch it should turn out to be—but of this I am
> extremely doubtfull [sic]—in the meantime I have com-
> menced two Shafts on the dip of the Main body, and am in
> hopes to Strike the coal at from 250 to 300 feet when those
> shafts are down, I shall do well for a considerable time, but it
> is a most tedious & expensive undertaking.[90]

Even when the coal seam was undisturbed, it occasionally plunged downward precipitously at sixty- or seventy-degree angles. Then the coal had to
be raised up this steep incline along an underground tramway, a process
which obviously hindered productivity.[91]

Most of the horizontal mines of Maryland and Pennsylvania held a
decided competitive advantage in this respect. In an 1849 official report of
the Phenix Mining and Manufacturing Company, which conducted extensive operations in the Cumberland coal field, the board of directors informed stockholders that the coal seam lay in a nearly horizontal direction,
with a slight incline toward the Potomac River. Because of this incline,

> The miners, working into the sides of the hills, will stand on
> dry floors, while the product of their labor will be carried, in
> loaded cars, over a tram road, of easy descent, to the mouth
> of the pits. In mines, thus situated, we shall not have to
> encounter the heavy expense usually attending on those
> which are worked through deep shafts, or where the strata lie
> vertically. There can be no necessity to employ mechanical
> power, for any purposes; the coal and drainage will pass over
> inclined planes, and with a free circulation of air through the

drifts, from opening to opening, the miners will be secure
from any danger of firedamps, or foul atmosphere.[92]

This natural incline increased productivity enormously. Water drained
itself from the mines, and coal cars delivered the coal to the mouth by
gravity plane, which eliminated the need for expensive machinery.
Moreover, slope mining often eliminated the necessity to dig expensive
shafts for air ventilation. Thus, elaborate circulation systems with underground furnaces to rarify the air and create drafts were not necessary.
According to the Phenix Company report, the "large number of men and
boys . . . constantly occupied in the superintendence of the complicated
system" utilized in deep shafts was rendered "completely superfluous" by
geology.[93] Writing under the pseudonym *Economicus,* a correspondent in
the *New York Columbian* recognized as early as 1811 that, given the state
of technology, slope mines held distinct advantages over shafts, since the
operator merely had to get the coal "started on an inclined plane, to travel
by its own gravity from the verge of the mine to the hold of the vessel."
Economicus wondered if anyone could "imagine any more promising and
productive occupation than our colliers and coasters would thus have. Is
there any thing that can more effectually fasten and dove tail the union?"[94]
This particular nationalist would have to wait for half a century to see the
United States control its own coal markets, and much longer than that for
the Union to be "dove tailed."

A large percentage of the coal mined from the Richmond field was
transported to Richmond by batteaux, either down the James River or via
the James River Canal. As a result of overhandling, this mode of portage
created severe economic difficulties for Virginia operators. The handling of
bituminous generally followed numerous damaging steps. After hoisting
the coal out of the pits and heaping it near the pit, coal was generally
shovelled into a cart and conveyed to the river or canal bank, reshovelled
into wheelbarrows, and dumped into the barges. In other cases, the carts
were drawn out over a scaffold, or tipple, erected over the water, and
emptied into the waiting batteaux. These boats normally carried two
hundred bushels, but during the dry season when the river was low, loads
had to be reduced to half that amount. Obviously, this procedure increased
transportation costs because coal boats paid a flat toll of $1 per load.
Half-loads cost the same but brought in only half the revenue. On arrival at
Richmond, coal yard slaves stockpiled the fuel for sale to local purchasers.
Coal designated for export was then reloaded and wheeled to the city
wharves, and was once again emptied into coastal vessels destined for
Atlantic ports. Since the canal was located on the north side of the James,
mines south of the river seldom used the facility. Instead, they waggoned
their product to the wharves at Richmond. While this mode of conveyance
reduced handling, the jarring movement of the wagon rumbling over rough

roads tended to break the lumps, which greatly reduced the coal's marketability. Either way, the excessive handling damaged the product so badly that it frequently sat on northern wharves without buyers or sold at a very low price.[95]

Water conveyance cost about seven cents per bushel. In 1820, the report of the Virginia Board of Public Works concluded:

> It will be perfectly safe to say, that if the coal could be got to market, nearly in the condition it is delivered from the mine, that the average sales would be five cents per bushel higher. It results then, that the collier pays seven cents in actual charges, and suffers by the present mode of conveyance five cents deterioration, making twelve cents per bushel cost, between the waters [sic] edge near the mine, and the vessel which carries it to market: and it is also to be remembered, that the freight of a cargo of inferior coal, will be equal to a cargo of that which will sell for the highest price.[96]

The board believed that with improved methods and reduced handling transportation charges could be reduced to about three cents per bushel.

Since lack of economical transportation was the foundation of so many of the financial difficulties which confronted the Virginia colliers, internal improvements dominated their concerns during the 1820s and 1830s. In 1824, the miners south of the James River petitioned the Virginia General Assembly to improve the river so that batteaux could be fully loaded year-round. The colliers observed that "the coal trade is at present languishing under great and burthensome expense in the Transportation of that article from all those valuable Mines situated in the said county of chesterfield." They informed the legislators that considerable savings would result from an improvement to the James River. The petitioners judged that the mines produced about one million bushels of coal annually. With that rate and land transportation costs of ninety cents per bushel, the southside colliers estimated that annual conveyance costs totaled $90,000. With an improvement to the river, the colliers believed that expenses would be reduced to four cents per bushel, or $40,000 per year, for an annual savings of $50,000. The improvement also would enable the operators to preserve the quality of their product and thus to "undersell and destroy the Competition of Foreign Coal, which now constitutes about one half the Quantity consumed in the United States."[97] According to the miners, who again petitioned the Assembly in 1832, the canal offered no solution to their problems because the toll of one cent per bushel represented the highest canal fee in America or Europe. Unless some relief was afforded the colliers, future business would be "carried on under great disadvantages, if not wholly abandoned." Furthermore, the colliers complained, slaves still towed the canal batteaux rather than horses or mules, and that reduced efficiency still more. The mine operators had an even greater grievance. When the coal arrived at Richmond, canal crews encountered additional problems, for the locks were "in such a state of decay" that few boats could ever pass through them to tidewater. Consequently, the coal had to be dumped and hauled by wagon to the wharves for export. The rehandling caused further deterioration of the coal and reduced its market value.[98]

In an attempt to reduce costs and increase their competitive ability, the southside miners constructed a horse-drawn railroad from the pits to Richmond. The 13.5 mile long Chesterfield and Manchester Rail Road was completed in 1831 at a cost of about $140,000.[99] The Chesterfield Rail Road conveyed most of the coal bound for northern ports and in 1837 charged six cents per bushel from the mines to tidewater. According to its charter, as soon as its capital stock had been refunded, transportation charges had to be reduced to a level required for adequate maintenance and payment of a 6 percent dividend per annum.[100]

Even though the Chesterfield line offered the colliers a reduction in transportation charges, it still failed to provide a competitive edge in the marketplace. A company report issued by the Chesterfield board of directors in 1844 concluded that, between 1835 and 1843, an annual average of 1,267,069 bushels was shipped over the line at an annual cost of $31,641.12 to the colliers. This came to an average of 0.032 cents per bushel for haulage. However, steam-powered railroads, such as the Baltimore and Ohio or the Philadelphia and Reading, which were then expanding into the bituminous fields of western Pennsylvania and western Maryland, shipped coal at a significantly cheaper rate than that of the horse-drawn Chesterfield line. Furthermore, contemporary engineering studies confirmed that steam was not economically feasible for the short thirteen mile line. Hence, Virginia colliers paid double the haulage charges levied against their competitors in the Pennsylvania and Maryland fields.[101]

Still other difficulties, which generally had little impact on northern coal mines, might confound operations at southern coal mines. The semifixed nature of annually hired slave laborers could adversely affect the financial status of a coal company. In an 1837 memorial to Congress, Virginia colliers noted that the coal trade had been "reduced to extreme distress." For six months, "the coal mines were scarcely worked at all, and the laborers, who are necessarily hired by the year, were at wages and bound by the employers, who could make no use of them."[102] Even if the demand for coal remained high, a scarcity of bondsmen might also hinder production. In the same memorial, the colliers observed that "the price of labor in coal-pits (by no means a favorite occupation) has perhaps risen more than in any other pursuit, from the competition for laborers in public and private works, most of which have the preference as employments."[103]

Innumerable, unforeseen events produced an unsettling effect on a coal company's business position. In 1819, one of Harry Heth's partners lamented that "it seems our misfortunes are never to be at an end. James Bryson the man who was making our Engine is dead, and our advances to him are considerable, say $2722." Much worse, because no one knew how to assemble it, the engine parts had been sold.[104] Moreover, since the coal trade involved extended lines of conveyance, frequent accidents occurred which lay beyond the control of the operator. Regarding "the 3504 Bushels of coal sunk at Alexandria, I have been very unfortunate," wrote an agent to Heth in 1819; "the Vessel still remains as she was." After an earlier attempt had failed, the shipowner and the agent "agreed with a competent person to raise her for 1000 dollars."[105]

Mine accidents, such as explosions, rockfalls, and flooding, which were all too frequent in the Virginia mines, also had a detrimental impact on the economic status of coal companies. For example, the colliers complained to Congress in 1837 that the "caving in of two of the most productive mines on the south side of the James river" had caused great reductions in coal production. The pits of A. and A. Wooldridge, which in 1835 yielded 760,000 bushels, "have this year produced but 70,000 bushels; and since March last, have afforded no coal" at all, observed the miners. "The pits of the Black Heath Company of Colliers, in consequence of a similar accident have been less productive, by 100,000 bushels, than they would have but for this cause." When such accidents occurred, the export miners, such as the Heths and the Wooldridges, lost orders to foreign coal competitors. When production resumed, the Virginia colliers then found that they had no immediate markets, and stockpiles grew sometimes to over twenty thousand bushels.[106]

For the Virginia coal mine operator, the high-risk nature of his underground enterprise formed the most pervasive economic uncertainty. Refusing to pay an increase in coal royalties to the owners of a leased site, Harry Heth summarized the financially tenuous nature of mining in the Richmond Basin:

> Will you do me the favor Gentlemen to reflect a few moments, upon the last stock of money and enterprise which will be necesary to carry on your works successfully, after the termination of the present lease, & of the uncertainty which always are: and always will attend coal mines. 1st the sinking of one shaft, only 400 feet will require 2 or 3 years labor, & will cost from 5 to $8000. The steam engine of 32 horse power, which, thank God, I have only conditionally contracted for, will cost (in fact I have bought two) $1000 [?] all of which will be necessary for the vigorous prosecution of the works, on the new, and I may say grand scale—here there

is a stock of near $40,000 . . . for the prosecution of a busi-
ness, dangerous in the extreme, and upon which there must
ever exist some degree of uncertainty. Suppose on Sinking
the Shaft 400 feet I should discover that the coal had no . . .
value, by no means an improbable event. Are you liable for
any of the loss of time, labor & money . . .? Suppose the
Engine . . . chokes & thereby suffocate[s] and destroy[s] 40
of my Negro men, a circumstance which has lately actually
occurred in England, in two instances, are you bound to
replace my loss?[107]

James M'Killop, a knowledgeable Scottish miner, visited the Virginia
coal fields in 1869, and seven years later published his notes for private use.
M'Killop observed that before the Civil War "most of the miningwork had
been done by the slaves." That proved unfortunate, he implied, for nothing
could be "more wretched" than this "cheap system of labour." Furthermore, according to M'Killop, "instead of increasing the intelligence,
wealth, and prosperity of the state," slave-operated coal mines helped to
hold "the poor in ignorance and vice, and retarded the development" of the
state's mineral resources.[108]

Not all observers during the nineteenth century agreed with M'Killop's
dismal assessment. Many commentators stated their conviction that coal
mining could be a highly profitable undertaking with slave workmen. In
May 1814, Harry Heth informed a friend that at Black Heath Coal Pits "the
annual profit may be made to exceed $75,000." Even though management
of his pits occasionally had been "more or less embarrassed," Heth's
mines still yielded a "profit for many years of $50,000."[109] Likewise, the
prestigious *American Journal of Science and the Arts* reported in 1826 that
"the bituminous coal region of Virginia continues to be profitably
explored," and at least one "considerable proprietor is said to have
realized the past year a profit of forty thousand dollars from his coal
pits."[110] Mine operators in eastern Virginia continued to earn substantial
profits, according to an account published in an 1838 edition of the
Richmond Daily Compiler. The paper reported that, while some of the pits
had been abandoned "from want of capital, or energy, or something,"
nonetheless "those which have been systematically worked have realized
fortunes for their proprietors."[111]

Little doubt exists that at least some families, such as the Heths and
Wooldridges, accumulated considerable wealth from their slave-run coal
mines. But did this prosperity result *because* of slavery, or *in spite* of it?
Certainly not all mine operators who utilized slaves succeeded. Indeed, the
history of the Virginia coal industry is strewn with failures. Ultimately,
however, neither testimonials to accumulated wealth among miners nor a
reduction in specific operating costs by the use of slave labor comes to grips

with the crucial question of profitability. That is, compared with equivalent free whites, did slave miners produce below, at the same, or above the levels of efficiency achieved by their free white counterparts? Only a comparison of per capita productivity at free and slave-operated mines will answer that issue.

While the detailed records necessary for a definitive analysis do not exist, cost comparisons over time can be established which provide important indices of relative productivity. In mining a bulk resource such as coal, expenses are inversely correlated with the level of production. For example, in 1797 one Goochland County mine raised only 55,536 bushels of coal. At that level of production, labor costs were exceptionally high at nineteen cents per bushel. The following year, the miners raised 550,000 bushels, and expenses declined to a very competitive two cents per bushel, with labor representing by far the largest single outlay per unit of production.

Labor expenses in the Richmond Basin increased steadily during the antebellum era. In 1812, the owner of Black Heath Pits contracted Samuel Wooddy to raise coal from the mine with the labor of fifteen hands. Wooddy received "four cents per bushel, for all coal he may be able to raise," which included the labor and supervisory charges as well as profit. That meant labor costs must have been lower than three cents per bushel at Black Heath in 1812.[112] Similarly, in 1816 Heth's underground labor costs averaged about four cents per bushel. When profit is taken into account, labor costs probably came to slightly over two cents per bushel.[113]

In January 1836, when the Black Heath Company of Colliers and twenty-four other coal operators petitioned the Virginia Assembly for the right to build a railroad link with the James River, they calculated that coal "at the landing is sold at 14 cents per bushel."[114] That figure included the expenses of transporting the coal over the two or three miles to the river bank. Assuming that cost averaged a high four cents per bushel and that the operator realized a large profit of 50 percent, labor costs must have been near six cents per bushel. By the late 1850s, the cost of mining coal had increased dramatically, according to knowledgeable contemporaries, averaging "at least $2.50 per ton at the pits." Labor costs in the Richmond field then approached a very steep ten cents per bushel.[115] Thus, as the antebellum period progressed, the productivity of Virginia mines apparently decreased.

On the other hand, comparative data suggest that the opposite trend characterized the burgeoning bituminous fields of Maryland and western Pennsylvania. As discussed in Chapter 2, productivity cannot be considered in isolation from prevailing geological conditions. Thus, given available technology, the Maryland and western Pennsylvania slope mines had a natural advantage for miners since the coal seam was entered directly and presented few of the physical impediments to production which confronted Virginia colliers. The absence of social welfare costs for free white workers in northern mines probably played a significant role in reducing labor costs as well, but that conclusion can only be inferred. Whatever the reason, underground labor definitely represented a smaller expense in the free labor mines than in the slave pits of Virginia.

In 1809, Joshua Gilpin of Philadelphia toured western Pennsylvania and noted that coal was "taken from the drift of tunnells [*sic*], put into boats, landed at Pittsburgh on the opposite shore and carted to houses there for 5 cents per bushel." Across the Monongahela River, near the coal bank itself, Gilpin found factories erected so conveniently that coal cost no more "than the mere labor of throwing it a few yards from the pit to the furnace."[116] Estimating a conservative profit for the colliers at one cent per bushel and allowing two cents for delivery and middle-man profits, free white miners still delivered coal to the pit mouth at two cents per bushel.

Bituminous mining constituted a lucrative business from an early period in the Pittsburgh area. In 1814, Zadock Cramer recorded in *The Navigator* that forty or fifty coal mines operated near Pittsburgh, and "little short of a million bushels are now consumed annually in the city."[117] Some mines in western Pennsylvania produced coal much more cheaply than it could be raised in the Richmond Basin, for as early as 1815 the *Uniontown Genius of Liberty* advertised that Thomas Gregg would "deliver the stone coal into boats at the bank, for 2 cents per bushel." Assuming that Gregg earned only a meager profit, labor expenses must have been less than two cents per bushel.[118] In 1818, Thomas Hulme, the knowledgeable English traveler, visited a coal mine along the Ohio River near Wheeling and noted that coal cost

> 3 cents per bushel to be got out from the mine. This price . . .
> enables the American collier to earn upon an average, double
> the number of cents for the same labor that the collier in
> England can earn; so that as the American collier can, upon
> an average, buy his flour for one third the price that the
> English collier pays for his flour, he received six times the
> quantity of flour for the same labour.[119]

At other mines in the area, costs seem to have been still lower. Another English traveler, Adlard Welby, recorded in 1819 that coal in Washington and Canonsburg, Pennsylvania, could be purchased for "only two cents per bushel at the pit, and laid down at the door for two more." Labor costs, therefore, must have been close to one cent per bushel.[120] And twelve years later, in 1832, coal could be purchased at a Connellsville, Pennsylvania, mine for 0.015 cents per bushel.

Thus, at approximately the same time that mine operators in the Richmond Basin paid six to ten cents per bushel for underground slave labor, Pennsylvania and Maryland owners paid about one-third of that figure for the services of free white labor. The relative productivity of free and slave mine labor between 1800 and 1860 is estimated in Table 16.

Table 16

APPROXIMATE PER BUSHEL LABOR COSTS (IN CENTS) AT THE PIT MOUTH

Coal District	1800–1819	1820–1829	1830–1839	1840–1849	1850–1859
Pennsylvania (free)	2–3	2	1.5–2	2	3
Maryland (free)	—	2	—	1.5–2	1.5–2
Virginia (slave)	2	4	6	6–8	8–10

Source: Compiled by the author.

Since free labor mines achieved a greater reduction in per unit costs than did slave-operated mines, can it be claimed, therefore, that free workmen constituted a more profitable source of labor in bituminous coal mines? The answer must be qualified: possibly. Slave labor did compete well during the first two decades of the nineteenth century, and not until the 1830s and 1850s did an exaggerated divergence occur between slave and free labor productivity. It was during these two decades that dramatic increases in slave prices took place. Also, the erratic nature of the coal deposits in the Richmond Basin imposed numerous financial burdens upon mine operators in the field which were not duplicated in the bituminous mines further north. Although the extent cannot be determined, geologic considerations directly affected profitability. To surmount their problems, Virginia miners could only employ the most efficient techniques and equipment available. Although sound and progressive mine management was essential, that quality seems to have been the most telling deficiency in the Richmond field. Mine operators did not maintain the kind of data required for any thorough assessment, but numerous experts from free labor systems examined the mines in the Richmond Basin and expressed their consternation at the inefficient methodology utilized and at the firm resistance to basic technological improvements among the Virginia miners.

One report, commissioned by Christopher Quarles Tompkins, owner of Dover and Tuckahoe coal mines, summarized the general attitude of northern experts. Tompkins planned to purchase additional coal properties, and in 1858 he employed two well-known consultants from Pennsylvania to examine prospective pits in Goochland County. Although the mines had been operated by Maury and Company, a respected mining firm in the Basin, mining operations nevertheless had been "carried on in a very irregular manner, generally by Slave labor," most of whom had not received instruction in how to separate "slate or other impurities" from the coal, or in the selection of the right sizes for market purposes.[121] According to the consultants, it appeared that

> in no instance have the parties who worked these mines mined out the full size of the Vein, but have mined or dug holes in all directions without any system of management, or care of the coal in these Veins must be left standing, but in such a condition as to cost twice the amount to mine it out as it would in the first opening.[122]

Moreover, when the coal had reached the surface, it was "so handled as to reduce it nearly to dust." Whether they realized it or not, the consultants struck a sensitive nerve in planter-dominated Virginia when they declared that "mining has been considered secondary to farming, the hands have been employed in mining, when not required on the farm, consequently a regular supply to meet demand has not been furnished, nor a regular business established."[123] Nor had the Virginia operators utilized even the most rudimentary advancements in mining techniques. Many continued to sink shafts near the outcrops, then drifted with the descent of the seam toward the middle of the Basin; the slow and difficult work of hoisting the coal up an extended incline hampered productivity. "It will readily be perceived," noted the consultants, "how much more expensive, and inconvenient, and injurious to the coal by crushing it, the present mode of mining is, than if mined in the regular manner from the center of the basin, ascending with the dip." This method would have permitted the coal and water to flow with the gravity plane to the bottom of the shaft where one direct hoist could take the product to the surface. Even with "management so bad," however, the current operator had made a "large profit" and was "anxious" to renew his lease.[124]

Samuel Daddow, the superintending engineer of a large Pennsylvania coal firm and one of the most prominent members of the American Institute of Mining Engineers, examined numerous mines throughout the South in 1860. His assessment of management in the Richmond Basin confirmed the opinions expressed by the consultants employed by Christopher Q. Tompkins. Daddow considered the methods used by Virginia miners as "exceedingly primitive." Most of the "blunders and failures" made by the operators in the field resulted, he believed, from "ignorance." For example, only the Midlothian Company operated with "improved machinery," and even that firm did not employ "ordinary fixtures" for hauling the coal to the surface. The construction of a sophisticated $70,000 pump, when simple mechanisms costing less than one-third of that price would have sufficed, represented a typical management failure, according to Daddow. Even worse, the company had built the pump at a time when nearly all the coal accessible to the pit had been extracted. This case was indicative, Daddow believed, of "the want of practical knowledge in mining matters displayed by the miners of that District." Inevitably, mismanagement bore the fruit of low productivity, for the cost of producing coal was "at least double that of our anthracite or Western coal-fields" in Pennsylvania, Daddow reported.[125]

Although some Virginia coal mine operators realized substantial profits from their enterprises, the central issue lies in the comparative profitability of free and slave labor as alternative systems. And, while all things were not equal, free mines did operate at a higher level of productivity. In a very real sense, however, the problems associated with slave versus free labor existed within a larger matrix of social, political, and economic thought, both conscious and subconscious. That broader pattern of values and assumptions regarding the employment of black slave labor shaped the parameters of economic rationality—whether that labor was employed in the fields, the factories, or in the bowels of the earth.

NOTES

1. Robert S. Starobin, *Industrial Slavery in the Old South* (New York: Oxford University Press, 1970), pp. 148–49.

2. Ibid., pp. 148–53.

3. Ibid., p. 150.

4. York County Records, 1664–1672, and 1694–1702; Henrico County Records, 1677–1692, Virginia State Library, hereafter cited as VSL.

5. Arthur Cecil Bining, *Pennsylvania Iron Manufacture in the Eighteenth Century* (Harrisburg: Pennsylvania Historical Commission, 1938), p. 114.

6. Henry Bolingbroke, *A Voyage to the Demerary* (Philadelphia: M. Carey, 1813), pp. 84–86.

7. "Acct of Negroes," Principio Company Papers, 1723–1730, Maryland Historical Society, hereafter cited as MHS.

8. "Inventory of Ben Tasker of Negroes at the furnace, 1737," Carroll-Maccubbin Papers, MHS.

9. Unsigned memorandum in Dr. Carroll's handwriting, undated, Carroll-Maccubbin Papers, MHS.

10. Thomas J. Wertenbaker, *The Planters of Colonial Virginia* (New York: Russel & Russel, 1959), p. 127; Anne Bezanson, *Prices in Colonial Pennsylvania* (Philadelphia: University of Pennsylvania Press, 1935), p. 425.

11. Samuel G. Hermelin, *Report About the Mines in the United States of America*, trans. by Amandus Johnson (Philadelphia: John Morton Memorial Museum, 1931), p. 52.

12. Ibid., pp. 61–63. For the percentage of increase in wholesale prices for the war period, see *Historical Statistics of the United States: Colonial Times to 1957*, prepared by the Bureau of the Census (Washington, D.C.: U.S. Government Printing Office, 1961), p. 119. For the exchange rate of colonial currency to English pounds sterling, see Anne Bezanson, *Prices and Inflation During the American Revolution, Pennsylvania, 1770–1790* (Philadelphia: University of Pennsylvania Press, 1951), p. 346.

13. Hermelin, *Report About the Mines*, pp. 52–53; Bezanson, *Prices and Inflation During the Revolution*, p. 346.

14. Dr. Charles Carroll, "Proposals," in "Extracts from Account and Letter Books of Dr. Charles Carroll of Annapolis," *Maryland Historical Magazine* 25 (September 1930):299; unsigned memo in Dr. Carroll's hand, undated, Carroll-Maccubbin Papers, MHS.

15. Hermelin, *Report About the Mines*, p. 54.

16. Unsigned memo in Dr. Carroll's handwriting, undated, Carroll-Maccubbin Papers, MHS.

17. William Byrd, "Progress to the Mines," as reproduced in Louis B. Wright (ed.), *The Prose Works of William Byrd of Westover: Narratives of a Colonial Virginian* (Cambridge, Mass.: Belknap Press of Harvard University Press, 1966), p. 360.

18. Unsigned memo in Dr. Carroll's handwriting, undated, Carroll-Maccubbin Papers, MHS. It is impossible to say precisely how many whites were hired by the amount allotted for white labor expenses, but it is very unlikely that the number exceeded fifty men at this time. "Account of Persons employed at the Baltimore Iron Works, April 30, 1734," Carroll-Maccubbin Papers, MHS.

19. Keach Doyel Johnson, "The Establishment of the Baltimore Iron Company: A Case Study of the American Iron Industry in the Eighteenth Century" (Ph.D. dissertation, State University of Iowa, 1949), pp. 152, 162–63.

20. Bining, *Pennsylvania Iron Manufacture*, p. 49; Keach Johnson, "The Genesis of the Baltimore Ironworks," *Journal of Southern History* 19 (May 1953): 92, 95.

21. Stephen Onion to Charles Carroll, July 16, 1734, Carroll-Maccubbin Papers, MHS.

22. Dr. Carroll to his son, undated [probably February 1753], in "Account and Letter Books of Dr. Charles Carroll," *Maryland Historical Magazine* 25 (1930):68–69, 74, 75.

23. Hermelin, *Report About the Mines*, pp. 61–63.

24. Dr. Carroll to Edmond Quincy, July 9, 1748, in "Account and Letter Books of Dr. Charles Carroll," *Maryland Historical Magazine* 24 (1929):374–75.

25. "Rough state of My Acct with Mr. Price," in Charles Carroll's handwriting, November 15, 1755; "General Imports of Baltimore Pigg iron from Charles Carroll Esq," February 1754; "Account of Sales, 1754" by John Price and William Perkins, all in Carroll-Maccubin Papers, MHS.

26. Keach Johnson, "The Baltimore Company Seeks English Markets: A Study of the Anglo-American Iron Trade, 1731–1755," *William and Mary Quarterly* 16 (January 1959):58.

27. See, for example, Dr. Carroll to Charles Carnan, July 15, 1751, and to William

Black, November 18, 1753, in "Accounts and Letter Books of Dr. Charles Carroll," *Maryland Historical Magazine* 24 (1929):191, and 26 (1931):236.

28. Charles Carroll to his son, January 9, 1764, in "Extracts from the Carroll Papers," *Maryland Historical Magazine* 12 (1917):27.

29. Correspondence reprinted in Kate M. Rowland, *The Life of Charles Carroll of Carrollton, 1737–1832* (New York: G. P. Putnam's Sons, 1898), Vol. 1, p. 61.

30. "Journal of a French Traveller in the Colonies, 1765," *American Historical Review* 27 (October 1921):73.

31. Charles Carroll to his son, January 9, 1764, "Extracts from the Carroll Papers," *Maryland Historical Magazine* 12 (1917):27.

32. Daniel Dulany to George Fitzhugh, November 11, 1783, Dulany Papers, MHS.

33. Charles Carroll to Clement Plumsted, February 18, 1731, and Plumsted to Carroll, April 20, 1731, Carroll-Maccubbin Papers, MHS.

34. Ralph Falkner to Charles Carroll, February 20, 1733, Carroll-Maccubbin Papers, MHS.

35. Jackson T. Main, "The One Hundred," *William and Mary Quarterly* 11 (July 1954):363.

36. David Ross to Robert Richardson, hereafter cited by last name only, November 10, 1812, David Ross Letterbook, 1812–1813, Virginia Historical Society, hereafter cited as Ross Letterbook, VHS.

37. Ross to Richardson, February 19, 1813, Ross Letterbook, VHS.

38. Ross to Juliana Ross, August 29, 1813, Ross Letterbook, VHS.

39. Ross to Richardson, n.d. [probably December 1812], Ross Letterbook, VHS.

40. Ibid., November 10, 1812.

41. Ibid.

42. Ibid., February 19, 1813.

43. Ibid., November 10, 1812.

44. Ibid., February 19, 1813.

45. Ibid., November 10, 1813.

46. Ibid., n.d. [probably December 1812].

47. Ibid.

48. Ibid., October 30, 1812.

49. Ibid., November 10, 1812.

50. Ibid., November 12, 1812.

51. Ibid., November 10, 14, 1812.

52. Ibid.

53. Ibid., n.d. [probably December 1812].

54. Ibid., January 5, 1813.

55. Ibid., n.d. [probably December 1812].

56. Ibid., February 19, 1813.

57. Ross to William Dunn, n.d. [probably April 1813], Ross Letterbook, VHS.

58. Ibid., July 2, 1813.

59. Ibid., July 4, 1813.

60. Ross to Thomas Evans, August 10, 1813, and to Richard Netherland, August 17, 1813, Ross Letterbook, VHS.

61. Ross to John Staples, September 14, 20, 1813; Bond V. Ross, 3 Fed. Cas. 842

(1815); Ross to Jefferson, August 7, 1813, all in Ross Letterbook, VHS.

62. "Last Will and Testament of David Ross," April 24, 1817, typed copy, VSL; Campbell County Personal Property Tax Books, VSL.

63. Ross to Richardson, n.d. [probably December 1812], Ross Letterbook, VHS.

64. Ibid., November 10, 1813.

65. Ross to Thomas Evans, June 24, 1812, Ross Letterbook, VHS.

66. Andrew Burnaby, *Travels Through the Middle Settlements in North America in the Years 1759 and 1760 with Observations upon the State of the Colonies* (London: T. Payne, at Mews-Gate, 1775), p. 115.

67. *Journal of the Proceedings of the Commissioners Appointed to Preserve Confiscated British Property, 1781, and 1781–1782*, Maryland Hall of Records, hereafter cited as HR.

68. "List of Slaves at Oxford Iron Works," William Bolling Papers, Duke University, hereafter cited as Duke.

69. Charles B. Dew, *Ironmaker to the Confederacy: Joseph R. Anderson and the Tredegar Iron Works* (New Haven, Conn.: Yale University Press, 1966), pp. 29–30.

70. "List of Slaves at Oxford," William Bolling Papers, Duke.

71. Ridwell Furnace, Ledger, 1805–1809, University of North Carolina, hereafter cited as UNC; James C. Dickinson to William Weaver, January 2, 1828, Weaver-Brady Papers, University of Virginia, hereafter cited as UVa; "A register of the black Hands at C. Forge for 1830," and "Register of Furnace for 1830," Jordan and Irvine Papers, State Historical Society of Wisconsin, hereafter cited as SHSW; Henry A. McCormick to William Weaver, December 29, 1855, Weaver-Brady Papers, UVa; James Coleman to William Weaver, February 5, 1856, William Weaver Papers, Duke; James C. Davis to W. W. Davis, January 7, 1856, Jordan and Davis Papers, SHSW; S. Sydney Bradford, "The Negro Ironworker in Ante Bellum Virginia," *Journal of Southern History* 25 (May 1959):196.

72. See, for example, Ulrich B. Phillips, *American Negro Slavery: A Survey of the Supply, Employment and Control of Negro Labor as Determined by the Plantation Regime* (Baton Rouge: Louisiana State University Press, 1966, originally 1918), pp. 395–97; Fabian Linden, "Repercussions of Manufacturing in the Ante-Bellum South," *North Carolina Historical Review* 17 (October 1940):328; Eugene D. Genovese, *The Political Economy of Slavery: Studies in the Economy and Society of the Slave South* (New York: Random House, 1965), p. 181.

73. Starobin, *Industrial Slavery in the Old South*, p. 179.

74. "Daniel Dulaney, Negroes to be put into the works as per Agreement," and "Inventory of Ben Tasker, Negroes at the Furnace, 1733," Carroll-Maccubbin Papers, MHS.

75. See Chapter 3 and Bradford, "The Negro Ironworker," p. 195.

76. Starobin, *Industrial Slavery in the Old South*, pp. 157–58.

77. Ibid., p. 162.

78. James D. Norris, *Frontier Iron: The Maramec Iron Works, 1826–1876* (Madison: State Historical Society of Wisconsin, 1964), pp. 37–41.

79. Ibid., pp. 41, 43–44.

80. The discussion of Tredegar relies primarily upon the analysis of Charles B. Dew, *Ironmaker to the Confederacy*, pp. 29–34, and additional sources cited.

81. Joseph Anderson to Harrison Row, January 3, 1848, Tredegar Letterbooks, Tredegar Company Papers, VSL. This letter is also reproduced in Kathleen Bruce, *Virginia Iron Manufacture in the Slave Era* (New York: Augustus M. Kelley, 1960, originally 1930), pp. 237–38.

82. Dew, *Ironmaker to the Confederacy*, p. 29.

83. *Richmond Dispatch,* March 30, 1860; *Baltimore Daily Exchange,* March 10, 1860.

84. *The Crescent Iron Manufacturing Company with Statistics of Other Manufacturing Companies, Wheeling, Virginia* (Boston, 1815), p. 2; Archer & Co. to McKinney & Boss, October 16, 1858, Tredegar Letterbooks, Tredegar Company Records, VSL.

85. "Corporate Holdings, 1866," Manuscript Tredegar volume, p. 6, Tredegar Company Records, VSL.

86. Samuel Sydney Bradford, "The Ante-Bellum Charcoal Iron Industry of Virginia" (Ph.D. dissertation, Columbia University, 1958), pp. 65–67; Peter Temin, *Iron and Steel in Nineteenth-Century America: An Economic Inquiry* (Cambridge, Mass.: MIT Press, 1964), pp. 52, 57–62, 83–85.

87. Henry Howe, *Historical Collections of Virginia; Containing a Collection of the Most Interesting Facts, Traditions, Biographical Sketches, Anecdotes, etc. Relating to its History and Antiquities* (Charleston, S.C.: Babcock & Co., 1845), p. 230.

88. Agreement, Harry Heth and Daniel French, November 30, 1811, Heth Family Papers, UVa.

89. U.S. Congress, House, *Coal Trade—Richmond,* petition, 24th Cong., 2nd Sess., 1837, p. 2.

90. Harry Heth to Thomas Railey, July 7, 1812, Heth Family Papers, UVa.

91. Mssrs. Fenton, Murray & Wood to Harry Heth, November 26, 1818, Heth Family Papers, UVa.

92. *Documents Relating to the Phenix Mining and Manufacturing Company: Comprising Extracts From Various Official Reports* (New York: Sibell & Mott, 1849), p. 7.

93. Ibid., p. 18.

94. *New York Columbian,* 1811, quoted in Howard N. Eavenson, *The First Century and a Quarter of American Coal Industry* (Pittsburgh: By the Author, 1942), p. 68.

95. See numerous such complaints scattered throughout the Heth Family Papers, UVa.

96. Virginia Board of Public Works, *Annual Report,* 1820, VSL.

97. Memorial, December 15, 1824, Chesterfield County Petitions, VSL.

98. Memorial, January 28, 1832, Henrico County Petitions, VSL.

99. *Report of the Committee Under a Resolution of the Stockholders of the Chesterfield Railroad Company* (Richmond: Shepherd & Colin, 1844), pp. 1–7.

100. U.S. Congress, *Coal Trade—Richmond,* petition, 1837, pp. 5–6.

101. *Report . . . of the Chesterfield Railroad Company,* pp. 8–9.

102. U.S. Congress, *Coal Trade—Richmond,* petition, 1837, p. 6.

103. Ibid., pp. 4–5.

104. Ben. Sheppard to Harry Heth, October 12, 1819, Heth Family Papers, UVa.

105. Andrew Ramsey to Harry Heth, March 7, 1819, Heth Family Papers, UVa.

106. U.S. Congress, *Coal Trade—Richmond,* petition, 1837, p. 5.

107. Harry Heth to Sirs [?], October 10, 1815, Heth Family Papers, UVa.

108. Eavenson, *First Century and a Quarter of American Coal Industry,* pp. 129–33.

109. J.P. Pleasants to Harry Heth, May 5, 1814, enclosure, Heth Family Papers, UVa.

110. "Practical Remarks on Bituminous Coal Formation," *American Journal of Science and Arts* 11 (October 1826): 57–58.

111. John B. Chapman to Isaac Lea of Philadelphia, reproduced in the *Richmond Daily Compiler,* June 5, 1838.

112. Agreement, Harry Heth to Samuel Wooddy, January 21, 1812, Heth Family Papers, UVa.

113. Harry Heth to Thomas Railey & Brothers, October 17, 1816, Heth Family Papers, UVa.

114. R. C. Taylor, *Statistics of Coal: Including Mineral Bituminous Substances Employed in Arts and Manufactures; With Their Geographical, Geological, and Commerical Distribution, and Amount of Production and Compensation on the American Continent* (Philadelphia: J. W. Moore, 1855, originally 1848), p. 52.

115. John D. Imboden, *The Coal and Iron Resources of Virginia: Their Extent, Commercial Value and Early Development Considered* (Richmond: Clemmitt & Jones, Printers, 1972, originally 1872), p. 8.

116. Joshua A. Gilpin, "Journal of a Tour from Philadelphia in 1809," *Pennsylvania Magazine of History and Biography* 52 (1928):49–50.

117. Zadock Cramer, *The Navigator; Containing Directions for Navigating the Monongahela, Allegheny, Ohio and Mississippi Rivers* (Pittsburgh: Cramer, Spear & Eichbaum, 1814), pp. 108–109.

118. *Uniontown Genius of Liberty,* October 18, 1815.

119. Thomas Hulme, *Hulme's Journal of a Tour in the Western Counties of America—September 30, 1818–August 8, 1819,* as reproduced in Reuben Gold Thwaites (ed.), *Early Western Travels, 1748–1846,* Vol. 10 (Cleveland: Arthur H. Clark Co., 1904), pp. 37, 77.

120. Adlard Welby, *A Visit to North America and English Settlements in Illinois, with a Winter Residence at Philadelphia* (London: J. Drury, 1821), as reproduced in Thwaites (ed.), *Early Western Travels,* Vol. 12, pp. 201–202.

121. "Report of Smelhurst and Vivian," December 22, 1858, Tompkins Family Papers, VHS.

122. "Report of Sampson Vivian," December 22, 1858, Tompkins Family Papers, VHS.

123. "Report of Smelhurst and Vivian," December 22, 1858, Tompkins Family Papers, VHS.

124. Ibid.

125. Samuel Harries Daddow and Benjamin Bannan, *Coal, Iron, and Oil; or, the Practical American Miner* (Philadelphia: J. B. Lippincott & Co., 1866), pp. 397, 401.

The Social Politics of   7
Industrial Slavery

Here . . . capital will be able to control labor, even in manufactures with whites, for blacks can always be resorted to in
case of need.
                       —James Hammond, 1851

While the rest of the nation experienced dynamic economic growth during the first two decades of the nineteenth century, the Chesapeake region suffered from soil exhaustion and depressed tobacco prices. By the 1820s the planter aristocracy, which had guided the region to its earlier political prominence in the nation's affairs, now found its dominance eroded.[1] Looking back over the history of this general demise from the vantage point of the 1870s, one Virginian suggested that these problems stemmed from the fact that

> land and negroes were the aspiration of the Virginian of the past, and not mines, mills and furnaces, and we didn't want people amongst us who did not concur in or adopt our social and political ideas. Therefore, all these great national re-
> sources not only remained buried, but very few amongst us even knew the extent to which we possessed them.[2]

Tidewater planters resisted the national trend toward industrialization because they believed their way of life was being threatened not only by the broader national thrust toward protective tariffs, banks, and government-financed internal improvements which accompanied the process, but also by the "Jacobinical" reformers in the western part of the region.[3]

When the state constitution was framed in 1776, the Eastern Shore counties of Maryland had the largest percentage of that state's white population and the vast majority of the black slaves, while the western counties contained few inhabitants and they were predominantly white. According to the constitution,[4] however, each county had the same number of representatives in the legislature. Each elected four members to the House of Delegates, while Baltimore and Annapolis elected two apiece. On the other hand, the Senate was chosen by electors. Together the two bodies elected the governor and Council. During the years following adoption of the constitution, the population of the western counties grew significantly until the western section of the state was grossly underrepresented in the affairs of state government. Accordingly, in 1837 Kent and Calvert, two eastern counties with a combined population of only 19,401, were apportioned the same number of delegates as Frederick and Washington, two western counties with a combined population of 71,056. Moreover, Kent and Calvert counties each had twice as many representatives as were allotted to the city of Baltimore, whose population totaled 80,625. The legislature elected the executive who then appointed nearly all the civil officeholders in the state government. Consequently, a minority of one-fourth of Maryland's 470,019 people controlled the governmental machinery.[5]

Given this background of disproportionate representation, in 1836 Marylanders were "up in arms," demanded "reform or revolution," as the government leaders characterized it, and held mass demonstrations to show their displeasure. In November 1836, a reform convention met in Annapolis and quickly drafted proposals that called for such measures as the popular election of the governor, of one senator from each county and from Baltimore, and of certain other public officials; a reapportionment of the House of Delegates according to the population; and the abolition of offices for life. In March 1837, the legislature, coerced by the public uproar, passed most of the measures into law.[6] Accordingly, the plantation gentry's influence was significantly diminished, and Maryland was spared the deep cleavages that split Virginia during this era.

Although the Virginia constitutional convention of 1829-1830 turned out to be little more than a forensic exhibition, the debates themselves revealed the divisiveness within the state over fundamental social, political, and economic issues. The dissident western section of the state charged that Virginia's decline stemmed from the lack of an adequate transportation system and an undemocratic constitution. The state constitution, framed during the Revolutionary era, maintained the traditional principle that property qualifications were necessary to hold office and for the exercise of the franchise. It also apportioned representatives in the General Assembly, composed of a Senate and a House of Delegates, to the cities and counties on the basis of property and white population. This propertied assembly elected the judges of the higher courts, the governor, and nearly all state officials of importance. The governor then appointed the members of the county courts.[7]

Virginia Tidewater planters insisted that the foreign ideas of industrialism, tariffs, and internal improvements had infiltrated the state through the political reformers beyond the Blue Ridge Mountains. The gentry viewed the westerners as advocates of "mobocracy," which they believed at some point would develop into abolitionism.[8] Since the vast majority of slaves in Virginia were in the eastern Tidewater and Piedmont areas, the planters feared that a loss of political power would necessarily result in a loss of control over blacks. An insurrection would certainly result from any changes in the status quo. During the 1820s, Tidewater planters charged time and again that the western reformers wanted political power only in order to abolish slavery by the imposition of heavy taxes on slaves or even by direct emancipation.[9] Given this state of mind, it was little wonder that the planters emitted such a paranoiac response when Nat Turner launched his uprising in 1831 and seemingly gave credence to the gentry's worst fears that threats to the social order would lead to slave revolt.[10]

During the three decades between 1830 and the Civil War, the gentry felt further threatened by the rising tide of industrial and commercial growth in the nation generally and in their region specifically. The Chesapeake planters opposed all internal improvements on transportation, a banking system to provide sufficient capital for economic expansion, and a protective tariff to shield industrial enterprises from foreign competition. All these measures assumed the existence of a strengthened central government. Traditionally, the Democratic party represented the Chesapeake gentry, while the Whigs generally spoke for industrial and commercial interests.[11] By the 1840s, the bonds between the planters and the Democratic party had grown even stronger. They feared that to yield on any of these measures would set a dangerous precedent for the federal government to rule against slavery in the future. The gentry associated Democrats with southern nationalism and states' rights, two forces that would guard against the encroaching power of a federal government dominated by northerners opposed to slavery.[12]

The broader political struggle between the gentry and the industrial-commercial interests of the South was typified in microcosm by the attempt of Chesapeake ironmasters and colliers to gain a concession for a protective tariff and internal improvements. The rise of iron manufacturing in Richmond during the antebellum era and the growing use of coal as a furnace fuel united Chesapeake iron and coal producers during the 1840s in an attempt to increase the protective tariff on coal and iron.[13] Iron companies, which drew upon their own deposits in nearby fields, and the western iron men, who still relied on charcoal for fuel, found the prospects of such increased tariffs to their mutual advantage. Whatever advantages Calhoun and his South Carolina followers had wrested from Congress during the 1833 Nullification Crisis, such as the downward revision of the tariff schedules,[14] a residue of problems remained for the upper South. Both the planters who hired their excess slaves to industries and the aspiring industrialists felt the impact. By 1837, colliers complained that reduced tariff schedules for imported coal undermined their competitive effectiveness in the marketplace. That year, the leading colliers presented a memorial to the U.S. Congress which argued for an increase in the tariff. The Virginia coal operators reminded Congress that most of the bituminous fuel mined in the field went to fire the furnaces of industry along the eastern seaboard. Therefore, an inexpensive source of domestic coal was vital in the national struggle for industrial self-sufficiency.[15] The colliers reminded Congress that dependence on foreign coal imports would result in a loss of control over the price of the fuel. Even now, English coal had a "peculiar advantage" in American markets, lamented the colliers. In addition to possessing a cheap and abundant supply, English colliers transported their product practically commission-free as ballast in trading ships bound for America. If that coal then entered U.S. ports duty-free, American bituminous would not be able to compete and the industry would inevitably fall.[16] The Virginia petitioners were convinced that England would ship cheap coal only until American coal production had been destroyed, at which time the price would rise dramatically. There was probably some basis for this fear. Certainly the volume of British bituminous entering the market suggested the worst. Between 1822 and 1841, Virginia colliers watched the volume of imported coal rise from three million bushels to eighteen million bushels, respectively, or an increase of 600 percent. On the other hand, Virginia shipped six million bushels in 1822 and only nine million bushels in 1841, an insignificant increase compared with British imports.[17]

Over the years, numerous coal agents along the Atlantic Coast expressed similar fear of foreign competition. F. S. Taylor of Norfolk, who sold Black Heath coal in that city, informed Harry Heth in 1819 that "two vessels with coal are daily expected from Liverpool which will deprive me of some of my customers, more particularly in it is an experiment to put down the price of your coal. The importers saying they can furnish it as cheap or cheaper from Liverpool than they can be supplied from Richmond."[18] While this may not have constituted an orchestrated effort by the English colliers to "destroy" American coal producers, Virginia miners realized that without a protective tariff an open market would achieve the same result. In June 1817, Heth lamented that the "vast importations of foreign coal, now selling in New York, Philadelphia & Baltimore one at 25 & 26 cents per bus. on a credit of 4 & 6 months," had all but ruined his business for the year. Moreover, Heth still had "upwards of 200,000 bus. on hand & not one solitary [*sic*] order from any of the great towns of the North & East as usual, at this season of the year, on the contrary, all my letters state, that they are supplied with foreign coal on much better terms than I can possibly afford." Similarly, Heth informed one correspondent, in Baltimore a customer had purchased foreign coal at a rate which was 25 percent cheaper than Virginia coal, and the customer had refused to deal with Heth.[19] By 1843, when the *Miners' Journal* compiled a study of the coal trade, English bituminous had flooded eastern cities and had forced American producers to compete at "ruinous rates." Foreign coal had all but driven domestic coal out of the market, and "these facts speak much louder than all the fine spun theories of free-tradists," the *Journal* concluded.[20]

In like manner, southern ironmasters had already experienced serious difficulty in competing against British iron when the passage of the Tariff of 1833 compounded their disadvantage by permitting English rails to enter the United States duty-free. The ironmasters in the Valley of Virginia also became alarmed in the 1840s as they watched the tariff duties on pig iron decline according to the provisions of the 1833 tariff bill. During the spring of 1841, iron and coal producers finally realized that they had to shelve their differences and pool their energies if any impact was to be made toward reducing the tariff. They met in Lexington where they prepared and sent a memorial to Congress protesting the decline in the protective schedules.[21] Apparently, they received little satisfaction, for the following year the colliers and ironmasters met once again, this time in Richmond. A committee of nine drew up a memorial which claimed that it was to the advantage of the planters to support the demands of the industrialists for a protective tariff:

> Agriculture can only be relieved or aided by directing to other occupations a portion of the labor applied to it and by increasing at the same time the domestic market for its products. No branch of industry in the country has, therefore a clearer interest in the due encouragement and support of home manufactures than agriculture.[22]

The industrialists could not have analyzed the interests of the gentry more clearly. Like most planters of the South, those in Virginia constantly complained about the high prices paid to northerners for manufactured goods, the lack of home markets, and the need for "self-reliance."[23] It is significant that the planters rejected the industrialists' argument, for it indicated the extent to which they were forced into economic irrationality by the fear that any compromise with the industrialists would set a precedent for further erosion of their dominance. The next time the "alien forces" might act against slavery itself. Therefore, the planters rejected the proposal. Thomas Ritchie, editor of the *Richmond Enquirer* and a leader in the Virginia Democratic party, continued to denounce the course of action proposed by the Virginia industrialists.[24] The industrial interests, represented by the *Richmond Daily Whig and Public Advertiser,* castigated Ritchie's anti-business editorials as the work of a "loud-mouthed" reactionary. "The Agricultural and laboring population of Virginia have been humbugged long enough," the *Whig* chided in 1846. Favoring an increase in the protective tariff on imported coal, rather than the proposed decrease, the *Whig* informed its readers that

> the commerce of the city alone is indebted for its prosperity of these Coal Mines more than it is possible to calculate—yet you are told by that concern, the Enquirer, that the men who are engaged in these mining operations are oppressing the people in and around the city. I wonder if every man, woman and child in this neighborhood would not like such robbery and oppression as these Mines inflict continued all their lives? . . . There is no telling how many houses have been put up in the city of Richmond and vicinity from funds arising out of these Pits;—how many firms in the many departments of business depend directly or indirectly upon these Mines to carry on their operations and for support. The amount of capital which they put in motion is several millions, and the number of persons directly or indirectly depending on them may be put down in round numbers of ten thousand. . . . Should the proposed tariff pass, it would be more destructive to the prospects of every man than the overthrow, by conflagration, of one half of the city.[25]

The political debate over the protective tariff for iron and coal continued to rage in some quarters as late as March 1849, when John Anderson wrote to his brother Frank (both brothers were prominent ironmasters in Botetourt County) that he had heard a political speech delivered by a member of the Edmundson family, a leading slaveowner and pillar of the gentry class. Edmundson "made a violent attack upon the Manufacturers & particularly the iron men," denounced them as "great monopolists" who supported the tariff policy and as "oppressors of the farmers," and "dragged the private affairs of our firm before the people as he did in Fincastle." John suggested that Frank, who at that time was running for state office, should expose Edmundson as being "against all protection & in favor of European paupers doing all our Manufacturing" when Frank spoke in the western county of Greenbriar, "as it is a Strong tariff county."[26] The following year, by order of the "convention of Delegates, representing the Mining and Manufacturing interests of Virginia, held in Richmond on the 5th and 6th December, 1850," a memorial was sent to the U.S. Congress which once again outlined the complaints against the low import duties levied against foreign coal, iron, and other manufactured goods. They complained that, while other industries of the South had fallen on hard times, the condition of the coal and iron trades constituted an even more "depressed and discouraging" state of enterprise. Coal had dwindled to one-half its amount in 1856, and the fifty blast furnaces of Virginia produced only one-fifth of their potential capacity.[27] The industrialists received little relief from Congress, however. By 1858, Samuel McDowell Reid, an ironmaster of Rockbridge County, wrote that he did not "suppose that any good can come from keeping the Forge lands & waiting for Congress to increase the tariff on iron altho' there is some stir in the papers. I have no confidence in the pretenses of the Democrats on that subject."[28]

The Whigs won support for their policy of a liberal funding of internal improvements primarily from inhabitants of the western section of the state, for whom transportation connections with eastern markets were economically vital, and from those along prospective sites who expected to gain from the increased trade.[29] The most important internal improvement that Virginia industrialists secured before 1860, and then only after a hard fight, was a canal through the Blue Ridge Mountains. Prior to 1847, the James River and Kanawha Canal had been completed to Lynchburg; early that year, the Assembly rejected a plan to extend the operation beyond that point. The vote on the bill can be seen in Table 17. Two ironmasters from Botetourt County, Francis T. Anderson and his brother John Anderson, both active Whigs, led the abortive attempt.[30] From their furnaces in the Valley of Virginia, they supplied their brother Joseph Anderson's Tredegar works in Richmond with pig iron. Passage through the mountains was difficult and expensive, however, and improved transportation facilities became increasingly critical if western iron men were to remain competitive. Accordingly, when the bill to extend the canal through the mountains failed to gain approval from the planter-dominated legislature in January 1847, the Andersons summoned interested parties in the western counties to meet the following month.

The resolutions passed by the western representatives at the February 1847 convention left little to the imagination of the legislators: the Assembly had to appropriate funds to extend the Kanawha Canal through the mountains, approve a right of way to a railroad company for the construction of a line from Winchester to the James River and on to the Ohio, or face a secession movement in the western section of the state for separate statehood in the Union.[31] By March 2, 1847, the Virginia legislature had reversed its policy and had appropriated $1,236,000 for extending the waterway to Buchanan. At least part of the reason for this compromise by the eastern planters no doubt arose from their unwillingness to face a loss of a good slave-hiring market. Even though the ironmasters of the western counties owned many slaves, at this time about six hundred additional blacks were hired each year from the gentry east of the Blue Ridge Mountains. "Thus were three counties in the Valley [Rockbridge, Allegheny, and Botetourt] paying in the form of slave hire to the East, an amount almost equal to the entire slave tax of Eastern Virginia."[32]

Table 17

VOTE ON THE JAMES RIVER AND KANAWHA CANAL
EXTENSION, 1847

Affirmative

Delegates from
  The West and Southwest   30
  East of the Blue Ridge   21
  The extreme Northwest, the region attached
    to the interests of Wheeling   7
  The counties interested in the "Right of Way"
    to the Baltimore and Ohio Railroad   _2_
                                                    60

Negative

Delegates from
  The West and Southwest   8
  East of the Blue Ridge   47
  The extreme Northwest, the region attached
    to the interests of Wheeling   0
  The counties interested in the "Right of Way"
    to the Baltimore and Ohio Railroad   _8_
                                                    63

Source: Richmond Times and Compiler, January 28, 1847; Kathleen Bruce, *Virginia Iron Manufacture in the Slave Era* (New York: Augustus M. Kelley, 1960, originally 1930), p. 272.

The canal opened up a two-way cross between Richmond and the Valley of Virginia. By January 1851, the number of slaves in Botetourt County had increased by 2,812. "The explanation may doubtless be found," noted the *Times and Compiler,* "in the fact that slave labour is peculiarly adapted to the iron business which is destined to make Botetourt one of the most important counties in the state."[33]

Throughout the period 1790 to 1860, many southerners realized that it was expensive for the South to depend upon others for their secondary goods and acknowledged the need for economic diversification.[34] Historians Donald L. Robinson and Robert Russel argue that the South failed to develop industrially because its sparse and poor population restricted the home market. Moreover, an inadequate transportation system, streams too sluggish to generate power, great distances between urban markets, and the lack of raw materials, all added to the formidable handicaps that prevented the growth of southern industry.[35] But Russel fails to mention one other vital noneconomic consideration: the will of the gentry was set against industrialization. The planters held the reins of power in a society based on plantation slavery, and basic social change would weaken their ability to control the machinery that maintained the black population in a subordinate status.[36] The gentry's position contained an inherent contradiction. Maintenance of a distinctive South independent of the North required the development of urban, industrial centers in the nineteenth-century pattern, a development which the planters feared and most distrusted. Cities threatened their control of society as they knew it. In his study of antebellum southern cities, Richard C. Wade succinctly summarizes the planters' quandary when he observes that slavery "required a high degree of order, the careful regulation of Negro affairs, and a fixed status for bondsmen. On the other hand, the city demanded fluidity, a constant reallocation of human resources, and a large measure of social mobility."[37] The planters viewed the prospect of a fluid and open society as inimical to their control, and throughout the 1830s and 1840s, such a prospect motivated their vigorous opposition to measures, such as internal improvements, which would foster such a trend.

After 1847, the hostility of the Virginia gentry toward industrialists weakened significantly. Not only did the planters begin to see that slavery was a common bond between the men of industry and themselves, but also national events jolted the planters into the realization that they needed political allies. Following the question of the annexation of Texas in 1845 and the Mexican War in 1846, the issue of slavery's expansion into the newly acquired territories and the compromise debates of 1850 inflamed the nation. The South became more conscious than ever of its political vulnerability and of its dependence upon the North for finished products. Before long, the South viewed itself as a regional and cultural entity under attack.[38] In this atmosphere of southern "cultural nationalism," opposition toward industrialization became muted, for the South could hardly expect to control its affairs without a manufacturing base of its own. The question became one of what *kind* of labor force southern industry should employ rather than whether or not the South should have industry at all.[39]

The planters had long feared the rise of an economically independent and politically powerful urban middle class. Beyond that, during the late antebellum era there arose in the South a general debate over which form of industrial labor was preferable, black slaves or free whites. Fired by a growth in manufacturing of such items as tobacco products, textiles, coal, and iron, the debate did not center on the *profitability* of slaves versus free labor. Southern white leaders had already convinced themselves that slavery was both profitable and essential in a biracial society. The debate took a rather different turn: could the South permit the rise of a class of urban factory slaves or of white proletarians, either of which might prove fatal to the region's traditional social system?[40]

Proponents of black industrial workers usually maintained that slaves were just as economical, and since slaves lacked mobility, on a seasonal basis they provided more stability than whites. Furthermore, whites wasted time by drinking or by engaging in meetings, musters, elections, and similar activities denied to slaves. Samuel D. Morgan, a prosperous Tennessee iron manufacturer, flatly stated in 1852 that slaves did not strike or demand wage increases.[41] In addition, manufacturers did not have to educate slaves and therefore had "their uninterrupted services from the age of eight years," as another prominent industrialist argued. Even though antebellum manufacturers encountered difficulty persuading planters to invest in industry, they found slaveowners willing to lease their excess slaves.[42] This diverted an unprofitable surplus of hands from agriculture into industry and guaranteed against a labor surplus and declining slave prices. Thus, in 1846 a local Whig declared that the Midlothian mines were of "incalculable benefit" to the nearby farmers, for they hired excess slaves to the pits "who would otherwise be idle and a burthen on their hands."[43] As economist Claudia Dale Goldin explains in *Urban Slavery in the American South, 1820–1860,* the fluctuation of slaves employed in southern industrial centers resulted from the varying elasticities of demand between the urban and agricultural sectors. As prices for agricultural goods fell, slaves brought better prices in the cities, and when agricultural prices regained lost ground, bondsmen tended to be reallocated to the rural sector. Urban did not necessarily mean industrial, of course, but in Richmond, the southern city with the greatest industrial base, the two terms came to be nearly synonymous.[44]

Industrial slavery not only provided planters with an outlet for their surplus slaves, but it also reduced the necessity of fostering the development of a white industrial proletariat who might generate civil unrest and agitate against the status quo. At the same time, planters feared the consequences of industrial slavery. Slave factory workers might be preferable to free white labor, but training and incentive systems were necessary, both of which made the gentry more uneasy about slave control.[45] Planters were unnerved when they saw blacks in the Virginia tobacco industry hiring themselves to the highest bidder, acquiring their own food and lodging, and earning wages for overwork,[46] or Tredegar slaves who lived "pretty much on the basis of free labor" as long as they did their jobs as expected.[47] In 1849, James H. Hammond, the leading planter of South Carolina, summed up the fears created by the spectre of industrial slavery: "Whenever a slave is made a mechanic he is more than half freed, and soon becomes, as we too well know, and all history attests, with rare exceptions, the most corrupt and turbulent of his class."[48] In Richmond, the authorities attempted to curb the relative freedom of movement, and consequent loss of control, of slaves who worked in the city. In 1852, the *Daily Dispatch* reported that some slaves, especially those who worked in the tobacco factories, received between seventy-five cents and one dollar per week to provide for their own board and that the city council was considering legislation restricting the practice.[49] By 1859, Richmond had passed a city ordinance which prohibited the payment of money in lieu of board. The 1859 law stipulated that every "hirer, owner or other employer of slave labor" must provide food and lodging for slave workers "upon his own premises, or by engaging board and lodging for them with some free person."[50]

Proponents of white factory labor based their primary arguments on the assumption that it was the social responsibility of self-respecting leaders to bring poor whites into the mainstream of southern life. That is, industrial expansion should be based on white labor, with industry absorbing and uplifting the multitudes of poor whites by providing them with the "proper supervision" and "moral instruction." In the process, the entire cultural life of the region would ultimately be elevated.[51] James H. Hammond clearly expressed the reasoning behind this approach:

> It has been suggested, that white factory operatives in the South would constitute a body hostile to our domestic institutions. If any such sentiments could take root among the poorer classes of our native citizens, more danger may be apprehended from them, in the present state of things, with the facilities they now possess and the difficulties they have now to encounter, than if they were brought together in factories, with constant employment and adequate remuneration. It is well known, that the abolitionists of America and Europe are now making the most strenuous [sic] efforts to enlist them in their crusade, by encouraging the exclusive use of what is called "free labor cotton," and by inflammatory appeals to their pride and their supposed interests. But all apprehensions from this source are entirely imaginary. The poorest and humblest freeman of the South feels as sensibly, perhaps more sensibly than the wealthiest planter, the barrier which nature, as well as law, has erected between the white and black races. . . . Besides this, the factory operative could not fail to see here, what one would suppose he must see, however distant from us, that the whole fabric of his own fortunes was based on our slave system.[52]

Concern for the traditional social-political structure spawned and fed this debate. Nearly a century before the antebellum controversy, however, ironmasters and then colliers had already convinced themselves that slavery provided the most preferable form of labor. By the antebellum era, the use of slaves in the iron industry had a tradition nearly as old as the peculiar institution itself, and ironmasters recognized as clearly as planters that slavery was the cement of southern society as they knew it.

Aubrey C. Land has studied the Chesapeake social structure during the colonial era and suggests that "the men of first fortune functionally belonged to a class whose success stemmed from entrepreneurial activities as much as, or even more than, from their direct operations as producers of tobacco." They included names such as the Taskers, Carrolls, and Dulanys of Maryland, and the Spotswoods, Washingtons, and Tayloes of Virginia. Even though they lived on plantations, their success came from business enterprise, such as land speculation, moneylending, the sale of imported goods, and the legal profession. Their business activities included shipbuilding, cooperage, flour milling, mining, and the manufacture of iron.[53]

The owners of the first ironworks in the Chesapeake region had already made their fortunes before turning to the "mysteries" of making iron. All the original ironmasters in the area were also large slaveowners. Charles Carroll of Annapolis was probably the most affluent of the original entrepreneurs. By 1764, his annual net income was at least £1,800, and he estimated that the total worth of his estate ran to £88,380. His estate included "285 slaves, each worth, on the average, £30 sterling," which totaled £8,550 in slave property.[54] Therefore, it was perfectly natural for Carroll and other early ironmasters to use slave labor upon erecting the first ironworks.

Natural, perhaps, but not automatic. Labor was the most scarce of the factors of production in the Americas. Men who migrated to the colonies during the eighteenth century found that their neighbors also sought laborers rather than become workers themselves. Lacking a surplus population, entrepreneurs could only import indentured servants and convicts from Europe,[55] or black slaves from Africa. Over time, the number of free workers increased steadily. Compared with slaves and indentured servants, however, free labor was excessively expensive and frequently undependable. The two or three shillings per day demanded by unskilled free workmen in America (a specie-scarce economy) seemed outlandish compared with the one shilling per day paid to skilled artisans in England. Colonial craftsmen sometimes demanded eight shillings per day.[56] Dr. Charles Carroll promoted the development of an iron industry in the colonies. His plan called for the mother country to pay a bounty on iron made in America. In 1753, he justified his views by noting that

> it is true that the Article of Wood for Coal is Cheaper here than in Gr: Br: but then all Labour is double or more than there Founders Hammermen finers & Coaliers very scarce as are all other Tradesmen necessary for Carrying on Such Works as Furnaces & Forges, whereby the making Bar Iron

is rendered far Dearer in the plantations & therefore requires
a national Encouragemt [sic].[57]

The first entrepreneurs of the embryonic southern iron industry quickly came to believe that slave labor, though relatively scarce, might best counter high wages and labor instability. Extant business records are insufficient to permit a definitive answer to the perennial question about the relative profitability of slavery in the iron industry. The question, however, diminishes in causal importance because from the 1720s until the end of the Civil War, industrialists assumed, and acted affirmatively on the assumption, that normally it was more profitable to employ slaves than free whites. This conviction is best illustrated among ironmasters.

Alexander Spotswood and Mr. Chiswell both informed William Byrd in 1732 that the use of slave labor kept costs to a minimum.[58] Reluctant to use slaves in the beginning, the British owners of Principio quickly changed their minds, and the company manager was ordered to buy "Negroes both for Principio and Virginia works (Accokeek) too for no works can carry on without them."[59] Certainly few ironmasters would have disagreed with Dr. Charles Carroll, manager of the Baltimore Iron Works, when he advised a prospective ironmaster that "as soon as he Can conveniently do it to get Young Negro Lads" to work under the skilled craftsmen, as well as to acquire "a certain number of able Slaves" to do the heavy unskilled manual labor.[60]

David Ross believed that the Oxford Iron Works could "afford to work as cheap as others" because "every branch of the business is carried on by the Servants belonging to the Estate."[61] A letter addressed to a white plantation overseer at Oxford Iron Works in 1812 illustrates Ross's firm belief in the economic effectiveness of using slaves in all occupations, including supervisory positions. Upon learning that one of his managers had hired a white assistant, Ross wrote that within six months the assistant would

> get a wife and her relations to be maintained—in three months more, he would get a mare and colt and in six months more, he would get a Studd horse, all to be maintained out of my corn—if your honesty and character compelled you to take notice of such abuses this young rascal would be ready to gouge out your eyes. . . . Take I say again and again one of my most faith[ful] servants give him some encouragement or fourth part of what you must give to a white lad [and] take my word for it you'll find him ten times better than any you can hire—he will labour day by day he has ten time[s] more experience and [is] a much honester man, he will receive your instructions with patience and humility & if a reprimand becomes necessary he will receive it without putting out your eyes.[62]

Like David Ross, Joseph Anderson of the Tredegar works believed that black labor was indispensable. In 1848, shortly after he had placed slaves at most of the skilled positions in the rolling mills, Anderson wrote that slave labor "enables me, of course, to compete with other manufacturers." [63]

Industrialists preferred slaves to white labor for several reasons. Masters considered whites unstable and disorderly workers. Quite as urgently as their modern counterparts, the first ironmasters yearned for predictability, although their means for achieving it differed. Even if the first iron entrepreneurs did procure a sufficient number of free and indentured whites, excessive turnover seriously hindered production at the Baltimore Iron Works which for many years was in blast only half the time because not enough hands could be found to keep the furnace in operation. [64] The problem included unskilled and skilled workers alike. The ironmaster at Principio, John England, lamented to one of the British partners that he did not trust "our founder Robert Durham, he is a very loose, careless Drinking man and I fear when the furnis [*sic*] Cometh to blow there will be no Dependence upon him." [65]

The number of white runaways at Chesapeake ironworks was staggering. In July 1734, Stephen Onion, the first manager of the Baltimore Iron Works, noted that some servants stole a boat, a square sail, and oars, and made their escape down the Patapsco River. [66] In August 1737, Onion wrote that he had intended to employ an agent to go after a runaway from the Principio Iron Works. [67] Many reasons lay behind this excessive runaway problem. Frequently, whites took flight in order to escape debts accumulated at the company store. Such was the case with two miners who ran away from the Baltimore Iron Works in June 1735: Francis Allinder owed £6 10s.8d., and Joseph Reardon owed £2 2s.9d. [68]

Harsh working and living conditions as well as the stern policy of ironmasters toward white servants undoubtedly created many labor problems. This attitude appeared in a letter sent to the ironmaster of Northampton Furnace in 1787 by an agent dispatched to Pennsylvania to track down a band of fugitive white workers:

> I have the pleasure to inform you that the Seven Servants that Runaway the 4th of this Instant is Just Now Brought home. They were taken up in York County near the Pidgion [and] the taking of them up and Bringing them home will cost upward of thirty Pounds. . . . wish we had a proper place provided to Sock them up in at Night. am just going to flog the Seven & five of the others—I hope you will send up more money. . . . I rode upwards of two hundred Miles after the Servants, I was up Susquehana to Sunsbury. . . . You may depend the servants made a great push and had it not been for the Snow that fell they would have given us much more

trouble. They were Tracked neare 30 miles in the Snow and was taken Wading Down a Creek like as many Spaniel Dogs.[69]

Along with other colonists, early ironmasters believed that the use of slave labor would reduce rapid turnover in the work force and would overcome the high wages demanded by free white mechanics in the labor-scarce colonies.[70] The use of black slaves was also more advantageous than the use of white indentured servants. After the 1660s, slaves were held in perpetuity rather than for a fixed term[71]; in time, they were judged less expensive to maintain than free labor, and under proper conditions their numbers increased by natural reproduction.[72] The use of slaves actually undermined the demand for indentured servants in the southern colonies, and as the number of skilled blacks became a larger part of the available labor force, the demand for free white artisans also declined.[73] Even though the weight of colonial law was on the side of the masters, little could be done to stem the tide of runaway whites, free and indentured, and to prevent them from losing themselves in the larger society once they had escaped. Conversely, blacks could be identified more easily and therefore be subjected to more control. During the period before the 1790s, a large percentage of the black slaves in the Chesapeake area were born in Africa and therefore were less able than whites to cope with the problems of geography, language, and survival in an alien society. Consequently, even if a slave escaped in this era he tended to "sulk about" the neighborhood and often was retrievable or, out of necessity, forced to return to the place of employment.[74]

Behavioral problems of white workers also presented a formidable un-settling element in maintaining a steady work force. Custom and necessity dictated that white ironworkers be supplied food and lodging because, in their master's view, they were "generally Such Idle Drunken Fellows that otherwise they would make no Provision and not be able to Goe on with theire work."[75] The problem was widespread. In 1734, Stephen Onion wrote to Charles Carroll that "too much strong Liquid dayly disordered more or less of the workmen and is the Occasion of Bad language and Quarell." Onion concluded that more caution had to be taken in the distribution of rum.[76] The time books of Northampton Furnace indicate that many days of labor were lost during the 1770s by rowdy intoxicated whites. Benjamin Leggett, for example, "got drunk in town yesterday—sick this day," and Martin Pollis "went to sleep Because of liquir [*sic*]" and "swore he would work no more."[77]

An act passed by the Maryland Assembly and signed into law by Gover-nor Samuel Ogle on August 8, 1732, attempted to quell the problems created by drunkenness among ironworkers in the colony. The act pro-vided that no "ordinary-keeper, Victualler, or Public House-Keeper" could "harbour or entertain" the employees of an ironworks or give them more than five shillings credit per year without first obtaining the employer's written consent. Violation of the law entailed "the same Losses, Pains, and Penalties" stipulated by the act "restraining Victuallers and Keepers of Public Houses, from entertaining Sailors, to the Prejudice of Trade and Commerce."[78]

By no means was the problem confined to the Chesapeake iron industry. In Pennsylvania, the colonial Assembly passed acts in 1726 and 1737 that forbade liquor sales near iron furnaces.[79] The New Jersey legislature enacted a law in 1769 which made it illegal to sell liquor within four miles of an iron furnace. Despite this regulation, New Jersey ironworkers found ways to procure enough liquor to hinder furnace production.[80] The problem of labor instability went unabated into the early nineteenth century. At Birdsboro Forge in Pennsylvania, one man missed work from being "drunk frolicken and Idle all this week," and not far away at Hopewell Furnace another ironworker had his wages docked "for getting intoxesitated [*sic*]" and missing work.[81] In New Jersey, an ironmaster recorded continuous laments, such as "all hands drunk" and "molders all agree[d] to quit work and went to the beach." On another day "Edward Rutter [was] off a-drinking."[82] Laws to regulate the behavior of white workmen notwithstanding, Euro-Americans had privileges and safeguards that were denied or only irregularly available to their Afro-American counterparts, such as freedom of movement, legal protection from physical abuse, access to property ownership, and a fixed limit on the length of their bondage if they were servants. In short, only whites had a range of civil and political rights which ironmasters were forced to recognize and honor.

Throughout the eighteenth century and years before the late antebellum debate over slave versus free white labor, ironmasters concluded that Africans best suited the needs of industrial stability. Unlike the case with white mechanics, the lives and working behavior of blacks were relatively controlled and therefore more predictable. As the nineteenth century progressed, northern industrial and commercial society adopted the individualistic patterns of nineteenth-century liberal capitalism, emphasizing the autonomy of the individual in the marketplace and the assumption that social progress was predicated on individuals serving their own private interests. The South, however, retained a preference for the traditional, organic society which stressed communal responsibility and the maintenance of established relationships and responsibilities. Moreover, the existence of a large slave population within its borders forced whites of Maryland and Virginia, and the South generally, to maintain a more rigid class hierarchy and social regulation over its members. Cemented together by the need to control the black population, conservative southern planters believed that the emphasis upon fluidity of class and capital in a rising,

modern industrial society constituted a direct threat to the very foundations of southern culture.[83] In their traditional reliance on slave labor, both
as owners and hirers, industrialists did not differ markedly from the gentry
in the conviction that a white-dominated society must be preserved.

Had the planters not been so paranoiac about maintaining the traditional
social and political status quo, they would have realized that the industrialists constituted no fundamental threat to southern society. Iron men
had no intention of undermining slavery, which was the very foundation of
southern culture. Joseph R. Anderson clearly revealed this attitude in his
reaction to the strike by white workers at Tredegar in 1847.[84] Anderson not
only perceived a menace to his authority and profits in their attempt to
block the employment of slaves in skilled rolling mill positions, but he also
believed that the white strikers threatened the principle of slaveownership
and hence slave society itself. Anderson therefore fired them. "It must be
evident," Anderson commented, "that such combinations are a direct
attack on slave property; and, if they do not originate in abolition, they are
pregnant with evils."[85] A Tidewater planter could not have advanced a
more proslavery position. Even the Whigs were not the social rev-
olutionaries conjured up by a nervous gentry. For example, the Whig
Richmond Times and Compiler stated that the principle behind the strike
attacked "the root of all the rights and privileges of the master, and if
acknowledged, or permitted to gain foothold, will soon wholly destroy the
value of slave property."[86]

Planters might have seen that industrial slaves were also used for restraining the white proletariat, the class that the planters most feared would
create turmoil and demand the abolition of slavery. Blacks were easier to
control because the entire might of the slavocracy, legal and institutional,
lay in the hands of slaveowners. To conservative southerners, the white
workers' struggle to gain economic security in jobs and pay presented an
unsettling threat to the status quo. In essence, industrialists and planters
alike used black slaves to control white workers; whites in positions of
authority employed the economic and political means at their disposal to
maintain the social status quo. In 1851, James Hammond pointed out that
"in all other countries, and particularly manufacturing states, labor and
capital are assuming an antagonistical position. Here it cannot be the case;
capital will be able to control labor, even in manufactures with whites, for
blacks can always be resorted to in case of need."[87] Frustrated in their
attempts to improve their economic position through the slaveowning elite,
white mechanics turned their attention to excluding politically vulnerable
free blacks from employment competition. In 1857, for example, white
mechanics in Richmond organized toward this end. They made it clear to
the elite, however, that "we do not aim to conflict with the interest of slave
owners, but to elevate ourselves as a class from the degrading positions

which competition with those who are not citizens of the commonwealth entails upon us."[88]

White workmen who did not adhere to accepted racial etiquette immediately encountered stiff opposition from local white residents with an economic or psychological stake in maintaining the established system of race relations. During his visit to the Midlothian mines in 1855, Frederick Law Olmsted was informed of a case which vividly illustrates the point. Olmsted reported the story which involved an English miner who broke the code:

> The white hands are mostly English or Welchmen. One of them, with whom I conversed, told me that he had been here several years; he had previously lived some years at the North. He got better wages here than he had earned at the North, but he was not contented, and did not intend to remain. On pressing him for the reason for his discontent, he said, after some hesitation, that he had rather live where he could be more free; a man had to be too "*discreet*" here: if one happened to say anything that gave offense, they thought no more of drawing a pistol or knife upon him, than they would of kicking a dog that was in their way. Not long since, a young English fellow came to the pit, and was put to work along with a gang of negroes. One morning, about a week afterwards, twenty or thirty men called on him, and told him that they would allow him fifteen minutes to get out of sight, and if they ever saw him in those parts again they would "give him hell." They were all armed, and there was nothing for the young fellow to do but to move "right off."
>
> "What reason did they give him for it?"
>
> "They did not give him any reason."
>
> "But what had he done?"
>
> "Why I believe they thought he had been too free with the niggers; he wasn't used to them, you see, and he talked to 'em free like, and they thought he'd make 'em think too much of themselves.[89]

Whatever political differences existed between industrialists and the planter gentry, both groups responded alike to the acid test of Union or slavery. Even though most men of industry were Whig nationalists on economic matters, when the time came to choose between the southern slave system or the modern, open industrial society, they chose the former. Like old guard planters, the industrialists viewed with horror "Black Republicanism" and all that the term symbolized because it threatened white domination of black people.

Joseph Anderson, for example, was an ardent Whig during the 1840s and early 1850s who enthusiastically supported the measures identified with that party. But during the election of 1856 when the Republican party showed itself a major force in national politics, as Charles B. Dew has observed, Anderson changed from a "Whig nationalist to a Democratic sectionalist" nearly overnight. During the election, the Tredegar ironmaster and a number of prominent Richmond businessmen announced themselves in support of the Democratic candidate for president, James Buchanan, rather than the Republican candidate, John Fremont.[90] In 1857, Anderson won a seat in the General Assembly as a Democrat and wrote to his brother Frank that he should also become a Democrat, for it was "the only means of defeating the Black Rep. party."[91] Following John Brown's raid on the Harpers Ferry Arsenal in October 1859, Anderson advanced to the forefront of the movement for southern, industrial self-sufficiency.[92] The episode confirmed the suspicions of Chesapeake slaveowners about the Republicans and symbolized the inevitable results of disturbing the social-racial status quo. Brown's raid touched a long-standing and sensitive cultural nerve among whites who feared that a general slave uprising would result from any loss of control by white slaveowners. That Harpers Ferry was located in their own region made the symbolism even more dramatic to whites of the Chesapeake.

The iron men of western Virginia had traditionally been ardent unionists and Whig nationalists. When in their minds the alternatives became slavery or Union, however, ardent nationalists quickly became southern sectionalists like Joseph Anderson. James D. Davidson, a Lexington attorney who represented several ironmasters in the western county of Rockbridge, wrote in December 1859 that "I am one of those, who, but a short time ago, thought it Treason almost even to speak of disunion. But late events & developments . . . have taught the South, to look to its own interests," and now "that word Disunion" was on the minds of Rockbridge County residents. He noted that "the great family of this Union is unfortunately divided in sentiment, upon slavery, that great institution of the South, which was planted here . . . by God himself." Davidson believed that "political Spoilsmen & Fanatical Preachers, have brought us under this impending ruin Prostituting, as they do, the unholy zeal of the Northern Masses." The Republicans were agitating the discord with their "Hell Broth" from public forum and pulpit. Davidson hoped that the Union could be saved, but whatever the outcome, the South should "stimulate its industry & develope its resources" to protect its social institutions.[93] As late as January 8, 1860, he was calling for "conservative" people to "cherish their Union," but he had little doubt that in any choice between Union and slavery, he would opt for slavery.[94] The same held true for the operator of Dover Pits, Christopher Q. Tompkins. Even though he had graduated from West Point, served as an officer in the U.S. Army for many years, and opposed secession, when the war finally came, Tompkins enlisted in a regiment and campaigned in western Virginia before he resigned his Confederate commission in order to labor full-time raising coal to fuel the iron furnaces of Richmond.[95]

When disunion became reality in 1861, the ironmasters enthusiastically supported the war and quickly switched to the production of iron for Confederate ordnance. Southern entrepreneurs were not the vanguard of a modern industrial order, thwarted by a reactionary planter class. A great deal of conflict did exist over how the region's human and financial resources should be employed, but in the final analysis, both industrialists and planters were social conservatives. Neither group seriously questioned the economic value and social necessity of slave labor as the foundation of southern society.

Southerners believed that developments beyond their control—the abolitionist movement, political opposition to the extension of slavery, northern control of Congress, and the rise of the Republican party to national power—all threatened the continued existence of their slave culture. This sense of impending calamity caused Virginia industrialists and planters alike to opt for disruption of the Union rather than lose white domination of the region's social structure. Maryland ironmasters had no real opportunity to act on their convictions because the Union Army occupied their state during the siege of Fort Sumter and remained for the duration of the war. For Virginians, however, if industrialization was necessary to maintain the South's social institutions, then slavery must be adapted to industrial expansion. If the Civil War had not disrupted the process, the Chesapeake coal and iron industries would have provided excellent models for the South's adjustment to a more industrialized society. And although full industrialization along northern or European lines is difficult to envision in a slave society, in 1861 Southerners clearly had not reached the point where they were able to conceive of that development within a free-labor model.

NOTES

1. Avery Odelle Craven, *Soil Exhaustion as a Factor in the Agricultural History of Virginia and Maryland, 1606-1860* (Urbana: University of Illinois Press, 1926), p. 124; Theodore M. Whitfield, *Slavery Agitation in Virginia, 1829-32* (Baltimore: Johns Hopkins University Press, 1930), p. 48; Robert S. Sutton, "Nostalgia, Pessimism, and Malaise: The Doomed Aristocrat in Late-Jeffersonian Virginia," *Virginia Magazine of History and Biography* 76 (January 1968):41.

2. J.D. Imboden, *The Coal and Iron Resources of Virginia: Their Extent, Commercial Value and Early Development Considered* (Richmond: Clemmitt & Jones, Printers, 1972, originally 1872), p. 24.

3. Henry H. Simms, *The Rise of the Whigs in Virginia, 1824-1840* (Richmond: William Byrd Press, 1929), p. 14; Sutton, "Nostalgia, Pessimism, and Malaise," p. 42.

4. J. Thomas Scharf, *History of Maryland: From the Earliest Period to the Present Day 3* (Hatboro, Pa.: Tradition Press, 1967, originally 1879), 187–88; Jeffrey R. Brackett, *The Negro in Maryland: A Study of the Institution of Slavery* (New York: Negro Universities Press, 1969, originally 1889), pp. 246–47.

5. Scharf, *History of Maryland*, 3:188; Donald B. and Wynelle S. Dodd, *Historical Statistics of the South, 1790-1970* (University: University of Alabama Press, 1973), p. 30. The total population figure for Maryland is for 1840.

6. Scharf, *History of Maryland*, 3:189-95; Sutton, "Nostalgia, Pessimism, and Malaise," p. 42.

7. Simms, *Rise of the Whigs in Virginia*, p. 12; Francis Newton Thorpe (ed.), *The Federal and State Constitutions, Colonial Charters, and Other Organic Laws of the States, Territories, and Colonies Now or Heretofore Forming the United States of America*, vol. 7 (Washington, D.C.: U.S. Government Printing Office, 1909), pp. 3819-29. Not until the reform convention of 1850-1851 was Virginia's constitution revised to make it more democratic. Property qualifications to hold public office and to exercise the franchise were eliminated. Moreover, the governor, as well as state judges, henceforth would be elected directly by the people (ibid., pp. 3829-50). Most of these reforms were enacted to appease the western section of the state, and although the eastern planters acquiesced to allay the danger of western secession, deep feelings of mutual hostility and suspicion remained; Charles Henry Ambler, *Sectionalism in Virginia from 1776 to 1861* (Chicago: University of Chicago Press, 1910), pp. 270-72.

8. Simms, *Rise of the Whigs in Virginia*, p. 12; Sutton, "Nostalgia, Pessimism, and Malaise," pp. 46-47, 49, 53-54.

9. Sutton, "Nostalgia, Pessimism, and Malaise," pp. 51-53.

10. Herbert Aptheker, *Nat Turner's Slave Rebellion* (New York: Grove Press, 1966), pp. 57-71. Also see Herbert Aptheker, *American Negro Slave Revolts* (New York: International Publishers, 1963, originally 1943), pp. 293-324. For a discussion of the literature relating to the Turner Revolt, see Henry Irving Tragle, *The Southampton Slave Revolt of 1831: A Compilation of Source Material* (Amherst: University of Massachusetts Press, 1971).

11. Kathleen Bruce, *Virginia Iron Manufacture in the Slave Era* (New York: Augustus M. Kelley, 1960, originally 1930), pp. 260-63. See Bruce's tables 1 through 8, pp. 458-60.

12. Prospectus of the *Southern Standard*, a Democratic newspaper published in Richmond, sent to Francis T. Anderson, July 28, 1847, Anderson Family Papers, University of Virginia, henceforth cited as UVa.

13. Bruce, *Virginia Iron Manufacture*, p. 264. Also see the *Richmond Examiner*, July 22, 1842, and the *Richmond Times and Compiler*, September 2, 1842.

14. William W. Freehling, *Prelude to Civil War: The Nullification Controversy in South Carolina, 1816-1836* (New York: Harper & Row, Publishers, 1965), pp. 292-97; William W. Freehling (ed.), *The Nullification Era: A Documentary Record* (New York: Harper & Row, Publishers, 1967), pp. xv-xvi.

15. U.S. Congress, House, *Coal Trade—Richmond,* petition, 24th Cong., 2nd Sess., 1837, pp. 3-4.

16. Ibid., pp. 6-7.

17. *Report of the Committee Under a Resolution of the Stockholders of the Chesterfield Railroad Company* (Richmond: Shepherd & Colin, 1844), p. 8.

18. F. S. Taylor to Harry Heth, September 11, 1819, Heth Family Papers, UVa.

19. Harry Heth to Thomas Railey & Brothers, June 16, 1817, enclosures, Heth Family Papers, UVa.

20. Quoted in the *Richmond Compiler,* February 17, 1843.

21. Eugene D. Genovese, *The Political Economy of Slavery: Studies in the Economy and Society of the Slave South* (New York: Random House, 1965), p. 167; Bruce, *Virginia Iron Manufacture,* p. 264.

22. *Richmond Enquirer,* June 28, 1842; Bruce, *Virginia Iron Manufacture,* p. 265.

23. James D. Davidson to Messrs. Baron & Baskerville, December 19, 1859, James D. Davidson Papers, State Historical Society of Wisconsin, hereafter cited as SHSW; Genovese, *Political Economy of Slavery,* pp. 159-73.

24. Bruce, *Virginia Iron Manufacture,* p. 265. Also see the *Richmond Enquirer,* June 20, 1843, and July 30, 1844. The manner in which the slavery issue spilled over into all aspects of economic and political life has been cogently discussed by C.L.R. James, "The Atlantic Slave Trade and Slavery: Some Interpretations of Their Significance in the Development of the United States and the Western World," as reprinted in John A. Williams and Charles F. Harris (eds.), *Amistad I* (New York: Random House, 1970), pp. 141-48, 160-62.

25. *Richmond Daily Whig and Public Advertiser,* June 26, 1846.

26. John Anderson to F. T. Anderson, March 21, 1849, Anderson Family Papers, UVa.

27. "Memorial of the Miners' and Manufacturers' Convention of the State of Virginia, to the U.S. Congress, December 6, 1850," photocopy at the Virginia State Library, hereafter cited as VSL.

28. Samuel McDowell Reid to Mr. Alexander, December 24, 1858, Reid-White Papers, Washington and Lee University.

29. Charles Grier Sellers, Jr., "Who Were the Southern Whigs?," *American Historical Review* 59 (January 1954):343.

30. *Richmond Times and Compiler,* February 22, 1847; Bruce, *Virginia Iron Manufacture,* p. 272.

31. *Richmond Times and Compiler,* February 22, 1847; Bruce, *Virginia Iron Manufacture,* p. 273.

32. *Richmond Times and Compiler,* January 13, 1847; Bruce, *Virginia Iron Manufacture,* pp. 273, 274.

33. *Richmond Times and Compiler,* January 15, 1851, cited in Bruce, *Virginia Iron Manufacture,* p. 274, n. 49.

34. Donald L. Robinson, *Slavery in the Structure of American Politics, 1765-1820* (New York: Harcourt Brace Jovanovich, 1971), p. 46.

35. Ibid.; Robert R. Russel, "The General Effects of Slavery upon Southern Economic Progress," *Journal of Southern History* 4 (February 1938):47.

36. Robinson, *Slavery in the Structure of American Politics,* pp. 46-47, 50-51.

37. Richard C. Wade, *Slavery in the Cities: The South, 1820-1860* (New York: Oxford University Press, 1964), p. 262.

38. Bruce, *Virginia Iron Manufacture,* p. 274; Rollin G. Osterweis, *Romanticism and Nationalism in the Old South* (New Haven, Conn.: Yale University Press, 1949), p. 6.

39. Robert S. Starobin, *Industrial Slavery in the Old South* (New York: Oxford University Press, 1970), Chap. 6; Genovese, *Political Economy of Slavery,* Chap. 9.

40. Genovese, *Political Economy of Slavery,* pp. 181, 221; Starobin, *Industrial Slavery in the Old South,* pp. 205-206.

41. Thomas P. Jones, M.D., "The Progress of Manufactures and Internal Improvements in the United States and Particularly on the Advantages to be Derived from the Employment of Slaves in the Manufacturing of Cotton and Other Goods," originally published in *American Farmer* 9 (November 30, 1827):290-91 and reproduced in *Textile History Review* 3 (July 1962):156; Genovese, *Political Economy of Slavery,* p. 222.

42. Genovese, *Political Economy of Slavery,* pp. 222-23.

43. *Richmond Whig and Public Advertiser,* June 26, 1846.

44. Claudia Dale Goldin, *Urban Slavery in the American South, 1820–1860: A Quantitative History* (Chicago: University of Chicago Press, 1976), pp. 7-10, 26-27, and Chap. 5.

45. Genovese, *Political Economy of Slavery,* pp. 224-25, 231, 233.

46. Joseph Clarke Robert, *The Tobacco Kingdom: Plantation, Market, and Factory in Virginia and North Carolina, 1800-1860* (Gloucester, Mass.: Peter Smith, 1965, originally 1938), p. 203.

47. Bruce, *Virginia Iron Manufacture,* p. 252 n.89.

48. *DeBow's Review* 7 (June 1850):518.

49. *Richmond Daily Dispatch,* October 25, 1852.

50. *Charters and Ordinances of Richmond,* 1859, pp. 196-97, VSL.

51. *DeBow's Review* 12 (January 1852):42-49; Genovese, *Political Economy of Slavery,* pp. 227-28.

52. *DeBow's Review* 8 (June 1850):519-20. The same argument was advanced during the late nineteenth century by prominent whites anxious to prevent joint efforts among poor whites and blacks. See C. Vann Woodward, *The Strange Career of Jim Crow* (New York: Oxford University Press, 1966), Chap. 3.

53. Aubrey C. Land, "Economic Base and Social Structure: The Northern Chesapeake in the Eighteenth Century," *Journal of Economic History* 25 (December 1965):646-47, 648-52; Aubrey C. Land, "Economic Behavior in a Planting Society: The Eighteenth-Century Chesapeake," *Journal of Southern History* 33 (November 1967):475-76, 479-80. For a detailed account of the early entrepreneur, see Aubrey C. Land, "Genesis of a Colonial Fortune: Daniel Dulany of Maryland," *William and Mary Quarterly* 7 (April 1950):255-69.

54. Charles Carroll to his son, January 9, 1764, in "Extracts from the Carroll Papers," *Maryland Historical Magazine* 12 (March 1917):27.

55. Abbot Emerson Smith, *Colonists in Bondage: White Servitude and Convict Labor in America, 1607-1776* (Chapel Hill: University of North Carolina Press, 1947), p. 26; Richard B. Morris, *Government and Labor in Early America* (New

York: Columbia University Press, 1946), pp. 22-33, and Chap 8.

56. Smith, *Colonists in Bondage,* pp. 27-28. Smith concluded that "Even more troublesome than the price of free labor was its uncertainty" (p. 28).

57. Dr. Carroll to his son, probably February 1753, in "Extracts from Account and Letter Books of Dr. Charles Carroll of Annapolis," *Maryland Magazine of History* 25 (1930):73.

58. William Byrd, "Progress to the Mines," as reproduced in Louis B. Wright (ed.), *The Prose Works of William Byrd of Westover: Narratives of a Colonial Virginian* (Cambridge, Mass.: Belknap Press of Harvard University Press, 1966), p. 360.

59. William Chetwynd to John England, August 19, 1726, Principio Iron Company Papers, 1725-1726, VSL.

60. Dr. Charles Carroll, "Proposals," probably 1753, in "Extracts from Account and Letter Books of Dr. Charles Carroll of Annapolis," *Maryland Historical Magazine,* p. 299.

61. D. Ross to John Staples, September 16, 1813, David Ross Letterbook, Virginia Historical Society, hereafter cited as VHS.

62. D. Ross to Reuben Smith, March 27, 1812, David Ross Letterbook, VHS.

63. Joseph Anderson to Harrison Row, January 3, 1848, cited in Bruce, *Virginia Iron Manufacture,* pp. 237-38. Charles Dew concluded that the use of slave labor did produce some limited reduction in labor costs. See Charles B. Dew, *Ironmaker to the Confederacy: Joseph R. Anderson and the Tredegar Iron Works* (New Haven, Conn.: Yale University Press, 1966), p. 29.

64. Stephen Onion to Charles Carroll, January 30, 1736, Carroll-Maccubbin Papers, Maryland Historical Society, hereafter cited as MHS; Keach Doyel Johnson, "Establishment of the Baltimore Iron Company: A Case Study of the American Iron Industry in the Eighteenth Century" (Ph.D. dissertation, State University of Iowa, 1949), pp. 72, 87-88.

65. John England to Joseph Farmer, January 1724, Principio Company Papers, MHS.

66. Stephen Onion to Charles Carroll and Company, July 1, 1734, Carroll-Maccubbin Papers, MHS. Also see colonial newspapers serving the region, such as the *Maryland Gazette* and the *Virginia Gazette.* For a discussion of the extent of the runaway servant problem and the legal machinery devised to cope with it, see Morris, *Government and Labor in Early America,* Chap. 9.

67. Stephen Onion to Charles Carroll, August 7, 1737, Carroll-Maccubbin Papers, MHS.

68. Johnson, "Establishment of the Baltimore Iron Company," pp. 76-77; Charles Daniell to Charles Carroll, June 25, 1735, Carroll-Maccubbin Papers, MHS.

69. George Ashman to Charles Ridgely and Thomas Crowell, February 16, 1787, Ridgely Family Papers, MHS.

70. Leonard P. Stavisky, "Negro Craftsmanship in Early America," *American Historical Review* 54 (January 1949):317-18; Marcus W. Jernegan, "Slavery and Industrialism in the Colonies," *American Historical Review* 25 (January 1920):226-27, and his *Laboring and Dependent Classes in Colonial America, 1607-1783* (Chicago: University of Chicago Press, 1931), p. 9.

71. In 1662, Virginia passed an act which stipulated that children of slave mothers were considered slaves, presumably for life. William Waller Hening (ed.), *The Statutes at Large, Being a Collection of All the Laws of Virginia,* vol. 2 (Richmond: By the Editor, 1810-1823), p. 170. Two years later, in 1664, the Maryland Assembly passed a law declaring that, henceforth, blacks became servants *Durante Vita,* for the duration of their lives. William H. Brown et al. (eds.), *Archives of Maryland,* vol. 1 (Baltimore: Maryland Historical Society, 1883-1930), pp. 533-34.

72. Samuel G. Hermelin, *Report About the Mines in the United States of America,* trans. by Amandus Johnson (Philadelphia: John Morton Memorial Museum, 1931), pp. 52-55.

73. Smith, *Colonists in Bondage,* pp. 29-30; Hermelin, *Report About the Mines,* p. 54.

74. Gerald W. Mullin, *Flight and Rebellion: Slave Resistance in Eighteenth-Century Virginia* (New York: Oxford University Press, 1972), Chap. 2. Darold D. Wax, "Preferences for Slaves in Colonial America," *Journal of Negro History* 58 (October 1973):371-401, refutes the "widely-held notion" (374) that plantation owners generally preferred "seasoned" slaves over blacks imported directly from Africa. Nevertheless, the traditional interpretation seems more applicable for the colonial iron industry.

75. Clement Plumsted to Charles Carroll, April 20, 1731, Carroll-Maccubbin Papers, MHS, cited in Keach Johnson, "The Genesis of the Baltimore Ironworks," *Journal of Southern History* 19 (May 1953):167.

76. Stephen Onion to Charles Carroll and Company, July 1, 1734, Carroll-Maccubbin Papers, MHS.

77. Ridgely & Co. Account Book, 1774-1780, Northampton Furnace, Ridgely Account Books, Library of Congress, hereafter cited as LC.

78. Browne et al. (eds.), *Archives of Maryland* 37:441-42, 515, 540-41.

79. Arthur Cecil Bining, *Pennsylvania Iron Manufacture in the Eighteenth Century* (Harrisburg: Pennsylvania Historical Commission, 1938), pp. 37-38.

80. *Session Laws of New Jersey,* 1736, Chap. 19, p. 109, cited in Charles S. Boyer, *Early Forges and Furnaces in New Jersey* (Philadelphia: University of Pennsylvania Press, 1931), p. 93.

81. Joseph E. Walker, *Hopewell Village: A Social and Economic History of an Iron-Making Community* (Philadelphia: University of Pennsylvania Press, 1966), pp. 266-67.

82. "The Martha Furnace Diary," cited in Arthur Dudley Pierce, *Iron in the Pines: The Story of New Jersey's Ghost Towns and Bog Iron* (New Brunswick, N.J.: Rutgers University Press, 1957), pp. 96-105; Herbert G. Gutman, "Work, Culture, and Society in Industrializing America, 1815-1919," *American Historical Review* 78 (June 1973):545.

83. These ideas have been expressed by Rowland Berthoff, *An Unsettled People: Social Order and Disorder in American History* (New York: Harper & Row, Publishers, 1971), pp. 172-73, 175, 177, 183-84, 284-87.

84. For a Discussion of the Tredegar strike, see pp. 31–33, 231–232.

85. *Richmond Enquirer,* June 12, 1847.

86. *Richmond Times and Compiler,* May 28, 1847.

87. *DeBow's Review* 11 (August 1851):130.

88. *Richmond Enquirer,* August 27, 1857.

89. Frederick Law Olmsted, *A Journey in the Seaboard Slave States, with Remarks on Their Economy* (New York: Mason Brothers, 1859), pp. 47-48.

90. Dew, *Ironmaker to the Confederacy,* pp. 38-41.

91. Ibid., pp. 41-42; Joseph Anderson to F. T. Anderson, June 6, 1857, Anderson Family Papers, UVa.

92. Dew, *Ironmaker to the Confederacy,* pp. 42-43.

93. James D. Davidson to Messrs. Baron & Baskerville, December 19, 1859, James D. Davidson Papers, SHSW.

94. J.D. Davidson to Governor John Letcher, January 8, 1860; and James D. Davidson to Messrs. Baron & Baskerville, December 19, 1858, James B. Davidson Papers, SHSW.

95. William M. E. Rachal (ed.), "The Occupation of Richmond, April 1865: The Memorandum of Events of Colonel Christopher Q. Tompkins," *Virginia Magazine of History and Biography* 73 (April 1965):189; Ellen Wilkins Tompkins (ed.), "The Colonel's Lady: Some Letters of Ellen Wilkins Tompkins, July-December 1861," *Virginia Magazine of History and Biography* 69 (October 1961):387-88.

APPENDIXES

Appendix 1

EXPORTS OF PIG IRON FROM THE AMERICAN COLONIES TO GREAT
BRITAIN, 1720–1755 (in tons, cwts., qrs., lbs.)

Year	Carolina	New England	New York	Pennsylvania	Maryland-Virginia
1720					
1721					
1722					15.02.03.22
1723					202.09.00.00
1724					137.06.03.19
1725					
1726				32.11.03.22	263.00.03.03
1727				72.13.02.26	407.09.03.13
1728				243.01.03.01	645.06.00.24
1729	5.1.0.0			274.06.01.21	852.16.01.11
1730	0.10.3.1			188.16.00.20	1526.15.01.15
1731				169.03.02.15	2081.01.00.27
1732				106.11.01.15	2226.03.02.00
1733				95.05.01.18	2309.11.03.22
1734	7.0.0.0			147.07.03.11	2042.02.02.03
1735	3.9.0.0	0.6.0.0		195.11.02.22	2362.08.00.17
1736				270.19.01.19	2458.00.00.03
1737		27.5.0.0		168.16.00.01	2119.16.01.25
1738		14.0.0.0		228.00.02.10	2112.18.03.19
1739	1.9.2.27	3.18.1.0		170.05.03.19	2242.02.02.14
1740	2.0.0.0	94.0.1.12		159.04.02.22	2020.02.00.22
1741		42.16.1.16		153.04.01.25	3261.08.01.05
1742		5.0.0.0		143.16.03.18	1926.03.01.75
1743	18.19.0.16	25.11.1.17	81.4.2.7	62.12.00.23	2816.01.01.15
1744	20.1.0.19		5.16.0.0	87.15.00.00	1748.04.01.03
1745	25.9.3.0	2.0.0.0	18.12.0.0	97.07.01.07	2130.16.01.10
1746			29.0.0.0	103.01.03.11	1729.01.00.02
1747			13.0.0.0	24.14.03.20	2119.00.03.24
1748	1.4.1.21		22.9.1.80	114.10.00.00	2017.11.03.10
1749			16.10.3.0	166.11.03.17	1575.05.01.27
1750		21.1.12.0	75.12.1.0	318.09.03.17	2508.16.01.00
1751	17.4.0.0	9.16.2.0	33.0.3.0	199.15.02.00	2950.05.03.00
1752 —	20.0.0.0 _	—	41.5.0.0 _	156.08.02.00 _	2762.08.00.00
1753	10.0.0.0	40.10.1.0	97.4.3.0	242.15.01.00	2347.09.02.00
1754	20.0.0.0	4.16.0.0	115.16.2.0	512.19.03.00	2591.04.03.00
1755	14.13.0.0		457.8.0.0	836.06.01.00	2132.15.01.00

Source: Adapted from Arthur Cecil Bining, *British Regulation of the Colonial Iron Industry*
(Philadelphia: University of Pennsylvania Press, 1933), pp. 128–32.

Appendix 2

MARYLAND IRONWORKS ERECTED PRIOR TO 1776

FURNACES

Principio
Kingsbury
Lancashire
Baltimore/Gwynn's Falls
Baltimore/Charles Run
Onion's Gunpowder River
Snowden's Patuxent
Nottingham
Ridgely's Northampton
Dorsey's Elk Ridge
Dorsey's Curtis Creek
Bush River
Legh
Antietam
Mount Etna
Mount Etna/Leitersburg
Green Spring
Catoctin

FORGES

Principio
North East
Baltimore/Gwynn's Falls
Baltimore/Mount Royal
Onion's Gunpowder #1
Onion's Gunpowder #2
Snowden's Patuxent
Ridgely's Long Calm #1
Ridgely's Long Calm #2
Unicorn
Elk
Hockley
Rock
Cumberland
Antietam/Potomac River
Rock/Great Rock
Hughes'/Antietam Creek
Jacques/Licking Creek

Source: Michael W. Robbins, *Maryland's Iron Industry During the Revolutionary War Era* (Annapolis: Maryland Bicentennial Commission, 1973), p. 10; James M. Swank, *History of the Manufacture of Iron in All Ages* (Philadelphia: American Iron and Steel Association, 1892), pp. 240–57.

Appendix 3

VIRGINIA IRONWORKS ERECTED PRIOR TO 1782

FURNACES

Falling Creek
Germanna
Massaponux
Bristol
Fredericksville
Accokeek
Neabsco
Vestal's
Buckingham
Occoquan
Archibald Cary's
Carter's Bridge
Olds
Oxford
Mossey Creek
Marlboro
Bear Garden
Hardware River
Redwell
Hunter's (several)
Albemarle (three)
Stonewall

FORGES
Occoquan
Providence
Grymes'
Pine
Oxford
Mossey Creek
Marlboro
Westham Foundry
Fredericksburg Arms Factory
Hunter's (several)

Source: Kathleen Bruce, *Virginia Iron Manufacture in the Slave Era* (New York: Augustus M. Kelley, 1968, originally 1930), pp. 3–79, 454; James L. Bishop, *A History of American Manufacturers from 1608–1860* (Philadelphia: Edward Young & Co., 1866), pp. 595–609; Swank, *History of the Manufacture of Iron in All Ages,* pp. 258–71.

Appendix 4

IRON FURNACES IN ANTEBELLUM VIRGINIA

Australia	McCormick's
Aetna	McKiernan's
Barren Spring	Moore's
Bath	Mount Hope
Beauregard	Mount Torry
Bill and Kincannon	Mount Vernon
Buena Vista	Oakland
California	Oxford
Callaway's	Paddy
Canada	Panther Gap
Caroline	Paramont
Carron	Paulina
Catawba	Pine Hope
Catharine	Popular Creek
Catoctin	Porter's
Clifton	Potomac
Cloverdale #1	Ravenscliffe
Cloverdale #2	Rebecca
Columbia	Retreat
Cotopaxi	Roaring Run
Craig's Creek	Rocky Mount
Davidson's	Rough and Ready
Deane's	Rumsly's
Dolly Ann	Sanders
Elizabeth	Shelor's
Elk Creek	Shenandoah
Estilene	Smith Creek
Fort	Speedwell
Georgetown	Stonewall
Glenwood	Taylor
Grace	Union
Gray Eagle	Van Buren #1
Isabella	Van Buren #2
Jane	**Vesuvius**
Lagrange	Victoria
Liberty	West Fork
Lucy Salina	Westham
Manakin	White's
Margaret Jane	Wilkinson's
Marion	Yeatman's

Source: Adapted from Bruce, *Virginia Iron Manufacture*, Appendix I, p. 452, facing sheet.

Appendix 5

IRON FURNACES IN ANTEBELLUM MARYLAND

Antietam	Lonaconing
Ashland Iron Company	Maryland #1
Catoctin #1	Maryland #2
Catoctin #2	Mount Savage #1
Cecelia	Mount Savage #2
Cedar Point #1	Muirkirk
Cedar Point #2	Nassawango
Chesapeake #1	Oregon
Chesapeake #2	Patapsco
Curtis Creek	Patuxent #1
Elba	Patuxent #2
Elk Ridge	Rough and Ready #1
Greenspring	Rough and Ready #2
Gunpowder	Sarah
Harford	Savage #1
Lagrange	Savage #2
Laurel	South Baltimore
Locust Grove	

Source: Adapted from J. P. Lesley, *The Iron Manufacturer's Guide to the Furnaces Forges and Rolling Mills of the United States with Discussions of Iron as a Chemical Element, An American Ore, and a Manufactured Article, in Commerce and in History* (New York: John Wiley, Publisher, 1859), pp. 23–24, 46–51, 83–84.

Appendix 6

IRON MANUFACTURES OF THE UNITED STATES IN 1840

States and Territories	*Cast-iron*		*Bar-iron*	
	No. of Furnaces	Tons Produced	Bloom-eries, Forges, and Rolling Mills	Tons Produced
Maine	16	6,122	1	—
New Hampshire	15	1,320	2	125
Massachusetts	48	9,332	67	6,004
Rhode Island	5	4,126	—	—
Connecticut	28	6,495	44	3,623
Vermont	26	6,743	14	655
New York	186	29,088	120	53,693
New Jersey	26	11,114	80	7,171
Pennsylvania	213	98,395	169	87,244
Delaware	2	17	5	449
Maryland	12	8,876	17	7,900
Virginia	42	18,810	52	5,886
North Carolina	8	968	43	963
South Carolina	4	1,250	9	1,165
Georgia	14	494	29	—
Alabama	1	30	5	75
Louisiana	6	1,400	2	1,366
Tennessee	34	16,129	99	9,673
Kentucky	17	29,206	13	3,367
Ohio	72	35,236	19	7,466
Indiana	7	810	1	20
Illinois	4	158	—	—
Missouri	2	180	4	118
Michigan	15	601	—	—
Wisconsin	1	3	—	—
TOTAL	804	286,903	795	196,963

States and Territories	Tons of Fuel Consumed	Men Employed Including Mining Operations	Capital Invested (Dollars)
Maine	285	48	185,950
New Hampshire	2,104	121	98,200
Massachusetts	199,252	1,097	1,232,875
Rhode Island	227	29	22,250
Connecticut	16,933	895	577,300
Vermont	388,407	788	665,150
New York	123,677	3,456	2,103,418
New Jersey	27,425	2,056	1,721,820
Pennsylvania	355,903	11,522	7,781,471
Delaware	971	28	36,200
Maryland	24,422	1,782	795,650
Virginia	36,588	1,742	1,246,650
North Carolina	11,598	468	94,961
South Carolina	6,334	248	113,300
Georgia	630	41	24,000
Alabama	157	30	9,500
Louisiana	4,152	145	357,000
Tennessee	187,453	2,266	1,514,736
Kentucky	35,501	1,108	449,000
Ohio	104,312	2,268	1,161,900
Indiana	787	103	57,700
Illinois	240	74	40,300
Missouri	300	80	79,000
Michigan	451	99	60,800
Wisconsin	1	3	4,000
TOTAL	1,528,110	30,497	20,432,131

Source: Harry Scrivenor, *History of the Iron Trade, from the Earliest Records to the Present Period* (London: Longman, Brown, Green, & Longman, 1854), p. 232.

Appendix 7

COAL PRODUCTION IN SELECTED STATES, 1800–1865 (in tons)

Year	Kentucky	West Virginia	Virginia	Alabama	Maryland	Tennessee	Pennsylvania	Estimated U.S. production
1800	100	2,700	18,000	....	200	....	87,000	108,350
1801	100	2,700	22,000	....	300	....	89,000	114,450
1802	100	2,800	26,000	....	500	....	92,000	121,750
1803	200	2,800	29,500	....	500	....	94,000	127,500
1804	200	2,900	40,500	....	500	....	97,100	141,750
1805	300	3,000	42,000	....	500	....	100,100	146,700
1806	400	3,100	43,000	....	600	....	104,200	152,050
1807	500	5,600	44,000	....	600	....	108,200	159,800
1808	500	5,700	45,000	....	600	....	112,300	165,600
1809	600	5,700	46,000	....	700	....	116,600	171,500
1810	700	6,100	47,000	....	700	....	120,700	178,500
1811	800	6,300	48,000	....	700	....	130,800	190,200
1812	900	6,500	50,000	....	800	....	143,000	205,200
1813	1,000	6,700	52,000	....	800	....	155,100	220,250
1814	1,100	6,900	54,000	....	800	100	169,300	237,550
1815	1,200	7,300	56,000	....	900	....	183,600	255,050
1816	1,300	7,500	57,000	....	900	....	205,900	279,900
1817	1,400	8,700	58,000	....	900	....	228,000	305,100
1818	1,500	10,500	59,000	....	1,000	....	251,300	332,300
1819	1,600	16,700	60,000	....	1,400	....	232,900	323,350

1820	2,000	27,200	62,000	....	1,800	....	225,600	333,765
1821	2,100	34,400	64,000	....	2,200	....	233,900	353,066
1822	2,300	42,800	54,000	....	2,600	....	243,000	365,633
1823	2,400	50,100	43,966	....	3,000	....	251,200	380,172
1824	3,100	58,500	67,040	....	3,400	....	260,400	429,118
1825	6,700	66,200	66,720	....	3,800	....	270,050	480,389
1826	7,500	74,600	88,641	....	4,200	....	294,680	554,414
1827	8,500	82,900	84,720	....	4,600	....	320,850	611,577
1828	9,600	74,200	100,080	....	5,000	....	347,500	672,424
1829	16,000	83,100	93,350	....	6,800	....	372,100	756,637
1830	18,900	78,300	102,799	10	8,500	....	397,700	880,899
1831	21,700	89,500	104,320	100	10,200	....	425,340	953,418
1832	23,400	103,200	132,033	100	12,000	....	450,940	1,273,124
1833	26,600	128,900	159,697	200	12,000	....	437,240	1,486,031
1834	34,700	165,400	124,000	200	12,000	3,000	504,540	1,423,469
1835	36,000	172,000	201,600	300	12,000	6,000	531,640	1,819,155
1836	40,300	186,800	124,000	300	12,000	6,000	607,420	1,991,680
1837	58,200	203,100	112,000	400	12,000	6,000	575,260	2,234,281
1838	74,300	206,700	107,999	500	12,000	6,000	618,263	2,118,761
1839	63,200	202,000	96,000	600	12,000	7,000	731,322	2,323,667
1840	62,700	304,900	88,000	700	12,000	8,000	699,994	2,474,319
1841	64,700	202,600	79,600	800	12,000	8,000	783,515	2,617,633
1842	66,700	234,300	77,000	900	12,000	8,000	833,900	2,914,133
1843	68,800	252,700	95,606	1,000	12,421	9,000	887,100	3,271,586
1844	70,500	230,100	115,313	1,000	18,345	10,000	981,500	3,921,281
1845	71,800	279,800	134,603	1,200	30,372	18,000	1,130,000	4,722,932
1846	71,800	325,800	124,669	1,400	36,707	25,000	1,255,500	5,359,854
1847	72,700	292,400	126,422	1,500	65,222	30,000	1,466,900	6,357,482

Year	Kentucky	West Virginia	Virginia	Alabama	Maryland	Tennessee	Pennsyl-vania	Estimated U.S. production
1848	73,400	309,500	120,747	1,600	98,032	40,000	1,767,300	7,081,250
1849	74,200	320,700	138,801	1,700	175,497	52,000	1,952,500	7,689,535
1850	75,500	348,400	138,017	1,700	242,517	60,000	2,147,500	8,355,739
1851	76,800	339,300	136,523	2,000	317,460	70,000	2,403,300	10,403,606
1852	78,800	344,000	106,087	2,100	411,707	75,000	2,719,200	11,321,444
1853	82,200	360,700	101,726	2,300	657,862	85,000	2,944,800	12,753,124
1854	85,800	411,063	132,554	2,300	812,727	90,000	3,230,800	15,027,076
1855	107,600	381,004	125,977	2,700	.735,137	100,000	3,429,700	16,149,677
1856	114,200	330,597	106,150	7,000	817,659	115,000	3,695,786	16,951,939
1857	118,600	336,933	114,826	8,000	654,017	125,000	4,335,039	17,393,689
1858	122,900	349,043	113,734	9,000	722,686	135,000	4,383,560	17,654,110
1859	127,000	336,986	106,338	10,000	833,349	150,000	4,504,000	19,218,810
1860	131,400	364,754	112,473	15,000	438,000	165,300	4,710,400	20,040,859
1861	45,450	323,859	94,697	5,000	287,073	150,000	4,562,000	19,000,663
1862	4,200	266,822	115,495	18,000	346,201	140,000	4,995,600	19,570,544
1863	4,100	276,489	112,068	18,000	877,313	100,000	5,332,600	22,747,407
1864	104,100	313,398	111,742	20,000	755,764	100,000	6,051,600	24,441,998
1865	106,500	484,215	73,730	8,000	1,025,208	100,000	6,372,900	24,426,344

Source: Howard N. Eavenson, *First Century and a Quarter of American Coal Industry* (Pittsburgh: By the author, 1942), pp. 426–434. Adapted and reprinted with permission.

Appendix 8

MINES IN THE EASTERN VIRGINIA COAL FIELD BEFORE
THE CIVIL WAR

Anderson Pits
Barr's Pits
Blackheath Coal Pits
Black Heath Company of Colliers
Burton
Carbon Hill Mining Company
Chesterfield
Clover Hill
Coal Brook
Coal Brook Colliery
Creek Company of Colliers
Crouches & Snead
Cunliffe's Pits
Deep Run Pits
Dover Pits
Edge Hill Colliery
English Coal Company
Etna Coal Company
Gowrie Colliery
Graham Colliery
Heth Pit
Heth's Drop Shaft

Huguenot Springs
Lauree Pits
Midlothian Coal Mining Company
Mills' & Reeds'
Moody & Johnson
Murchie, Brander, & Brooks
Powhatan
Railey's Pits
Salle's Pits
Scott's Pitts
Springfield Pits
Stonehenge
Tippecanoe
Townes & Powell
Trabue's Pits
Tuckahoe Pits
Union Coal Company
Waterloo
Wills, Brown, and Company
Wills' Pit
Winterpock

Source: Compiled by the author. *Richmond Daily Dispatch*, January 11, 1858, December 31, 1859, January 5, 1861; "Report on Gowrie Gallery, December 29, 1850," by A. F. Hopper and John Steele for Christopher Quarles Tompkins, Tompkins Family Papers, Virginia Historical Society, hereafter cited as VHS; "Report of Thomas S. Foizey to Abraham S. Wooldridge, October 22, 1855, William B. Phillips Papers, VHS; "Analytical Table," Tompkins Commonplace Book, 1863–1867, Tompkins Family Papers, VHS; "Coal Trade—Richmond," House of Reps., 24th Cong., 2d Sess., Doc. 94.

Appendix 9

COAL OR COAL AND IRON COMPANIES
INCORPORATED IN MARYLAND (1828–1849)

Maryland Mining Company
Savage Coal and Iron Company
Town Hill Mining,
    Manufacturing & Timber Company
Boston and New York Coal Company
Allegany Mining Company
George's Creek Mining Company
Cumberland Coal Mining Company
Clifton Coal Company
Maryland and New York
    Iron and Coal Company
Western Coal and Iron Company
Western Coal and Iron Mining Company
Mining and Manufacturing
    Company of Hibernia
Cumberland Coal and Iron Company
Potomac Coal and Iron Company
Barrellville Mining Company
Frostburg Coal Company
New York Mining Company
John Brant's Iron and Coal Company
Washington Coal Company
Borden Mining Company
Valley Mining and
    Manufacturing Company
Preston Coal Company
Buena Vista Coal Company
    of Allegany County
Withers Mining Company
Parker Vein Coal Company
Westernport Coal Company
Swanton Coal and Iron Company
Astor Coal Mining Company
People's Mining Company
Llangollen Mining Company

Source: Katherine A. Harvey, *The Best-Dressed Miners; Life and Labor in the Maryland Coal Region, 1835–1910* (Ithaca, N.Y.: Cornell University Press, 1965), pp. 375–76.

Selected Bibliography

PRIMARY SOURCES

MANUSCRIPTS

DUKE UNIVERSITY, DURHAM, NORTH CAROLINA

F. T. Anderson Letters and Papers
Anonymous Ledger, 1849-1850, Columbia Furnace
William Bolling Papers
Robert Carter Papers
John Jordan Daybook, 1826-1834
John Jordan Ledger, 1814-1824
John Jordan Papers
Samuel M. Lantz and J. P. Rinker Daybooks and Ledgers, 1823–1875
William Weaver Papers

HALL OF RECORDS, ANNAPOLIS, MARYLAND

Caleb Dorsey & Company, Elk Ridge Furnace, Journal for Ledger C, and Journals
      AA, BB, CC, 1761-1772
Journals of the Proceedings of the Commissioners Appointed to Preserve Confis-
      cated British Property, 1781, and 1781-1782
Patuxent Iron Works, Journal (A) & B, 1767-1794
Patuxent Iron Works Ledger, 1767-1769
Sale Book of Confiscated British Property, 1781-1785

HISTORICAL SOCIETY OF PENNSYLVANIA, PHILADELPHIA, PENNSYLVANIA

The Isaac Zane Papers

LIBRARY OF CONGRESS, WASHINGTON, D.C.

Bush Town (Maryland) Iron Works Journal, 1747-1773
Bush Town Store Ledger, 1765-1766
Cumberland Forge, Maryland, Day Book, 1802, and Account Book, 1796-1797
Miscellaneous Manuscripts, Ferdinando Fairfax to Wilson Cary Nicholas, Feb-
      ruary 5, 1808

Shenandoah Furnace Ledger C, Account Book A, and Journal B, 1809-1811
Time, Ore, Coal, Iron Book, of Charles Ridgely (Capt.), Darbey Lux, Daniel
      Chamier, Pleasance Goodwin, of the Company of Maryland, 1774-1780

MARYLAND HISTORICAL SOCIETY, BALTIMORE, MARYLAND

Aquila Hall (Sheriff), Assessment Ledger, Baltimore County, 1763-1764
Bond Family Papers
Stephen Bordley Letterbooks, 1727-1759
Carroll-Maccubbin Papers
Carter Papers
Dulany Papers
Joseph Hughes, Harford County Collection
Industrial Notes
Meredith Papers
Principio Company Papers, 1723-1730
Ridgely Account Books
Ridgely Family Papers
D.S. Ridgely Papers
Scharf Papers
Robert and William Smith Papers
Washington Family Papers

UNIVERSITY OF NORTH CAROLINA, CHAPEL HILL, NORTH CAROLINA

Fredericksburg, Virginia, Account Books, #2208, Volumes 4, 5, 6
Ridwell Furnace Record Book, 1805-1809
Shenandoah County, Virginia, Account Books, #2934, Volumes 2-8

STATE HISTORICAL SOCIETY OF WISCONSIN, MADISON, WISCONSIN

Daniel C.E. Brady Journals, 1860-1865
James Dorman Davidson Papers
Jordan and Davis Papers
Jordan and Irvine Papers
Cyrus Hall McCormick Papers

UNIVERSITY OF VIRGINIA, CHARLOTTESVILLE, VIRGINIA

Anderson Family Papers
William Davis Papers
Graham Family Ledgers & Papers
Heth Family Papers
McCaw Journal, 1834-1880
Rinker-Lantz Papers
Weaver-Brady Papers

VIRGINIA HISTORICAL SOCIETY, RICHMOND, VIRGINIA

Henry Banks Papers
Archibald Cary Papers
Preston Davie Papers
Edmundson Family Papers and Account Book 1838
Commonplace Book of Isaac Hite
Thomas Mann Randolph Letters
William B. Phillips Papers
Preston Family Papers
Lilburn Rogers Railey Papers
Redwell Furnace Account Books, 1791-1816
David Ross Letterbook, January 1812-October 1813
Tayloe Family Papers
Tayloe Letterbook and Account Books
Tompkins Commonplace Book, 1863-1867
Tompkins Family Papers
Bickerton Lyle Winston Manuscript Slave Account Book
Woolfolk Family Papers

VIRGINIA STATE LIBRARY, RICHMOND, VIRGINIA

Auditor's Item 214, Account Books of the Manufactory of Arms, 1811-1821
Executive Papers of Virginia
Principio Iron Company Papers, 1725-1726
Public Foundry (Westham), Miscellaneous Papers, and Westham Ledgers, 1776-
    1781
Tredegar Company Records
Isaac Zane, Marlboro Iron Works Papers

WASHINGTON AND LEE UNIVERSITY, LEXINGTON, VIRGINIA

The Reid-White Papers
Rockbridge County Historical Society Files

NEWSPAPERS

Lexington (Virginia) *Gazette*
Maryland Gazette
Maryland Journal
Maryland Journal and Baltimore Advertiser
Richmond Daily Courier
Richmond Daily Dispatch
Richmond Daily Whig and Public Advertiser
Richmond Enquirer

Richmond Examiner
Richmond Times and Compiler
Virginia Gazette
Virginia Gazette and Weekly Advertiser

BOUND VOLUMES

"An Account of the Coal Mines in the Vicinity of Richmond, Virginia, Communi-
    cated to the Editor in a Letter from Mr. John Grammar, Jun." *American
    Journal of Science* 17 (July 1834):273-82.
Acrelius, Israel. *A History of New Sweden; or, the Settlements on the River
    Delaware,* W. M. Reynolds, trans. Philadelphia: Historical Society of
    Pennsylvania, 1874.
Acts of the General Assembly of Virginia. Richmond: Samuel Shepherd & Co.,
    1846.
Ansted, D. T. *Scenery, Science and Art; Being Extracts from the Notebook of a
    Geologist and Mining Engineer.* London: J. Van Voorst, 1854.
Betts, Edwin Morris, ed. *Thomas Jefferson's Farm Book with Commentary and
    Relevant Extracts from Other Writings.* Princeton, N.J.: Princeton Uni-
    versity Press, 1953.
Beverley, Robert. *The History and Present State of Virginia.* Edited by Louis B.
    Wright. Chapel Hill: University of North Carolina Press, 1974.
Black, Leonard. *The Life and Sufferings of Leonard Black, a Fugitive from
    Slavery.* New Bedford, Mass.: Benjamin Lindsey, 1847.
Bolingbroke, Henry. *A Voyage to the Demerary.* Philadelphia: M. Carey, 1813.
Browne, William H., et al., eds. *Archives of Maryland.* Baltimore: Maryland
    Historical Society, 1883-1930.
Burnaby, Andrew. *Travels Through the Middle Settlements in North America in
    the Years 1759 and 1760 with Observations upon the State of the Colonies.*
    London: T. Payne, at Mews-Gate, 1775.
Byrd, William. "Progress to the Mines." As reproduced in Louis B. Wright, ed.
    *The Prose Works of William Byrd of Westover: Narratives of a Colonial
    Virginian.* Cambridge, Mass.: Belknap Press of Harvard University
    Press, 1966.
Cappon, Lester J., ed. *Iron Works at Tuball: Terms and Conditions for Their
    Lease as Stated by Alexander Spotswood on the Twentieth Day of July
    1739.* Charlottesville: Tracy W. McGregor Library of the University of
    Virginia, 1945.
Catterall, Helen T., ed. *Judicial Cases Concerning American Slavery and the
    Negro.* Washgon, D.C.: Carnegie Institution, 1926-1937.
"Coal Trade—Richmond." 24th Congress, 2nd Session, House Document 93,
    1837.
*A Collection of All Acts and Parts of Acts of the General Assembly of Virginia,
    from October 1, 1784, Down to the Session of 1829-30, Inclusive, Relating
    to the James River Company.* Richmond: Samuel Shepherd & Co., 1830.
Coxe, Tench. *A View of the United States of America, in a Series of Papers Written*

at Various Times, Between the Years 1787 and 1794, Philadelphia: Wrigley & Berriman, 1794.

Cramer, Zadock. *The Navigator; Containing Directions for Navigating the Monongahela, Allegheny, Ohio and Mississippi Rivers*. Pittsburgh: Cramer, Spear & Eichbaum, 1814.

The Crescent Iron Manufacturing Company with Statistics of Other Manufacturing Companies, Wheeling, Virginia. Boston, 1815.

Daddow, Samuel Harries, and Bannan, Benjamin. *Coal, Iron, and Oil; or, the Practical American Miner*. Philadelphia: J.B. Lippincott & Co., 1866.

DeBow, James D.B., ed. *DeBow's Review and Industrial Resources, Statistics, etc., of the United States and More Particularly of the Southern & Western States*. New York: Augustus M. Kelley, 1966, originally January 1846 through April 1862.

Documents Relating to the Phenix Mining and Manufacturing Company: Comprising Extracts from Various Official Reports. New York: Sibell & Mott, 1849.

Dodd, Donald B., and Dodd, Wynelle S. *Historical Statistics of the South, 1790-1970*. University: University of Alabama Press, 1973.

Donnan, Elizabeth, ed. *Documents Illustrative of the History of the Slave Trade to America*. Washington, D.C.: Carnegie Institution, 1930-1935.

Douglass, Frederick. *Life and Times of Frederick Douglass Written by Himself: His Early Life as a Slave, His Escape from Bondage, and His Complete History*. London: Collier-Macmillan Ltd., 1962, originally 1892.

DuBois, Henry A. *Report to the Board of Directors and Stockholders of the Virginia Cannel Coal Company*. New York: Van Norden & Amerman, 1853.

Dunn, Matthias. *A Treatise on the Winning and Working of Collieries; Including Numerous Statistics Regarding Ventilation and Prevention of Accidents in Mines*. London: By the Author, 1852.

"Eighteenth Century Slaves as Advertised by Their Masters." *Journal of Negro History* 1 (April 1916):163-216.

"Extracts from Account and Letter Books of Dr. Charles Carroll of Annapolis." *Maryland Historical Magazine* Vols. 3 through 27 (1908-1932).

"Extracts from the Carroll Papers." *Maryland Historical Magazine* 14 (1919).

"Extracts from the Dulany Papers." *Maryland Historical Magazine* 14 (1919).

Fitzpatrick, John C., ed. *The Writings of George Washington*. Washington, D.C.: U.S. Government Printing Office, 1939.

Force, Peter, ed. *American Archives*. Washington, D.C.: By the Editor, 1837-1853, fourth and fifth series.

Ford, Paul Leicester, ed. *The Writings of Thomas Jefferson*. New York: G.P. Putnam's Sons, 1892-1899.

Frederick County Superior Court Will Book. Vol. 1, Virginia State Library.

Gallatin, Albert. *Report on Roads and Canals*, April 6, 1808, 10th Congress, 1st Session, Senate, American State Papers, Vol. 37.

Gilpin, Joshua A. "Journal of a Tour from Philadelphia in 1809." *Pennsylvania Magazine of History and Biography* 51 (1927):351-75, and 52 (1928):29-58.

Great Britain. *Journals of the House of Commons, 1640-1800*. London: 1803, Vols. 2-42.

———. *Journals of the House of Lords*. London, 1810-1826.

Green, William. *Narrative of Events in the Life of William Green*. Springfield, Mass.: L.M. Guernsey, Printer, 1853.

Hazard, Samuel, ed. *Pennsylvania Archives*. Philadelphia: Published for the State, 1852-1914.

Heinrich, Oswald J. "An Account of an Explosion of Fire-Damp at the Midlothian Colliery, Chesterfield County, Virginia." *Transactions* of the American Institute of Mining Engineers 5 (May 1876-February 1877):148-61.

———. "The Midlothian Colliery, Virginia." *Transactions* of the American Institute of Mining Engineers 1 (May 1871–February 1873):346–59.

———. "The Midlothian, Virginia, Colliery in 1876." *Transactions* of the American Institute of Mining Engineers 4 (May 1875-February 1876):308-16.

Helper, Hinton Rowan, *The Impending Crisis of the South: How to Meet It*. George M. Frederickson, ed. Cambridge, Mass.: Belknap Press of Harvard University Press, 1968, originally 1857.

Hening, William Waller, ed. *The Statutes at Large, Being a Collection of All the Laws of Virginia*. Richmond, By the Editor, 1810-1823.

Henrico County Records, 1677-1692. Virginia State Library.

Hermelin, Samuel G. *Report About the Mines in the United States of America*. Amandus Johnson, trans. Philadelphia: John Morton Memorial Museum, 1931.

Holland, John. *The History and Description of Fossil Fuel, the Collieries, and Coal Trade of Great Britain*. London: Whittaker & Co., 1841.

Howe, Henry. *Historical Collections of Virginia; Containing a Collection of the Most Interesting Facts, Traditions, Biographical Sketches, Anecdotes, etc. Relating to Its History and Antiquities*. Charleston, S.C.: Babcock & Co., 1845.

———. *Memoirs of the Most Eminent American Mechanics*. New York: A.V. Blake, 1844.

Hulme, Thomas. *Hulme's Journal of a Tour in the Western Counties of America—September 30, 1818-August 8, 1819*. As reproduced in Reuben Gold Thwaites, ed. *Early Western Travels, 1748-1846*, Vol. 10. Cleveland: Arthur H. Clark Co., 1904.

Ingraham, Joseph Holt, *The South-west. By a Yankee*, Vol. 2. New York: Harper & Brothers, 1835.

Jefferson, Isaac. "Life of Isaac Jefferson of Petersburg, Virginia Blacksmith Containing a Full and Faithful Account of Monticello & the Family There, with Notices of Many of the Distinguished Characters that Visited There, with His Revolutionary Experiences & Travels, Adventures, Observations & Opinions, the Whole Taken Down from His Own Words." Edited and with commentary by Raford W. Logan. *William and Mary Quarterly* 8 (October 1951):561-82.

Jefferson, Thomas. "Notes on Virginia." Albert Ellery Bergh, ed. *The Writings of Thomas Jefferson*. Washington, D.C.: Thomas Jefferson Memorial Association of the United States, 1907, Vols. 1 and 2.

Jones, Hugh. *The Present State of Virginia: From Whence Is Inferred a Short View of Maryland and North Carolina*. Richard L. Morton, ed. Chapel Hill: University of North Carolina Press, 1956.

Jones, Thomas P., M.D. "The Progress of Manufactures and Internal Improvements in the United States and Particularly on the Advantages to be Derived from the Employment of Slaves in the Manufacturing of Cotton and Other Goods." Originally published in *American Farmer* 9 (November 30, 1827):290-91, and reproduced in *Textile History Review* 3 (July 1962):155-61.

"Journal of a French Traveller in the Colonies, 1765." *American Historical Review* 27 (October 1921):70-89.

Lacock, Abner. *Great National Object. Proposed Connection of the Eastern & Western Waters, By a Communication Through the Potomac Country.* Washington, D.C.: By the Author, 1822.

Lesley, J. P. *The Iron Manufacturer's Guide to the Furnaces, Forges and Rolling Mills of the United States; with Discussions of Iron as a Chemical Element, an American Ore, and a Manufactured Article, in Commerce and in History.* New York: John Wiley, Publisher, 1859.

"The Letters of Charles Carroll, Barrister," *Maryland Historical Magazine* Vols. 21 (1936) through 38 (1943).

Loguen, Jermain Wesley. *The Rev. J. W. Loguen, as a Slave and as a Freeman. A Narrative of Real Life.* Syracuse: J.G.K. Truair & Co., Printers, 1859.

Lyell, Sir Charles. *Second Visit to the United States of North America.* New York: Wiley & Putnam, 1855, originally 1849.

————. *On the Structure and Probable Age of the Coal-Field of the James River, near Richmond, Virginia.* London: By the Author, 1847. Xeroxographic copy at the Virginia State Library, Richmond, Virginia.

Manuscript Population and Slave Schedules, Rockbridge and Henrico Counties, Virginia, Eighth Census of the United States, 1860, National Archives Microfilm Publications, M653.

Martin, Joseph. *New and Comprehensive Gazetteer of Virginia.* Charlottesville, Va., 1835.

Maxcy, Virgil, ed. *The Laws of Maryland with Charter Bill of Rights, Constitution of the United States,* Baltimore: Philip H. Nicklin & Co., 1811.

McIlwaine, H. R., ed. *Journals of the Council of the State of Virginia.* Richmond: Virginia State Library.

Memorial of the Miners' and Manufacturers' Convention of the State of Virginia, to the Congress of the United States. Richmond, December 6, 1850. Xeroxographic copy at the Virginia State Library, Richmond, Virginia.

Mordecai, Samuel. *Richmond in By-Gone Days: Being Reminiscences of an Old Citizen.* Richmond: George M. West, 1856.

Morrison, James L., Jr., ed. *The Memoirs of Henry Heth.* Westport, Conn.: Greenwood Press, 1974.

Olmsted, Frederick Law. *A Journey in the Back Country.* London: S. Low, Son & Co., 1860.

————. *A Journey in the Seaboard Slave States, with Remarks on Their Economy.* New York: Mason Brothers, 1859, originally 1856.

Pennington, James W. C. *The Fugitive Blacksmith; or, Events in the History of James W.C. Pennington formerly a Slave in the State of Maryland, United States.* London: C. Gilpin, 1850.

Pennsylvania Colonial Records; Minutes of the Provincial Council and the Supreme Executive Council. Harrisburg: By the State of Pennsylvania, 1852-1853.

Perdue, Charles, Jr., Barden, Thomas E., and Phillips, Robert K., eds. *Weevils in the Wheat: Interviews with Virginia Ex-Slaves.* Charlottesville: University Press of Virginia, 1976.

Personal Property Tax Books. Campbell and Chesterfield Counties, 1800-1820. Virginia State Library, Richmond.

"Practical Remarks on Bituminous Coal Formation." *American Journal of Science and Arts* 11 (October 1826):57-58.

Proceedings and Debates of the Virginia State Convention of 1829-30. Richmond: Samuel Shepherd & Co., 1830.

Report of the Committee Under a Resolution of the Stockholders of the Chesterfield Railroad Company. Richmond: Shepherd & Colin, 1844.

Report of the President of the Virginia Cannel Coal Company to the Stockholders. Cincinnati: Joseph B. Boyd, 1865.

Rochefoucauld-Liancourt, Duc de La, Francois Alexandre Frederick. *Travels Through the United States of North America, the Country of the Iroquois, and Upper Canada, in the Years 1795, 1796, and 1797; with an Authentic Account of Lower Canada.* Vol. 3. London: R. Phillips, 1799.

Rogers, William B. *Report of the Geological Reconnaissance of the State of Virginia.* Philadelphia: Desilver, Thomas & Co., 1836.

Rudolph, Adam. *Report of the Dora Coal and Iron Mining and Manufacturing Company.* New York: Baker, Godwin & Co., 1854.

Ruffin, Edmund. "Visit to Graham's Coal Pits." *Farmers' Register* 5 (August 1, 1837):315-19.

St. John, I. M. *Notes on the Coal Trade of the Chesapeake and Ohio Railroad, in Its Bearing upon the Commercial Interests of Richmond, Virginia.* Richmond: By the Author, 1878.

Schoepf, J. D. *Travels in the Confederation, 1783-84.* Alfred J. Morrison, ed. Philadelphia: University of Pennsylvania Press, 1911' originally 1785, Vol. 2.

"The 1716 Journal of John Fontaine." *Iron Worker* 27 (Autumn 1964):8-12.

Shepherd, Samuel, ed. *The Statutes at Large of Virginia, 1792-1806.* Richmond: S. Shepherd, 1935-1936.

Taylor, R. C. *Statistics of Coal: Including Mineral Bituminous Substances Employed in Arts and Manufactures; With Their Geographical, Geological, and Commercial Distribution, and Amount of Production and Compensation on the American Continent.* Philadelphia: J.W. Moore, 1855, originally 1848.

Thorpe, Francis Newton, ed. *The Federal and State Constitutions, Colonial Charters, and Other Organic Laws of the States, Territories, and Colonies Now or Heretofore Forming the United States of America.* Vol. 7. Washington, D.C.: U.S. Government Printing Office, 1909.

Tocqueville, Alexis de. *Democracy in America.* Francis Bowen, trans. New York: Alfred A. Knopf, 1945.

Tuomey, M. "Notice of the Appomattox Coal Pits." *Farmers' Register* 10 (1842):449-50.

Tyson, J. Washington. *Report of the Board of Directors of the Hampshire Coal and Iron Company of Virginia*. Baltimore: John Murphey & Co., 1856.

U.S. Congress. House. *Coal Trade–Richmond*. 24th Congress, 2nd Session, House Document 93, 1837.

Virginia Board of Public Works. *Annual Report, 1820*. Virginia State Library, Richmond.

Virginia Cannel Coal Company. Reports, Acts of Incorporation, etc. New York: Van Norden & King, 1851.

Votes and Proceedings of the House of the Province of Pennsylvania, 1682-1776. Philadelphia: By the Colony, 1752-1776.

Welby, Adlard. *A Visit to North America and English Settlements in Illinois, with a Winter Residence at Philadelphia*. London: J. Drury, 1821, as reproduced in Reuben Gold Thwaites, ed. *Early Western Travels, 1748-1846*, Vol. 10. Cleveland: Arthur H. Clark Co., 1905.

Weld, Isaac, Jr. *Travels Through the States of North America and the Provinces of Upper and Lower Canada During the Years 1795, 1796, and 1797*. London: John Stockdale, Piccadilly, 1800.

Wooldridge, A. S. "Geological and Statistical Notice of the Coal Mines in the Vicinity of Richmond, Va." *American Journal of Science and Arts* 43 (October 1842):1-14.

Wright, Louis B., ed. *Letters of Robert Carter, 1720-1727: The Commercial Interests of a Virginia Gentleman*. San Marino, Calif.: Huntington Library, 1940.

York County Records, 1664-1702. Virginia State Library, Richmond.

SECONDARY SOURCES

BOOKS

Alexander, John. *The Iron Industry of Wythe County from 1792*. Wytheville, Va.: Southwest Virginia Enterprise, 1942.

Ambler, Charles Henry. *A History of Transportation in the Ohio Valley, with Special Reference to Its Waterways, Trade, and Commerce from the Earliest Period to the Present Time*. Glendale, Calif.: Arthur H. Clark Co., 1932.

————. *Sectionalism in Virginia from 1776 to 1861*. Chicago: University of Chicago Press, 1910.

————. *Thomas Ritchie: A Study in Virginia Politics*. Richmond: Bell Book & Stationery Co., 1913.

Aptheker, Herbert. *American Negro Slave Revolts*. New York: International Publishers, 1963, originally 1943.

————. *Nat Turner's Slave Rebellion*. New York: Grove Press, 1966.

Armes, Ethel. *The Story of Coal and Iron in Alabama*. Birmingham, Ala.: Chamber of Commerce, 1910.

Ashton, Thomas Southcliffe. *Iron and Steel in the Industrial Revolution*. New York: Augustus M. Kelley, 1968, originally 1924.

Ballagh, James Curtis. *A History of Slavery in Virginia*. Baltimore: Johns Hopkins University Press, 1902.

Barker, Charles A. *Background of the Revolution in Maryland*. New Haven, Conn.: Yale University Press, 1940.

Berlin, Ira. *Slaves Without Masters: The Free Negro in the Antebellum South*. New York: Vintage Books, 1974.

Berthoff, Rowland. *An Unsettled People: Social Order and Disorder in American History*. New York: Harper & Row, Publishers, 1971.

Binder, Frederick Moore. *Coal Age Empire: Pennsylvania Coal and Its Utilization to 1860*. Harrisburg: Pennsylvania Historical and Museum Commission, 1974.

Bining, Arthur Cecil. *British Regulation of the Colonial Iron Industry*. Philadelphia: University of Pennsylvania Press, 1933.

————. *Pennsylvania Iron Manufacture in the Eighteenth Century*. Harrisburg: Pennsylvania Historical Commission, 1938.

Bishop, James L. *A History of American Manufactures from 1608-1860*. Philadelphia: Edward Young & Co., 1866.

Blassingame, John W. *The Slave Community: Plantation Life in the Antebellum South*. New York: Oxford University Press, 1972.

Boyer, Charles S. *Early Forges and Furnaces in New Jersey*. Philadelphia: University of Pennsylvania Press, 1931.

Brackett, Jeffrey R. *The Negro in Maryland: A Study of the Institution of Slavery*. New York: Negro Universities Press, 1969, originally 1889.

Brewer, James H. *The Confederate Negro: Virginia's Craftsmen and Military Laborers, 1861-1865*. Durham, N.C.: Duke University Press, 1969.

Brown, George T. *The Gas Light Company of Baltimore: A Study of Natural Monopoly*. Baltimore: Johns Hopkins University Press, 1936.

Brown, Robert E., and Brown, B. Katherine. *Virginia 1705-1786: Democracy or Aristocracy?* East Lansing: Michigan State University Press, 1964.

Brown, Sterling A., Davis, Arthur P., and Lee, Ulysses, eds. *The Negro Caravan: Writings by American Negroes*. New York: Arno Press, 1970.

Bruce, Kathleen. *Virginia Iron Manufacture in the Slave Era*. New York: Augustus M. Kelley, 1960, originally 1930.

Bruce, Philip Alexander. *Economic History of Virginia in the Seventeenth Century*. New York: Macmillan & Co., 1896.

Callahan, James Morton. *Semi-Centennial History of West Virginia*. Charleston, S.C.: Semi-Centennial Commission of West Virginia, 1913.

Channing, Edward A. *A History of the United States*. New York: Macmillan & Co., 1905-1925.

Clark, Victor S. *History of Manufactures in the United States 1607-1860*. Vol. 1. New York: Peter Smith, 1949, originally 1929.

Cole, Arthur Charles. *The Whig Party in the South*. Gloucester, Mass.: Peter Smith, 1962, originally 1914.

Conley, Phil. *History of the West Virginia Coal Industry*. Charleston, S.C.: Educational Foundations, 1960.

Conrad, Alfred H., and Meyer, John R. *The Economics of Slavery; and Other Studies in Econometric History*. Chicago: Aldine Publishing Co., 1964.

Craven, Avery Odelle. *Soil Exhaustion as a Factor in the Agricultural History of Virginia and Maryland, 1606-1860*. Urbana: University of Illinois Press, 1926.

Crowl, Philip A. *Maryland During and After the Revolution: A Political and Economic Study*. Baltimore: Johns Hopkins University Press, 1943.

Daniels, Jonathan. *The Randolphs of Virginia*. Garden City, N.Y.: Doubleday & Co., 1972.

David, Paul A., Gutman, Herbert G., Sutch, Richard, Temin, Peter, and Wright, Gavin. *Reckoning with Slavery: A Critical Study in the Quantitative History of American Negro Slavery*. New York: Oxford University Press, 1976.

Davis, David Brion. *The Problem of Slavery in Western Culture*. Ithaca, N.Y.: Cornell University Press, 1966.

Davis, Rebecca Harding. *Life in the Iron Mills*, with a Biographical Interpretation by Tillie Olsen. Old Westbury, N.Y.: Feminist Press, 1972, originally 1861.

Degler, Carl N. *Neither Black Nor White: Slavery and Race Relations in Brazil and the United States*. New York: Macmillan Co., 1971.

Delaplaine, Edward S. *The Life of Thomas Johnson: Member of the Continental Congress, First Governor of the State of Maryland, and Associate Justice of the United States Supreme Court*. New York: Frederick H. Hitchcock, 1927.

Dew, Charles B. *Ironmaker to the Confederacy: Joseph R. Anderson and the Tredegar Iron Works*. New Haven, Conn.: Yale University Press, 1966.

Dickerson, Oliver M. *The Navigation Acts and the American Revolution*. Philadelphia: University of Pennsylvania Press, 1951.

Dodson, Leonidas. *Alexander Spotswood, Governor of Colonial Virginia, 1710-1722*. Philadelphia: University of Pennsylvania Press, 1932.

Dorman, James H., and Jones, Robert R. *The Afro-American Experience: A Cultural History Through Emancipation*. New York: John Wiley & Sons, 1974.

Du Bois, W. E. Burghardt. *The Suppression of the African Slave-Trade to the United States of America, 1639-1870*. New York: Social Science Press, 1954, originally 1896.

Dunaway, Wayland F. *History of the James River and Kanawha Canal*. New York: Columbia University Press, 1922.

Eaton, Clement. *The Growth of Southern Civilization, 1790-1860*. New York: Harper & Row, Publishers, 1961.

Eavenson, Howard N. *The First Century and a Quarter of American Coal Industry*. Pittsburgh: By the Author, 1942.

Elkins, Stanley M. *Slavery: A Problem in American Institutional and Intellectual Life*. Chicago: University of Chicago Press, 1959.

Fairbanks, W. L., and Hamill, W. S. *The Coal-Mining Industry of Maryland*. Baltimore: Maryland Development Bureau of the Baltimore Association of Commerce, 1932.

Fisher, Richard Swainson. *The Progress of the United States of America, from the Earliest Periods: Geographical, Statistical, and Historical*. New York: J.H. Colton & Co., 1854.

Flinn, M. W. *Men of Iron: The Crowleys in the Early Iron Industry*. Edinburgh, Scotland: Edinburgh University Press, 1962.

Fogel, Robert William, and Engerman, Stanley L. *Time on the Cross: The*

Economics of American Negro Slavery. Boston: Little, Brown & Co., 1974.

Foner, Philip S. *American Labor Songs of the Nineteenth Century.* Urbana: University of Illinois Press, 1975.

Frazier, E. Franklin. *The Free Negro Family.* New York: Arno Press and the *New York Times,* 1968, originally 1932.

Frederickson, George M. *The Black Image in the White Mind: The Debate on Afro-American Character and Destiny, 1817-1914.* New York: Harper & Row, Publishers, 1971.

Freehling, William W. *Prelude to Civil War: The Nullification Controversy in South Carolina, 1816-1836.* New York: Harper & Row, Publishers, 1965.

————. ed. *The Nullification Era: A Documentary Record.* New York: Harper & Row, Publishers, 1967.

Genovese, Eugene D. *The Political Economy of Slavery: Studies in the Economy and Society of the Slave South.* New York: Random House, 1965.

————. *In Red and Black: Marxian Explorations in Southern and Afro-American History.* New York: Random House, 1971.

————. *Roll, Jordan, Roll: The World the Slaves Made.* New York: Vintage Books, 1976, originally 1974.

————. *The World the Slaveholders Made.* New York: Vintage Books, 1969.

Goldin, Claudia Dale. *Urban Slavery in the American South, 1820-1860: A Quantitative History.* Chicago: University of Chicago Press, 1976.

Gray, Lewis C. *History of Agriculture in the Southern U.S. to 1860.* Washington, D.C.: Carnegie Institution of Washington, 1933.

Greene, Evarts B., and Harrington, Virginia D. *American Population Before the Federal Census of 1790.* New York: Columbia University Press, 1932.

Greene, Jack P. *The Quest for Power: The Lower Houses of Assembly in the Southern Royal Colonies, 1689-1776.* Chapel Hill, N.C.: University of North Carolina Press, 1963.

Gutheim, Frederick. *The Potomac.* New York: Rinehart & Co., 1949.

Gutman, Herbert G. *The Black Family in Slavery and Freedom, 1750-1925.* New York: Pantheon Books, 1976.

————. *Slavery and the Numbers Game: A Critique of Time on the Cross.* Urbana: University of Illinois Press, 1975.

Hartley, E. N. *Ironworks on the Saugus: The Lynn and Braintree Ventures of the Company of Undertakers of the Ironworks in New England.* Norman: University of Oklahoma Press, 1957.

Harvey, Katherine A. *The Best-Dressed Miners: Life and Labor in the Maryland Coal Region, 1835-1910.* Ithaca, N.Y.: Cornell University Press, 1969.

Humphrey, H. B. *Historical Summary of Coal-Mine Explosions in the United States, 1810-1958.* Washington, D.C.: U.S. Department of Interior, Bureau of Mines, 1960.

Imboden, John D. *The Coal and Iron Resources of Virginia: Their Extent, Commercial Value and Early Development Considered.* Richmond: Clemmitt & Jones, Printers, 1972, originally 1872.

Jackson, Luther P. *Free Negro Labor and Property Holding in Virginia, 1830-1860.* New York: D. Appleton-Century Co., 1942.

Jenks, Leonard. *The Migration of British Capital to 1875.* New York: Alfred A. Knopf, 1927.

Jernegan, Marcus W. *Laboring and Dependent Classes in Colonial America, 1607-1783.* Chicago: University of Chicago Press, 1931.

Jones, Meriweather. *A Report of the Richmond Coal Field.* Richmond: By the Author, 1916.

Jordan, Winthrop D. *White Over Black: American Attitudes Toward the Negro, 1550-1812.* Chapel Hill: University of North Carolina Press for the Institute of Early American History and Culture at Williamsburg, Va., 1968.

Kemble, Frances Anne. *Journal of a Residence on a Georgia Plantation in 1838-1839.* London: Longman, Green, Longman, Roberts, & Green, 1863.

Land, Aubrey C. *The Dulanys of Maryland: A Biographical Study of Daniel Dulany, the Elder (1685-1753) and Daniel Dulany, the Younger (1722-1793).* Baltimore: Johns Hopkins University Press, 1955.

Lebergott, Stanley. *Manpower in Economic Growth: The American Record Since 1800.* New York: McGraw-Hill Book Co., 1964.

Lynd, Staughton. *Class Conflict, Slavery, and the United States Constitution.* New York: Bobbs-Merrill Co., 1967.

May, Earl Chapin. *Principio to Wheeling, 1715-1945: A Pageant of Iron and Steel.* New York: Harper & Brothers, Publishers, 1945.

Mellon, Matthew T. *Early American Views on Negro Slavery from the Time of the Founding of the Republic Until 1830.* Boston: Meader Publishing Co., 1934.

Middleton, Arthur Pierce. *Tobacco Coast: A Maritime History of Chesapeake Bay in the Colonial Era.* Newport News, Va.: Mariner's Museum, 1953.

Mitchell, Broadus. *William Gregg, Factory Master of the Old South.* New York: Octagon Books, 1966.

Morris, Richard B. *Government and Labor in Early America.* New York: Columbia University Press, 1946.

Morton, Louis. *Robert Carter of Nomini Hall: A Virginia Tobacco Planter of the Eighteenth Century.* Charlottesville: University Press of Virginia, 1941.

Morton, Oren F. *A Centennial History of Alleghany County, Virginia.* Dayton, Va.: J.K. Ruebush Co., 1923.

———. *A History of Rockbridge County, Virginia.* Staunton, Va.: McCluer Co., 1920.

Moynihan, Daniel P. *The Negro Family: The Case for National Action.* Washington, D.C.: U.S. Department of Labor, 1965.

Mullin, Gerald W. *Flight and Rebellion: Slave Resistance in Eighteenth-Century Virginia.* New York: Oxford University Press, 1972.

Norris, James D. *Frontier Iron: The Maramec Iron Works, 1826-1876.* Madison: State Historical Society of Wisconsin, 1964.

Osterweis, Rollin G. *Romanticism and Nationalism in the Old South.* New Haven, Conn.: Yale University Press, 1949.

Pearse, John B. *A Concise History of the Iron Manufacture of the American Colonies Up to the Revolution and Pennsylvania Until the Present Time.* Philadelphia: Allen, Lane & Scott, 1876.

Phillips, Ulrich B. *American Negro Slavery: A Survey of the Supply, Employment* and Control of Negro Labor as Determined by the Plantation Regime. Baton Rouge: Louisiana State University Press, 1966, originally 1918.

————. Life and Labor in the Old South. Boston: Little, Brown & Co., 1929.

Pierce, Arthur Dudley. Iron in the Pines: The Story of New Jersey's Ghost Towns and Bog Iron. New Brunswick, N.J.: Rutgers University Press, 1957.

Pinchbeck, Raymond B. The Virginia Negro Artisan and Tradesman. Richmond: William Byrd Press, 1926.

Quarles, Benjamin. The Negro in the American Revolution. Chapel Hill: University of North Carolina Press, 1961.

Randolph, Edwin Archer. The Life of Rev. John Jasper, Pastor of the Sixth Mt. Zion Baptist Church, Richmond, Virginia: From his Birth to the Present Time, with His Theory on the Rotation of the Sun. Richmond: R.T. Hill & Co., 1864.

Rawick, George, From Sundown to Sunup: The Making of the Black Community. Westport, Conn.: Greenwood Publishing Co., 1972.

Robbins, Michael W. Maryland's Iron Industry During the Revolutionary War Era. Annapolis: Maryland Bicentennial Commission, 1973.

Robert, Joseph Clarke. The Tobacco Kingdom: Plantation, Market, and Factory in Virginia and North Carolina, 1800-1860. Gloucester, Mass.: Peter Smith, 1965, originally 1938.

Robinson, Donald L. Slavery in the Structure of American Politics, 1765-1820. New York: Harcourt Brace Jovanovich, 1971.

Rowland, Kate M. The Life of Charles Carroll of Carrollton, 1737-1832. New York: G.P. Putnam's Sons, 1898.

Roy, Andrew. A History of the Coal Miners of the United States, From the Development of the Mines to the Close of the Anthracite Strike of 1902, Including a Brief Sketch of Early British Miners. Westport, Conn.: Greenwood Press, 1970, originally 1905.

Russel, Robert Royal. Economic Aspects of Southern Sectionalism, 1840-1861. New York: Russel & Russel, 1960, originally 1924.

Scharf, J. Thomas. History of Maryland: From the Earliest Period to the Present Day. Vol. 3. Hatboro, Pa.: Tradition Press, 1967, originally 1879.

Schubert, H. R. History of the British Iron and Steel Industry. London: Routledge & Kegan Paul, 1957.

Scrivenor, Harry. History of the Iron Trade, from the Earliest Records to the Present Period. London: Longman, Brown, Green, & Longmans, 1854.

Sheppard, Muriel Early. Cloud By Day: The Story of Coal and Coke and People. Chapel Hill: University of North Carolina Press, 1947.

Simms, Henry H. The Rise of the Whigs in Virginia, 1824-1840. Richmond: William Byrd Press, 1929.

Smith, Abbot Emerson. Colonists in Bondage: White Servitude and Convict Labor in America, 1607-1776. Chapel Hill: University of North Carolina Press, 1947.

Spero, Sterling D., and Harris, Abram L. The Black Worker: The Negro and the Labor Movement. New York: Atheneum, 1972, originally 1931.

Stampp, Kenneth M. *The Peculiar Institution: Slavery in the Ante-Bellum South.* New York: Alfred A. Knopf, 1956.

Starobin, Robert S. *Industrial Slavery in the Old South.* New York: Oxford University Press, 1970.

Stover, John F. *American Railroads.* Chicago: University of Chicago Press, 1961.

Swank, James M. *History of the Manufacture of Iron in All Ages.* Philadelphia: American Iron and Steel Association, 1892.

Sydnor, Charles Sackett. *The Development of Southern Sectionalism, 1819-1848.* Baton Rouge: Louisiana State University Press, 1948.

_____. *Slavery in Mississippi.* Gloucester, Mass.: Peter Smith, 1965, originally 1933.

Taylor, George R., and Neu, Irene D. *The American Railroad Network, 1861-1890.* Cambridge, Mass.: Harvard University Press, 1956.

Temin, Peter. *Iron and Steel in Nineteenth-Century America: An Economic Inquiry.* Cambridge, Mass.: MIT Press, 1964.

Thomas, Emory M. *The Confederate State of Richmond: A Biography of the Capitol, 1861-65.* Austin: University of Texas Press, 1971.

Thomas, James W., and Williams, T.J.C. *History of Allegany County, Maryland.* Vol. 2. Baltimore: Regional Publishing Co., 1969.

Tragle, Henry Irving. *The Southampton Slave Revolt of 1831: A Compilation of Source Material.* Amherst, Mass.: University of Massachusetts Press, 1971.

Tryon, Rollo Milton. *Household Manufactures in the United States, 1640-1860: A Study in Industrial History.* Chicago: University of Chicago Press, 1917.

Vandiver, Frank E. *Ploughshares into Swords: Josiah Gorgas and Confederate Ordnance.* Austin: University of Texas Press, 1952.

Wade, Richard C. *Slavery in the Cities: The South, 1820-1860.* New York: Oxford University Press, 1964.

Walker, Joseph E. *Hopewell Village: A Social and Economic History of an Iron-Making Community.* Philadelphia: University of Pennsylvania Press, 1966.

Wayland, John W. *A History of Shenandoah County, Virginia.* Strasburg, Va.: Shenandoah Publishing House, 1927.

Weinstein, Allen, and Gatell, Frank Otto, eds. *American Negro Slavery: A Modern Reader.* New York: Oxford University Press, 1968.

Wender, Herbert. *Southern Commercial Conventions, 1837-1859.* Baltimore: Johns Hopkins University Press, 1930.

Wertenbaker, Thomas J. *The Planters of Colonial Virginia.* New York: Russel & Russel, 1959.

Whitfield, Theodore M. *Slavery Agitation in Virginia, 1829-32.* Baltimore: Johns Hopkins University Press, 1930.

Williams, John A., and Harris, Charles F., eds. *Amistad I.* New York: Random House, 1970.

Woodward, C. Vann. *The Strange Career of Jim Crow.* New York: Oxford University Press, 1966.

ARTICLES

Anderson, Ralph V., and Gallman, Robert E. "Slaves as Fixed Capital: Slave Labor and Southern Economic Development." *Journal of American History* 64 (June 1977):24-46.

Aufhauser, R. Keith. "Slavery and Technological Change." *Journal of Economic History* 34 (March 1974):36-50.

Bailey, Clay. "Joseph R. Anderson of Tredegar." *The Commonwealth* 12 (November 1959):2, 36, 38.

Barksdale, S. "Coal Mining Thrives on Virginia's Last Frontier." *The Commonwealth* 2 (June 1949):30-32.

Bateman, Fred, Foust, James, and Weiss, Thomas. "The Participation of Planters in Manufacturing in the Antebellum South." *Agricultural History* 48 (April 1974):277-98.

Bateman, Fred, and Weiss, Thomas. "Comparative Regional Development in Antebellum Manufacturing." *Journal of Economic History* 35 (March 1975):182-215.

Bauer, Raymond A., and Bauer, Alice H. "Day to Day Resistance to Slavery." *Journal of Negro History* 27 (October 1942):388-419.

Bining, Arthur Cecil. "The Iron Plantations of Early Pennsylvania." *Pennsylvania Magazine of History and Biography* 57, No. 2 (1933):117-37.

Bradford, S. Sydney. "The Negro Ironworker in Ante Bellum Virginia." *Journal of Southern History* 25 (May 1959):194-206.

Brainerd, Alfred F. "Colored Mining Labor." *Transactions* of the American Institute of Mining Engineers, 14 (June 1885-May 1886):78-80.

Brydon, G. MacLaren. "The Bristol Iron Works in King George County." *Virginia Magazine of History and Biography* 42 (April 1934):97-102.

Buck, William J. "History of the Early Discovery of Coal." *Potter's American Monthly* 4 (January 1875):180-82.

Cappon, Lester J. "Iron Making—A Forgotten Industry of North Carolina." *North Carolina Historical Review* 9 (October 1932):331-48.

————. "Trend of the Southern Iron Industry Under the Plantation System." *Journal of Economic and Business History* 2 (February 1930):353-81.

Cassell, Frank A. "Slaves of the Chesapeake Bay Area and the War of 1812." *Journal of Negro History* 57 (April 1972):144-55.

Collins, Herbert. "The Southern Industrial Gospel Before 1860." *Journal of Southern History* 12 (August 1946):386-402.

Condit, William Ward. "Virginia's Early Iron Age." *Iron Worker* 23 (Summer 1959):1-7.

Conley, Phil. "Early Coal Development in the Kanawha Valley." *West Virginia History* 8 (January 1947):207-15.

Dew, Charles B. "David Ross and the Oxford Iron Works: A Study of Industrial Slavery in the Nineteenth-Century South." *William and Mary Quarterly* 31 (April 1974):189-224.

————. "Disciplining Slave Ironworkers in the Antebellum South: Coercion, Conciliation, and Accommodation." *American Historical Review* 79 (April 1974):393-418.

Dowd, Mary Jane. "The State of the Maryland Economy, 1776-1807." Part 1. *Maryland Historical Magazine* 57 (June 1962):90-132.

_____. "The State of the Maryland Economy, 1776-1807." Part 2. *Maryland Historical Magazine* 57 (September 1962):229-58.

Eaton, Clement. "Slave-Hiring in the Upper South: A Step Toward Freedom." *Mississippi Valley Historical Review* 46 (March 1960):663-78.

Eavenson, Howard N. "Notes on an Old West Virginia Coal Field." *West Virginia History* 5 (January 1944):83-100.

_____. "Some Side-Lights on Early Virginia Coal Mining." *Virginia Magazine of History and Biography* 50 (July 1942): 199-208.

Fishwick, Marshall W. "John Jordan, Man of Iron." *Iron Worker* 21 (Autumn 1957):1-8.

Frazier, E. Franklin. "The Negro Slave Family." *Journal of Negro History* 15 (April 1930):198-259.

Frederickson, George M., and Lasch, Christopher. "Resistance to Slavery." *Civil War History* 13 (December 1967):315-29.

Giddens, Paul H. "Trade and Industry in Colonial Maryland, 1753-1769." *Journal of Economic and Business History* 4 (May 1932):512-38.

Green, Fletcher M. "Duff Green: Industrial Promoter." *Journal of Southern History* 2 (February 1936):29-42.

Griffin, Richard W. "Ante Bellum Industrial Foundations of the (Alleged) 'New South.' " *Textile History Review* 5 (April 1964):33-43.

Gutman, Herbert G. "Work, Culture, and Society in Industrializing America, 1815-1919." *American Historical Review* 78 (June 1973):531-88.

Hatch, Charles E., Jr., and Gregory, Thurlow Gates. "The First American Blast Furnace, 1619-1622: The Birth of a Mighty Industry on Falling Creek in Virginia." *Virginia Magazine of History and Biography* 70 (July 1962):261-96.

Haywood, C. Robert. "Economic Sanctions: Use of the Threat of Manufacturing by the Southern Colonies." *Journal of Southern History* 25 (May 1959):207-19.

Hudson, J. Paul. "Augustine Washington." *Iron Worker* 25 (Summer 1961):1-13.

_____. "Iron Manufacturing During the Eighteenth Century." *Iron Worker* 21 (Autumn 1957):9-13.

_____. "The Story of Iron at Jamestown, Virginia—Where Iron Objects Were Wrought by Englishmen Almost 350 Years Ago." *Iron Worker* 20 (Summer 1956):1-14.

Jackson, Luther P. "Religious Development of the Negro in Virginia from 1760 to 1860." *Journal of Negro History* 16 (April 1931):168-239.

Jernegan, Marcus W. "Slavery and Industrialism in the Colonies." *American Historical Review* 25 (January 1920):220-40.

Johnson, Keach. "The Baltimore Company Seeks English Markets: A Study of the Anglo-American Iron Trade, 1731-1755." *William and Mary Quarterly* 16 (January 1959):37-60.

_____. "The Baltimore Company Seeks English Subsidies for the Colonial Iron Industry." *Maryland Historical Magazine* 46 (March 1951):27-43.

_____. "The Genesis of the Baltimore Ironworks." *Journal of Southern History* 19 (May 1953):157-79.

Laing, James T. "The Early Development of the Coal Industry in the Western Counties of Virginia, 1800-1865." *West Virginia History* 27 (January 1966):144-55.

Land, Aubrey C. "Economic Base and Social Structure: The Northern Chesapeake in the Eighteenth Century." *Journal of Economic History* 25 (December 1965):639-54.

_____. "Economic Behavior in a Planting Society: The Eighteenth-Century Chesapeake." *Journal of Southern History* 33 (November 1967):469-85.

_____. Genesis of a Colonial Fortune: Daniel Dulany of Maryland." *William and Mary Quarterly* 7 (April 1950): 255–69.

Lander, Ernest M., Jr. "The Iron Industry in Ante-Bellum South Carolina." *Journal of Southern History* 20 (August 1954):337-55.

Lee, Ida J. "The Heth Family." *Virginia Magazine of History and Biography* 42 (July 1934):273-82.

Lewis, Ronald L. "Slave Families at Early Chesapeake Ironworks." *Virginia Magazine of History and Biography* 86 (April 1978):169-79.

_____. "Slavery on Chesapeake Iron Plantations Before the American Revolution." *Journal of Negro History* 59 (July 1974):242-54.

_____. "The Use and Extent of Slave Labor in the Chesapeake Iron Industry: The Colonial Era." *Labor History* 17 (Summer 1976):388-405.

_____. "The Use and Extent of Slave Labor in the Virginia Iron Industry: The Ante-Bellum Era." *West Virginia History* 38 (January 1977):141-56.

Main, Jackson Turner. "The Distribution of Property in Post-Revolutionary Virginia." *Mississippi Valley Historical Review* 41 (September 1954):241-58.

_____. "The One Hundred." *William and Mary Quarterly* 11 (July 1954):353-84.

McKenzie, Robert H. "The Shelby Iron Company: A Note on Slave Personality After the Civil War." *Journal of Negro History* 58 (July 1973):341-48.

Morris, Richard B. "Labor Controls in Maryland in the Nineteenth Century." *Journal of Southern History* 14 (August 1948):385-400.

_____. "The Measure of Bondage in the Slave States." *Mississippi Valley Historical Review* 41 (September 1954): 219-40.

Moss, Roger W., Jr. "Isaac Zane, Jr., A 'Quaker for the Times.' " *Virginia Magazine of History and Biography* 77 (July 1969):291-306.

Phillips, Ulrich B. "Slave Crime in Virginia." *American Historical Review* 20 (January 1915):336-40.

Rachal, William M. E., ed. "The Occupation of Richmond, April 1865: The Memorandum of Events of Colonel Christopher Q. Tompkins." *Virginia Magazine of History and Biography* 73 (April 1965):189-98.

Ramsdell, Charles W. "The Natural Limits of Slavery Expansion." *Mississippi Valley Historical Review* 16 (September 1929):151-71.

Rice, Otis K. "Coal Mining in the Kanawha Valley to 1861: A View of Industrialization in the Old South." *Journal of Southern History* 31 (November 1965):393-416.

Russel, Robert R. "The Economic History of Negro Slavery in the United States." *Agricultural History* 2 (October 1937):308-21.

_____. "The General Effects of Slavery upon Southern Economic Progress." *Journal of Southern History* 4 (February 1938):34-54.

Sellers, Charles Grier, Jr. "Who Were the Southern Whigs?" *American Historical Review* 59 (January 1954):335-46.

Shelly, Fred. "The Journal of Ebenezer Hazard in Virginia, 1777." *Virginia Magazine of History and Biography* 62 (October 1954):400-23.

Smith, George Winston. "Ante-Bellum Attempts of Northern Business Interests to 'Redeem' the Upper South." *Journal of Southern History* 11 (May 1945):177-213.

Spencer, Richard Henry. "Honorable Daniel Dulany, The Elder (1685-1753)." *Maryland Historical Magazine* 13 (March 1918):20-28.

_____. "Honorable Daniel Dulany, The Younger (1722-1797)." *Maryland Historical Magazine* 13 (June 1918):143-60.

Starobin, Robert. "Disciplining Industrial Slaves in the Old South." *Journal of Negro History* 53 (April 1968):111-28.

Stavisky, Leonard P. "Negro Craftsmanship in Early America." *American Historical Review* 54 (January 1949):315-25.

Stealey, John Edmund, III. "Slavery and the Western Virginia Salt Industry." *Journal of Negro History* 59 (April 1974):105-31.

Sutton, Robert P. "Nostalgia, Pessimism, and Malaise: The Doomed Aristocrat in Late-Jeffersonian Virginia." *Virginia Magazine of History and Biography* 76 (January 1968):41-55.

Tompkins, Ellen Wilkins, ed. "The Colonel's Lady: Some Letters of Ellen Wilkins Tompkins, July-December 1861." *Virginia Magazine of History and Biography* 69 (October 1961):387-419.

Turner, Charles W. "The Early Railroad Movement in Virginia." *Virginia Magazine of History and Biography* 55 (October 1947):350-71.

_____. "The Louisa Railroad, 1836-1850." *North Carolina Historical Review* 24 (January 1947):35-57.

Walker, Joseph E. "Negro Labor in the Charcoal Iron Industry of Southeastern Pennsylvania." *Pennsylvania Magazine of History and Biography* 93 (October 1969):466-86.

Wax, Darold D. "Preferences for Slaves in Colonial America." *Journal of Negro History* 58 (October 1973):371-401.

Whitely, William G. "The Principio Company: A Historical Sketch of the First Iron-Works in Maryland." *Pennsylvania Magazine of History and Biography* 11 (1887):63-68, 190-98, 288-95.

Whitten, David O. "Slave Buying in 1835 Virginia as Revealed by Letters of a Louisiana Negro Sugar Planter." *Louisiana History* 11 (Summer 1970):231-44.

Wish, Harvey, "The Revival of the African Slave Trade in the United States, 1856-1860." *Mississippi Valley Historical Review* 27 (March 1941):569-88.

Woodman, Harold D. "The Profitability of Slavery: A Historical Perennial." *Journal of Southern History* 29 (August 1963):303-25.

Woodworth, J. B. "The History of Conditions of Mining in the Richmond Coal-Basin, Virginia." *Transactions* of the American Institute of Mining Engineers 31 (1902):477-84.

UNPUBLISHED SECONDARY SOURCES

Bradford, Samuel Sydney. "The Ante-Bellum Charcoal Iron Industry of Virginia."
    Ph.D. dissertation, Columbia University, 1958.
Cappon, Lester J. "History of the Southern Iron Industry to the Close of the Civil
    War." Ph.D. dissertation, Harvard University, 1928. Microfilm copy of
    earlier draft, University of Virginia Library.
Holland, Francis R., Jr. "Three Virginia Iron Companies, 1825-1865." M.A.
    thesis, University of Texas, 1958.
Johnson, Keach Doyel. "Establishment of the Baltimore Iron Company: A Case
    Study of the American Iron Industry in the Eighteenth Century." Ph.D.
    dissertation, State University of Iowa, 1949.
McKenzie, Edna Chappell. "Self-Hire Among Slaves, 1820-1860. Institutional
    Variation or Aberration?" Ph.D. dissertation, University of Pittsburgh,
    1973.
Robbins, Michael Warren. "The Principio Company: Iron-Making in Colonial
    Maryland, 1720-1781." Ph.D. dissertation, George Washington Univer-
    sity, 1972.

Index

Contributions in Labor History
SERIES EDITORS: Milton Cantor and Bruce Laurie

———————————About the Author———————————

RONALD L. LEWIS is Assistant Professor of Black American
History at the University of Delaware in Newark. He is the co-editor
of *The Other Slaves: Mechanics, Artisans, and Craftsmen* and of
*The Black Worker: A Documentary History from Colonial Times to
the Present* (8 volumes) and has contributed to such journals as
The Crisis, *Labor History*, and the *Journal of Negro History*.